What Others are Saying about This Book...

"A most inspirational memoir by a man who's had more ups and downs than the mountain ranges he traversed during his incredible walk across America."

—**Alan M. Dershowitz**
Internationally acclaimed author, criminal defense and civil liberties lawyer, and Felix Frankfurter Professor of Law at Harvard Law School

"Walking is an American tradition, but the compelling story that Don Brown tells about his formative years and his life experiences is an extraordinary read. Anyone who loves walking, this great country, and the great sense of triumph overcoming tragedy must read Don Brown's new book. It is a page-turner and a compelling lesson about humility, justice, equality, and faith. I recommend it enthusiastically!"

—**Charles Ogletree, Jr.**
The Jesse Climenko Professor of Law and the founder and executive director of the Charles Hamilton Houston Institute for Race and Justice at Harvard Law School. Author of *The Presumption of Guilt: The Arrest of Henry Louis Gates, Jr.*, and *Race, Class, and Crime in America*, and others

"You have done it and I must confess that I am both impressed and envious. Impressed because you have stayed with a very large   :d personal experience into a quit   ?

—**Derrick Bell**
The late profes   rican American
to be granted tenure at Harvard Law School, where he established a course in civil rights law and wrote *Race, Racism and American Law*, a standard law school textbook nationwide. He was also the first African American

dean of the University of Oregon Law School. He was an acclaimed author of both fiction and non-fiction, including the books *And We Are Not Saved* and *Faces at the Bottom of the Well*

"A fascinating and compelling story—part *Blue Highways*, part *Rocky*—to mix a few art forms. It is a travelogue, but moreover a human interest story and a treatise on the importance of never giving up, no matter how many times you are knocked down, no matter what anybody tells you. I kept my road atlas by my side as I read this and I felt like I, too, walked across the country—but without the bugs, blisters and boiling temperatures! This is an amazing memoir with the capacity to uplift and inspire people to achieve their own dreams."

—Christine Belleris
Editor of the original *Chicken Soup for the Soul* series,
and president of Beyond Words, Inc.

"Savor this really special story."

—Leon Logothetis
Author of *Amazing Adventures of a Nobody*

To the students of Dennison University

Enjoy!

THE
MORPHINE
DREAM

DONALD L. BROWN

BYB

BETTIE YOUNGS BOOKS

Disclaimer: This is a true story, and the characters and events are real. However, in some cases, the names, descriptions, and locations have been changed, and some events have been altered, combined, or condensed for storytelling purposes, but the overall chronology is an accurate depiction of the author's experience.

About the cover: The author on Pacific Coast Highway in Northern California near Trinidad, California on his walk across America
Cover design by Tatomir Pitariu
Text design by Min Gates
Photo of Donald L. Brown by J. Kramer Photography

Bettie Youngs Books are distributed worldwide. If you are unable to order this book from your local bookseller or online, or from Espresso, or from Read How You Want, you may order directly from the publisher.

BETTIE YOUNGS BOOK PUBLISHERS
www.BettieYoungsBooks.com

ISBN: 978-1-936332-25-0
Library of Congress Control Number: 2012934494

1. Brown, Donald L. 2. Bettie Youngs Books. 3. Family Relationships. 4. Harvard. 5. Harvard Law School. 6. Running. 7. Mental health. 8. Self-image. 9. Walking.

Printed in the United States of America

Dedication

To the unforgettable Nick Charles;

To Lou Mitchell, an extraordinary man;

To my late mother, Anita Katherine Butterfield Brown: though you are resting, enjoy reading about my odyssey, and thank you for instilling in me the importance of reading. I miss you!

To the late Professor Derrick Bell, the kindest and most compassionate man I have ever known.

And finally, to my sons, Nicholas Alexander Brown and Louis Mitchell Brown: you have made my life complete. My greatest wish is that my efforts while walking the USA will always remind you both that you, too, can do anything you put your mind to; just keep moving forward, one step at a time.

Contents

Foreword by Margaretha C. Kress Hertle, MD   ix

Acknowledgments   xi

Prologue   xiii

Part One: No Longer a Dream   1

1. One Step at a Time 2. Training 3. My Heartbreak Hills 4. Sea of Uncertainty 5. Some Things Are Written in Our Blood 6. The Basket 7. Blisters on Blisters 8. The Itinerary 9. Pushing the Envelope 10. My Prairie Schooner 11. Live Free or Die 12. The Morphine Dream 13. Nick 14. My Last at Bat 15. Maize and Second Skin 16. Nightmare 17. Fate, the Phone Rang 18. "Donna" Goes to College 19. Another Crossroad 20. Kicking Ass 21. Serendipity 22. The Hobo 23. *Que Sera, Sera* 24. *Terras Irradient* 25. Henry Steele Commager 26. I Can Do This 27. To the Green Mountains 28. Hogback

Part Two: From the Mountains   135

29. The Preparation 30. I Love New York 31. Coopers Town 32. The "Old Boy" Network 33. Tragedy Strikes 34. Amherst Again

Part Three: The Rust Belt   157

35. The Other Apple 36. Liquid Thunder 37. Knee Alert 38. The Mistake by the Lake 39. Cortisone 40. Columbus Bound 41. Lou Mitchell 42. The $600,000 Cab Ride 43. Princessa Vanessa 44. Baseball 45. Motown 46. Soccer School 47. It Ain't Over Till It's Over 48. Battle Creek

Part Four: Crossroads of America   223

49. The House That Rockne Built 50. Football 51. A Mild-Mannered Reporter 52. The Brickyard 53. Ian Vanderwall 54. Place of the Smelly Onion 55. Brew Town 56. Bob Ferrari 57. Mary in the Morning 58. The Fall from Grace 59. Family Reunion 60. The Day the Music Died 61. Mall Walking 62. Twin Cities 63. Changing of the Guard

Part Five: To the Prairies   **287**

64. Mosquito Rain 65. Sunflowers 66. The Pied Piper 67. The Big
Muddy 68. *Mato Tanka* (Big Bear) 69. Grades Are Random 70. Red
Cloud 71. Rambo 72. He Died with His Boots On

Part Six: Purple Mountains Majesty   **327**

73. The Last Best Place 74. Coeur d'Alene

Part Seven: Amber Waves of Grain   **353**

75. Drysiders 76. Hotel Waterville 77. Wetsiders

Part Eight: To the Oceans, White with Foam   **371**

78. War of the Woods 79. Land of the Giant Trees 80. San Francisco
81. Big Sur

Part Nine: From Sea to Shining Sea   **417**

82. San Simeon *(Las Cuestas Encantada)* 83. Finally

Epilogue   **429**

The Best and Worst of Walking USA   **435**

Sources   **443**

About the Author   **447**

Other Books by Bettie Youngs Book Publishers   **449**

Foreword

What makes the difference? What enables people in the worst of situations to pull through, change, move on, and do what they have to in order to surmount the impossible, to succeed and fulfill their dreams? Of course, first they have to have a dream. And then they have to have a lot of support, both practically and in terms of role models or examples. Finally, a spark has to be ignited that kindles the enthusiasm to go on.

During my thirty years working directly with patients in the medical field, the latter half of which I have worked as a family practice physician, I have occasionally witnessed people succeeding through tremendous adversity in life and circumstance. The turning point was almost always a moment where a trusted friend, often their doctor, really saw who they were, who they could become, and posed a question that allowed them to engage and envision a new potential for themselves.

The stories of people who have done the impossible are a strong catalyst both for formulating a new dream and providing the motivation to attempt it. That is true for those in desperate situations as well as those plodding along in everyday life. *The Morphine Dream* is just such a story, and its interest and relevance to people from all different walks of life makes it a powerful catalyst for anyone who reads it.

This is the story of a fifty-two-year-old man, Donald Brown, who walked across America, from Boston, Massachusetts, to San Simeon, California, in four and a half months in 1997, raising money for children's charities in the process. This is a chronicle of that walk and of Don's experiences as he got to know America and her people on foot. And, it is the story of a man who surmounted overwhelming obstacles in pursuit of his dreams.

At the age of thirty-five, having done well in his career as a professional athlete, an injury forced Don to retire from a career as a professional athlete. With a ninth-grade education, finding a job was difficult. The only job he could find was that of a laborer; he was on that job when his right knee was destroyed in an industrial accident. He was told he would not walk again. Life as he had known it was over. But, as he drifted in and out on morphine after one of his many surgeries, he dreamt of doing the impossible: going to Harvard Law School, and walking across America.

As a doctor, I know both dreams were virtually impossible. As a close friend who has seen him do the impossible on many occasions, I knew that if anyone could, it would be Don. In the years that followed, Don did both—against all the odds and despite everyone's skepticism.

This is the story of the realization of those dreams and it has the power to inspire anyone struggling against small or large obstacles in life. It illustrates how you can do anything you set your heart on—*one step at a time.*

It is an adventure story of an arduous journey with its own challenges, crises and rewards as Don describes his daily struggles against the weather, his own medical problems, deadly dangers and personal tragedy.

It holds interest for those dealing with their own medical problems, as they learn how he addresses the challenges posed by his own diabetes, depression, and various orthopedic problems.

It is a human interest story for all with many moving personal experiences and unforgettable characters that have made a large difference in the author's and other people's lives.

It is a practical guide and compelling narrative for the many millions of regular walkers and hundreds of thousands of long-distance walkers, for anyone interested in becoming a walker and for those who prefer to just dream about it.

And it is of interest to anyone planning to travel to the areas Don walked through as he describes the local attractions, overnight accommodations and memorable dining experiences. In this vein, it follows in the footsteps of several highly successful books by other adventurers including: *Walk Across America, The Walk West, Into Thin Air* and *Travels with Charley* to mention a few . . .

If you have a dream that you have put on the shelf because you think it is too late, that you are too old, that you don't have the resources or the education or the time . . . then find your inspiration in the pages of Don Brown's amazing journey. All you have to do is take the first step.

—Margaretha C. Kress Hertle, MD

Acknowledgments

I am profoundly grateful for the kind assistance I received from the following people in preparing this book: Professor Charles Ogletree, of Harvard Law School, Liam Hales, Robin Chafetz, Carolyn Rieder, Nicholas Brown, Louis Brown, Cathy Hales, Kenny Martin, Violet Foster, and the late professor Derrick Bell. Also, to Professor Jim Ellis, thank you for your literary observations. Dr. Margaretha Kress Hertle, along with Larry Qualteri, your guidance helped immensely.

My beloved sister, Nancy Pawlyshyn, along with her late husband John, helped from the very beginning and planted the seeds of this book. I am especially grateful to my writing mentor, a fellow Amherst alum and author of many books, the late Bill Tapply, without whom there would be no book. Bill's patience and empathy were truly noteworthy as I struggled in my early attempts at writing a book.

And especially to Gary S. Chafetz, your encouragement before you agreed to help with the book was most important of all. You kept after me—always in a kind and compassionate way—and you succeeded in motivating me to get it done. I will be forever grateful to you.

Thank you also to Bettie Youngs Book Publishers and in particular, Christine Belleris, Min Gates, Tatomir Pitariu, Jazmin Gomez, and most importantly, Bettie Youngs. Your encouragement, dedication was simply remarkable, and gave this book spirit. Thank you for believing in me.

Prologue

The title for this book, *The Morphine Dream,* is not merely an analogy but was in fact a real event. It occurred while I was a patient in the New England Baptist Hospital on Mission Hill in Boston in 1981. I was just waking up after the latest of several knee surgeries designed to keep me out of a wheelchair for the rest of my life. The prognosis was not good. The doctors were saying I still might not walk again. Worse, I was in terrible pain. Lying in my hospital bed on that warm summer night so long ago, even the slightest movement made me wince. It seemed this was yet another failed attempt to get me walking. A nurse came in and said "Do you need some pain medicine, honey?"

I had just gotten a shot of morphine in the recovery room, but what the heck. I said, "Absolutely, the more the merrier." Fifteen minutes later I got my injection.

Perhaps an hour later, a different nurse came in and said, "Did you get your shot?"

I said, "No."

Shortly afterwards, I got my second shot of morphine. Then there was a shift change and a different staff came on duty. Soon another nurse came into my room. She asked, "How are you doing tonight?

"I'm not doing too well; I need some pain medicine."

I got my third shot. Now, I was in a different world. My thoughts were scrambled. When a different nurse appeared a little while later asking me if I needed medication, I said, "Yes," again. I was sky high on morphine. For the first and only time in my life, I was under the influence of drugs.

I knew I would have many hours laid up in bed during my stay so I had brought some motivational tapes with me to productively kill the time. I popped one into the tape player and the speaker queried: "Where do you want to be in five years? Write it on the top of a pad." I wrote down "Harvard Law School." It was a strange thing for me to write because I had never thought of Harvard Law School in my entire life prior to that moment.

The next suggestion was "Make a list of the things you have to do to get there."

I wrote my list. Number one was "Get a GED." That was really a stretch because I didn't even know what a GED was. My second item was "Go to community college." That was equally strange because I had no idea what the difference was between colleges and universities or community colleges and junior colleges. Third was different as I was very familiar with the concept. I wrote the letters "K" and "A", which stood for Kick Ass—something taught to me as a young boy by my stern taskmaster of a father. One thing for sure, he certainly taught his children how to work hard. He toiled longer and harder than anyone and set the example.

Then the speaker said: "Now turn the page and write about where you want to be in *ten* years."

I wrote "Walking USA." I then sketched maps of the United States and drew on them different routes I could follow. Having been told I would likely never walk again it was pretty foolish, but the morphine was at work on my mind. Unlike attending Harvard Law School or getting a GED, this actually was a longstanding dream. From the time I was seven or eight years old, I had wanted to walk across America. As a lad of five or six, I used to dream about walking to Niagara Falls, the Rockies, the Grand Canyon, the Redwood Forests, and the Big Sur. Every month when the *National* Geographic would show up in our mailbox, I would add places to my dream list. Now, in my drug-induced state, I traced the lines I had drawn with my fingers that would take me to these many special places. Maybe this was my way of deciding I *would* walk again, mentally overcoming the emotional blow dealt by my doctors.

After all this, I finally fell into a deep and long sleep, not knowing if what preceded it was real or imagined. I tossed and turned all night, dreaming of Harvard Law School and walking across the country. I dreamed of walking through cities. I dreamed of walking across the Great Plains and the "amber waves of grain." I dreamed I would walk among the gargantuan trees of the redwood forests and through the Big Sur. I dreamed of the Green Mountains of Vermont and of the Rockies in all their "purple mountains majesty." I dreamed that I walked "from sea to shining sea" and it was beautiful, indeed.

I woke up the next day thinking about my marathon dreams. I was surprised to see that the legal pad was right beside me on the bed and I had, indeed, written about Harvard, getting a GED and Walking USA. The handwriting was mine so that part was not a dream. Still, now that

I was fully conscious, that seemed to be nothing more than a flight of fancy. That would quickly change.

The doctor and a nurse arrived to do their post-breakfast rounds. Coming up to my bedside, the doctor asked, "How are you doing this morning?"

"I'm great! I have decided I'm going to Harvard Law School and I am going to walk across the country." He raised his eyebrows; surely that was not the answer he expected.

Turning to the nurse, he said, "I don't know how much morphine you've been giving him, but stop. He's delirious; he thinks he's going to Harvard Law School."

I had never accepted that I couldn't do something—especially if someone *told* me I couldn't do it. The notion of going to Harvard Law School and walking across the country began to sink in and take form. I told myself: *You can do it—go for it!*

So, with only a ninth grade education and a knee beyond surgical repair, I focused on making my morphine dream come true. From the outside my goals seemed absurd and downright ridiculous. Maybe because I was pushed against a wall, focusing on the morphine dream was my private and personal last-ditch effort at hope. I could give up or go all out. I chose the latter. I had already failed at everything else so what did I have to lose?

What follows is the story of a long walk—physical, figurative, and at times, metaphysical—across multiple landscapes in the long prelude to a different life. It is the story of the trials and tribulations I confronted as I set about pursuing the morphine dream. Now that you have the book in your hands or on your Nook, take the journey with me. If you find yourself beginning to dream about your own future, don't be afraid to "go for it—you can do it".

Make your own dreams come true. Take it from me—it is never too late. If you have hope, you can have a dream. If you have a dream, you can make a plan. If you have a plan, you can get where you want to go. Don't wait; make it happen.

Part One
No Longer a Dream

The key to realizing a dream is to focus not on success but significance, and then even the small steps and little victories along your path will take on greater meaning.
—Oprah Winfrey

Chapter One
One Step at a Time

Follow your dream.
Take one step at a time and don't settle for less,
Just continue to climb.
Follow your dream.
If you stumble, don't stop and lose sight of your goal
Press to the top.
For only on top can we see the whole view,
Can we see what we've done and what we can do;
Can we then have the vision to seek something new,
Press on.
Follow your dream.

—Amanda Bradley

On another summer day, far removed from that hospital bed, dawn broke in all her glorious splendor. I was standing on my own two feet at my *alma mater,* Harvard Law School. Breathing in the fresh morning air, I was anxious to take my first steps on the final part of an improbable journey. It was 6 A.M. on July 4, 1997, nearly sixteen years to the day since my morphine-induced dream—but this was not a fantasy. It was the culmination of a dream fulfilled. I was finally launching my improbable—but meticulously planned—walk across America.

Was I ready for this? I hoped so as this was a moment I had waited for my whole life. My home, my creature comforts, my regular work routine, would be replaced by new sights, sounds and experiences each and every day for the next five months. I was sorry to be leaving my wife and children behind but I knew that I would come back a different person and hoped that they, too, would gain from my experience.

I would not be trekking across the country alone. I'd hired a young Brazilian man named Charles as my trainer, driver, and companion. Charles was a Brazilian soccer star who became a nurse's aide after a career-ending leg injury in a motorcycle accident. I had only found Charles a few days earlier at the recommendation of his cousin Marco, who had helped my family move into our home in Newton. Without a support "crew" I knew my plans were in jeopardy, so I was relieved beyond words when Marco told me about Charles and he came to see me about the job. It seemed a good fit. He was eager to see America and spend time with his family members here in the States.

Charles sat behind the wheel of a brand new, shiny white Ford van that my eight-year-old son, Nicholas, fluent in Spanish and English, had named *"candida"* meaning "pure white." The vehicle was stuffed with enough equipment to outfit a sporting-goods store. My wife, Estela, whom I met when I was a first-year student in law school and she was a visiting student from Honduras studying computer science at UMASS Boston, snapped photographs.

I had two starting points—one that was significant to me personally and one that was better for media and a grand send-off. I started at Harvard Law School because that is the first goal I set on my notepad when I was in the hospital. After my unofficial starting point there, I would walk to the Hatch Memorial Music Shell, on the "Esplanade," on the banks of the Charles River near downtown Boston.

This five-mile stretch down Mass. Ave. from Cambridge to Boston took me about an hour. On July 4th every year, the Boston Pops Orchestra celebrates the nation's birthday with a concert at the Hatch Shell, followed by a thrilling fireworks display. On this particular early holiday morning, the banks of the Charles River alongside Storrow Drive was decorated with blankets: people staking claim to prime seating for the evening's concert. Along the river's edge, hundreds of inline skaters, walkers, joggers and bicyclists—all ages, sizes and shapes—glided by, a freeway of fitness enthusiasts and people-watchers.

Many people came by to wish us well; others to check out the E-150 Ford van. It was customized for my adventure, converted into a portable hotel room. The vehicle, a "high top" conversion van, had a double bed, television, computer, VCR, vast storage bins, and four roomy captain's chairs, among other amenities. The abundant storage space allowed Charles and me to load everything we needed for my long walk. The van was the most expensive and intriguing vehicle I'd ever owned, but I would not be driving it. That was Charles' job. He would follow me at a snail's pace wherever I walked.

Charles generated curiosity, too, especially among the young women who seemed to swirl around him. He was a tall, dark-skinned, curly-haired young guy, with an athletic build and calm demeanor. No wonder he was so popular with the ladies.

I had added a six-mile loop around the Charles River to my original plan for the first day before heading to my official starting line in

Copley Square. A small group of friends walked the first mile with me. Among them were my sons, some of their classmates, their moms, Estela, and Gladis, my mother-in-law.

As I took the first step, my eyes welled up with tears that soon streamed down my face. Speaking was impossible; I was so overcome with emotion. This moment was my liberation from years of frustration and uncertainty. I was thrilled to begin at last, but was not without apprehension. Though I had accomplished so much, would I be able to complete this last figurative step? This journey would take me over 5,000 miles and would be far from easy, either physically or mentally. I was overweight, over fifty, and a diabetic. My knees would never be 100 percent—I was lucky to be walking at all. Would I humiliate myself? Plus, I was sad about leaving Estela and my boys behind.

After the first mile, our friends dropped out as planned. Estela and Nicholas walked with me for the remaining five miles around the Charles River. Louis, my younger son, walked the first mile and then rode his bicycle the rest of the way.

My completed loop around the river brought me back to the Hatch Shell. I bid *adieu* to everyone who had come to see me off and headed for Copley Square.

Officially, my walk across America—which was also a desultory tour across my checkered life—began at the finish line of the Boston Marathon in Copley Square. I would walk the grueling marathon route in reverse. I had walked it each fall for the previous eight years, coming from the opposite direction, as a participant in the annual Jimmy Fund Marathon Walk. I had also run twice in the marathon many years before, as a youngster. The first time I finished in about four hours. The second time I had to drop out at the notorious "Heartbreak Hills" in Newton because of severe blistering.

Standing on the Boston Marathon emblem, I knelt and kissed the ground, like I was greeting the Pope.

I crossed the three-foot-wide yellow-stripe finish line that stretched from curb to curb on Boylston Street. Those were the first official steps in a 5,004-mile journey: If all went well, in 26.2 miles, I would arrive at the official starting line of the Boston Marathon in Hopkinton, a line identical to this one.

Two miles away, Charles waited for me in Kenmore Square. By then, I had already walked twelve miles and I needed a break. My clothes were soaked. I changed into dry duds and climbed into the back of the van. It was pushing 90 degrees outside, but the temperature in the air-conditioned van was a refreshing 65. My blood sugar was very low; I hadn't eaten enough. The diabetes I had struggled with for years caused me to be extra vigilant about my sugar levels. I knew that low blood sugar meant "feed the body." I snacked on salted peanuts and sipped a Diet Coke as an antidote. It was important for Charles to recognize when I was potentially in trouble from diabetic-related symptoms, so I had explained to him, in detail, the problems that occur to diabetics, especially with extreme exercise. I was glad that he had some medical training.

Any long-distance walker will tell you that no matter how carefully planned your journey, you can be stopped dead in your tracks; not by your cardiovascular system or sore muscles, but by the blisters on your feet. I lay down in my new bed as Charles attended to my feet under the watchful eye of my virtual podiatrist, Nicholas. During my twelve weeks of training, upon my arrival home after walking twenty-five to forty miles, Nicholas would carefully minister to me. He'd cut my nails, drain my blisters with a syringe, apply ointments, and massage my feet with a moisturizing cream. I was amazed how that little guy could handle adult responsibilities so well.

Charles also knew what he was doing. After stripping off my socks and shoes, he cleansed my feet with alcohol and sprayed them with a coolant while looking for potential problems. He noted two latent blisters and put tubular toe bandages on each.

Estela, Gladis, and my boys chatted with me while I rested. This was the last time I would see them until Labor Day weekend when Estela and the kids would fly to Peoria, Illinois, and walk with me into Des Moines, Iowa.

With fresh socks and shoes, I was rejuvenated and ready to go. I said a final good-bye to my family, and set off on a small side trip: a jaunt around Fenway Park, home of the Boston Red Sox, where I had once dreamed—like millions of other kids—of playing professional baseball.

The lap around Fenway brought back many memories, the foremost of which was Ted Williams, "The Splendid Splinter." "Teddy Ballgame." "Mr. Baseball." Whichever name you preferred, he was the best. He was the second coming. He was forever . . . I thought. Those were not the days of great Red Sox teams. While the team always had its notables to complement Williams, like Jimmy Pearsall, Frank Malzone, Jackie Jensen, Vic Wertz, Bill Monboquette, Mickey Vernon, Dick Stuart, Sammy White and others (Boy does that sound like an all-star team!), they usually had among the worst records in baseball. I didn't care.

I remembered one year when the Sox had catcher-pitcher combinations of Ike and Nixon (Delock and Russ), Sullivan and Sullivan (Frank and Hayward) and Hillman and Tillman (Dave and Bob). The fun I used to have with those names.

In ensuing years, there had been three league championships and many very good teams. Several superstar players had spent some or all of their careers here. But for me, the years from the mid-fifties to 1967, the year of "Yaz" and the "Impossible Dream" held the most wonderful of memories. No matter how many great players come along—the likes of Fred Lynn, Jim Rice, Carlton Fisk, Mo Vaughn and Roger Clemens, Nomar, Big Papi, Manny and Dustin, no Sox team will ever overshadow the "Cardiac Kids" of 1967.

It was past noon and I had thirty-four miles to the end of my day in Marlboro.

It was definite that I'd be walking long into the dark, but I knew that when I agreed to the starting time of 10:00 A.M. in Copley Square because of press obligations.

I headed back to Beacon Street. I knew I was in the right place because of the giant Citgo sign that looms high over Kenmore Square and the ballpark. All over the country, that spectacular sign is recognized by the "Red Sox Nation." It is also a great place for the brave fans that climb up on it to watch the game from the most perilous of seats.

When I reached Cleveland Circle, I had completed fifteen miles with thirty-two to go. It was almost 2 P.M. and I felt new blisters forming. I had already changed my sneakers twice because of discomfort. This was not a good sign this early on in my journey!

A few more blocks and I walked by the entrance to Boston College, and soon ambled down the Heartbreak Hills of Newton, the famous nemesis for many Boston Marathon runners each year. The hills begin at about the eighteen-mile marker (when coming towards Boston) of the race and continue for almost two miles. They are so steep that many runners drop out. But for me, there was no problem; I was walking *down* those hills.

Crossing Route 128 meant I was halfway to Hopkinton. My pace had picked up. I got a second wind heading west. Crossing the Charles River on Route 16, we entered Wellesley. Soon thereafter, I walked by the very house where, working with my friend Slim nineteen years earlier, I'd been pruning bushes when he urged me to go and find myself.

As I reached Wellesley Hills Square, it hit me how much Wellesley had been a part of my life. I only lived here for five years, but I had worked in the town for eight more years. I saluted the folks at the Maugus Restaurant as I passed by. I had been eating the culinary delights of the "Maugie" for almost forty years. Over those forty years and thousands of meals the Maugie was an indelible part of my life. That memory served only to make me feel very old. For much of that time it was owned by only one family serving simple, home-cooked food with a side of warmth and friendliness.

Many people of enormous wealth call Wellesley home. When I was in my teens, some of my friends chided the wealthy, resenting them for their material success. What I had found, living and working there is, most of the people, wealthy or not, were decent, friendly folks who were very aware of the fact they were privileged to live in such a unique town.

During a break for supper, I reclined on the double bed in the back of the van. I turned on the Channel 4 News to watch my earlier interview with reporter Mary Ellen Burns at the Hatch Shell before we had departed. Charles had never seen himself on television and he was beaming—or maybe it was because he seemed smitten by the beautiful blonde reporter.

After more than an hour's rest, Charles checked my feet so I could get back on the road. I had so many tubular bandages and blister patches on my feet that I was beginning to wonder if I could tolerate forty miles a day. The heat was on the attack. There were no days like this during my training. My new shoes didn't seem to fit well, although they were comfortable earlier in the day when I first laced them up. As the day progressed, the shoes became uncomfortable. Charles drained several new blisters and applied antibiotic cream, which made me feel better at least temporarily. I began walking again and the pain came back but I pushed through it. I said to myself, *Just keep going, one step at a time*. I couldn't slow down now. Darkness was approaching.

Chapter Two
Training

*The purpose of training is to tighten
up the slack, toughen the body, and
polish the spirit.*

—Morihel Ueshiba

It had only been three months since I had set the date for my journey and begun training in earnest. It was April 1, April Fool's Day, and I knew that only a rigorous walking schedule beforehand would allow me to complete the trek. As they say, there is no fool like an old fool: and at the age of fifty-two, I'd be walking 5,000 miles, through all sorts of weather and terrain, at a rate of about forty miles a day. A walk of that magnitude requires a thorough conditioning regimen no matter what your age. I had only ninety days to get my 325-pound body ready to march out of Boston on our nation's birthday.

Though I had been walking several miles a week, I hadn't walked more than five miles in a day since the Jimmy Fund Marathon (26.2 miles) the previous September. I set out a rather simple schedule: I'd walk five miles a day for the first few days. Then, I increased my program to five miles twice a day, with five hours of rest in between. Then I quickly increased my jaunts a mile each day for each walk, until I was doing two twenty-mile walks a day, with a one-hour rest in between. It sounds a lot easier than it was.

I had four reasonably new pair of Rockport Professional Walkers. By alternating pairs each day of my training, I was comfortable and had little difficulty with foot problems. Blisters seemed to be a part of walking, so I was not really bothered by them and Nicholas helped minister to any problems that cropped up. I ordered four new pair of Rockports, which would be shipped at the end of June—just in time for the beginning of the walk.

The raw and often wet springtime weather had made walking somewhat uncomfortable. I knew I needed to get used to the varying conditions, good or bad. I knew that once I started my trip, the weather could be much worse in Montana and beyond, so I trained without complaint.

I also needed to think a lot about my pace. I considered a twelve- to fourteen-minute mile optimum. That's power walking, at least for me.

I usually walked at that pace for a marathon walk or shorter events. The next level "strider," is a fourteen- to sixteen-minute mile, while "fitness walking" is at a rate of sixteen to eighteen minutes a mile. I needed to work at all three paces. I had to always know how fast I was walking, without any gadgets like pedometers or stopwatches, which are pretty much useless. I needed to know when and how much to slow down, and when to gear up a little. It was necessary to be able to set internal clocks to keep me on schedule.

As I continued to add miles to each of my two daily walks, I began to add obstacles like those I expected to encounter when I walked across the country. I walked hilly routes; the more hills, the better the training. I walked in terribly inclement weather, regardless of the temperature. I regularly walked as far as possible without water and food, to build endurance. As my walks increased to twenty miles a day, I began to encounter insects. At the same time, my rest periods were shortened more each day.

I learned long ago from the noted distance walker Rob Sweetgall that, while distance walking, if I completed an arduous and lengthy walk one day, and then repeated it the next day without difficulty, I'd be prepared for that distance—regularly. I needed to see how ready I was.

April 20, 1997, the day before the Boston Marathon, I left my home in Newton and walked to the house of an old friend, Al Waterman, twenty-five miles away in Sharon. I had spoken to Al that morning, telling him only that I'd see him later in the day. It was a rainy, bleak day, the temperature in the high forties. Some call it the right weather for an extreme walk or run, but I prefer warm sun over raw, wet and dreary conditions. I purposefully selected a route that included many long hills so that I could continue to build stamina for the terrain I'd encounter when walking the USA. I showed up at Al's, drenched, beat, and looking like an old man *should* look after twenty-five miles. Al was flabbergasted that I'd walked all the way to his house from my home in Newton. He said, "I guess you really are serious about this walk."

The next day, April 21, was the 101st Boston Marathon. I showed up at the starting line in Hopkinton at 6:00 A.M. My plan was to walk the marathon route, finishing before the runners got to Boston. If I could complete the twenty-six miles after doing twenty-five the previous day, I would be comfortable about my conditioning level.

I set out on the course that I had walked many times in the past as a participant in the annual Jimmy Fund Marathon Walk that benefited children with cancer. When dawn broke, it was warm and sunny: perfect conditions in my playbook. It was a special time of the year to be walking. The grass was greening up, the buds and leaves on the trees were coming to life, and tulips and daffodils filled the air with their sweet fragrance. Along the route, many people were outside working in their yards.

When I reached Kenmore Square, one mile from the finish line, the Boston Police ordered me off the marathon route. Rather than try to defy the police I decided to end my walk in Kenmore Square. It was more important for me to complete twenty-five miles without rest or significant nourishment two days in a row.

As I stepped up my training, I was faced with significant problems. I regularly found myself out of water and snacks, with no idea where I might find some. Going to the bathroom was always difficult simply for want of an adequate place. Often, the biggest problem was finding a place to rest. With ants, moisture, and the worry of what's hiding in the weeds, the ground was often not a great place to take a break, and I usually had no idea how far away relief was. I had nobody to help me. This was planned deprivation, though. I needed to establish my ability to keep walking, in spite of whatever obstacles I encountered.

Walking fifteen miles twice a day, with a two-hour rest in between, I found the physical demands less challenging than the mental. To keep pushing myself for long distances was a mental process. By this time my legs operated as if they were a machine, but I had to force myself to ignore the signals my brain was sending me. "You can stop now," it told me. "You've done enough today." Those messages I had to quash, and it wasn't easy. Some days I gave in. I realized that it was the mental challenge which would make or break "Walking USA."

By the middle of May, I had moved up to the optimum of twenty miles a day, twice a day, with only a one-hour rest period. After a few days at that level, I was walking pretty much problem-free. I decided it was time to cut back; I didn't want to be worn out by July 4th.

With my training curtailed, I walked only ten miles, twice a day. As mid-June approached I cut my distance back to ten miles each morning. That was my schedule until Friday June 27, when I again walked forty miles a day for four days. In mid-May though, ten miles each morning seemed like a stroll. Now that summer was in full bloom, with temperatures reaching into the seventies, I was out early, when the birds were singing and I could hear the "peepers." The scent of newly cut grass was my companion on my morning walk. It was a pleasant time of year to be meandering around the Newton area at dawn.

On June 27, I was left with one more week to prepare my now 298-pound body to walk the daily forty miles that I had scheduled. I was delighted that I had lost twenty-seven pounds while training. I felt a lot different in spite of the fact that I was still size "double extra fat." With that in mind, two twenty-mile strolls each day for the next four days should be enough to get me in prime condition.

Forty miles a day, for four days, I'd managed to do without difficulty. Three days remained until I was to begin my adventure, and I had a lot of chores to do. I wanted to rest my legs, and five miles a day seemed appropriate to keep my muscles alive and yet little enough to allow me plenty of rest and leisure time to attend to all the final details of the last three days. I was ready. Or at least I thought I was.

Chapter Three
My Heartbreak Hills

Boston's legendary course has the reputation of being both gorgeous and nasty at the same time. Its hills have swallowed even the most elite runners

—Mike Morrison

Although I had whizzed down Newton's Heartbreak Hills, the hills leading into Hopkinton were my personal heartbreakers. Now it would be uphill all the way.

I was exhausted, soaked to the bone, with blisters upon blisters. I didn't know if I could finish the day, never mind the trip. How could I endure hundreds of days and thousands of miles of this punishment? I pushed myself up another steep hill and there it was—the three-foot-wide yellow stripe across the road. I was there, finishing my reverse marathon. I leaned down, with my palms resting on the stripe, kissed the line, and shouted as loud as I could, "I MADE IT!"

Laughing, Charles pulled up. I climbed into the back of the van for another rest.

"What's wrong?" he asked.

I was overwhelmed with emotion. "I crossed the starting line," I told him. "Do you have any idea what that means?"

I couldn't explain. *I* was not quite sure what it meant. After the strain of my Heartbreak Hills, I needed to rest before the final eight miles to Marlboro. Lying there in the quiet of the evening, I could hear the sounds of 20,000 pairs of sneakers smacking the pavement on marathon morning. It's the sound you hear in Hopkinton every year in mid-April—and it's one you never forget.

I remembered when I ran the marathon long ago, back in the late fifties. In those days there were less than 500 runners, and even then the distinctive sound of sneakers slapping the pavement was something you could only have heard in Hopkinton

At 9:30 P.M. I still had eight miles to go. On Route 85, two police cars approached, one from each direction. It turned out someone had called to say "some whacko" was walking down Route 85 in the dark. Thankfully, the police—who reminded me of Andy Griffith and Don Knotts—were polite and respectful. They realized what I was doing as soon as they saw the van. Furthermore, when they saw that among the listed charities I was raising money for was C.O.P.S. (Children of Police Survivors), they thanked me profusely. They urged me to be careful on the narrow road at night. I assured them that I was an experienced walker and would be vigilant.

Fearful, Charles looked on. Because of his temporary visa, he was nervous.

Pushing on to Marlboro, I desperately wanted to lie down. I passed under the Massachusetts Turnpike. Half an hour later, when I passed Route 9, I knew I was getting closer to the end of this arduous day. My hips ached and rashes under my arms stung from perspiration and friction. I had a headache. My feet were taking a beating. With several miles to go, I felt like I should have already given up for the day. But I realized I must push on, or else the notion of quitting when things got tough would rule the walk.

I needed to focus my mind on something else. If I continued to bemoan the difficulty of the next few miles, I would never finish the day. I began to think back about my life. I was soon lost in thought.

Chapter Four
Sea of Uncertainty

The quest for certainty blocks
the search for meaning. Uncertainty
is the very condition to impel man
to unfold his powers.

—Erich Fromm

One night I grew up. I was thirteen. My father had committed suicide. I didn't know that night that he had killed himself. The younger kids were told he had a heart attack. I only knew he was gone—forever.

He left behind my mother and seven children, ranging in age from four to twenty-one. He was diagnosed bipolar, also known as "manic depressive," but in the 1950s no one knew how to treat that illness.

While my dad was harsh and abusive by today's standards, he was a good and decent man. He was extremely strict and demanding because he wanted his children to be focused and achieving. He was highly intelligent, but for some inscrutable reason, he never found himself. He worked as a granite cutter in Quincy, a bricklayer on the Harvard campus, a florist, and a landscaper. He was good at everything he did; he had been a superior student in high school and an excellent football player. Yet he always seemed in limbo, adrift in a sea of uncertainty. There was a strong seasonal component to his illness. He was missing for much of our lives, especially in the winter months when he was often in a state hospital. According to my mother, who finally told me about his death a couple of years later, he attempted suicide more than forty times during their twenty-five-year marriage.

In his final attempt, he had stuck a garden hose in the tailpipe of his pickup truck and ran it into the passenger compartment. He was only forty-four. My older brother Dickie had searched for him for hours and found him in his truck at an estate where we had been working. During the last week or two before he died we had all been working at that place. After that, I could never bring myself to go there again.

He left too soon. I never got to know him and it certainly seemed like he never wanted to know me. It seemed to go far beyond his role as taskmaster to make us stronger adults. My relationship with him was hollow and empty. He barely ever spoke to me or acknowledged me, let alone have the kind of heart-to-heart conversations kids want from their dads. I have heard stories that he believed my mother conceived me during an affair with another man and that I was not his son. Perhaps, if the stories were true, it could have caused an emotional rift when I was born that lasted throughout the rest of his life. I do not know anything about my mother engaging in that behavior. I doubt she did. But it was his thoughts—truth or fantasy—that left him distanced from me for life. I was left with the sense that I never had a father. To this day, I wish I had one.

By dying, he made all of my siblings anxious and insecure. Why would he do that to his children and his wife? How could he leave us forever, without a father to help us grow up?

In an instant, I became a man, thirteen going on thirty-five. It was the beginning of my own long journey—a long and often miserable journey, drifting and treading water in that same sea of uncertainty. It apparently ran in the family.

My father's suicide forced me to find work. There was no money. There never had been. Now, there was no food. Growing up there often was nothing—no heat, no electricity, no clothes, except old and ragged hand-me-downs. I had to get a job . . . several jobs.

For my mother, always at home with her brood, it was time to get a job so she could keep her family together. She soon was working the soda fountain at the Rexall Drug in town. She would get off at 4:00 P.M. and come home, only to go to straight to bed for a few hours because she had to work the overnight shift at the local mental hospital from 11 P.M. to 7 A.M. Her third job—as if two were not enough—was working on the weekends as a hostess at the Howard Johnson's in the neighboring town. In essence, my father's death took my mother from me, too. All my life, until that point, my mother had been home—for me and all her children. Now, she was virtually an absentee mom.

My siblings' lives seemed reasonably stable. My two older sisters continued on in college. My older brother took over my father's landscaping business. My other brother was away at high school. My two younger sisters were too young to work or contribute. We were all alone in the world. My father's family ignored us. I think they blamed my mother for his death. There was no counseling in those days—we all just had to live with it.

I did find employment. In the early morning hours, I'd walk a mile in the dark to the news agency arriving by 4 A.M., where I prepared bundles of newspapers for delivery to paperboys, to the street corners of my own routes, and to stores throughout Westwood. I'd then walk ten miles each morning, from street to street, picking up my bundles, then going house to house, pulling my little red Radio Flyer wagon, delivering the local "rag" to the scores of homes on my route.

This job also came with a big perk. There were often coupons in the newspapers for free loaves of bread. I'd cut some of them out of my customer's copies, hoping they wouldn't notice, and take the coupons to the supermarket, exchanging them for as many as fifty loaves that I would proudly give to my mother. It was amazing how she could "stretch" that bread out to make all kinds of things: bread pudding, sandwiches, bread broken into small pieces with sugar and milk in a bowl for breakfast, two loaves stacked on the table for dinner, toasted bread slathered with butter and cinnamon for snacks. It was our major food group—sometimes our only food group. We lived the phrase "our daily bread."

I enjoyed the walking that came with my job. It got me out of the house and away from the misery that often enveloped it. I would lose myself in thought, walking my early-morning paper route. I often wondered what it would be like to walk all the way to Boston and back.

I had been to Boston only once, about a year earlier when my father was given tickets, enough for the entire family, for the Green Bay Packers and New York Giants exhibition game at Braves Field. The trip into Boston mesmerized me. Although only twenty miles it seemed a world away. I was astonished by the buildings I saw, many with familiar names. I got to see the Warren Spahn Diner, a place I had heard about often on the radio listening to baseball games. The diner was named after one of the Braves' greatest pitchers in history, who was also one of my baseball heroes. The stadium was like a holy place to me.

It was my first sighting of trolley cars, my first encounter with blacks, and my first time seeing so many thousands of people in one place at one time. It was the first time I heard the hawkers shouting, "Hot dogs heeeere!" or "Popcorn, peanuts and crackerjacks!" The cacophony of sounds was like a symphony. The colors, as I looked around the stadium, were dazzling. The aroma of all the different foods and beer was an experience I had never sensed. The football, although a special event, was secondary to my having the experience of going to the city.

Weekday mornings after I was finished with my paper route, I'd reluctantly show up at school. Although I was wide awake and alert after walking ten miles every morning, most of my classmates had just gotten out of bed and come right to school. My four hours of walking had my brain far more stimulated than most of the kids.

When school began in September, after my father had died, I was in a fog, not at all interested in studying. The teachers often repeated the same material I had been exposed to throughout elementary school. It was hard not to be bored. I remember thinking to myself, *Not this shit again.* If school hadn't been compulsory I wouldn't have gone. In fact, I often did not. With my father gone, I had no strict overseer like before. Missing this kind of guidance, the truant officer and I became well acquainted. The teachers' lectures about how I'd never go anywhere if I didn't get an education went in one ear and out the other.

School simply didn't interest me. Earning money, playing baseball, and walking were the only things that mattered. Maybe it is because my family and I were in "survival" mode after my father died and I could not project out to the future—or did not want to. I was living for the here and now and just trying to get by.

I also barely had time for homework and studying. After school I had other jobs. I would rush off to the hardware store or the dry cleaners where I earned fifty cents an hour as a helper, sweeper, or stock boy. My job there included going through the pockets of the clothing to remove pens, pencils, candy, and anything that could foul up or damage the dry-cleaning machines. Naturally, I also found lots of coins and sometimes dollar bills. My record one-day haul was $30, which was a lot of money back then. I would take the windfall home to my mother, whose eyes lit up like a Christmas tree.

One of my "helper" duties was delivering the cleaned clothing, time which I used to promote my other sidelights. I would slip a piece of paper with my name and phone number into customers' pockets, offering my services for babysitting, lawn-mowing, yard work or snow-shoveling, depending on the season.

Besides walking, my other love was the baseball diamond, which held magical properties for me. Despite going to school and working I always found time to play the game. A distant relative of my mother, Pete Daley, was a catcher with the Boston Red Sox. Of course, I became a catcher. I dreamed of being on the Red Sox, too, tipping my cap to the crowd at Fenway Park as I jogged around the bases after hitting a home run. I never thought of any other career, and it wasn't just a pipe dream. I could hit with power and run, throw, pitch or catch as well as anyone. It was the only time I felt really good about myself. My idol was Ted Williams. I always wore his number 9. Baseball was empowering for me. It gave me purpose.

When I was fourteen I met Alice, my first romantic love. She gave me something else to feel good about. She was gentle, considerate, intelligent and beautiful. Her family became my family. Her father became a father figure for me. I even called him "Daddy" for the next thirty-five years, until the day he died. I would eventually have many such mentors, without whose kindness, compassion and guidance I would have faced a bleak future.

Alice was two years older than I was, which created some peer problems for her, though she tried not to let it bother her. You never fall as hard as you do for your first love, and that was certainly true in my case. So what happened next absolutely crushed me and changed the trajectory of my life.

In her senior year of high school, Alice suddenly vanished. I never found out why. I reran in my mind all the moments we shared. Not a day passed (even years later) that I didn't think of her, confounded and confused by what had happened. I am sure that not having resolution with my father's suicide contributed to this pain, though I could not see this for myself at the time. I decided to escape my emotional anguish by getting my "duty to serve my country" out of the way.

In the 1960s, with the U.S. becoming entrenched in Vietnam and mired in the Berlin crisis, every able-bodied young man faced military conscription to battle the scourge of communism. I had seen young professional baseball players, like Ted Williams, interrupt their careers because they'd been drafted or had enlisted. I didn't want to interrupt my career. I would serve my country first and *then* become a professional baseball star.

I wanted to join the Marines on my sixteenth birthday but when I tried, I found out you had to be seventeen. I waited the agonizingly long year until then, suffering through uninspiring teachers and dreary texts. The grades I received—all F's (all well-deserved)—reflected my increasingly diminished interest in academics. To be fair, some of my teachers were excellent educators. The problem was me: I didn't study; I didn't bother with homework; therefore I flunked all my courses. I'd already suffered the humiliation of repeating the ninth grade, each day surrounded by younger kids with whom I couldn't relate. I felt isolated. I counted the days to my next birthday so I could flee.

Unfortunately, my stint in the Marine Corps was exceptionally brief. About six weeks into boot camp our squad was instructed to move from the first floor to the second floor of the barracks. As we were carrying our heavy footlockers up a long flight of stairs, someone in front of me tripped and fell against me. Like a domino chain I and everyone below me went tumbling down the stairs. On my way down, I knocked over many of my fellow recruits and somehow I ended up at the bottom of the heap beneath many of them. My knees, back, neck, and shoulders were injured, for which I should have had surgery. Instead, I got whirlpools, physical therapy, and a medical discharge. Worse, my left arm was useless and would remain useless all of my life. That caused big obstacles for me as I was left-handed. I had to learn to do everything right-handed.

Soon after, my knees had recovered enough to engage in physical activity, I travelled to Southern California to try out for the Los Angeles Angels' farm system, but I didn't make the cut. I returned to Boston where I played semi-professional baseball in the Boston Park League. There, I honed my skills playing with and against many of the most talented athletes in the area—guys like Tony Conigliaro, Tommy Bilodeau and Mike Fornieles. Life was good. I enjoyed hitting home runs. Nicknamed "Line Drive," I usually crushed the ball. As a catcher, I relished picking runners off at first or third base, never mind those trying to steal second. When I had been left-handed, I was blessed with a strong arm and could throw out runners without getting up from the crouching position. My right-handed throwing turned out to be even stronger. The future looked promising.

However, by the time I turned twenty, I found myself no longer able to hit a fastball. I didn't realize it, but my eyesight was deteriorating from incipient diabetic retinopathy and macular degeneration. Of course I knew nothing about those afflictions until several years later when they worsened. My career plans were slowly wasting away. In baseball, when you can't hit a fastball, it's over. I struck out too frequently; five times in one game. I tried to hang on. I was only twenty-two when I was eventually cut from the team that had signed me. What was I going to do? How was I going to support myself? I had pinned all my hopes and dreams to baseball without a thought that I could not do it and certainly had no alternate plans.

I started driving a truck, making home deliveries for Lechmere Sales, a large retail store in Cambridge. I also decided to try out for a local professional football team, the South Boston Chippewas of the New England Conference. I was never into football and didn't know what to expect, but I made the team.

Once again, sports gave me the opportunity to have fun. As a defensive lineman and designated pass rusher, I found that sacking the quarterback was as thrilling as hitting a home run. Football became the new focus of my life.

It was at Lechmere Sales that I met a beautiful young girl, Louise. For the second time in my young life, I fell in love, or so I thought. Louise was tall, almost as tall as me. Her hair was always so attractively styled. I absolutely loved her sense of humor and she could get a laugh from any situation. We enjoyed so much together. Hockey was our mutual passion. We loved going to Bruins games or watching them on television. We also liked to go out, and we frequently found our way to clubs where we could see the live performances of many outstanding music groups. We were like groupies, always looking for the new talent that regularly showed up in Boston area clubs.

After more than a year of dating, I did what most people who are young, in love, and irrational do: I got married and started a family. Louise and I were soon blessed with two beautiful daughters, Nancy and Dawn Marie. Now, I was the sole supporter of four people. I drove trucks in the daytime and taxis at night. I also worked security jobs on alternate nights. I pumped gas on weekends. In short, I was always working. I hardly ever saw my family. I was taking care of my responsibilities but felt like I was just treading water. I discovered that what all my teachers had told me was true: When you don't have an education, earning an adequate living is extraordinarily difficult. Football season was the only time I felt satisfied. The game had become my passion. I made more money from each game than I did in a month of driving. The jobs were only the means to support my family.

Despite, or maybe because I had patched together all these jobs, my family wanted for nothing. My mother-in-law, Gert, was always there to help out. My girls were so spoiled by Louise's mother and other relatives, I was amazed. We bought a beautiful two-family home, and renovated the first-floor apartment for Gert. On the surface, life was a huge improvement over what I had experienced growing up. Beneath the surface was a different story. My relationship with Louise had steadily deteriorated from the beginning. We were never on the same page and we were like strangers to each other. It was evident to us both that the marriage just wasn't working. This was certainly not what I wanted but I could never figure out a way to make our life together more harmonious; something I regret to this day.

I felt restless and adrift. When I lost baseball, I had lost my dream and therefore my goal and my sense of purpose. Getting married had only made me responsible for other people when I had not yet reconciled my own emotions. Like perhaps many other folks, I had no idea how difficult life after marriage was. It was certainly life-changing in a totally unexpected way. Something inside me was seething but I did not know how to direct it into something positive. I only knew that this life was not what I wanted but I had no idea how to fix it.

Chapter Five

Some Things Are Written in Our Blood

Bipolar robs you of that which is you.
It can take from you the very core
of your being and replace it with
something that is completely
opposite of who and what you truly are.

—Alyssa Reyarsk

When my brother David—like my dad—developed bipolar problems other family members pressured me into running his business. He was only about thirty and suffering from the same types of behavior that had plagued our father. My sister Fran and her husband had put significant amounts of money into it to help out. Although I was reluctant to take over I felt obligated to the family. My sister quickly convinced me that I needed to step up and help so that the business and their investment were protected.

While this was not something I wanted to do for work, it did pay the bills—barely. At least, the tasks varied with the seasons. I mowed law,ns in the summer, raked leaves in the autumn and, when winter came, plowed snow. At least I was plowing instead of shoveling. I liked mowing lawns because I got to walk many miles a day. I enjoyed the scent of newly mowed grass and being outside in the fresh air. It was as good as a menial job could get. I sang as I worked, serenaded by the high-pitched whir of the lawnmower. Perry Como's famous song, "Faraway Places with Strange Sounding Names" was one of my favorites. Crisscrossing the yards, making patterns in the grass, had an almost meditative affect and I daydreamed about taking long walks to those "faraway places" that I had always dreamed of visiting. I could see myself walking in the mountains, the prairies and the great forests of America.

I struggled with the business for more than a year. The demands on me had multiplied. I was fully responsible for not only my family of four, but his family of six. He had four children: the oldest was eight and the youngest a newborn. David had run up enormous bills during the previous twelve months because of his illness. He was the force behind the business. Without him at the helm, it was difficult to maintain the necessary revenue streams. To make matters worse, he had done some crazy financial deals that left the business without capital.

When I couldn't take the stress anymore, I asked my sister and her husband for permission to seek a sale of the company. They granted it and I put the company up for sale. My brother was in no condition to make decisions and my sister controlled the majority interest in the company. The conditions I had set for the sale protected my brother's interest in that the sale would supply him with the necessary cash to buy a house for his family and provide him with a new vehicle and a well-paying position with the successor company.

Ron "Slim" Slamin, a close friend of my brother's, owned a competing business: Slim Landscape Gardener. He agreed to purchase our company, for which I was relieved and grateful, but there was a catch: I had to work with him for two years to ensure that all of our customers would remain his customers.

The last thing I wanted to do was continue cutting grass, raking leaves, fertilizing lawns, and doing tree work. I was in my early thirties, not getting any younger, and this was demanding work that I knew I could not do forever. I also had a delusional vision that greater things were in store for me. I had no clue what they were. I vaguely sensed I was meant to dance to a drummer whose beat I could feel, but couldn't hear.

I became irritable, depressed, and grew into an unpleasant husband and father. My marriage continued to suffer but Louise certainly wasn't to blame. Maybe the writing had been on the wall all along but after eight years together, she and I finally separated and divorced. I was really floundering now.

A lonely year passed. I missed Louise and my daughters. I was wrong to leave; I should have worked at my marriage instead of just capitulating. My mantra was "life sucks," which just pulled me down further into the vortex of depression. I didn't want to be like this but it seemed that there was always something going wrong, and I kept slipping into the rut. Forlorn beyond belief, I often cried myself to sleep.

Then I met Susan, who was in the process of getting a divorce. She had three small children, Amy, seven, April, five, and Chuck three. She had come along when I really needed something to give meaning to my life. Football, which had once given me so much pleasure, had lost its magic. Besides, it was a young man's sport and the young men who keep playing it age exponentially. I didn't want to be a cripple from years of mindlessly sacking the quarterback.

Susan was a far better companion than men on the gridiron. She and I hit it off immediately. She was a great homemaker, a lovely friend and companion, and a tender lover. She was a cook of magnificent repute, rivaling my mother's cooking, and she could make anything taste awesome. Every day she and the kids waited for me to get home to have dinner with them. I liked that. In the mornings, I would get up at 4:30 A.M. because I had a commute of more than an hour. Susan would get up with me, cook breakfast, and sit with me while I ate. I had never experienced that kind of caring and felt downright spoiled.

My divorce from Louise had been acrimonious and thus emotionally taxing. Still, I was ready to try again so Susan and I married two years after we met. Sadly, the nature of my split from Louise was so bad that I lost touch with my daughters. Susan's children helped fill that void, though I missed my own daughters terribly. I tried my best to be happy and make this relationship work. For a while, in the early years of our marriage, I was content. Or maybe I was just distracted from the angst of what was missing in my life. Whatever it was.

Chapter Six
The Basket

Sometimes we must lose
Ourselves to find ourselves

—Unknown

The two-year commitment with Slim drifted by. While I had finished my required time working with him, I had nowhere to go, no other options. I was now a foreman, which simply meant I didn't cut lawns anymore. Instead, I supervised the lawn crews, sending them out each day on their routes, making sure they were properly equipped and staffed to complete the daily task list. Slim and I would then go together to the homes of customers with our own list of chores. Usually we pruned shrubs at the numerous estates throughout Wellesley, Massachusetts.

Early one morning in late June 1978, Slim and I were doing a job at a stately colonial home. I was pruning bushes on the right side of the house; Slim was pruning bushes on the left. After a few minutes, I became lost in thought, almost catatonic. I had put down my tools and was just sitting there on the wet grass, motionless. I thought, *What am I doing here? Why am I pruning bushes, sitting on this wet grass—in Wellesley? I belong somewhere else; anywhere but here. Will I ever discover what I really should be doing with my life? How will I ever get off this treadmill to nowhere?*

Suddenly, I heard Slim's booming voice: "Brownie, take the rest of the summer off and find what you're looking for, whatever it is."

I couldn't believe it. He'd read my mind. With tears in my eyes, I asked, "Why do you think I need the summer off?"

"You're lost. You're in a fog. I can see you don't belong here. Come up to the office tonight and get your check. I'll pay you up to Labor Day. Go wherever you have to go, but find out what you want. Come back and see me on Labor Day and let me know how you've made out."

I didn't have to ponder his offer for long. The freedom to go exploring and to be paid for the privilege was a deal I couldn't refuse. Now I just had to convince my wife.

I went home and asked Susan, "Can you get your mother to take care of the kids so we can go away for the summer?"

"Why, what is going on?" she asked.

"I want to take you on a mystery expedition."

She raised her eyebrows and I could tell that the prospect of an "expedition" was exciting and might seal the deal. "Where are we going?" she asked.

"I don't really know where," I told her. "The where doesn't matter. We have an eight-week paid vacation compliments of Slim."

Susan seemed as happy as I was to go on our spontaneous voyage. She went to the kitchen to call her mother

A few minutes later she was back, beaming. "My mother agreed to come up from Duxbury to take care of the kids for the summer. She'll be here in a few hours," she said happily.

We packed the car and left the next day.

We visited Susan's "Aunt" Susan in Pennsylvania. She wasn't really Susan's aunt; she was Susan's mother's best friend and had never had children of her own. Susan was even named after her. Aunt Susan's lovely smile and elegance immediately reminded me of my mother.

Next, we visited my sister Beryl in Oklahoma. My second oldest sister, she had graduated from nursing school and had joined the Air Force, to "see the world," but she had only gotten as far as Tinker Air Force Base. Nursing was her real passion—she thrived on helping people—and she was everyone's favorite in my family.

After Oklahoma, we drove directly to Arizona, where I fully expected to find what I was looking for. Oddly, I still hadn't a clue what it was, but I was convinced it would be there, that I would have some sort of epiphany right there in the desert between the scorpions and the saguaro cactus plants. I couldn't have been more wrong. Our experience there was miserable. The summer heat was intense, rising to 115 degrees during the day. It was so hot you couldn't walk on a sidewalk, even with shoes on, because the heat burned right through your soles. People there also didn't like what they called "tire kickers." Too many folks like us showed up there looking but not staying. Consequently the people we met weren't friendly, plus the job market wasn't promising. I could have gotten a job cutting grass but why would I go 3,000 miles to do that—especially in that heat? After two weeks, we left Arizona in the rearview mirror.

We headed east and spent a lot of time sightseeing. Back in Oklahoma City, we stayed again with Beryl, who told us we could stay as long as we liked and insisted that we weren't imposing on her. However, there was nothing for me to do there. Oklahoma City was not for us. I realized that the solution to my restlessness was not geographic, but abstract—and abstractions can be elusive. We headed home, more uncertain than before.

While on an interstate in Arkansas, we saw a sign advertising "Baskets for Sale" at the next exit. Susan said, "Brownie, get off here, I want to get a basket." I immediately turned off the road. While Susan shopped I killed time by looking through a Strout Realty catalog I'd picked up in the lobby, which listed farm properties for sale all across the country. I turned to the Massachusetts pages and found an ad for a place that sounded appealing:

**Former barn, remodeled into a
Colonial house—with woodstoves.
Blueberry bushes, lilac bushes,
Apple trees, 2 acres, Priced to sell!**

I looked up. Susan had her basket. Little did I know, stopping for that basket would alter my life.

"Susan, look at this," I said as I showed her the listing. She was as intrigued as I was and we decided to drive directly to Orange, Massachusetts, in the western part of the state—a thirty-hour drive—to see the property. Orange was only seventy-five miles from Wellesley where we were living, but it was like a different world. It was rural, mostly farmland with small mountains surrounding the town. It was charming and was idyllic. Living here would certainly be quiet and peaceful, without congestion, noise and traffic jams. We both loved the ambience of the area. It was exactly the kind of place where we had both lived when we were children.

We arrived on Labor Day morning, not expecting to see the property because of the holiday. We drove to see it anyway, and found that the house was unlocked. We knocked and wandered in. An older man, dressed in old-fashioned overalls, was cutting trim and baseboard, hammering, and measuring.

I asked him, "Do you know where we can find the person selling this house?"

"A-yep, I guess I can," he said, with a Maine accent. "That's me. Name's Ron Stone. I am just finishing getting it ready."

"In the ad, it says 'priced to sell.' What's the asking price?"

"Well, I guess I could let it go for $35,000, and with an extra acre of land it would be $37,500."

I looked at Susan whose face lit up. She didn't need to say a word; her expression told me she was thrilled by the place, giving me unwritten permission for my next move.

"Sold," I said impulsively. I wrote out a check for the deposit.

At last, I'd found the answer. I was sure of it. I'd stumbled on what felt like "home" for the first time in my adult life. Every place I had lived in before was just that: a place to live. This home was different. It fit us. It was surrounded by the things we loved: deer in our backyard, apples to pick, fragrant, purple lilacs each spring. We had mountain views from every window. One of the best features was there was plenty of room for a vegetable garden.

Susan ran from room to room, making notes about wallpaper, paint, colors, and furniture. She was ready to move. We drove directly back to Wellesley, talking all the while about papering and painting together, to make it *our* house. When we arrived home, we immediately told the kids that we were moving to a new house—our first real home.

A few days later, Slim's crew helped us pack our belongings into a rental truck and we drove back to Orange. It was such a magnificent and peaceful place. Deer wandered into our backyard every morning, eating leaves off our apple trees. Rolling green hills surrounded us and there was a pristine lake only a mile or so up the road. The plaintive coo of mourning doves woke us up each day. It was like a dream. We loved being there.

The kids were thrilled with their new home. They loved their new school, as it was much less crowded than the schools in Wellesley. Susan enjoyed her role of house manager and loved providing for all of us. There remained one problem—what was I going to do for work?

In Orange, there was essentially one employer, the Rodney Hunt Company, which designed and produced goods for the textile and water-control industries. (There was also a parachuting and skydiving business, but I'm afraid of heights.) The Rodney Hunt Company was the largest manufacturer of water-control products in the world. It seemed like a booming business, as their facilities covered what looked like hundreds of acres. I filled out an application but there were no openings. I went to neighboring towns. No luck. I went as far as Worcester and Springfield, which were fifty miles away; still, no luck.

Finally, after a two-month search, the Rodney Hunt Company called to offer me a job as a factory laborer. The pay was reasonable, the people seemed friendly, and it appeared to be a decent place to work. I accepted and began a new career as a factory laborer.

The Basket

It didn't take long to find myself dissatisfied again. Mowing lawns had actually been a step higher up on the employment ladder. At least in that job I was outside and I enjoyed the endless walking. My new job was physically demanding and dirty, as in filthy. My shift was typically 3:00 P.M. to 1:00 A.M. Often we had mandatory overtime which had us working until 3:00 A.M. I assembled and painted giant cast-iron sluice gates. The end of every shift left me coated with a fine layer of paint all over my face and hair. The paint was so toxic that the label on the cans warned, "In case of skin contact, go directly to the nearest hospital." Given this description it felt like I was working in a Superfund site. Not only was I covered with the disgusting paint, I also breathed it into my lungs every day. I couldn't wait to get home in the wee hours of the morning after my shift to take a shower. I'd get out of the tub and look at the thick patina of black paint in the stall. When I'd blow my nose, black paint filled my handkerchief. It was scary and it was repugnant.

Working that crazy shift wasn't good for family life, and I never saw the kids much. They would be off at school when I was sleeping. I would be gone at work by the time they got home. Susan was supportive, but not being home together as a family was tough for her. I made it worse by going to play golf most days with my new friends from the factory. They had a routine of hitting the course by 10:00 A.M. and getting in eighteen holes before it was time to report for our shift. I should have been more aware that my marriage would certainly suffer from the unusual schedule I was on.

The job kept us afloat financially, at least, and Susan and the kids loved our new home. Still, something kept gnawing at me. I still felt like something major was missing from my life. I was often semi-catonic—in a fog—opining over what was missing. Ever since I was thirteen—after my father's suicide—I'd been treading water in that same sea of uncertainty. I sensed that something just beyond the horizon was tugging me, like the moon pulled at the tides.

The answer was obvious. It was staring me in the face. Yet I was clueless.

Chapter Seven
Blisters on Blisters

March on. Do not tarry. To go
forward is to move toward perfection.
March on, and fear not the thorns,
or the sharp stones on life's path.

—Khalil Reyarsk

I trained for this odyssey in comfortable, worn shoes and mostly cooler weather. I had not prepared adequately for a forty-mile day in the heat of a New England summer. It was certainly a mistake to try and break in new sneakers on this very hot day. I had started with eight pair of shoes: four old and worn pair and four brand new pair. My plan was to alternate them and slowly break in the new ones.

A church bell struck midnight as I reached Marlboro Square. I took over the wheel from Charles, who was exhausted. As I was to later realize, it was an enormous ordeal to drive a van at three-and-a-half miles an hour for thirteen hours a day. Staying alert was a real challenge. The stress of the effects on traffic and how badly we interfered with drivers was constant.

We drove straight to the Holiday Inn. In spite of being frazzled and overtired, Charles decided that he would repack the van. He was having difficulty locating gear and supplies. I couldn't help him. My feet were covered with blisters. My legs were tight and sore; my hamstrings ached. "I'll deal with the equipment problems in the morning, if I survive the night," I said to Charles. If this was the way I felt on the very first day, I didn't see how I would make it out of Massachusetts, never mind to Big Sur.

I was bewildered. I had trained long and hard, so I thought I was prepared. I knew this walk would not be easy but I certainly did not expect to be knocked out like this on day one in my home state.

Six hours of sleep was hardly enough. My legs were stiff and aching. My feet, shoulders, hips, and back told me that my training was insufficient. I couldn't put on my socks or shoes. It hurt too much to bend my legs. Charles helped me, like a father getting his son ready for school in the morning—but a kid certainly would have felt better than this!

It was already nearly 90 degrees at 8:30 in the morning. I started walking from Marlboro to Hudson, passing through several small towns and villages, and then on to the cities of Lowell, Lawrence and Haverhill. I had programmed my body to walk, but it was not responding. My legs were like prosthetics. Both shoulders sagged under an Atlas-like load. My feet were on fire with combustible fluids and sadistic abrasions. I tried to think only ten minutes ahead at a time. If I thought about miles or hours, I would surely give up, so I set ten-minute goals.

Charles seemed skeptical: "I no think you can do this. Your feet very bad."

Maybe he was right. I was quite heavy, weighing in at 298 pounds, and I felt every gram of fat in this heat. I decided to strip away some of the weight I was carrying. A fanny pack with thirty-two ounces of water was the first to go, along with my half-gloves, which I wore to protect the back of my hands from the sun. I even tossed my little hand towel into the van. All of those items didn't add up to much, but every little bit helped. I felt the difference, even if it was psychological. My legs were livelier; my hips weren't nearly as sore. There was a bounce in my step.

The walk on Route 85, north from Marlboro, took me through a rural area. The traffic was now so thin that I walked in the middle of the road. It was the best place because it was flat.

Walking with a "sag wagon" definitely had its advantages. Training was lonely and creature comforts were non-existent. Now, Charles was always nearby with a cold drink, a snack, a meal, medicine, a change of clothes, fresh sneakers and socks. I had my own personal mini mall only 100 feet behind me.

Charles was a bright young guy, and I enjoyed having company, but we sometimes had a language barrier. Before we left I bought him some tapes: "Learning English for Portuguese Speakers." Charles used his thirteen hours a day behind the wheel, inching along behind me, to improve his English. I hoped it would. It would be nice to have someone to talk to. As a former nurse's aide, he also seemed to understand my physical ailments better than I did. He was observant and missed nothing. He quickly understood my diabetic problems.

In the heat, passing drivers often noticed my suffering. Some of them stopped with water, sodas, ice cream and other snacks. We didn't need these kind offerings, but it was impossible to refuse the kindness of strangers.

The blisters were getting worse. Charles cut four two-inch slits in the older pairs of sneakers I was wearing, two on each side. Rockport, the shoes' manufacturer, would cringe if they saw what he was doing.

I taught Charles to recognize more of the warning signs of my diabetic problems, as well as heat exhaustion and heat stroke. My aggressive pace created the threat of heat stroke. With his background, Charles seemed to understand.

My goal was forty miles a day, but on the second day, it seemed like I would actually be walking forty-eight miles, because of detours and miscalculations. At 4 P.M. I still had seventeen miles to go. Nevertheless, I picked up the pace. I didn't want to be walking until midnight again. Route 110 took me through Methuen and into Lawrence and back into Methuen.

A lady stopped to say hello, holding out a cool and frosty Gatorade. "How nice of you," I said.

She had read the "Walking USA" plastered all over the van and was curious. She asked: "Where are you going to end up?"

"The Big Sur in California" I replied.

"I think you are headed the wrong way—you are going Northeast instead of Southwest."

"Once I reach Portland, Maine, I will be headed back across Maine and New Hampshire, back into Massachusetts and then Vermont and Upstate New York and westward," I explained to her.

"You certainly are making it hard for yourself."

"It may seem that way, but I have an agenda."

"Please stay safe and watch out for the crazies," she said as she rolled up her window and drove away.

Chapter Eight
The Itinerary

*Even if you walk exactly the same
route each time—as with a sonnet—
the events along the route cannot
be imagined to be the same from
day to day, as the poet's health,
sight, his anticipations, moods,
fears, thoughts cannot be the same.*

—A.R. Ammons

I was not taking a beeline for the Big Sur. It was not about "sea to shining sea" or a direct route. It was about the places I wanted to walk to and through. I had some personal detours to make. For example, up on the hill to my left was the Holy Family Hospital, where I had my last back surgery. That was in 1993, only four years earlier, when I thought I'd have to bury my walking dream forever.

I had laid out a map of the United States and stuck a little pin into different places I wanted to see for the first time, places that had been special for me, and places where people I wanted to visit lived. It was to be an awesome opportunity to see and visit locales I had thought about throughout my life; the "Big Sky" of Montana, the redwood forests of California, Motown, Chicago, Milwaukee, the Great Northwest, and much more.

I spent hundreds of hours over three years wrestling with maps and guides. They were helpful, but there was too much left to chance. I had heard that there were computerized maps, so I decided to try one. I found a Microsoft product called "Trip Planner." It would give me all the route guidance I needed while still at the comfort of my desk. I knew that if the route wasn't plotted correctly and exactly it could mean many extra miles.

While my planned route was 5,000 miles, averaging 40 miles per day, I knew that variables would confront me each day. While I needed a plan, I also needed to be flexible.

Weather was a major consideration. I wanted to walk in "comfortable" weather for as many months, weeks and days as possible. For me, heat and rain, while not optimal, still fit into that category.

The weather I needed to avoid was cold, specifically below thirty-five degrees, and the possibilities of snow or ice. These conditions could greatly interfere with my daily progress—along with being just plain miserable.

I also needed to study terrain. I would need to climb mountains regardless of any route I planned. As I looked at all the possibilities, arranging a schedule that had me walking through Montana and Idaho as early as feasible in the fall was a good choice since autumn storms were a strong possibility. The northern route across the country would result in my walking through six of the top twelve most mountainous states in the country, coming one right after the other: first Wyoming, then Montana, Idaho, Washington, Oregon and California. My legs needed to be up to that formidable task.

After leaving the Boston area, I would head north through the old mill cities of Massachusetts, through a portion of coastal New Hampshire, and into Maine. I would then leave from Portland, Maine, to central New Hampshire, and on to Keene. From Keene, it would be back to Massachusetts to Gardner, Athol and Orange, and then over the mountain on Route 202 to Amherst. After Amherst, Northampton, and then to Greenfield, and finally to Brattleboro, Vermont. From Brattleboro, west over Hogback Mountain, finishing the New England leg of the walk.

I would then head west, through upstate New York, Erie, Pennsylvania, and through the "Rust Belt": Cleveland, Columbus, Detroit, Indianapolis, Chicago, Milwaukee and Peoria. Then I would head to Des Moines and north to the Twin Cities, Minneapolis and St. Paul. Once in Minnesota, it would be mostly westward after that. Through the Great Plains, South and North Dakota, a corner of Wyoming, all the way across the Big Sky country of Montana into the "purple mountains majesty." I would cross Idaho at the panhandle and into Spokane, Washington. Then I would traverse through the "amber waves of grain" in Central Washington, winding my way down into the Columbia River Valley and then quickly climb into the Cascades. Once through the Cascades, I would be in Seattle and turn south, walking alongside Mt. Rainer, Mt. St Helens and into Portland. Then I would again turn west and make my way to the splendor of the Oregon coast.

As I mapped the route from the California/Oregon border to San Francisco, the vastness of this country and California in particular, stood out. I would walk for eleven days, traveling 450 plus miles, and I would at all times still be in Northern California. The final miles from San Francisco to San Simeon, where the walk would end on the southern tip of "The Big Sur," at the Hearst Castle, were all on the Pacific Coast Highway, except for the two times it turned into freeway for specific portions.

In most places there were people I wanted to see; people who had been my friends. Many folks in most of the places I was going had been classmates, either at community college, Amherst College or Harvard Law School. Some were relatives. Many of the cities or towns I had chosen to walk through were picked merely because of my curiosity. It wasn't just filling in the route; it was about places and people I felt I had to see.

With a printout of each day's walk, along with an "itinerary" printed from the trip-planner program, I had a three-ring binder that would prevent me from ever getting lost. In addition, the software and the computer were going along for the ride, just in case.

Chapter Nine
Pushing the Envelope

*Too much of a good
thing can be taxing.*

—Mae West

Somehow I had made a big mistake in plotting the route from Marlboro to Haverhill. The route covered fifty miles, not forty, and that extra ten miles was a killer. The sun was finally setting at the end of a brutally hot day and the temperature changed from scorching to chilly in a matter of minutes. I was only in Lawrence and still had three hours to go after already walking for thirteen hours.

Finally finished we drove a mile out on Route 125 to a Best Western. It was nearly midnight and we had a lot of work to do. We were having such difficulty finding stuff that Charles went to a K-mart next door to the motel—thank God it was open all night—to buy a storage unit for the top of the van and a Walkman for me.

I checked us into the motel then retreated to the swimming pool. The cool water on my sunburned skin was shocking, but a welcome relief. Next to the pool was a small hot tub—a great way to soothe my sore body.

I woke up at 5:00 A.M. Charles suggested an early morning swim and convinced the front desk clerk for permission to use the pool before its usual opening time. It helped loosen my muscles somewhat. When I returned to the room, Charles had re-packed the van and was ready to go. Even with the new purchase, he was frustrated and said, "Van sucks."

I dressed quickly and examined my feet: blisters galore, especially under my toes. Charles wanted to try something new, a thick layer of Vaseline on the front half of my feet. He proceeded to use a whole jar, packing the area between the arches and the bottom of my toes. I pulled on my socks, laced up my sneakers, and discovered that walking was going to be "squishy" that day. It was worth a try.

Chapter Ten
My Prairie Schooner

Fortress, ambulance, amphibious home
on wheels—the humble covered wagon
stands as the symbol of the winning of the West.
—**George R. Stewart**

In spite of the complaints from Charles about the van, I loved it. For many weeks prior to buying the vehicle, I was certain that a standard Ford minivan would serve my purposes. After looking at a couple and comparing the prices and accessory packages I decided to check out full-size conversion vans. I was quick to realize that a conversion van would be far more appropriate than a minivan. I got more bang for the buck as far as standard equipment plus the vast cargo area was just what I needed for this journey.

The Ford Econoline had heavy-duty brakes, shocks, generator, and alternator. There were electric outlets everywhere and it had two batteries. It also had a rear overhead air/heat system, which would be an enormous help during the dog days of summer and the biting cold of winter that I expected to encounter. The pleated shades on all the windows except for the driver's area made it possible to provide privacy when needed and to block out the sun so the van would be easier to cool or heat. Overhead cabinets throughout made for easy storage for the small things I used regularly.

The van had a television, enabling me to watch the news, and it was also equipped with a VCR, which would allow me to watch my collection of movies: the *Rocky* series, *Rudy*, and most importantly, videos of my sons. Whenever I might feel overworked or depressed, I could simply pop in a tape to help me feel connected to my children or a movie to inspire me.

There was also an AM/FM cassette/CD player with six speakers in the driver's area alone, for great sound. A portable vacuum cleaner and electric outlets located appropriately throughout the van would help to keep it clean. The electric outlets would give me the capacity to plug in my computer at will to post my daily summaries on the Walking USA Web page. I had a telephone line to plug into that, which would allow me to connect to the Internet. Most importantly, the van had a bench seat that converted to a double bed with plenty of storage underneath. Trading in my Lincoln, a car I had always dreamed of owning since I began driving, for a high-top van meant that there was no turning back.

Chapter Eleven
Live Free or Die

Is life so dear, or peace so sweet, as to be purchased
at the price of chains and slavery? Forbid it, Almighty God!
I know not what course others may take; but as for me,
give me liberty or give me death!

—Patrick Henry

To my surprise, I felt really good as I began the third day, despite the high humidity, which would make things miserable once the sun was up. I moved along briskly and for the tenth time in three days, I crossed Interstate 495. I walked another mile towards Amesbury, paused for a cold drink, and continued my rapid pace, now headed east, towards the Atlantic Ocean. I promised myself I would walk twenty miles before noon. For the first time, I was beginning to feel like I was in the zone.

The music coming from my new Sony—appropriately named—Walkman that Charles bought me the night before, helped me maintain a faster pace. I loved Motown music. The beat kept me strutting at twelve minutes a mile, or five miles an hour—a pace for success.

A car pulled up. The driver was a young, very attractive woman, dressed in skimpy beach clothing, her face slathered with sun cream. Charles, of course, couldn't take his eyes off her. She brought me a *Boston Sunday Globe*, a liter of ice water, and an ice cream bar. I thanked her profusely.

"I saw you on Channel 4 yesterday," she said. "Are you seriously going to walk all the way to California?"

"That's the plan. Would you like to come with us?" I said jokingly.

"I wish. Will you pay my rent and car payment?" she said.

"I can barely pay mine," I answered. She sped off as I enjoyed the cold treats she gave me.

A few miles farther up, another car pulled alongside. The driver, who resembled Lurch from the Addams Family, brought me a liter of Diet Coke. I wasn't thirsty but I was grateful.

By 11:30 A.M., I had walked the twenty miles from Haverhill to Amesbury and into Salisbury, the last town before crossing into New Hampshire. In Salisbury Center, I turned off Route 110 onto the old Route 1. I would be heading north for the rest of the day.

Drenched with perspiration, I changed clothes every hour. The heat slowed me down to about 3.5 miles per hour. The severe pain on the bottom of my right foot made me wince with every step I took. Charles packed the area again with gobs of Vaseline a couple of times, which gave me short-term relief. But after an hour or so, it started to throb with excruciating pain. I had to find a better way to deal with my feet, or I would surely fail.

As I crossed the New Hampshire border, I was three days and 118 miles into my journey. This was my first state border, with many more to come.

I choked on this thought and pressed on. I was so lucky to be walking after all I had been through with knee injuries. I reflected back on how this had all come to pass.

Chapter Twelve
The Morphine Dream

Morphine
Call your doctor at once if you have a serious side effect:
confusion, unusual thoughts or behavior; or
sleep problems (insomnia), strange dreams.

—Drugs.com

Come January 1980, I'd been working the night shift at the Rodney Hunt Company as a spray-painter for fourteen months, still working the night shift and covered in black paint. On January 30, around 9 P.M., just before my scheduled "lunch" break, I looked up just in time to see an industrial fork lift coming right at me. The driver, Ray L. was joking around, trying to scare me. I attempted to leap out of the way but fell over backwards. Unfortunately, my right foot was caught under a piece of cast iron weighing many thousands of pounds. My body fell one way but my foot stayed where it was. My right knee felt like it exploded. I was a veteran of many knee injuries—so many I'd lost count. Most had occurred while I was playing baseball or football. This one, however, was distinct. The pain was absolutely excruciating, off the charts in its intensity. On the one to ten scale it was about a thirty.

With the help of my co-worker Brian Sibley, I got on my feet. The pain did not abate. I could walk, but only gingerly, as with each step it felt like somebody was hitting me in the knee with an ax. I spent the next few minutes trying to walk off the effects of the injury. I felt enough relief to go off to the lunchroom with my co-workers. When it was time to return to work, I had trouble getting out of the chair. My co-workers realized that I was in real trouble as several came over to my table to help me up. My knee was swollen, had stiffened, and wracked with stabbing and continuous pain, especially when I tried to put any weight on that leg. On my way back, Jim Carey, my foreman asked, "What's wrong with your leg?"

Jim was a roly-poly little man—five-feet tall and three-feet wide— a real gem of a person, and he seemed genuinely concerned. I related the details of the injury. I was fuming. I said, "Ray is out of his mind to be creating situations like this." I continued, "Something has to be done. Take him off duty as the fork truck driver."

Jim said, "He was way out of line to be fooling around, trying to scare people as he drives around the plant, and he's been doing it for years." Jim continued, "I assure something will be done about it. Please be extra careful, ease up some and let me know if it gets any worse."

I said, "Of course," and returned to work. Taking Jim's advice, I eased up quite a bit from my usual pace, mostly because the pain prevented me from pushing myself. Only a few minutes later Jim came by to tell me, "I sent Ray home and suspended him from working until an investigation is completed about the incident."

"Thank you," I said. "He deserves to be punished."

Somehow, I finished the night. I went home and wrapped my knee with an ice-filled towel. I swallowed several ibuprofen but my throbbing knee prevented me from sleeping very well.

Susan was awakened by my moaning and groaning and asked me, "What's the matter?"

Grimacing, I said, "I had a bad accident at work and my knee is really messed up." She got up, came around to my side of the bed and checked out my knee.

"Oh my God!" she said. "It's about twice its normal size." She went downstairs and got another ice bag and helped me to position my knee in a way that would allow me to sleep. She carefully re-wrapped the ice bag in a towel and then put it around the swollen knee.

For over a year I had toiled in the middle of the night, at great expense to my personal life. I had waited patiently for a transfer to the more coveted day shift, from 7:00 A.M. to 3:00 P.M, but, as luck would have it, my new schedule started today—when I needed to rest my injured knee as long as possible.

With only three hours of fitful sleep under my belt, I tried to get out of bed. I realized that I had damaged my knee far worse than I'd originally thought. I could barely walk, the pain was horrible, and my knee was swollen grotesquely. In spite of the difficulties, I managed to get dressed to go to work.

Susan was really upset with me. "You should not be going to work. You should be going to the hospital!"

I told her, "My job is our means of living, I have to go."

"You're going to make things worse and then we will all be in a bad situation. Your health is more important than going to work."

She was really mad, but I had a sense that if I called in sick, unable to be at work, there would be harsh consequences. I said to Susan, "Please calm down and trust me. I am sure I am doing the right thing."

At the plant, I explained to the day foreman about my accident the night before. He had seen the report from the previous shift foreman and he, too, seemed genuinely concerned. He advised me to find something I could do sitting down, at least for a couple of hours, to give the knee time to recuperate. After parking myself on a stool for the entire morning, doing mindless handwork, the plant manager—a guy who looked like Alfred Hitchcock and was as abrasive as Nikita Khrushchev—ordered the foreman to get me back to work. All puffed up he said, "I am not going to have a lost-time accident in my plant!" I returned to my regular duties, hoping my "light duty" had helped. Within a couple of hours I could no longer stand.

Finally, the foreman, who had been watching me struggling to keep performing my tasks, had the sense to send me to the company nurse. She immediately sent me to the Franklin County Hospital in Greenfield, twenty miles away. The doctors there determined that I had suffered a "severe internal derangement of the knee." They sent me home with instructions to stay in bed and see an orthopedic surgeon as soon as possible.

When I got home, I immediately called Dr. James Gibbons, my longtime orthopedic surgeon in Cambridge. I had known him since my days as an athlete and he had performed my first knee surgery in 1966. "I'm sorry, Dr. Gibbons is on vacation. He can see you in a month," said the receptionist.

I couldn't wait. I located an orthopedic surgeon in a neighboring town, who in turn sent me to the Henry Heywood Hospital in Gardner for an arthroscopic examination. This revealed that the damage to my knee was, indeed, serious. The doctor said the impairment level was such that an artificial knee would normally be considered. But he ruled that out as an option because of my age, thirty-five, and weight, 260 pounds. He told me, "You need complete bed rest for at least six weeks, while doing some light physical therapy." He continued "You should make an appointment to see me in six weeks."

"What am I supposed to do for six weeks?" I said, dumbfounded by the bad news.

"Stay in bed, take the medication I have given you for pain, and do these exercises daily, in bed, until I see you next," he said handing me a sheet of instructions.

I went home disheartened, not only because I was under orders to stay in bed, but because I was going to be out of work indefinitely. I would still get paid on disability, but a "lost-time accident," as it was referred to at the Rodney Hunt Company, was the worst thing for your reputation. Throughout the community you were regarded as a malingerer.

Perhaps more discouraging was the fact that I had no idea what the future held for my knee and I was still in a great deal of pain. I was afraid. How was I going to provide for my family? How many knee surgeries would I need? I worried most about whether I would ever walk again. Would I be in a wheelchair or on crutches for the rest of my life?

Susan and the kids were in a state of shock. They had never seen me unable to do normal things around the house. They were used to working with me in the yard, cutting wood for our woodstoves, or mowing the lawn. Now I was an invalid. There was a cloud of limbo in which we were all victims. Everyone pitched in and helped me as best they could. Susan was a real trooper, not only working with me on the exercises but also giving me encouraging pep talks, promising that I would get better. Certainly this unfortunate turn of events was no fault of my own, yet I felt defeated and guilty. In my mind, I had let my family down—again. I felt a complete disconnect with the kids. Worse, there was no intimacy with Susan any longer, as I was in so much pain, I had no desire.

After several weeks in bed, my knee had not improved at all. I had become withdrawn. I was like a recluse. The kids barely talked to me anymore. Susan, although still very attentive to my needs, had become distant also. I wasn't much fun to be around so who could blame them? Growing more despondent and depressed, I sought refuge in food. Ice cream and candy made up much of my diet. I would often eat huge portions of meat and potatoes. I quickly gained thirty pounds in just a few weeks. I had maintained 260 pounds as my weight for several years and now I was up to 290 pounds. I decided to hold on until Dr. Gibbons came back from vacation. If anyone could help me he could.

In early March, Dr. Gibbons finally examined me. He studied the X-rays and the arthrogram, and left the room with Susan. I waited, like a defendant awaits a verdict. After a while, the two returned. I could tell from Dr. Gibbons that he was about to deliver bad news.

"Donald, what do you want me to tell you?" he asked. The tone of his voice, and starting the conversation with a question, made it obvious this was bad news.

I answered, "I want to know when my knee will be back to normal so I can walk and get back to work."

His response haunted me for years. "Your knee will never be back to normal," he said. "You must stay off your legs permanently. You need artificial knees, but that surgery is about twenty years down the road."

He explained that this was the kind of surgery performed when a person was in his late fifties or sixties, so the artificial knees wouldn't wear out in that person's lifetime. "Any other kind of surgery," he added, "would be a waste of time."

I was dazed. This prognosis was so life-shattering that Dr. Gibbons might as well have given me a lethal injection right then and there. My physical strength and prowess had helped me earn a living and my years as a professional athlete had filled me with pride. Rounding the bases after a home run, sacking a quarterback, throwing out runners stealing a base—that's what my life had been all about. Now, it was over. Even walking across the room was apparently out of the question.

Dr. Gibbons was probably inured to these situations and he continued on. He said very matter-of-factly, "You need to make another life for yourself. Go back to school. You have a fine mind. Put it to work for yourself. It's time to rely on your intellect, not your body. Put the energy and passion you've always had during your athletic career to work for your mind."

Easier said than done, I thought. But when Dr. Gibbons spoke, I listened.

On crutches for months, my left knee—which was not involved in the accident—began to really bother me. I suffered, kept awake by stabbing pain in my balloon-sized knees. As a last resort, Dr. Gibbons sent me to Dr. Theodore Potter, another renowned orthopedic surgeon in Boston, for a second opinion. Dr. Potter was famous for having operated on the likes of Mickey Mantle, Joe Namath and Pete Maravich. I was thrilled just to have an appointment with him.

Perhaps Dr. Gibbons just sent me to Dr. Potter to pacify me, but it threw me one last lifeline. After Dr. Potter examined me, he asked if I'd be willing to be a guinea pig. He wanted to perform experimental reconstructive surgery on my knee. If it worked, I would walk again. I immediately agreed, and the surgery was promptly scheduled for Independence Day weekend at the New England Baptist Hospital in Boston. I was elated, hopeful that I might walk again.

The surgery took over six hours. When I awoke in the recovery room, I had a harder time than with my earlier surgeries. The usual people dressed in blue were milling around, and I heard an occasional scream from nearby beds. I couldn't catch my breath and I couldn't feel my leg. I tried to speak but I couldn't. The nurse wiped the tears from my face and said, "You're doing fine; everything's all right. I am giving you a shot of morphine for the pain." I never felt the needle, but suddenly, I realized there were tubes in my nose, throat, and other unmentionable places.

Back in my room and on morphine, I was transported to another galaxy, the loveliest in the universe, where I drifted from one halcyon world to the next. And once again, food got my attention. I hadn't eaten since the day before the surgery. Even hospital food tasted good. As soon as I was finished eating, a nurse appeared to give me a shot of morphine for dessert.

Perhaps, for the first time, the obvious dawned on me. My life had been only a physical one. Now, I was in a bind. I would have to find a new way to provide for my family. But what would I do? I didn't have a single idea. I had no "Plan B."

This is when the morphine kicked in and I sketched out my seemingly impossible and grandiose future on the very pedestrian legal pad—first the GED, then a diploma from Harvard Law, and finally the walk across America.

Dr. Potter never showed up that evening to check on me, so I had no one to tell about my new goals. Later, however, my youngest sister, Nancy, a tenured professor at Simmons College, with her then-husband, George, an eccentric teacher at Boston Latin School, came by to visit. After we had exchanged pleasantries, I handed her the legal pad and watched her reaction.

Once she realized I was serious, she said, "Don't set goals that are so out of reach. But I suppose it's helpful to do this stuff to pass the time." She was right. It was as if I'd decided to walk to the moon and then, on the way back, devise a unified theory for general relativity and quantum mechanics.

I found out later that after they'd left my room, my sister turned to her husband and said, "I don't know what kind of drugs they're giving him, but he's having the craziest of thoughts; he thinks he's going to Harvard Law School."

My mother, always the most important person in my life, was next. I called her, as I did every night. At first we made small talk and chatted about my surgery. Finally I mustered up the courage to say, "I've made up my mind what I'm going to do with the rest of my life, and it means a lot of studying. I'm going to Harvard Law School and then I'm going to walk across America."

There was a deafening silence. Finally, she said, "Don't be ridiculous!"

"Watch me!" I said defiantly.

After hanging up the phone, I fell into a deep sleep. I slept for twelve hours. Suddenly, I woke up. The pain in my knee felt like a knife had ripped open my leg to mid-calf. I rang the nurse's bell. She appeared instantly.

"I'm in pain you wouldn't believe," I said.

My knee was in traction. Once she had lowered my leg back onto the bed, the pain subsided a little. The nurse stripped the Velcro straps from the cast and removed the top. Wouldn't you know it? Some son of a bitch *had* stuck a knife in the middle of my thigh and ripped my leg open to mid-calf. Scores of sutures and staples held it all together. It was grotesque.

After breakfast, I picked up the yellow pad and doodled some more, drawing possible routes from the Atlantic to the Pacific. Obviously, the journey would begin in Boston. More specifically, I decided I would begin my cross-country jaunt at the starting line of the Boston Marathon. But where would I end it? San Francisco? Los Angeles? In my youth, I used to pour over every issue of the *National Geographic* I could get my hands on. For me, the most stunning photos of all were those taken in Big Sur, California. I'd always wanted to see it in person. Well, this was my chance. I would end my imaginary journey there, with the mighty Pacific crashing into the cliffs. Furthermore, I found something pleasing about the alliteration: Boston to Big Sur. Yes, start and finish were all set. Now, I kept tinkering with and tweaking the route between those two points. I calculated that my walk would probably take four to six months. Morphine dreams were such fun.

However, once the painkiller wore off, the view from my wheelchair wasn't so rosy. Back at home, after I was told it would take several months for me to recover from the surgery, I really struggled. Physical therapy every other day was extremely painful and difficult to tolerate. On the other days I didn't get out of bed except to go to the bathroom. The doctor had said it would be twenty years before they could replace my knees. *Why bother with P.T.?* I thought.

One morning, after carefully climbing down the stairs on crutches to make breakfast, I sat staring at my soggy cereal. I had the urge to vomit. I abandoned my breakfast and with difficulty made it back upstairs, back to bed. I hugged the pillows, afraid to let go. I was sinking fast. Suicide seemed an attractive option. All I did was lie on my bed all day long, staring at the cracks in the ceiling. I was tired of the struggle. I was hurt by the cloud that hung over my stepkids and

Susan. Everybody always had a sad face and sad eyes. There was no laughter, there was no excitement, like there always had been. There was no affection among anyone. The difference in the atmosphere in our home after the injury was stark. It was a very tough time for all of us. It would be a relief to fall asleep and never wake up.

This was 1981. I was only thirty-six years old, and the painful idea that I might never walk again was starting to come into sharper focus. I clung irrationally to Dr. Gibbon's advice: develop a plan. The only plan I could conjure up was one that had no hope of becoming a reality—my morphine dream. I kept telling myself that I *would* walk again. I kept telling myself that I *would* get an education: maybe Harvard Law School, maybe ITT Tech, maybe Katie Gibbs Secretarial School. Something other than lying in my bed a hopeless cripple, wishing that I never woke up again.

I spent my days planning my suicide, the only practical solution to my monumental problem. My grim prognosis made this seem like a viable option. I just made everyone around me miserable—they'd be better off without me. Susan sensed my tenuous state of mind. I suffered but kept my thoughts to myself. At some point, I finally decided I had to tell her.

We were lying in bed one night when I blurted out, "I'm such a burden to everyone. I think I need to take a bunch of pills and get out of your way."

Susan was speechless. Tears rolled down her cheeks and she quickly turned away. Obviously she was afraid and she must have felt my pain.

The next morning, without my knowledge, Susan called Dr. Gibbons to alert him. A little later that morning Dr. Gibbons called me and asked me to come to the Mount Auburn Hospital in Cambridge to be evaluated by a psychiatrist. My first thought was, *I don't need a psychiatrist*. My second thought was, *What business is it of yours?* However, because of my great respect for Dr. Gibbons, I agreed to his request, and Susan immediately drove me the ninety miles to the Mount Auburn Hospital in Cambridge. For the entire two hour ride, she never said a word.

My evaluation resulted in my being admitted to the psychiatric ward of the Mount Auburn Hospital. It wasn't enough that I had worsening knee problems, now I was in the "funny farm" to boot. I was no sooner admitted than a doctor told me, "Did you know that your wife is contemplating moving out of your home?"

"What are you talking about?" I said. I was shocked, I knew that Susan had become very distant over the months since my accident, but I never thought she would want to end our marriage. I was beside myself. *Look at the damage I have done,* I thought. I couldn't even talk to her, because I wasn't allowed to make calls for several days.

When I finally got to call her, after some chit chat, I finally got up the courage to ask, "The doctor told me you are leaving, is that true?"

Susan responded, "I am fed up with what has happened to you. You are not the tough man I thought I married. Don't call me. If I change my mind, I'll call you."

I tried to reason with her, but she hung up on me. I was crushed. I guess "in sickness and in health" part of the marriage vows didn't really mean much. I was quick to realize there was little I could do to stop her from leaving me. I promised myself that I would get moving and show her that I was recovering and things would be better.

On the positive side, though I didn't know it at the time, I was beginning a metamorphosis that would dramatically change my life. I was being taught to focus on what I could do to make a life for myself based on my strengths, and to forget about things I couldn't do. I worked on getting my confidence back. I read many books on motivation. I began to realize that I had many strengths. I sensed that I could change the future by getting focused. The hospitalization was very good for me, for it had given me some things to feel good about. I had regained a high level of self-assurance. It was a level that I hadn't experienced since my days as an athlete. I had come to realize that my athletic career had been a result of incredibly hard work and focus. I knew I had to get engaged in a new future and work as hard as I did to be a professional athlete. I needed to focus the same way I did when I took on the challenges of high-level baseball and football.

I was discharged from the hospital about three weeks later. Susan had decided to give me a chance to prove I was on a better path, though she and the kids were still very distant. It wasn't really comfortable for any of us but at least we were trying.

I certainly could not work on the factory floor anymore and, as good fortune would have it, Rodney Hunt Company had a clerical job in the office for me. This assignment would keep me busy for the foreseeable future and the pay rate was the same that I had in my old job. This was very generous of the company. More importantly, I would once again be useful and keep occupied doing productive tasks—a key to my emotional recovery. I would no longer be lying around the house getting depressed.

I gladly accepted the job, of course, and started a few days later. I found the work fascinating. I was assisting in a project to clean up thousands of computer records. Although I had no previous knowledge of computers, I learned fast. I took out books from the library about them, their history, how they worked, and their role in the future. I read scores of those kinds of books, and began to acquire a deep understanding of the machines, still never having touched one. The company agreed to send me to a class entitled "Computers as Used in Business." While this should have excited me, I was actually afraid to go to school. I had, after all, been a miserable student and never even made it to high school.

It was just another fear added to the growing list I had developed since my accident. I was afraid of my failure to be the breadwinner. I was afraid of being tossed aside by my family because I was physically unable to do all the things I used to do. I was painfully afraid of what the future would be for a middle-aged man who was physically devastated. I was afraid of being destitute, as we were closing in on losing everything.

Chapter Thirteen
Nick

It no longer bothers me that
I may be constantly searching
for father figures; by this time,
I have found several and dearly
enjoyed knowing them all.

—**Alice Walker**

In Portsmouth, New Hampshire, walking north on Lafayette Road, I stopped outside the former home of an old and special friend, Nick Charles. Memories overwhelmed me as I stood there. I had planned my journey based on special places and people in my life, and Nick Charles was the reason I went through Portsmouth, a journey planned around special people and special places.

* * *

A few months after my father's suicide, my family moved to another part of Westwood, Massachusetts. We didn't even know we were moving. When my mother got home from work she said, "We are moving tonight."

My mother was struggling to keep a roof over our heads. The size of our family meant we needed a lot of space and there weren't many places that fit the bill. We couldn't afford a moving company, so we had to transport our belongings using my brother's pick-up truck. We must have made a hundred trips to get everything to the new house.

Our new next-door neighbors were the Charles family—Nick and Ginny, and their daughters, Peggy and Evan. Peggy, the oldest, was my age. She was my classmate and had been my buddy for a couple of years even before our move. Now I had the privilege of getting to know her family.

Westwood was a tiny rural town at that time, and all of the residents knew about my father's suicide. It was humiliating the way many people looked at me and my family. The Charles family was a welcome exception and treated us with respect and dignity instead of whispers and sideways glances.

When Peggy and I graduated from eighth grade, she won several awards for academic excellence and I won several for athletic achievements. After the ceremony I got a ride home from Peggy's father, Nick. Beaming with pride, he said words I'll never forget: "One of my kids gets the awards for brains and the other gets the awards for brawn." I don't know that my own father had ever made me feel so good about myself and yet Nick, not even a blood relative, had identified me as one of his own kids. In his eyes, I was special, and I smiled from ear to ear. Those words were even more important to me than the award that inspired them.

Watching the Charles family interact with one another was a joy. They were affectionate with and kind to one another—and with me. I never saw them argue or insult each other. This was in stark contrast to my home environment growing up. Discord, yelling, fighting and a general lack of civility were the norm. I was always treated kindly by my mother and one of my older sisters, Beryl, but the environment in our home otherwise had always been unstable. My family, for whatever reasons, appeared to me to be seriously dysfunctional, certainly when I experienced the way the Charles family treated one another.

One day shortly after the graduation ceremony, I was sitting on Peggy's front porch talking to her about my father's death. "You are so lucky you have a father," I said. "Since my father died, I have felt lost. Life without a father sucks."

Peg's dad, Nick was sitting nearby and overheard the conversation. Interrupting us he said, "Don't worry kid, I'll be your father now." I started to cry. I held back as best I could, because I would have unleashed a torrent of emotion. "Do you really mean it?" I said, with tears rolling down my cheeks and off my chin, creating wet spots on the porch floor.

"Of course," Nick said.

Peggy hugged me and said, "Now you are lucky, I'm going to share my father with you—and my mother and my sister, too."

From that day on, Nick was more of a father to me than my own father had ever been. He became my advisor and mentor, especially during my teens. He was the one who taught me to believe in myself and that I could succeed at anything. I wouldn't be walking across the country if not for Nick. He was a considerate and truly wise man. It is amazing how far a little human kindness can go.

Nick would be the first of several mentors in my life who became father figures to me. I was not so alone after all. It seemed like there were special people around me that understood my losses and wanted to provide me with some valuable guidance.

About the time I dropped out of middle school to enlist in the Marines, Nick and his family had moved from Boston to Portsmouth. If he had been around, he probably would have stopped me from quitting school. He would have been happy that I was going into the service, but not without completing high school. Once they moved I didn't see Nick or the rest of the family very much. As the years drifted by, we lost touch, but never in spirit.

The last time I saw him was in 1981, shortly after the accident that disabled me. Nick came to visit me in Orange Massachusetts, where I was living. We renewed our bond that day. We spent a lot of the day talking about jumpstarting my life. Nick encouraged me to get an education, a message I kept hearing from others, but to which I was deaf.

One summer Sunday, seven years later, I decided to take Estela, then five-months pregnant with our first child, up to Kittery, Maine, to the Outlet Center to shop for baby clothes. As we drove through Portsmouth, I decided to drop in on and surprise Nick.

I called his number about a mile from his house. I wanted to let him know I was doing well and was sad that I hadn't been up to see him in so long. I especially wanted him to see I had risen from my wheelchair. I also wanted him to meet my wife. I knew he would be proud of me. I *needed* him to be proud of me.

Nick's wife, Ginny, answered the phone. After a couple of minutes of chit chat, I asked, "How's Nick?"

The silence on the other end of the line was foreboding. "Oh, Donald," she said, "Nick died last year." I staggered back to the car, sobbing. I was devastated and guilt-ridden that I never got to tell him how much he meant to me. I was sad for the Charles family, who had lost their patriarch.

After hanging up we drove directly to Nick's house, and Ginny and I had a tearful reunion. She didn't know Estela or that we soon were going to have a child. Near the end of the visit I told Ginny, "Our baby is a boy, and on the way here we both agreed to name him Nick."

Ginny was beaming and crying at the same time. She was thrilled that we honored her husband in such a profound way. Undoubtedly, our visit dredged up all the painful emotions Ginny had of losing her husband. Wanting somehow to ease that sorrow, I hugged her and said, "We will have another Nick to love and cherish."

* * *

I left Nick's former house and walked through Portsmouth on Route 1. For the second time in the same day, I crossed a state line. Strutting across the bridge over the Piscataqua River into Maine, I realized that this was the first of only two times on my entire journey that I would walk in three states on the same day. It had also been three days since I left the Hatch Shell, and I had walked 128 miles. Only eighteen states left to conquer until I reached Big Sur and stuck my blistered toes into the salty Pacific

My memories of Nick Charles made me think of my own Nick and his brother. I wouldn't be seeing my boys for a long time and I really missed them. On the Maine side of the bridge, I saw in the distance two little boys walking towards me. They looked familiar, I squinted to get a better look, and as they got closer I realized they were my boys! Totally surprised, tears rolled down my cheeks. *It was a day for tears*, I thought. I walked faster and then ran to make up the space between us. I hugged and kissed them. I didn't want to let go. Tears started to flow again, which embarrassed them. "What's wrong Daddy?" asked Louis.

"I'm just so happy to see you."

"Why are you crying if you're so happy?"

Estela told me she realized that today was the last time my boys could see me until their summer vacation ended, so she loaded them into her van and brought them to Kittery to surprise me. The next afternoon they were all flying to Honduras to visit Estela's family, so they would spend their final night before leaving with me.

"We should have dinner and we'll find a place to stay," Estela said. I told her I had about ten more miles to walk and then we could meet up again.

The shoulders on the road through Kittery were steeply sloped, and it adversely affected my pace. I had sharp pains in my knees and hamstrings, which until then had been relatively good. The condition of my legs and feet was deteriorating. The last few miles were torture.

When I reached my daily goal of forty miles, I told Charles, "I am done. I can go no farther." I jumped into my captain's chair, saying, "Charles, put the pedal to the metal. We're off to join the family."

As we walked into the restaurant, it seemed closed because it was deserted. "I hope you are open for business because we're starving!" I said to the waitress, a jolly, full-figured woman.

"We're open, just not busy, as you can see," she said sweeping her hand through the air. "It's always this way on July 4th weekend."

"Phew, that's a relief," I said. "We'll take one of everything!" Estela ordered a giant baked stuffed lobster, and I had clam chowder, smooth and creamy, and brimming with clams and potatoes. It was so good I ordered a second bowl. Next, I consumed an immense order of fish and chips. The boys ravaged their clam plates. Charles couldn't believe the amount of food we were consuming. I kept asking the waitress for more water. My thirst was unquenchable.

After the long, hot day, I felt thoroughly satisfied, but only for a moment. Stupidly, I had eaten and drank too much. Besides suffering from heat exhaustion, I was nauseated. When I tried to stand, my legs felt rubbery. I hurried to the bathroom and deposited my delicious meal in the porcelain potty.

Fortunately, the motel Estela booked was just across the street. Otherwise, I doubt I could have made it. Once there, I literally had to peel off my soggy clothing. My feet were not happy. I showered and collapsed on the bed.

While finally having a chance to scan the Sunday *Globe*, I noticed that Charles Kuralt, an adventurer whom I had long admired, died July 4th. It was Kuralt, among others, who provided inspiration for my own dream to walk across the continent and to experience the majesty of this country. The obituary read: "Kuralt . . . who traveled the back roads and highways of America, celebrating its differences. . . ." I saw a confluence of the stars. My trek began on the very day he died. One slight difference is that I was walking and he drove.

When Estela and Charles came in to check on me, they discovered my feet were in terrible shape. The patches, meant to protect my skin, had gotten so hot that they had adhered to the blisters. We had to figure out how to get them off. We tried hot and soapy water, moisturizing creams, alcohol—but nothing seemed to help. Any attempt to remove the patches caused great pain. My son Nick worked for an hour, peeling one millimeter away at a time, until the blisters were uncovered. A thorough examination led everybody to conclude that the walk must end. They said my feet would not be able to endure the repeated punishment.

Nick said, "Daddy, I've never seen your feet look so bad."

Estela said, "You can't continue this; it's very dangerous."

Charles chimed in succinctly, using his broken English, "Not good."

In my head, I heard the voice of Winston Churchill, "Never. Never. Never give up."

Chapter Fourteen
My Last at Bat

The world ain't all sunshine and rainbows. It's a very mean and nasty place and I don't care how tough you are it will beat you to your knees and keep you there permanently if you let it. You, me, or nobody is gonna hit as hard as life. But it ain't about how hard ya hit. It's about how hard you can get hit and keep moving forward.

—Rocky Balboa

While recuperating from my surgery after my 1980 forklift accident, I'd learned that people with my kind of disability often remained physically and spiritually immobilized for life. No way was I going to let that happen to me. For me, it would be different. I didn't know how or what, but I knew I would make it happen. Quitting was never an option.

One evening shortly after my surgery, my friend Ed April dropped by with a framed gift for my desk. It was called "A Creed to Live By," written by American statesman Dean Alfange. I was stunned by its words because it expressed exactly what I had been feeling for weeks:

> **I do not choose to be a common man. It is my right to be uncommon, if I can. I seek opportunity, not security. I do not wish to be a kept citizen, humbled and dulled, by having the state look after me. I want to take the calculated risk to dream and to build, to fail and to succeed...It is my heritage to think and act for myself, enjoy the benefit of my creations and to face the world boldly, and say, "This I have done."**

My overall intention was to reverse my grim prognosis. I began assiduously using weights to increase my leg strength. I dieted and dropped twenty pounds. I knew if I could walk, I'd find a way to play softball again. I set a goal: I would go out and cut wood for my woodstove by New Year's Day.

By Christmas 1980, I was walking. It was painful, especially in my right leg, but I limped around pretty spritely for a guy who'd been told he'd never walk again. On New Year's Day, I had the chainsaw shrieking. The smell of burning wood and sawdust covering my clothes confirmed that I was back. Or so I thought.

By spring, I was playing softball again. Perhaps it wasn't judicious, but my sanity demanded it. I played catcher, so I wouldn't have to move much. When I was behind the plate, I bent over, instead of squatting. When I batted, I needed to crush the ball a long way just to be able to hobble to first base. Then a designated runner would replace me. One day, I smashed the ball with a vengeance. It traveled so far that I was able to shuffle all the way to third base, where the coach waved me home. On sheer instinct, I slid into home plate as the catcher caught the throw from the outfielder. "Out!" yelled the umpire. The catcher kindly dropped the ball. The umpire changed his call to "Safe."

Even though I couldn't get up without help, I felt great!

I didn't realize it but that would be my last "at bat," and my last home run. I had done more damage to my knees sliding like a moron into the plate. The following day, the ambulance came and took me back to the New England Baptist Hospital in Boston.

The pain in my knees was beyond excruciating. Dr. Potter explained: "The knee is the most problematic joint in the body. Your knees have been damaged far beyond the point of repair. All we can do is maintenance surgery for now, and we'll do it tomorrow."

The day after surgery, I had an intense itch inside my cast, which itself seemed extremely tight. I called the nurse to complain. "You've got to expect some pain," she said. Obviously she did not understand. This itching and pain seemed abnormal and had me ready to climb the walls.

A couple of hours passed. My doctor hadn't shown up. Now I felt dizzy and nauseated. My roommate looked at me and said, "Are you okay?" I couldn't talk. It felt like I was under the effects of anesthesia. I drifted off . . .

Through the mist I heard: "Get an arterial gas! Get cardiology down here and a respiratory therapist! Is Dr. Potter in the hospital? Cut the cast off, he's hemorrhaging! Get a pump going on his leg! Get some help!" The speaker blared "Code 99 stat 412 west." That was my room. What the hell was happening?

When I regained consciousness, I was surrounded by about twenty doctors, nurses, and other emergency technicians. My cast was off. A doctor was attaching some kind of machine near my ankle.

He shouted, "He's conscious; get his vitals!"

Like a porcupine, I had wires and tubes sticking in me everywhere. The tube in my throat made me gag. I was scared. A needle was rammed into my wrist. The stabbing pain lifted me like a rocket off the bed.

Dr. Potter walked in. I could hear the cardiologist say that my leg had been hemorrhaging badly for hours. "We almost lost him."

Dr. Potter came over and said, "You've had a close call, big guy, but you're doing fine."

I couldn't believe it. I came to the hospital for knee surgery and almost died.

All the surgeries on my knees were taking their toll, each one was worse than the last. Pretty soon, there wouldn't be anything left to operate on. At times, I would look at the future with confidence and determination. At other times, I felt hopelessly depressed, frustrated and angry. I couldn't take it anymore. I was on an emotional rollercoaster. I needed to get off the ride.

Not unsurprisingly, my marriage was going downhill fast. It seemed that Susan no longer was interested in being married to a cripple. "You aren't the man I married," she had said again to me. She was right.

My shoulders, arms, and hands were always sore from walking with crutches, which only fed the depression. I continued to think about ways to commit suicide. Then, a few minutes would pass, and suddenly I would be thinking positive and looking ahead to better days. Paradoxically, my dreams of walking across the country and going to Harvard Law School were the only things that kept me going, but I knew in my heart they were delusional.

And I had nothing to do but eat. I gained a lot of weight. I thought about going to the lake for a swim, or downtown just to hang out. But those excursions were out of the question. There was nobody to take me.

One afternoon, I had an urge for sweets. The craving was so powerful. I loaded my ever-expanding 305-pound body up on my lawn tractor. I was only 260 pounds at the time of my injury. It seemed like I was growing bigger by the minute. With my casts out straight across the engine cover, I drove two miles to a convenience store and bought a box of éclairs. *Enough to last a few days,* I thought.

By the time I got back home, the box was empty.

Chapter Fifteen
Maize and Second Skin

*Maize: A tall annual cereal grass bearing kernels
on large ears; widely cultivated in America
in many varieties; the principal cereal in
Mexico and Central and South America
since pre-Columbian times.*
— **wordnetweb.princeton.edu**

Charles stayed up half the night, treating my blisters. As long as I lay quietly in bed, my feet felt okay. However, any movement at all caused me great pain. I could barely get out of bed.

I began to realize that my legs and feet couldn't take much more. I was too old and too overweight to be doing so much. During my training I walked over 2,000 miles in ten weeks to condition myself. I had more cutting-edge equipment and supplies than you could imagine. My sneakers were the best that money could buy and I thought that alternating the old and new pairs hourly would help break them in. I was wrong.

My feet were a mess. I could only think that this was the result of the steep shoulders of the roads and had little to do with my sneakers. When walking with traffic, my left foot felt like I was wearing a high-heeled shoe, while my right foot felt like I was walking in a sandal. When I crossed the street and walked towards the traffic, the feeling was reversed. I was always off balance, like a ship between high waves. While training around my home, roads were flatter, not like the ones I experienced in New Hampshire and Maine.

I felt sad and discouraged when I woke up. I just lay in bed wondering what to do. Estela, Nicholas, Louis, and Gladis, Estela's mom, visiting from Honduras, were packing, getting ready to go home, and then on to Honduras. *By the time I finish walking today . . .* , I thought, "if *I can walk today, they will already be in Honduras.*" I gave my boys a bear hug and kisses before they departed. I told them not to worry.

Nicholas said, "You'd better quit if your feet get any worse." His eyes showed his concern.

"I'll be all right," I reassured him. I didn't want him worrying about me. What he didn't realize was that I was not quitting, no matter what. I would make it even if I had to crawl. I fought back tears as they piled into their van. This was not the way I wanted my sons to see me, alone and sad.

After they left, Charles decided to seize the day. His English was marginal, but what he seemed to be saying was that I needed "maize and second skin." I didn't know what maize and second skin was, but he kept repeating it.

I called a friend who spoke Portuguese, hoping to get a translation. After five minutes, the mystery was solved. "Maize," my friend told me, "is corn seed. Charles wants to fill all of your sneakers with corn seed and then add water. Over three or four days, the water will cause the seeds to expand and the sneakers will stretch, giving your feet more room. With more room, the blister problem should go away."

My friend continued: "The 'second skin' Charles is talking about is nothing more than nylons that come up to your ankle and go under your socks." He advised me to find a feed store and a Wal-Mart, and let Charles take care of the rest.

Charles learned all of this while playing soccer for the Brazilian National Soccer Team in his native country. I could imagine that soccer players, with the jolting stops they face, have an especially difficult time with the fit of their cleats. Because of the extraordinary stress they put on their equipment, they had discovered these rather unusual and unique methods to ease their foot difficulties.

Charles went shopping at Agway and soon returned with the supplies in tow. He wasted no time getting my feet ready. Even though it was obvious that I wasn't going to do much walking that day, Charles carefully prepared my feet. He slathered a heavy layer of Vaseline in the indentation between the ball of my feet and my toes. Gauze pads held it all in place. That part of my foot was taking a beating. I had never had a problem like this with my feet, and I had been a distance walker for twelve years. After he applied a thick coating of the gel to the rest of my foot, Charles put on the second skin—the new nylon stockings—and then my regular socks.

He took my four newest pairs of Rockport's into the bathroom and filled them with corn and water. I couldn't believe I was allowing him to do this to my most prized possessions. Next, he wrapped them in plastic bags and stashed them under the bed in the back of the van.

It was time to get back on the road, but I was in no mood to walk. However, I was afraid of what would happen if I didn't. We drove back to York where I had left off the day before. Gingerly, I began walking along Route 1 North.

I slowed my pace considerably and I took more rests.

"It's time for a change of sneakers," I said to Charles.

I was eager to see if the "second skin" made any difference. Once my shoes and outside pair of socks were off, Charles pointed to several spots where the nylons had worn thin.

Proudly, he said, "Second skin take rub, not you." He pulled off the nylons, examined my feet, and then announced, "First time feet not worse. Very good."

We found a small diner in Ogunquit and relaxed over a sandwich and a soda. As we were getting up to leave, a woman came in from the Bread and Rose Bakery across the driveway.

She asked: "Who's the walker?"

"You tell me," I said.

She pointed to Charles and said: "It looks like it should be you." Hesitating, she pointed at me and said, "That means it must be you."

"Charles," I said, "that's Maine logic," but he didn't really understand.

A few minutes later I was at the back of the van getting ready to begin anew when the same woman—with a smile as wide as the state of Maine—showed up with a couple bags of goodies, fresh from the Bread and Rose Bakery.

"It's folks like you who make my journey special," I said.

Hours later, when I eased myself into the van for a short break, I inhaled the aroma from the bakery bags. The smell of fresh baked blueberries reminded me of my favorite cook of all time, my mother. A quick peek into the bags and I saw blueberry muffins, a blueberry cake, and other berry treats. I was not hungry, but who could resist a fresh-baked blueberry muffin?

When I was a child I used to pick blueberries for my mother during the summer. As soon as I got the pail into the kitchen, she would start baking. Within a couple of hours there would be blueberry pies, blueberry muffins, blueberry donuts, and blueberry crumb cake. My siblings and I would quickly polish them off. Simply opening this bag, I realized the kindness of a stranger brought all those wonderful memories of my mother flooding back to me.

Fortified, I was back on the road. I planned to cut the walk short today to give my feet some extra TLC. Stopping early had other benefits. My sunburned skin was eternally grateful. My rash-covered arms and thighs welcomed the extra time to absorb a heavy application of moisturizing cream. My knees weren't particularly sore. My leg muscles were not screaming. Maybe I should quit early more often.

After dinner, Charles examined and treated my feet. He inspected the nylons, and said in his thick accent: "Second skin have more bad spots. Each will be blister. You must keep second skin." I wasn't going to argue with him. Clearly, the new foot treatment was making a huge difference. I was so lucky to have him.

The fifth morning was my best since I began the trek. My feet felt good well, better anyway. The sun was coming up on my right as I traveled north towards Kennebunk. Walking was easier today. No hills, no sloped shoulders, and there was enough space on the road for me to walk safely.

While I was looking up at a sign declaring "Welcome to Biddeford," I also saw a Dairy Queen. I couldn't resist. I ordered a giant chocolate cone and found a table, where a very old man was sitting.

"So you gonna walk across country, a-yuh?" he said.

"Yes," I replied, "Would you like to join me?"

"I would, but now's the time for gittin' in the wood." He added that he was in the midst of cutting trees into ten cords of firewood to heat his house for the winter. "First, I cut four-foot logs," he explained, "Then I split them and cut them twice more, into sixteen-inch sections."

"That's a lot of work for an old-timer," I said.

"Why don't y'all come back to the farm and help me cut some firewood." I declined his kind invitation and asked his age and name.

"How old do you think?"

"Ninety," I answered.

He laughed. "You're getting there. Ninety-four. Name's Henry or Hank, but most call me Henry."

"Unbelievable!" I said to Charles. "At ninety-four, when most people are dead, he's out cutting wood."

I bid Henry good-bye.

A few hundred yards up Route 1, I turned left onto Route 111 south. This road would take me to Rochester, New Hampshire, by day's end. Soon we stumbled upon a Wal-Mart. It looked like an airport, a vast terminal surrounded by acres of runways. I had never been in a Wal-Mart before. Charles said, "It has everything we need." We went in together. Here I was a fifty-two-year-old American who had never been in a Wal-Mart. But Charles had, just off the boat. Imagine that.

Later, Charles lugged in the plastic bags containing the sneakers that had undergone the corn-seed-and-water treatment for the past thirty-six hours. He emptied the wet corn from the shoes into a wastebasket. The sneakers looked bigger and roomier, and they felt softer as well. First, for comparison, I tried on the pair I'd had been wearing for the last two hours. They felt good, but snug. Next, I tried a pair that had undergone the "maize" treatment. They felt like slippers.

"Charles," I instructed, "Put corn in all the other pairs, too."

"There is only enough seed for one more pair." He said, "More maize, more maize."

There was no need to call anyone for a translation; this time I understood.

Chapter Sixteen
Nightmare

Those heart-hammering nightmares that start to lose coherence even as you're waking up from them, but that still manage to leave their moldering fingerprints all across your day.
—**Mike Carey**

Fighting the urge to rest too often was becoming a challenge. I yearned for a day off. The physical demands of walking twenty miles twice a day, with a one-hour rest period in between, was difficult, but the mental challenges were even greater. My legs usually operated on autopilot, but I had to force myself to ignore the evil messages my brain kept emitting: "You can stop now. You've done enough today. It's time to jump into the shower." Willpower defeated temptation, but my willpower reservoir was diminishing.

A slight impingement in the kneecap was also bothering me; it was tender to the touch and swollen so I tried a walking stick to reduce the strain on the joint.

These physical hurdles were not surprising. Actually, I had expected them, which is why the van was packed with supplies and equipment. However, all the supplies and equipment in the world couldn't help if I was not eternally vigilant; a simple fall could be walk-ending.

After a couple of hours, I felt better. I was moving at a good clip into a cool and refreshing headwind, even though the temperature was in the nineties. My 3.6 mile-per-hour to 3.9 mile-per-hour pace seemed to agree with my legs. I was saving a slightly faster pace for the flatlands of Ohio and Indiana. Surprisingly, my feet, though badly blistered, were feeling better.

The maize treatments and the incisions to the sides of my sneakers were a godsend. Maybe it was a placebo effect, but I thought the blisters weren't quite as bad. In four decades of sports activity, I had never had shoes that felt so comfortable. I checked them once in a while to make sure they weren't sprouting corn plants.

We met some locals at lunch who urged Charles to join in their pick-up soccer game. Intrigued to meet a real-life Brazilian soccer star, they wanted to see how he handled the ball. Charles, of course would have loved to scrimmage with them and display his talents.

Charles looked at me and I shook my head "no." Before we began our trek, we agreed that he would not play soccer on this trip, due to his own leg problems. As an athlete myself, I knew the desire to play your sport is always present. Charles was only twenty-four, and would have been in his prime playing days were it not for very significant injuries he'd sustained from his motorcycle accident. If he did play, it would jeopardize the walk. So when he looked at me again, obviously disappointed, I shook my head again, "No, I'm sorry Charles."

After lunch, my stiff legs didn't take the hills well. The sky was growing dark and ominous. Up ahead I could see lightning, thunder, and rapidly approaching rain. A few minutes later, a lightning "zap" was followed by a thunder "boom" uncomfortably close. We sought shelter in a mini-market attached to a gas station until the fast-moving storm had passed us by.

Forty-five minutes later, with steam rising off the macadam, I was walking again, behind schedule. Four miles later we reached Laconia, which would be our overnight pit stop.

At a local diner, we lingered over warm bread pudding topped with extra whipped cream. We chatted with a couple of truckers who gave us some useful information about the next day's route.

At 8 P.M., we hit the road again. After an hour of driving by a number of "no-vacancy" signs, we finally located a motel with a room available. As soon as we settled in, Charles removed my shoes and declared that my feet were "improving."

He noted, "Four more days, blisters go, and you feel better."

I hoped he was right.

I was not happy about asking him to take off my shoes, but I just couldn't do it myself. His job title really should have included "personal-care attendant." In the mornings and the evenings my legs were so stiff I couldn't reach my feet.

By day seven and I had walked 300 miles. Few thought I would make it this far. But I knew when I departed Boston that if I could make it through the first two weeks, I would complete the entire journey. As a distance walker, it had become very clear to me that what you do in a day, if you could do it again the next day, without trouble, then you have mastered that level. The same held true for a week. If you could do forty miles a day for a week and follow it with another week at forty miles a day, then you could basically do it weekly for as long as you'd like. The first week was now history. If I could get through one more week, I was sure I could make it all the way.

Nightmare

* * *

At 5 A.M. in the darkness of Laconia, walking on the shoulder, facing traffic, I soon arrived at the front gate of the New Hampshire International Speedway in Loudon. The sign at the entrance read: "Home of the Winston Cup."

Given the activity around the speedway, one would think the Super Bowl was being played here. Race day was still two or three days away, but you'd never know it with all the RVs, pick-up trucks, and tractor trailers in the parking lots.

Two Loudon police officers pulled up and, in a disturbing tone, ordered me to stop. What could they have wanted at 5:30 A.M.? Apparently they had nothing better to do than pester me. They swaggered out of their car; each sporting a blond crew cut and the demeanor of a Marine Corps drill sergeant. "Someone has complained about you walking on the highway," one said.

The other officer barked, "You can't walk on the highway."

Highway? I thought. *This was a two-lane country road.*

"I'm not walking on the highway, sir. I'm walking on the shoulder."

"You can't walk on the shoulder either."

I had no idea what motivated these guys to behave in such a rude manner at such an early hour. Besides, distance walkers know the law, not to mention I was an attorney. If there is no sidewalk, you can walk legally on the shoulder, except on limited-access highways like some interstates.

I asked, "Where should I walk?"

One officer pointed to the brush, where a brook was trickling parallel to the road, heading south.

I walked in the brush to avoid a proverbial "pissing contest with a skunk." A few minutes later, I was back up on the road. I doubted those arrogant cops would be checking up on me, but I was alert to the sounds of approaching vehicles, just in case.

Laconia to Concord was an ordeal of hills and steeply slanted shoulders. My legs ached and my feet were sore.

Thoughts of ending the walk, which in moments of weakness had been quite strong, had all but disappeared. Although my head constantly whispered, "Stop," my heart said, "Go." The heart was winning.

It was 3:45 A.M., July 12. I had trouble sleeping. I woke Charles up and said "I need to get moving early this morning."

He said, "Give me ten more minutes and I'll get up."

I was getting myself prepared to start walking much earlier than normal and I could tell Charles wasn't too happy about it. When the ten minutes had elapsed, I nudged him and he jumped right up and got ready to travel without complaint. I was on the road to Keene, New Hampshire, by 4:15 A.M. I was moving at a pretty good clip, probably four and a half miles per hour, a really rapid stride. I hit some hilly stretches, but I got in twelve miles before the sun came up, bringing with it the heat. The daily grind was becoming second nature. Out on the road this early meant fewer hours in the heat and more miles without traffic. I was ahead of my daily goal.

The early-morning start, much earlier than I normally started, gave me time for "mobile meditation." I was almost hypnotized by the solitude and majesty of walking alone, without people or cars. The trance I was in allowed me to put ten miles behind me before I could blink.

As the day ended, I realized that by the same time tomorrow, I would have left New Hampshire behind.

I needed to focus on the roads ahead, as the Keene area was a little confusing. I was going to finish my forty miles before 4 P.M., my earliest finish thus far. As a reward for finishing early, I said to Charles, "Let's go to Friendly's for a super-sized hot-fudge sundae."

There wasn't a vacant room anywhere in Keene, even though we were over seventy-five miles from the New Hampshire International Speedway. The motel folks called it an anomaly, due to the Winston Cup Race in Loudon tomorrow; I called it a "pain in the ass."

We drove five miles to the south and luckily found a place to stay. Along the way, we scouted my walking route for the next day. The road to the motel happened to be the one we would follow into Gardner, Massachusetts, tomorrow.

I collapsed into bed. I was not used to getting to bed before dark, though I was eager to rest. Unfortunately, our flophouse had no television, no telephone, no air conditioning, not even the usual one-inch sliver of soap. After my soap-less shower, I tried to sleep.

But my mind was racing; I realized how lonely I was. I had never been apart from my sons and I missed them desperately. Charles was also complaining about how much he missed his family.

Maybe the heat was to blame for my restlessness. An air conditioner would've helped. I got up, went outside, and folded myself into one of the lounge chairs by the pool and begin reading the local newspaper. The headlines were about a local businessman who committed suicide a couple of days before. Anytime I heard about suicide I got very anxious as it had been such a big part of my life. When it's in the news or in my community, I feel the dreaded sensations I felt when I lost my father. I doubt that those who take that last, desperate step realize how much pain they cause those left behind. The one who has died is not the only victim—so are their loved ones. They have to live with the anxiety and confusion caused by the suicide for the rest of their lives.

At midnight, Charles awakened me. I didn't even remember falling asleep. It was drizzling. I was soaked and shivering. That wasn't what was bothering me though; I had been having nightmares about my father. I was fragile and teary—eyed. Charles noticed and said, "Are you all right?

I couldn't answer him as I was on the verge of an emotional collapse. I needed to sleep. I lay down and covered my head with a pillow so Charles wouldn't hear me cry myself to sleep.

Chapter Seventeen
Fate, the Phone Rang

As we move through life, the force of fate creates events
that we only appreciate when we reflect on our existence.
—Ronald Harmon

It was a quiet and peaceful Sunday morning as I walked the final miles in New Hampshire. In that part of New England I could walk twenty-five to fifty miles without seeing a McDonald's, Burger King, Pizza Hut, Taco Bell, car wash or strip mall. The Wal-Marts, however, were ubiquitous, which explains their ranking as the number one retailer in the world. My tastes though, favor the mom and pop stores of yesteryear. It's very interesting that Wal-Mart's success was allegedly built on being a very well-run mom and pop store—the very kind of store they have put out of business from coast to coast.

Today was a 4H day. In my youth, 4H was a club for teenagers interested in farming. Now, however, it is my walker's code for a nightmare: hot, humid, hazy and hilly. So far, every day had been a 3H or 4H day. If not for the prospect of crossing back into Massachusetts, just up ahead, I would probably have given up early.

Late in the afternoon, I crossed back into Massachusetts and soon arrived in Gardner, which brought back a flood of memories. I was so fond of this quaint town. From 1981 to 1983, this was where I attended Mount Wachusett Community College and had gotten an Associate's Degree.

I walked by an elementary school near the center of town where a huge chair sat on the front lawn. At thirty feet tall it is billed as the largest chair on Earth, and stands as a symbol for Gardner's status as the "Chair City of the World."

If you've ever walked into a doctor's, lawyer's or professor's office and seen the distinctive black enameled chairs adorned with college emblems in gold, those are among the chairs manufactured in this town. In fact, most of the furniture manufacturers in Gardner—and there are a large number of them—specialize in the production of chairs.

Tom Malloy, one of my favorite professors at Mount Wachusett, gave me a six-inch replica of the giant chair at my graduation in 1983, along with a congratulatory card with the words "So you will always remember where it all began."

As if I could ever forget.

At so many of life's crossroads, serendipity often plays a key role. And I remember this particular coincidence as if it were yesterday.

Fate. The phone rang. It was 1981, shortly after one of my major knee repair attempts. I was not able to work my "desk job" at Rodney Hunt Company any longer due to the constant surgeries and subsequent recoveries. Susan, still hanging in and trying to adjust to all the changes that had worked their way into our lives, was off working as she had felt it was the best thing for us. She was lucky to land a job in the local high school library. This was just after the surgery resulting from when I reinjured my knee, stupidly, while trying to play softball again. The kids were in school. I was sprawled in my recliner mindlessly watching soap operas. I was depressed and near suicidal again. The phone rang incessantly. Those were the days when there was one phone, and it was on the wall in the kitchen. My wheelchair made it difficult for me to get there, not that it mattered since I had no desire to answer it. One day it kept ringing. Annoyed, I pulled myself into my wheelchair, maneuvered into the kitchen and ripped the receiver from its cradle.

I shouted, "What do you want?"

It was someone from Mount Wachusett Community College, cold-calling in an attempt to recruit students.

"We'd like to offer you a free course in the Division of Continuing Education at the Mount."

"No thanks." I slammed the phone down.

I thought, *College? Forget it!* I was too stupid and too old—and too cynical. At thirty-seven, and with the awful state of my emotions, I didn't think college was possible, especially since I hadn't finished high school. The idea of going to college was an abstract and frightening prospect; it was out of the realm of possibility for me, in spite of my "dream." While I had spent scores of hours since my accident contemplating the possibility of college, I was discouraged about my academic shortfalls. My confidence had waned as my physical situation was such a constant demoralizer. On the other hand, without college, how would I ever earn a living again? But the contemplation, at times positive, always seemed to turn negative. I was broken. I was in a wheelchair at times and on crutches the rest of the time. I was in the midst of losing my home, my marriage was falling apart, and there were many surgeries scheduled for the immediate future. It was increasingly difficult to put a smile on my face.

I will admit though, after having read a book about former President Harry Truman, who became a great statesman after being a nobody at forty, my mind was churning. Could I do it? My mind was constantly vacillating. At times I was sure I could; at other times I felt lost.

The thought of a free course, indeed a college course, had instantly become more attractive. I thought a lot about my dream, particularly that I wanted to go to Harvard Law School. The process needed to start somewhere, but I seemed incapable of taking the first step. The fact that I missed high school daunted me the most. It seemed an insurmountable obstacle in any of my dreams of going to college.

Interrupting my reverie was a knock on the door. I already knew who it was: my neighbor Jack Hewitt, who knew I was usually home alone and unable to get around much, coming by for his almost daily visit. His visits were a welcome relief from my dreary existence. Jack—quiet and unassuming—was older, perhaps sixty. (Though that doesn't sound so old now.) He was a professor of marketing at DePaul University in Chicago. Jack and his overenthusiastic and uninhibited wife Eileen owned a summer cottage a few doors away.

"Jack," I said "You won't believe it, I got a call from Mount Wachusett Community College offering me a free course."

He said, "Hell, you ought to do it."

I reminded him, "You forget, I never went to high school. It is pointless to even think about it."

Jack said, "The college would see to it that you got your GED."

I said, "By the way, what is a GED?"

"It is a High School Equivalency Diploma," Jack said. "While you're taking courses, they will prepare you for the GED test." Jack was really pushing. The more he pushed, the more I resisted. I just couldn't do college. I felt a mixture of shame and impotence.

I said, "Jack, you can't drive your car down the highway with no gas in the tank, right?"

"That's true," he said, "but that's not a proper analogy."

"There you go again with your goddamn foreign language. What the hell does 'analogy' mean?"

I tried to make him realize the many obstacles in my way, and that I didn't feel comfortable taking such an impossibly overwhelming step. He gave up and went off to do some errands. I hoped that was the end of it. I knew Jack meant well, but he just couldn't accept the fact that I was not qualified to take such a big leap.

From that conversation though, I had learned something. Jack had said you can get your GED—a General Equivalency Diploma—now I knew what a GED was. I had written "Get a GED" on the night of the Morphine Dream, not even knowing what it was.

That evening, Jack drove up to my house. He often came by to take me for rides at night because, with my casts, I was unable to get into most cars. Jack's car, however, was a full size gas-guzzler, big enough for me to slide in with room for my straightened legs across the back seat.

As usual, Jack was taking me out for an evening ice cream cone at the local Dairy Queen. We had driven for twenty miles tonight, however, and I began to wonder why he was taking me to one so far away. They were all pretty much the same so why go so far out of the way? Minutes later, I was shocked and irked to discover that I'd been misled. Instead of the promised ice cream, we drove up to the entrance of Mount Wachusett Community College.

"Jack, I don't want to do this!"

He responded, "Just go see what they have to offer."

"No!" I shouted.

"If you don't go in, you get no ice cream."

I wanted that ice cream.

Chapter Eighteen
"Donna" Goes to College

I want every individual who has the potential and qualifications to succeed in higher education to be given the opportunity to participate, whatever their family background.
—Gordon Brown, former British Prime Minister

Jack helped me into my wheelchair, and we found our way into the Division of Continuing Education Office. It was open late because it was the registration period just prior to the start of the fall semester. As I looked over the materials, I became fascinated. I signed up for the free course, without any further pitch from Jack. The only catch was I would have to complete my GED before I could be awarded official college credits.

To my astonishment, as I read the information I quickly became so enthused about taking other college courses. If I was successful, I could maybe make good on my self-promise of law school. On the spot, I decided to take three courses, instead of just the free one the college had offered. I signed up for English Composition, Accounting I and America Government.

"How will you be paying?" the lady asked.

This shocked me out of my reverie. I was so impulsive I hadn't even thought about the financial side of this. I had no money for the additional courses or to purchase books. Indeed, I couldn't even afford the books for the free course. I was terribly embarrassed. My face must have turned beet red. I was forced to own up to the situation though. "I don't have any money, so I guess I'll only enroll for the free course." I told the lady.

She said, "Give me a couple of minutes and I'll see if I can figure out a way to get you into the three classes."

I was excited. This felt like it was meant to be. "Thank you!" I gushed.

After a few minutes the woman was back. "How do you feel about registering as Donna Brown?"

I was confused. "What does that mean?" I asked.

"We have some funding for working women returning to college and we can sneak you into that program."

"That works for me," I declared.

A few minutes later the lady returned with the confirmation; I was now Donna Brown, a first semester freshman at Mount Wachusset Community College. It made me feel like a different person. I was filled with excitement and confidence. My eyes welled with tears of pure joy.

That program funded my two additional courses and all my books. The only requirement: I had to go by the name of Donna Brown.

Two hours later, I finally got what I wanted—ice cream. It was going to taste even better that night. We drove to the local Dairy Queen. Enrolling in college was the cherry on top of the sundae.

The next day I showed up at the book store. I selected all the appropriate materials for the three courses and got in the long line to charge them to my "Donna Brown" account. When I reached the front of the line, I told the clerk that I had an account set up by the Division of Continuing Education in the name of Donna Brown. The clerk gave me a look of "Okay Buddy, what are you trying to pull off here?" I explained to her that I was being funded by a woman's program and that it was the way they got me into college for this semester. She had to call the Admissions Office to clear the account. A few minutes later, she gave me a receipt and said "Good luck Donna."

Once home, I began to look over the texts. There was nothing in them that was unfamiliar to me. I spent a couple of hours looking through the books and was certain I could do the work.

Susan seemed uninterested. I started to tell her how good it felt to be heading off to college. All she could say was, "I don't know why you would want to go to college now, it makes no sense."

I was left speechless. I had no idea what would be an appropriate response to that statement. I didn't bring it up again; obviously she wasn't at all in a mood to discuss my plans.

So the phone call that initially made me so angry and annoyed me had changed the trajectory of my life. I had to wonder, *What if I hadn't been on the cold-call list? What if I'd owned an answering machine? What if the rep from the college hadn't let the phone keep ringing? What if I wasn't in a wheelchair and had a neighbor who was kind and felt sorry for me?* The questions went on and on . . . but led me to one answer: Everything does, indeed, happen for a reason and we don't often understand until we see these things in the rearview mirror.

Chapter Nineteen
Another Crossroad

I think you will agree that life's plans are not always tied up in neat little packages. Occasionally we find ourselves at unexpected crossroads with more than one opportunity from which to choose. Time itself is often the best indicator of which decision to make, for it can tell so many things that are now hazy.

—Linda Lee Chaikin

Three days later I arrived at Mount Wachusett for orientation. There were probably a thousand students in the auditorium, all entering the fall semester. At the podium stood the president, Arthur Haley.

President Haley opened the orientation by remarking, "If each of you looks to your left, then looks to your right, understand that two out of three of you won't be here at the end of the semester. If you, however, are the one that is left there are many opportunities here for entering students."

He went on to say, "To those of you who yearn for a four-year degree, this is the place to lay the groundwork. If you can do well here and distinguish yourself it will make a huge difference when you find yourself attempting to transfer to a bachelor's program at some four-year college."

"We have many awards here at the Mount including seventeen awards for the best student in each of the seventeen divisions of the college. If you push yourself and put yourself in position to win an award as the best student in your division, that distinction will help you immensely when you apply to the colleges of your choice. In addition there are about twenty other awards and scholarships that can also make a large difference in your future."

I sat there taking it all in. I was so eager to start. It was time to energize myself and get moving. There was nothing to be feared, I could do this. It was like a switch had been turned on. I was so pleased that I had been led here. The telephone call from out of nowhere and Jack Hewitt's insistence on bringing me to the college had literally changed my life.

Jack had accompanied me to orientation. I made myself a promise, which I shared with him: "I will win the award for the best student in the liberal arts division of the college." Whatever it took, I would do it.

I needed simply to focus. I needed to make a plan: that I would actually do the required work. Sometimes we just talk about what we hope to do. Those hopes and dreams are meaningless unless we focus on a plan and create an itinerary of just how we can reach the goals and make the dreams become an actuality.

Later, driving back home, Jack said of my resolve, "I expect you will win it; in fact, I'd be surprised if you didn't." He went on to say, "That is exactly the attitude that portends great success in school. Go for it."

* * *

My first class was accounting. On that night, I walked into the classroom and was intimidated by the size of the very crowded room. There were over a hundred seats in a semicircle, about fifteen per row, and somebody sitting in most every one of the chairs. I made my way up to the back row, trying to hide in the corner. I was very uncomfortable in the presence of so many people, most of whom were much younger, none of whom I knew.

When the professor walked in, he announced that his name was, "Joe Ruth, no relation to Babe." It became quickly obvious that Professor Ruth took his job seriously. He knew the details of everyone in his class. He had obviously studied our enrollment packages. His eyes searched the room and when they found me, he shouted, "Brother Brown, *Semper Fi*." Obviously, to me, that meant he was a Marine. Not an ex-Marine, because there is no such thing as an ex-Marine.

What he said next was something I never forgot in my entire academic career. "Brother Brown, those who sit front and center get A's."

I got up and went down to a front-and-center seat.

And sure enough, I got an A in his course. In fact, I got A's in most of my classes for the rest of my college career because, in part, I always sat front and center.

I was so thankful that Professor Ruth singled me out that night so long ago! After the first class he told me how he had learned I was enrolled as Donna Brown and he said, "Good job Marine—we Marines do whatever it takes."

My second course was English composition. As I entered the class I was totally afraid of what I would be required to do. This was a writing course and each student was expected to write a score of papers over the semester. Professor Cronin began the class by saying, "Tonight I'm going to sit outside the door in the corridor while you write a one-page paper on your favorite place in the world. As you finish your papers, bring them to me so that I can check them, and if you've done well enough, I am going to dismiss you and let you leave early."

Professor Cronin took up his seat outside the door and waited for students to come see him. It wasn't very long before students began to line up to have their papers checked and for the most part they were told they could leave.

When there was no one left in line I decided to go and see him as I had no idea what I was supposed to do. I sat down and explained to him, "I never went to high school and I've never written anything in my life. I have no clue what to do."

Prof. Cronin said rather calmly, "Just tell me about a special place that you really like."

I quickly responded, "Fenway Park."

"What would you tell me about Fenway Park?" he prodded.

"When you walk up the tunnel and come out at field level, you see all the different shades of green—the grass, the walls—and the spotless white uniforms—so white they almost blind you—contrasted against the greens and the red clay of the infield. It's just an amazing sight, and every time you go there, it strikes you the same way: the cacophony of colors, the smell of popcorn, the restless fans and the anticipation of 'play ball!'"

"Go back to your desk, sit down and start writing what you said."

I returned to my desk, still unsure of what I was doing. I started to write and it wasn't very long before I had filled the page. I felt as though I had done the best I could do.

I got up and took my paper out to see Dr. Cronin. He started to read my work and he gasped and said, "Oh my God, where did you learn to write like this?"

I thought to myself, *He must be smoking dope; I don't know how to write.*

Prof. Cronin said, "This is magnificent work. You don't have a problem writing."

I was shocked.

"Remember this," he said, "if you can talk, you can write. Just write what you would say to me."

I would never forget that statement either. I was really learning.

The assignment for the next class was to go home and write a paper on football. What an exciting way for my first composition class to end. I was really psyched. Finally, I knew how to do something well enough so that my professor was awed by what I wrote.

I found that I was quickly sucked into the academic world. I discovered that I liked reading assigned works and learning to think critically. Being "Donna Brown" was growing on me. I was having fun. I got my GED, as Jack had predicted, and began to feel confident. As my confidence grew, so did my motivation. For the first time in my life, I found myself mesmerized by the world of the mind. Academia allowed me to discover, isolate, and face the inadequacies within me. I had rediscovered hope, gained a sense of direction, and could think about creating *real* opportunities for myself, not delusional ones.

I also made a startling discovery. I was actually told I was reasonably smart—smarter than many of my classmates. My history professor, Tom Malloy, told me, "Donald, you can probably get into any college in the country."

I had wanted to escape my self-pity and depression, and I did just that because the classroom proved to be invigorating. Successful experimental operations on my knee also boosted my sense of selfcontrol. The "self" that emerged through this experience was firmly grounded and relatively consistent. I came to claim and accept this "self" as uniquely mine—not because I was resigned to remaining stationary or stagnant, or because I had given up all hope of improvement or progression, but because this experience had helped to make me aware of how I lived, moved, and acted within my realm.

This new self-recognition was cause for proclamation, an opportunity to place myself within some sort of framework, and a chance to make a case for myself. Arriving at self-recognition through acquiring knowledge that must be first realized, and then transformed into certainty by being claimed, allowed me to make what is perhaps the most profound, liberating statement of all: I exist! This is the ultimate affirmation; the ultimate claim. And what discovery, what knowledge, what certainty, what expression, could be more definitive and more thrilling?

In junior high school I had been officially classified as a total failure. "Uneducable," they said. "Quit and go into the service—education is not for you." I should have known better. I guess my problem was that I had mentally checked out of life when my father died. There was no guidance. I merely slipped into an almost cationic state. It was many years before I began to exude any confidence. I often have wondered why any teacher would ever discourage any kid in that way. I have seen the results of that kind of negativity in plenty of others over the years.

For so long I hadn't known what I was looking for, the "magic potion" that would make me happy. It was intangible and I couldn't even articulate what it was. I thought I would find it in the Arizona desert or some other far-flung corner of the world, or by marrying someone and letting her fulfill what I was lacking. When I married Susan, for quite some time, it seemed as though I had married a person who would fulfill my needs. But, in the end, it wasn't about a wife or a place; it was about life's lessons that I needed to learn

Now, I had realized that the answer was within me all along. I realized, perhaps for the first time in my life, that whatever was required for having a life of meaning had to come from within. I had to have a plan. I was on the right path. I was no longer uncertain. I felt as though I had turned a corner. I certainly wasn't done, but I was on my way.

Chapter Twenty
Kicking Ass

I have come here to chew bubblegum
and kick ass . . . and I'm all out of bubblegum.
—Roddy Piper in "They Live"

I had completed seven courses in my first two semesters at the Mount, all the while going through multiple surgeries. It was the summer of 1982 and I had been through eleven knee surgeries in two years, eight on the right knee and three on the left. I wasn't scheduled for any more surgeries in the foreseeable future. I began to focus on my college schedule. At this rate, I realized it was going to take me too long to graduate. It would take me at least six semesters if I was to continue at a part-time pace. I looked into the possibility of taking more than a full-time load so I could get out in one more year.

I decided I would see the academic counseling center about transferring into the day school rather than continuing part-time nights. I walked into the office of Barbara Graham, the transfer counselor, and asked her what I had to do to change to day school.

"It's no problem," she said. "Just help me fill out these papers."

Once we finished that process I told her, "I want to take seven courses instead of five in the fall semester and six instead of five in the spring semester so I can graduate this year."

Shaking her head, Barbara told me, "The college will not allow a student to take that many courses because it is a huge overload."

Pleading my case I said, "Last year, I completed seven courses going part-time nights, spending half of the time in the hospital. I got all A's even with that course load and all the outside distractions. I don't want to be your first 100-year-old graduate—which is what I believe will happen if I am not allowed to take the extra coursework."

Barbara laughed and said, "Let me pull your record."

After examining my file folder she said, "I see your point." She added, "If you did this kind of work in those classes, I believe you can handle the extra courses."

That was great news. I signed up for seven courses for my third semester—the seventh being macroeconomics.

That course was taught by Professor John Bassett and proved to be the toughest course of my eight years in college and law school. Dr.

Bassett also proved to be the most rigorous and demanding professor I would ever encounter.

In his first class, he announced how he graded. "You will have six quizzes, a mid-term, and a final. If you are satisfied with your grade at the end of the semester, and you have not missed a single minute of class during the semester, you will not have to take the final exam."

There was an excited mumble in the classroom.

He went on to say, "Given the fact that no one has *ever* passed my final, I would expect every one of you to be here every minute of every class no matter what. No excuses."

As the semester proceeded, it was amazing to see that at 8 A.M., every single one of my classmates was in his or her seat. Near the end of the semester in early December, we had a bad snowstorm. In spite of the weather, every single student was in the class on time, except for one of my friends, Keith Williams. He showed up about ten minutes late.

Dr. Bassett looked at him and said, "Sitting for the final, are we Keith?"

Keith groaned, then he pleaded, "But Dr. Bassett, I live far away and had to come all away from Athol in the snow, so I have a good excuse."

"Keith," Dr. Bassett responded, "I also came from Athol. End of discussion."

More than any other professor, Dr. Bassett instilled in me the concept that you have to work extremely hard to satisfy your professors, your bosses, your clients. You have to understand what they want, and you have to give it to them—*if* you want to succeed and excel.

With a course load of seven classes instead of the traditional five, being confined to a wheelchair made it extremely difficult to keep up with the simple demands of even getting to class. I was perplexed because of how some people looked at me in my wheelchair. Some darted away so they wouldn't have to look at me at all, or perhaps have to help me. Some of the students, however, went out of their way to make me feel accepted and to help me get around. I was out of the wheelchair after a few weeks, and back to my crutches for the rest of the semester. Getting around became much easier.

The semester was a real eye-opener for me. I found out I could excel in a math class. I had an exceptional professor who made math understandable. It was a course that demanded long hours of attention to the homework to be able to figure out the problems.

History, the subject I liked the most, was taught by Tom Malloy. He made studying history a lot of fun. He had a great sense of humor and in every session he would have the class rolling in laughter at least a few times. I learned so much about "False History" from this educator. It was the first time I ever heard many of the "fictions" of the way we as Americans are fed history lessons.

I took literature courses and found out how much fun it was to write all the time—a first for me. I was totally awestruck by the joy of writing. My skills were not the greatest, especially with regard to long-forgotten rules of grammar and style, but putting my thoughts on paper built my growing self-confidence.

Chapter Twenty-One
Serendipity

Vital lives are about action. You can't feel warmth
unless you create it, can't feel delight until you play,
can't know serendipity unless you risk.

—**Joan Erickson**

It was in the middle of that third semester at Mount Wachusett when, by chance, I was in the cafeteria having a snack. I noticed a folded cardboard advertisement on the table. It said something like, "If you have a GPA of 3.5 or higher, Boston University offers trustee scholarships for a four-year law degree—two years of undergraduate work and two years of law school." Because I was carrying seven courses and getting all A's, I thought it might be worthwhile to look into this further. B.U. wasn't Harvard, but it was law school, and only four years, and a full scholarship for both degrees.

What I learned was that each of the roughly 2,000 community colleges in the country got to nominate one student for a full scholarship to B.U. Then, after all 2,000 applicants were reviewed, twenty students were chosen from all across the country and awarded scholarships. The only obstacle was that I needed a recommendation from the president of the college. I had never met him, so I was at a loss as to how to go about getting that letter.

I said, "What the hell, nothing tried, nothing gained." I immediately went to the office of Arthur Haley, the Mount Wachusett Community College president, "President Haley," I said, "I need a recommendation from you to be considered for a Boston University Trustee Scholarship."

"I know nothing about you or your qualifications," he declared.

I handed him a copy of my transcript. He glanced at it and said, "I would be pleased to nominate you, but first you need to get all your professors to write letters of recommendation to me."

I visited each of my professors, and they all wrote enthusiastic letters of support to President Haley. A few days later, a copy of President Haley's nomination arrived in my mailbox.

I am pleased to nominate Mr. Donald L Brown for the B.U. Trustee scholarship. Mr. Brown will graduate from this college in June of 1983. His academic achievement for his tenure here so far is outstanding. The transcript will attest to that. His personal qualifications are equally exceptional. I know him personally and can report that he possesses a sense of integrity, a high energy level and maturity not found typically in the community college student. Not a recent high school graduate, he has been in the workforce for a number of years and, at great cost to himself, has returned to college. If you're looking for a student who has demonstrated his academic ability and achievement and has indicated his sincere wish to earn advanced degrees, you would pick Mr. Donald Brown. My opinion is shared by members of the staff of the college and in that regard I am appending five testimonies, which describe in greater detail Mr. Brown's potential for great achievement.

It is my hope that you will join us in encouraging Mr. Brown to pursue his studies further by making him a "Trustee Scholar"... And, of course, if additional information is useful I would be happy to oblige.

The following Monday morning when I arrived at school, I received a message to come see Barbara Graham, the college's transfer counselor. When I arrived, Ms. Graham asked, "Donald, do you *really* want to go to Boston University?"

I said, "No."

Ms. Graham seemed puzzled. She said, "Why did you have the president nominate you if you don't want to go there?"

"I hoped by getting that prestigious scholarship, I would be in a position to transfer into an even more prestigious school."

"Where would you like to go?"

"Clark University," I replied.

"Would you like to go to Amherst College?"

"Is it a good school?"

Ms. Graham looked at me with a wry smile and said, "It's the best liberal arts college in the country."

"I'd love to go there," I said, "but I'm sure I couldn't afford it."

Ms. Graham knew a great deal about Amherst College, because she had helped a couple of other students from MWCC transfer there. She gave me an Amherst College catalog to take home.

That night I was so excited I couldn't eat. Instead, I devoured the Amherst catalog, application materials, and other brochures. For the first time, I read the inspirational Amherst emblem: *"Terras Iradient,"* which means, "Illuminate the Earth."

I learned that the college had a "need-blind" policy on financial aid. That meant that whatever a student needed in financial aid, they simply gave it to you. Then I came across the description of the William M. Prest bequest program for which I was apparently a candidate:

> **Since the late 1960s, the college has established a strong tradition of admitting community college graduates, and veterans and other individuals whose experience in the work world will add a special dimension to student life. Regardless of age or previous academic achievement, successful candidates are those who have unusual curiosity about learning and the motivation needed to survive as a non-traditional student at Amherst . . .**

Apparently, if I could get accepted, the Prest scholarship would provide the funding for me to attend Amherst. I called my sister to tell her the news. Her husband, George, answered the phone. I blurted out to him, "I'm going to Amherst College for an interview, and it looks like I might get in."

He said, "You mean UMASS Amherst."

I said, "No, Amherst College."

George was befuddled. "Donald, Amherst College is one of the top colleges in the country and it's in the same town as UMASS Amherst, that's why you're confusing them."

I replied, "I'm not confused, I called there today and the operator said 'Amherst College' and the woman I called was Amy Johnson who is the Dean of Transfer Admissions at Amherst College, according to the catalog in my hand."

Now George was lost for words. He said, "I'll get Nancy."

My sister got on the phone and I said to her, "I have a good chance to go to Amherst College." She said, "You mean UMASS Amherst."

I said, "No," and told her the events of the day.

She said, "If you're right, it's one giant step forward."

The next afternoon I spent six hours exploring the Amherst campus. Frankly, I was overwhelmed that I actually had a chance to attend this rarified institution. If I got into Amherst, I might be able to get into any law school in the country, including Harvard. I confidently went to the college store and purchased a purple Amherst athletic jacket and a class ring with an '86 on it—my projected year of graduation. I still wear them to this day.

During the admissions interview, I hit it off with Dean Amy Johnson. We talked about my love of history. She was very curious about my success with Dr. Bassett, obviously very familiar with the rigor of his courses. She also seemed very interested in my lit classes. She wanted to know how I handled interacting with students much younger than me. "They are people too, and I have no problems with them," I responded.

After an hour or so of sparkling conversation, she asked, "Where else have you applied?"

"Nowhere else," I told her.

"That's not wise," she said. "It's smart to have a couple of places for a safety net."

"I'm coming here," I said.

She must have sensed I was not to be disabused of my cocky decision. All she did was smile. She then told me, "The decision usually hinges on the awards a student received from their community college."

As for my apparent grandiosity, something I've been accused of from time to time, Randolph Bourne wrote, "Vision must constantly outshoot technique."

I later learned that Dean Johnson had also been a late bloomer, getting her degrees at a much later than usual time in her life. Apparently she had gone to college and graduate school when her children were in college. Meeting with her would prove to be another instance of serendipity that regularly visited my life during those years.

In my final semester at Mount Wachusett, my hard work paid off. The award I had promised myself I would get was not given to me. I was pissed. I had a GPA of 3.89. I had done more extracurricular stuff than anybody in the college—and yet the award was given to somebody with only a 3.2 GPA. I went to visit my advisor because I was so troubled that I had not won the award—not because I needed awards for myself, but that significant awards would be a big factor in getting accepted at Amherst. My advisor told me, "You have won almost every award this college has to offer and they're just not going to give you that one." I had no clue that I had won many of the other awards.

Several nights later at the academic awards banquet I gathered ten academic awards and several scholarships to go along with my 3.89 GPA, which meant graduating with highest honors, graduating *summa cum laude*. I felt so grateful to all those who had believed in me, long before I believed in myself. And I had done it while enduring several operations, followed by long stints in wheelchairs, and on crutches.

And of course, I remember the day I ripped open the letter from Amherst College.

"Congratulations," it began. I didn't have to read the rest. I was crying and jumping with joy at the same time. I was so happy, it was embarrassing. While Susan and the children didn't seem to be thrilled, my mother was beside herself. She too, cried when I called to give her the news. My sister Nancy was thrilled for me. It took me hours to come back to earth. I piled the family into the car and drove to Amherst. They were not really interested, as Susan was stewing over my taking off from life to get an education. She was forever telling her children that she was on the verge of leaving. I shouldn't have even taken them, but it was too late to cart them home.

We walked around the Amherst College campus. I was astounded that I would be going there. I loved the campus; the stately brick buildings, the vast green lawns, the magnificent views, the aroma of freshly cut grass and the chatter of the students rushing from class to class. It had been one of the most incredible days of my life. I was so grateful.

I'd been accepted at arguably the best liberal arts college in the country. How many other high-school dropouts could claim that? My heart was pounding. I didn't know whether to laugh or cry. This was a major step on the way to realizing my dreams.

Little did I know at the time but it was also the final blow to my marriage. Susan and I called it quits and later divorced. We had tried to make it work after she had threatened to leave when I was suicidal. Now she booked, and although I could accept her decision intellectually, I was still devastated. My second marriage, again eight years long, was over.

Chapter Twenty-Two
The Hobo

The hobo was essentially a wanderer. A free spirited human, who put his personal freedom ahead of his desire for worldly gain...The real hobo is purely and simply a wanderer at heart and enjoys this way of life—to work a few days and get a few bucks in his pocket to pay his way, . . .

—Angelfire

And so, on the tenth day of "Walking USA," I strutted onto the campus of Mount Wachusett Community College. I stood there, gazing at the acres of beautifully groomed trees and manicured grass surrounding the college's two buildings. Tears welled up in my eyes as I reflected back on this place and how it changed my life. To the manor born, so to speak, but I couldn't linger. I had miles to go before I slept.

We dined on a thick, juicy prime rib and enjoyed a rejuvenating night's sleep at the Super 8 motel, the "Ritz" of Gardner.

In the morning, feeling refreshed, I skated on a frozen river of memories towards Athol.

Route 2 was an opportune place to pile on some miles. Walking on a highway allowed me to go at a brisk pace. It was boring only because I knew it so well. I must have driven it hundreds of times when I lived in the area. I was in the valley, surrounded by the mountains of Central Massachusetts. While it was hot and dry, the green abounded and the air was clean. The quickness of my stride compensated for the lack of novelty. I hurtled towards Athol.

As I walked by the Athol Memorial Hospital, I remembered spending many anxious moments in the emergency room with my mother. She had moved up to Orange to live closer to me and nearly died—not once, but twice—because of heart and kidney problems.

I walked west through Athol, anxious to pass by my former home, a two-acre mini-farm on Hillshire Road in Orange, where I had lived with my second wife Susan and her children. Revisiting the place I lived when I had the Morphine Dream and when I attended Mount Wachusett would bring back another flood of emotions.

While I looked at my old home, from under the giant maple tree in the front yard near the street, my former next-door neighbor, Ron

Stone, pulled up in his pick-up truck. He climbed out to exchange a hug and a handshake. He was the realtor/builder/developer who had sold the place to Susan and me. He said, "Never expected I would ever see you again—but then, you always were one to do the unexpected." Although it had been nineteen years since we first met, Ron looked remarkably the same as he had when I first shook his hand on Labor Day in 1978; it even looked like he was wearing the same overalls.

I told Ron, "I'm finally walking across the country," which is what I'd told him I'd planned to do many years ago, when I was still confined to crutches and a wheelchair.

I remembered, I'd been stranded in my garden with my heavy, ass-high casts, and couldn't get up and get back to the house. Another neighbor had rescued me and alerted Ron about my predicament. He had rushed to my house and found me in tears, helpless, unable to get up.

I told him, "I'll be fine. And when I get all fixed up, I'm going to walk all the way to Big Sur."

He had laughed and said, "You'd best get rid of them crutches and casts before you try that." He went on to say, "I don't know if any man could do that. It's an awful long walk."

Ron reminded me of a story he had told me years back. "During the Depression, there was no work in Orange, or anywhere else for that matter. I had just graduated from high school and decided to travel across the country to find work," he reminisced. Like everyone else in those days, he had no cash, so the only way he could travel was on the trains, as a hobo. "I crisscrossed the country for three or four years, finding work here and there."

He certainly understood the magnitude of what I was trying to do and appreciated the distances.

I could have talked to Ron for hours but instead bid him farewell. I had to "beat the mountain" that rose up to Amherst that afternoon. I found my way to Lake Mattawa, a mile or two down Hillshire Road. I dove in the frigid water, fully clothed. It was just what I needed on that blisteringly hot day. Charles thought it was so "cool" that I had jumped in, so he jumped in too.

This would be one of the most difficult legs of the walk: the Daniel Shays Highway, Route 202 South. The walk up the mountain through New Salem, Shutesbury and Pelham to Amherst was one I'd never been able to complete in a single day during my twelve years of distance walking. It was always too difficult. But I was confident. I started up the mountain, thinking, *Today is the day I will conquer it.* It was

2:00 P.M., a little late to be attempting to do the twenty miles up and over the mountain, but I was eager to get to Amherst.

Once again, however, the mountain was the victor. This time it was not exhaustion that prevented me from reaching the summit, but thick swarms of biting horseflies. They were relentless in their desire to consume me and my bug repellent, effective previously, seemed more like an aphrodisiac to them.

Chapter Twenty-Three
Que Sera, Sera

*Lord, help me to change the things that I can
and accept the things that I cannot, and give
me the wisdom to know the difference.*
—Reinhold Niebuhr

The next morning, I was back on the mountain, eager to get moving.

Hours later, I made my descent into the town of Amherst, framed by the distant foothills of the Berkshires. When I reached the town center, immediately I headed to the Amherst College campus. Diana Scriver, an old friend, had asked me to lunch at the college dining hall.

When Diana was an administrative aide in the Development Office at the school, she was responsible for arranging transportation for the school's deans, professors and the director of development to travel to airports, meetings, and lectures in Boston or New York and points further away. As a part of my work-study requirements, Diana "hired" me to chauffeur many of these people around. Soon I had become known as "Scriver's driver." During my three years at Amherst—Amherst did not accept my first year's course work at Mt. Wachusett Community College—I worked directly for Diana.

I was an hour early, so I parked myself on a stone wall across from the dining hall. It gave me a chance to think back to the fortuitous circumstances that brought me to this magical and elite school. Back when I was a student here, I often sat on this same spot, with my most special friend, Margaretha Kress.

* * *

My most significant Amherst memories were of people within the Amherst community. President Peter Pouncey was one of my favorites. My advisor and great friend, Frank Couvares, a historian and American studies expert, had been a rock for me. Frank was as left politically as one could go so we spoke the same language. He guided me through the academic rigors of Amherst. Barry O'Connell, an American literature professor, brought to life written works to me in such a meaningful way. Gordie Levin, a legend at the college, was an inspiration for me. Rebecca Hague got me interested in the classics, something I had never even thought of before. Susan Snively, the writing counselor, gave so freely of her time to tutor me in the nuances of writing. John Brown Childs, my first professor of African-American history, inspired me the most. He introduced me to what was to become the focus of my curriculum. Betty McQuillen and Peggy Stotz were also key figures in my time at Amherst College. Ray Decker, the postmaster, gave me the best shifts to work during my three years: 5:00 A.M. to 8:00 A.M. I could go on and on, because the list should probably contain a hundred names. Many fellow students were also a part of making my Amherst experience remarkable; none more than Margaretha Kress.

Early in my first semester I was sitting in my room very late one night with my door open. Margaretha had been visiting in the room next door. As she walked by my door she said, "Hello."

I smiled as I looked up and said, "Hello back to you. Thank you for being so considerate to stop and say hello. It is not the usual reaction of your fellow students." Older students like me, who were always transfer students, often had a rough time adjusting to the social life at the college. Many of the young students didn't readily accept our presence. I sometimes would hear remarks like, "How did *he* get in here, when my sister didn't get in?" Over time, I adjusted to the shunning and made many friends. I understood that the younger kids found it difficult to relate to someone the age of their parents. Yet there was a sizeable group of the younger set that had no difficulty being friendly and kind. Those were most commonly the friendships I enjoyed.

Margaretha came into my room to continue the conversation. She was a very elegant young lady; impeccable in her grooming, extremely intelligent, sophisticated, and dressed differently from typical students. She wore a long, flowing skirt with a beautiful sweater. Her dark hair was shoulder length with not a single hair out of place. Her smile was genuine. I had long ago learned to recognize authenticity, and she was the real deal. Margaretha was class-plus.

We began a long conversation about writing papers at the Amherst level. Margaretha was very well educated and had gone to the best of feeder schools that almost all Amherst students come from.

Beginning that night, and continuing on through my first year, it was Margaretha who taught me how to write my assignments for my professors.

After perhaps an hour of academic chat, we began talking personal matters. In a matter of minutes we were sharing the most intimate of details about each other's struggles. It was surprisingly easy to talk with her. I told her about my estranged wife and stepchildren. I told her how my pursuit of an education had caused such friction in our marriage that we had separated many months before, and the marriage was basically over.

We decided to head out to the local all-night diner for something to eat. As we sat there, I realized how attracted I was to this amazing young woman. But, she was so young, only twenty. I was thirty-eight. I felt like it was so inappropriate to be attracted to someone so young. But she was so mature and sophisticated, she seemed much older. She was a German major and planning to go to medical school. She was an exceptional student.

We had such a great time together that evening; we began to eat all our meals together in the college dining hall. People were beginning to notice, but we were oblivious to the chatter, because it didn't matter to either of us. We grew to be the best of friends. It seemed like we were headed to a permanent relationship. On one level, we had made a life commitment to one another, as friends who would always be there for one another, but I shuddered when I thought about the prospect of what her parents might think of our "relationship"—whatever it was or might have been in the future, and their daughter spending so much time with a student almost old enough to be her father.

After a year of spending most of our spare time with one another, I finally got to meet her parents, Bob and Hannah Kress, when they came to Amherst at the end of the school year to pick Margaretha up to travel back home. They were obviously shocked by the implications of our relationship. It was a very uncomfortable feeling for me. I wasn't positive about how they felt, but it seemed to me that they disapproved, and I couldn't blame them. I would later find out what extraordinary parents they were. I also learned from Hannah that they harbored no sense of something wrong with my relationship with Margaretha.

I made a decision to let go of whatever the relationship was, so Margaretha would be free to explore life's possibilities. I suddenly had a huge sense of loss. In the fall, I would have an opportunity to revisit my decision though, if Margaretha came back to school still wanting to continue what we had started.

Margaretha didn't come back to school. She took a year off because she was distraught about the relationship ending and was adrift in her own sea of uncertainty. She was confronting major life decisions. On occasion, I would drive to New Haven where she was working during her respite from school. Those stolen moments together would only remind us of the significance of our feelings for each other.

The next year, Margaretha was back at Amherst, at least for the first semester. Because I was so incredibly busy, living off campus and always away from Amherst on driving assignments, I had almost no contact with Margaretha. Occasionally, we would find some time to spend together, meaningful time. It was clear that the attachment was profound but circumstances seemed to interfere with any opportunity to advance it forward.

In the spring, Margaretha went to Germany for a semester abroad. I sensed that it was her parents who sent her away, guessing their motive was to remove me from the picture. Later I would learn that they hadn't been involved in her decision to go there.

I missed Margaretha. I thought about her all the time. I struggled over my choice to end the relationship. Margaretha was still abroad after I had graduated. I wanted to be with her.

I had remained in Amherst for the summer to work as a special assistant to the assistant treasurer of the college. I was back living alone in a dormitory when one evening, in early June, I decided to call Margaretha in Germany to tell her I wanted to be with her. It must have been about 4 A.M. in Europe when I got through to her. As soon as we began to talk, she blurted out, "I met a guy and I am engaged."

I blurted out, "Oh my God!"

Margaretha continued, "I'll be coming back to Amherst for the fall semester and he will be coming with me on a fiancée visa."

I was crushed and I didn't know what to say, but I couldn't let her know that. I certainly didn't want to cry, so I said, "I have to hang up, I'll talk to you soon."

As soon as I put the phone down, my emotions overwhelmed me. I cried for hours, off and on. I had finally gotten over the age issue; I felt that she was my soul mate. Neither of my ex-wives had ever made me feel the way she had. I had also finally decided that Margaretha's parents would just have to deal with our having a relationship. But I realized these things too late; I had lost her. It was almost too much to bear.

I had a restless night. I lay in bed thinking about how my own actions had caused me all this pain. The next day, after having time to think, I realized that in a way I was happy for Margaretha. Deep down

I knew that we were soul mates. I didn't believe that she wanted to be married to someone else. I was convinced that she would rather have been with me. But, I needed to move on. *Get over it!* I told myself. *Que sera, sera.* Whatever will be, will be.

When Margaretha returned to Amherst in the fall, I was then at Harvard Law School. Late at night, we often talked about her upcoming marriage. It was obvious that she was not sure she wanted to go through with it. One night we made plans for the following weekend. She was going to come to Harvard to stay for the weekend, with me, in my six-by-eight-foot dormitory room and spend the time together so she could decide what to do. For some unknown reason, she was unable to come. I've often wondered if things would have been different in both of our lives if she had made it that weekend.

As the months and years passed, I went on to finish at Harvard Law School and met and married Estela. Margaretha was at my wedding. It was a strange feeling—getting married—while someone I had such significant feelings for was dancing around the ballroom with her husband to be. Estela and I soon had our two boys. Margaretha also married, I was at her wedding. Again, I experienced a flood of emotions. There was the woman I cared so deeply for, and she was tying the knot with her fiancé. Margaretha went on to finish medical school and achieved her dream of being a doctor, all while also giving birth to the first of two sons. After med school she had her second boy.

Though long periods would pass when we had no face-to-face contact, the closeness of our friendship never diminished. On our birthdays, most years, we would call one another. Margaretha would always send me a birthday card, signed simply, "Love, M."

More than twenty-five years later Margaretha is still my closest friend and always will be. Unfortunately, her marriage, which was doomed before it happened, fell apart. I regularly spend holidays with her and her children and parents and often drive to south of Albany in upstate New York where she lives—just to visit.

When reflecting on our time at Amherst, I can say for certain that I never would have made it through Amherst if not for Margaretha's help. Margaretha says the same: "I would have never made it through Amherst without Don's help."

Those Amherst bonds are very strong. It is a place that permeates your being and remains with you for a lifetime. It seems like when you go there you experience a transfusion and the same Amherst blood flows through everybody in the Amherst community. It always had the overwhelming feeling of "family." I finally had a place, which I came to identify as my own. To this day, when I travel to Amherst, I feel like I am going home. It felt like my birthplace. In many ways, it was.

Chapter Twenty-Four
Terras Irradient

Let them give light to the world.
—Amherst College motto

When I graduated from Mount Wachusett, I was still dashing around in a wheelchair. It wasn't motorized, just the plain old push-the-wheels-with-always-aching-arms version. I was very aware that the campus at Amherst College was going to be a challenge for me, as getting around well in a wheelchair required knowing the terrain. I had earlier arranged to move into an Amherst College dormitory a few hours after graduation exercises at Mount Wachusett.

It was after 6 P.M. by the time I showed up at Amherst on Sunday, May 29, 1983. Reunion weekend had just ended. It was the end of that event that opened up a dorm room for me. I planned to stay for the summer, and then move into a permanent room when classes started in September. That time on campus would allow me to figure out how to navigate the hills and dales of the campus, get my syllabi and books, meet my professors and, most importantly, start reading.

By midnight I had finished arranging my belongings, making the bed, filling the dresser drawers, and setting up my study area. I was drop-dead tired. Collapsing on the tiny bed, I opened my now ragged-eared copy of the Amherst College course offerings. I had already circled 106 courses that I wanted to take, but I was limited to twenty-four because I was entering as a first-semester sophomore. My burning desire was to take classes taught by the world-renowned historian Henry Steele Commager.

In his sixty-year career, Professor Commager had either written or edited over 160 history books. They were used by educators in high schools, colleges and universities around the globe.

I soon discovered that in order to attend one of his classes, you had to obtain his permission. I had missed the registration deadline for the required enrollment interview a month before and I soon learned that his class was also filled to capacity. It appeared I would have to wait until my junior year to attend one of his classes. I was disappointed.

My dorm room happened to be located on the upper floors over the dining hall. Once up and dressed and painfully hungry, I made my way down the stairs on crutches, found my wheelchair, and cruised into the dining area. It was a pretty good selection for breakfast. It certainly wasn't like the typical institutional food I had tolerated in hospitals or the Marine Corps. With my tray brimming with food—as much as one wanted of anything and everything—I moved into the area where students ate their meals. There was only one table occupied and two young women sat there. I wheeled myself up to the table and asked for permission to join them. They welcomed me as if I was no different from them—though I was probably almost twenty years older and 200 pounds heavier, not to mention wheelchair bound.

We immediately began a conversation, the focus of which was to "educate" me about being a student at Amherst. The two students, Marie Tatro and Dorrin Rosenfeld, so young and confident, made me feel like I was just another student. They were warm, friendly, bright and engaging. They made my first morning on campus more than comfortable. It was to become a daily ritual. We had breakfast together for most of the mornings that summer. Amherst was growing on me already. Another student I met that summer in the cafeteria during lunchtime was a really special kid by the name of Anna Middleton. She was from an Amherst family, I learned. Her brother had preceded her by a few years and her father was also an alum. She was obviously from a far different socio-economic class than I was, but she was easily able to connect with me socially. We would become lifelong friends. I went to her wedding some years later and I had her crying on my shoulder after her divorce. Her father also became a potent influence in my life.

Breakfast and lunch my first day at Amherst was a prelude to the wonderful influence the college would have on my entire life. How privileged I felt.

Chapter Twenty-Five
Henry Steele Commager

What every college must do is hold up before
the young the spectacle of greatness in history,
literature and life.
—Henry Steele Commager

After breakfast, with my Type-A personality propelling me along, I decided to take a long ride in my wheelchair to Professor Commager's home. I rang the bell and a young and exquisite-looking woman answered the door. I wasn't expecting anybody young, as I knew Professor Commager was advanced in age.

"Is this the home of Professor Commager?" I asked.

"I am Mrs. Commager. Please come in."

Mrs. Commager was about my age. I was beginning to think that the professor couldn't be as old as I thought. His wife led me through the sun porch, filled with books, and into the kitchen, where I began to notice there were books everywhere, thousands of them, piled in every possible place. She took me into a den where I sat in a very comfortable overstuffed chair that had to be a hundred years old.

When Professor Commager came downstairs, I saw that he was indeed very old. He had a look of curiosity and his eyes glistened with energy.

He asked, "To what do I owe the pleasure of your visit, young man?"

To him I was young, even though I was twice the age of a typical student. I told him I had just arrived at Amherst as a transfer student and had been extremely disappointed to find that I was excluded from his class due to the interview and registration process, which had been completed long before I had arrived on campus.

Now I had his attention. He asked me several probing questions about early American history. He asked who my favorite founding father was. I answered, "Thomas Jefferson."

He liked that response, as he said, "Jefferson is also my favorite."

After about a half hour of back-and-forth discussion of American history, he said, "Well, I think we can arrange for you to be in the September class. I don't like to have more than twenty, but I think you will be a valuable addition because of your intellectual curiosity."

He instructed me to tell the registrar that he would sign the appropriate form to allow me in his class.

Of course I was thrilled and grateful. I looked around the room and said, "You are the only person I know who has more books than I do."

He smiled and said, "You haven't even seen anything. The entire house—every room—is filled with books."

I explained how much I loved to read. He then said something I've never forgotten: "Reading leads to thinking, thinking leads to writing, and being able to write is the most important accomplishment of mankind."

I had only been on campus for fifteen hours and had already learned one of the most important lessons of life.

The joy of spending a couple of hours with Professor Commager, my acceptance into his class, and our discussion of history and books was magical. As the oldest student on campus at age thirty-eight, I left his house feeling like I belonged and with an extraordinary sense of how much Amherst College was going to propel me. I realized I was learning so much and that meant I was growing. I wasn't quite sure of where I would wind up, but I was certainly in for a good ride.

When the fall semester began, I discovered that another transfer student was Commager's teaching assistant, also known as a "T.A." I also found out that he'd been accepted to Harvard Law School. After the first class ended, I introduced myself to him and asked what advice he could give me to help me go from Amherst to Harvard Law School.

He replied, "Get to be the T.A. to Henry Steele Commager. That will get you into any law school."

I filed that tip away, then wondered how on earth one goes about doing that.

* * *

Near the end of my second semester, a senior, who had been the work-study college chauffeur, asked if I would like to do some driving as he was too busy working on his senior thesis to take on all the assignments. I told him I'd be happy to. That was when I began working for Diana Scriver, picking up and dropping off visiting dignitaries to and from the campus at airports and train stations.

After school ended, I was summoned to the president's office. His secretary, Pat Mullins, an elegant woman who had worked for the college for many years, asked if I would be willing to drive to New York City to pick up the new college president.

Early the next morning, I drove to Manhattan in a college vehicle and picked up Peter Pouncey, Amherst's new president. This was, in fact, his first day in this role and he hadn't even moved into the president's house yet. During the ride, President Pouncey asked me what kind of issues I needed help with. I told him there ought to be off-campus housing for students like me who have such a terrible time living in the typical "closet" they call a dorm room.. He said he would look into it. I told him there should be more people like me from community colleges and different socio-economic backgrounds, the student body should have more minorities.

"I will change the color of the place," he promised.

And sure enough, he did—from 3 percent minorities to 11 percent, in the last two years that I was there.

We talked about my desire to go to law school. I told him I needed to figure out how to become Henry Steele Commager's T.A. As I dropped him at the president's residence, he said, "Donald, when it comes time to go to law school, I will write the letter that gets you in." I believed him. His interest in what I was trying to accomplish was obvious. I certainly felt blessed that I was the one chosen to go to New York and bring him to Amherst.

Within a week, the buildings and grounds department called me to announce that a college-owned house on the main street across from the athletic complex had been reserved for me to move into. I no longer had to suffer the indignity of living in a room the size of a closet and sleep on a bed made for a midget. The dorm rooms, I supposed, were okay for typical students, but for somebody my age, with all my difficulties, a house to live in was such a special gift. President Pouncey had certainly intervened, because previously when I had inquired about alternative housing, I had no response that was promising. I realized the new president was looking after the needs of older students. I was so impressed that he hadn't forgotten. It was not the only surprise from his office.

Three weeks later, I received a copy of a letter he'd sent to Professor Commager:

Felix,
I am writing to endorse Don Brown's application for the prestigious role of being your teaching assistant. He is a marvelous maverick on the

Amherst scene, as any thirty-eight-year-old, ex-Marine, high-school dropout, former semi-professional baseball player, who found himself here, is probably bound to be. What I think is particularly distinctive about him is (1) his hard-driving intelligence and determination to succeed, bearing fruit in an A- average; (2) his love of this place and his conviction about the values of the life of the mind which it professes; and (3) his enjoyment of, and easy acceptance by, a wide array of younger students—male and female, rich and poor, black and white. He has no axes to grind, and they appreciate his candor and natural sympathy and admire him, as we all do, for the strength of his motivation that is carrying him through such a challenge as this deferred undergraduate degree. He has so clearly found himself that he encourages the young and less certain to hope that they will in turn be able to wrest some confident future for themselves.

I recommend him most strongly to your stern scrutiny, because I know he will serve you and your class surprisingly well.

Peter

A few days after that, Professor Commager asked me to his home to discuss being his T.A. It was almost a full-time job. In addition to its usual duties, I was required to drive him to faraway places for speaking engagements.

During the rides, which were often several hours in length—New York City, Philadelphia, Boston—Professor Commager would discuss his upcoming speeches and would actually ask my opinion on various things.

On the way back, we'd discuss how his speech had gone and the comments and questions it had generated. Those trips were more educational than taking a college class. I was listening to arguably the most incredible historian of our generation discuss the many facets of history, especially constitutional history.

A student usually held Commager's T.A. position for a single semester. I managed to hold it for three. It was as if I had been awarded two Amherst College degrees.

Thanks to Professor Commager, I became grounded in a rudimentary appreciation of American history. More importantly, I had gained a measure of political thought that included, but was not limited to: the diverse and often opposing forces that began with the stewardship of Puritanism; Ben Franklin's sense of community duty; Tom Paine's anti-religious fervor; the conservative strains of James Madison, De Tocqueville, and James Fennimore Cooper; Thoreau's anarchism; Whitman's universalism; the unions; and the progressive movement in the 1930s; and, of course, the overreaction to it in the 1950s. Most important to me, however, was my understanding of racial injustice and sexism.

Chapter Twenty-Six
I Can Do This

"Man often becomes what he believes himself to be.
If I keep on saying to myself that I cannot do a certain
thing, it is possible that I may end by really becoming
incapable of doing it. On the contrary, if I have the
belief that I can do it, I shall surely acquire the capacity
to do it even if I may not have it at the beginning.
—Mahatma Gandhi

They say youth is wasted on the young. Maybe if I'd been in my late teens, I would have skimmed the course readings or read the *Cliff Notes*, or I would have pulled all-nighters on speed, writing papers mere hours before they were due. Thanks to my advanced age, I instead had an unquenchable thirst for knowledge. I was profoundly fascinated and thrilled by this rare opportunity to make up for lost time—to receive a superior education. I'm not embarrassed to say that I made the acquaintance of some astonishing people: Thoreau, Melville, Baldwin, Richard Wright, Ann Moody, Claude Brown, Socrates, Plato, and Thucydides.

But I must confess that in the beginning it wasn't easy. After I had started classes, I began to have doubts. I wasn't sure I was up to snuff. Everyone was so smart. I thought about taking some time off, dropping out.

I called Dr. Richard Shine at Mount Wachusett. He had been instrumental in helping me get accepted to Amherst. I needed a confidence boost.

He suggested I go to Amherst admissions and inspect my file. He told me that if I read it, I'd learn what wonderful things people had said about me and I'd feel better. It would help restore my confidence.

Taking his advice, I showed up at the admissions office and asked to see my file. They sat me in a conference room and gave it to me. Yes, there were letters from those who had said nice things about me. But I also found something troubling.

When the Amherst admissions committee had met to consider my application, every single person voted against me. The only exception was Amy Johnson, the transfer dean.

The Dean of Admissions, whose name I can't recall, had written in my file: "This man is not intelligent enough to make it at Amherst College."

Amy Johnson had replied: "This applicant will work ten times harder than any other Amherst student. He will graduate with honors. I stake my professional reputation on it."

During the admissions process, committee members apparently get one trump card per year. In other words, they can use it to grant admission to one student whom they believe in that others may not agree with. Amy Johnson exercised her trump card on my behalf, and so I was accepted into the class of 1986.

I was stunned to find this out. I hadn't gotten the boost I expected, but I certainly discovered that I owed Amy Johnson a debt I could never repay. From that day forward, I was committed to making sure I would never let her down. There was no way I would ever give up, because Amy Johnson had pushed for me and stood up for me. It was a very powerful motivator.

* * *

It wasn't long after that I settled in comfortably to a routine, which assured me that I would be able to compete with typical Amherst students. One night my sister called to ask, "How are you faring?"

I quickly responded, "I am completely confident that I can do this."

Beginning my third year and final year at Amherst I determined that I would apply to seven law schools, but not Harvard. While Harvard had long been my dream, I purposely didn't apply there because friends from Amherst who had gone there didn't like it. I chose the seven top law schools in the country, but by then I was only interested in Yale. On December 13, 1985, two days before the application deadline, I drove to Yale for a meeting with admissions and to drop off my completed application. Before my appointment at the admissions office, I dropped in on famed civil rights professor Burke Marshall, who was my reason for wanting to go to Yale. With my focus at Amherst in African American history, the logical next step was to study Race and the Law. Marshall was a Kennedy administration civil rights lawyer and assistant attorney general under Robert F. Kennedy. I had long ago identified him as someone whom I would like to study under.

Almost immediately Prof. Marshall said to me, "If your interests and passions are as I believe they are, you belong at Harvard Law School studying under Derrick Bell." I didn't even know who Derrick Bell was. But I knew if Burke Marshall said I should be studying with Derrick Bell maybe that was what I should have been planning all along.

I left Burke Marshall's office and thought a lot about what he had said. I decided that even though there were only two days left before law school applications were due, perhaps I should reconsider and apply to Harvard. The next day on the drive back to Amherst I gave it even more thought. Realizing that the following day, which was coincidently my birthday, was the final day for applications I had no idea how I could prepare all the necessary materials to complete an application for Harvard Law in just one day. I would need to provide an essay, fill out the myriad of forms, and get recommendations written directly for Harvard. It was a process that took many hours.

The next morning, the final day for applications, I went to the law school counseling office at Amherst College where I explained my predicament to Dean Clark. He said to me, "No problem, we'll get some folks energized to put everything you need together so you can drive your application to Harvard this afternoon."

Three or four hours later, I gathered all the papers, put them into a large envelope, and drove to Cambridge, to the Harvard Law School Admissions Office where I dropped off the package. Because I arrived at lunch time, the only person available to take my package was the Dean of Admissions. I put my application materials directly into her hands. Serendipity again.

I felt relieved. I had done everything I could to realize my dream of getting an education and presenting myself as an excellent candidate for law school. It was as if someone lifted tons off my shoulders. Now all I was faced with was the wait. I had seen many of my classmates at Amherst in a tizzy, waiting for responses from law schools or medical schools or other graduate programs. It was a time of great apprehension for many of them. I was relatively calm about the process. I had already gotten into a bunch of really good law schools: Yale (where I was number one on the waitlist), Vermont, Suffolk, Boston College and Columbia. I was satisfied that whatever Harvard's decision was, at least I had succeeded in getting myself into the top-tier law programs.

The letter that President Pouncey had said he would write was included with my application. At Harvard Law School, that same dean of admissions later told me, "I read the first sentence of Peter Pouncey's letter a few minutes after you left your application with me, and at that moment you were accepted to Harvard Law School."

Pouncey's letter began: "Donald L. Brown is as remarkable a student as I have encountered in my twenty-odd years at American colleges and universities."

The very next day I got my letter of acceptance from Harvard Law School. It was a great birthday present, even if only *I* knew it was my birthday. How fortuitous. Part one of "The Morphine Dream" realized. The second part had to be deferred, but it was definitely not forgotten.

* * *

A few months later, when Amherst College graduation rolled around, I had completed a double major, in history and American studies. I graduated with honors. My thesis committee declared that I would graduate *cum laude*. I was terrible disappointed, as I was sure I had earned *magna cum laude*. I was not only disappointed, I was angry. My advisor had voted for *magna cum laude*, but the other two professors on my thesis committee had voted for *cum laude*.

Seeing how upset I was, my advisor, Frank Couvares said "Come with me, let's go have a pizza and a cold drink."

We walked up town and settled into one of the pizza joints. As soon as our pizza and soda arrived, Frank went to work on settling me down. What he said to me was appropriate. "You came from nowhere, with literally no defined academic success and you are graduating with honors from the best college in the country." Further he noted, "And you are going off to Harvard Law School. You have absolutely no reason to complain, whether *cum laude, magna cum laude* or *summa cum laude*. Wake up and accept that you have done something remarkable."

On graduation day, I experienced one of the most emotional moments of my life. Additionally, I was informed that I was the oldest student to ever graduate from that famed institution.

The entire class had lined up in the gym to prepare to march to the quad for the ceremony. As we were waiting for the signal to march, someone gave us instructions. He said, "When you march down the middle of the quad, the faculty will be lined up on both sides. Occasionally, a faculty member you have had a significant relationship with will step out to shake your hand or hug you. Please be sure to keep those situations brief so the line moves as it should."

When we finally marched up to and around the quad, and then down the middle between the professors, every single instructor in the faculty lines stepped out to shake my hand, or hug me. I was blown away. Tears rolled down my cheeks and I was so overwhelmed I thought I might pass out. Then, when I was called up to receive my diploma, handed to me by my friend, President Peter Pouncey—who had been there for me several times during my time at Amherst—the entire board of trustees gave me a standing ovation. Pouncey declared to the audience in his well-known British accent that "Donald Loring Brown has the distinct honor of being the oldest student to ever graduate from this fine institution."

Those moments are seared eternally into my soul and my memory. After the ceremony, the same dean who had voted against my application for admission came up to me and said, "I said you'd never make it here." He shook my hand warmly, adding, "I just want you to know how wrong I was. You have done an outstanding job and you deserve all the credit in the world."

The real thanks go to Amy Johnson. I'll never forget her!

Many of my friends and family had come from great distances to share this special day. After the graduation ceremony was over, my family hosted a grand party for me at a local function room. Many of my classmates came to wish me well. My mother was as happy as I'd ever seen her. She was beaming, thrilled to see that I had finally accomplished unimaginable goals.

That evening I spent a couple of quiet hours lying in a chaise lounge as the sun began to set over the trees. I reflected on the amazing series of events of the previous five years. I had gone from despair and thoughts of suicide to graduating from one of the best colleges in the country. I was going on to Harvard Law School. I hoped I wasn't going to wake up and find that I had been dreaming. At the same time, I realized that it had been a dream that led me to this grandest of days

I wished I could have stayed at Amherst forever. But I had a burning desire to be a lawyer.

* * *

I had been sitting on the wall for quite a bit more than an hour. Diana was late. I was enjoying the quiet time of peaceful reflection and suddenly Diana arrived and we made our way to Valentine, the dining hall. Diana was full of news. She told me who had retired and who had passed away at Amherst. I enjoyed so much being back on the campus and connecting with her and other friends. I was shocked by how much had changed in the eleven years since I had graduated.

Most of the professors I enjoyed were no longer teaching. More new buildings had been built. The dining hall, always good, was even better. The campus was beautifully manicured. We sat by the big windows of Valentine, looking out over acres of the pristinely landscaped grounds. The lunch was excellent.

After our long visit, I strolled over to the Jeffrey Amherst bookstore where I spent another hour in the air-conditioned comfort of the office of my former Amherst classmate, Ty Lorenzo, who ran the college bookstore.

Ty had also been an older student at Amherst, but somewhat younger than I, who also had a family to support while trying to complete his degree. We had quickly become close friends. It was Ty who taught me the ropes of being an older student and how to survive at a young person's college.

Like Ty, I had survived. In those final days I had spent at Amherst, I had a sense that, after all my years on this earth, I was becoming the person I was meant to be. I had come to believe we all have a calling inside of us. My calling was to become a lawyer and help those less fortunate than me. Amherst had given me what I needed to go to the next level. For the first time in my life I knew for certain that whatever it would take to become a more productive human being had been inside of me all along. I was ready for the rigors of law school.

Ty reminded me of the early days on campus when I was somewhat apprehensive about my chances of success. "When you think back" he said, "How lucky we were."

"Not lucky—blessed" I retorted.

Chapter Twenty-Seven
To the Green Mountains

The woods are lovely, dark and deep.
But I have promises to keep,
And miles to go before I sleep,
And miles to go before I sleep.

—**Robert Frost**

These wonderful memories had delayed me at Amherst College long enough. It was time to move on. I started back on the walk, and headed toward Northampton, westbound on Route 9.

I enjoyed walking through Whatley, and its sprawling green cornfields. The heat was my only problem. Hunger gnawed at me, but water was far more important at that moment. On hot days like that, I drank more than six gallons of fluid—four gallons of water, the rest fruit juices—every day.

If nothing else, the first two weeks of the walk had given me insight into how to pace myself, and how much to eat and drink. I didn't have to worry much about my caloric intake, because I was burning far more calories than I could eat. I had always been concerned about my feet, so I was paying lots of attention to what foot-care products worked and to the regular cleaning and cooling of my feet to prevent blisters. There was much to learn. None of the planning and training prepared me for the problems I had encountered over the first 500 miles.

Around 8 P.M., exhausted from the heat, humidity, and too much uphill walking, I took a break to check my blood sugar. I was feeling a little woozy.

My thrice-daily blood-test results were the best they'd ever been, from which I inferred that extreme exercise was all I needed to regulate my insulin levels. As a result, I rarely used my oral diabetes medications. I had learned well. The lessons of drinking water and warming up before starting in the morning; eating high-carb, low-fat foods; ample water throughout the day; regular rest periods; getting to bed early enough to get at least eight hours of sleep; and avoiding milk and sugared drinks, all helped me to feel healthy.

The Morphine Dream

* * *

Later the following day, I left Bernardston, Massachusetts, and crossed the border into Vermont. It was the fourth state of my walk, only seventeen to go. It had been thirteen days and I was 527 miles from the finish line of the Boston Marathon. Crossing another state border—just an arbitrary and imaginary line—filled me with pride. For a moment I forgot all the aches and pains. To the east, I saw the Connecticut River, which separated Brattleboro, Vermont, from New Hampshire. Part of me preferred to be headed east, to familiar places.

I was finally in Vermont: the Green Mountain State. The name came from the French *vert mount,* which means "green mountain." It is a special place and has long had a reputation for its majestic landscape. Many authors, artists and activists live here, especially in Brattleboro and Bennington. The rolling hills and quaint villages are a joy to behold in an age of over-commercialization. Visiting this corner of America feels like going back in time. I wished I was going to be in Vermont for more than two days.

Brattleboro has special meaning for me. One of my friends from Amherst College, David Foster Wallace, (class of 1985), who was a wonderful free spirit and talented writer when I knew him, wrote about Brattleboro in his thoroughly enjoyable novel *Infinite Jest*. I am thus a little more familiar with Brattleboro. Unfortunately, David took his own life in 2008, and the world lost an exceptional artist. It has been said he suffered from severe depression. I never saw any evidence of this while we knew each other at Amherst. I do know what depression can do to someone. David seemed remarkably mature for a young college student. All I saw when I used to sit with him in the college snack bar was a big smile and a propensity to speak his mind on a host of issues. He, like me, was a confirmed liberal with a capital L. He sometimes would get into arguments, acting as if he was very angry. But after making his points, he would simply laugh. He just loved to ring people's chimes.

We booked into our motel on the southern outskirts of Brattleboro. We got some Big Macs, french fries and a Diet Coke and settled in at the pool to relax and get ready for some serious mountain climbing. Charles said, "Two weeks are done. You do very good."

The fact that I had reached the two-week mark and was still standing tall was notice that I would complete the entire trip. It had been a tough two weeks at times. My foot and leg problems had definitely been more severe than ever before in my distance-walking career. But for the last couple of days, my feet seemed to have improved, for which Charles deserved all the credit. Without the serendipity of his presence, I would have been forced to call it quits a week ago. Charles tended to my feet so methodically that my blisters were showing signs of beating a hasty retreat.

For me, two weeks meant, "I've got it made." Many of my friends speculated I'd only last a week; other, more generous people, stretched it to two weeks—but that was the limit. The naysayers believed the extreme day-after-day exertion would eventually whittle down my resolve. One friend said, "Walking forty miles a day, day after day, will kill you. No one can do that."

I told her, "Not only can I do it, I have been doing it for several weeks."

My doctor told me, "Your knees cannot take the constant strain and you will develop significant problems within a week or so."

I heard all the negative comments, but I didn't listen to them, I had no doubt about my ability to focus and accomplish what I set out to do. People sometimes forget how a human being has the innate ability to overcome the most incredible obstacles and achieve lofty goals.

Recalling the skepticism made me more determined than ever.

Chapter Twenty-Eight
Hogback

I love Vermont because of her hills and valleys, her scenery and invigorating climate, but most of all because of her indomitable people. They are a race of pioneers who have almost beggared themselves to serve others. If the spirit of liberty should vanish in other parts of the Union, and support of our institutions should languish, it could all be the little state of Vermont.

—Unknown

I slept twelve hours, so I got up late in the morning. I wanted to give my legs more time to recover. I was sleeping more than ever. In the past, I had never slept more than five or six hours a night.

Before I left for the trek up Hogback Mountain, I called my boys, who by now were vacationing at their grandmother's coffee plantation in Honduras. The time-zone difference, however, made it hard to reach them. It was two hours earlier there. Usually I was already on the road before they got up, and sleeping soundly before they got back to *la casa* in the evening. I reached them just as they were leaving for the day. Nick said, "Dad, are you really still walking?"

"Of course," I told him. "I am walking tall and enjoying the adventure."

Even Nick was surprised that I had kept going. "Why are you so skeptical?" I asked.

Nick responded, "After seeing your feet last week, I thought you would have to quit."

I guess I was surrounded by skeptics. Nick said, "I'm having a great time, but I wish you were here. It's not the same without you." He continued, "Louie wants to talk to you, here he is."

Louis came on the phone. "I can't believe you're still walking."

I said, "I will finish, there is no doubt about that."

"We'll see," he told me skeptically.

"Are you getting along with everybody?" I asked.

"I'm playing baseball every day. My cousins like to play as much as I do," he responded.

"I am happy that you are enjoying the summer, and getting to spend time with your cousins. Please behave and be respectful to all your relatives," I said, imagining his carefree days and nights.

"I guess I'll see you in Illinois in a few weeks," he said, brightening my spirits.

"You certainly will. By then I will have walked almost halfway to California!" It sounded impressive, even to me.

I hated to hang up, but it was obvious that LouLou, my nickname for him, wanted to get outside for baseball. "I love you buddy."

"Love you too," said LouLou.

By 9 A.M., I was moving briskly down the steep hills toward downtown Brattleboro. While it was commonly referred to as a city, Brattleboro is smaller than many New England towns. The downtown was an anachronism. Chain stores had not yet inveigled their way into the quaint commercial district. Noticeably absent were golden arches and their meretricious iterations.

I breakfasted at the Chelsea Royal Diner on Route 9. Before climbing Hogback Mountain, I needed fuel. Waiting for my pancakes, I chatted up a few old-timers. Some were lifelong residents of "Brat," as they called it, and some were dedicated walkers. They were proud of the diner and quick to point out that it had been rated "The best place for breakfast" in the Brattleboro area for two consecutive years. For all I knew, this may have been the *only* place around here to get breakfast.

We commiserated about the commercial clutter on Route 5 coming from Massachusetts, and on Route 9, where the diner was located. The old timers said that this type of growth was being challenged, more now than in years past. They warned me that there would be more clutter as I headed west on Route 9, but promised it would soon vanish in the hills, forests, and pastures of the Green Mountains.

The rest of the day's walk, a forty-mile up-and-down-the-mountain journey, was as tough as any I would encounter on the entire trip. Lately, in my mind, I had been dividing each day's walk into four ten-mile walks. Four tens made the day seem easier than one forty or two twenties. Today, the first ten had me a few miles short of the summit of Hogback.

Hours later, I was there. It was a glorious summer day. At the top of Hogback, I felt like one of Ethan Allen's Green Mountain boys, running along the mountain tops on their way to capture Fort Ticonderoga during the Revolutionary War. It was worth every step of the ordeal to get there.

At some places along the switchbacks on Route 9, I had a five-state view of Vermont, New Hampshire, Massachusetts, Connecticut and New York. A wall-to-wall forest carpeted the distant hills in varying hues of green. The view from the coin-operated binoculars at the tourist overlook wasn't as good as the view with the naked eye. When there were no vehicles around, I heard only the whoosh of the breeze and the vocabulary of birds overhead. At times I heard absolute silence, a rare delight.

At the Skyline Restaurant, I lunched on a too-thick turkey club sandwich and hot cream of broccoli soup. I was seated next to a large plate glass window with the same five-state view.

I could imagine the leaves in their fiery autumn splendor, for which Vermont was famous. In a few months, thousands of tourists would flock to Hogback in the early fall. Vermonters called them "leaf peepers." As I looked out over the millions of acres of trees, I pictured the same view smothered with winter snow. *I will come back someday to experience it, but not on foot*, I thought.

The view impressed Charles. He said, "In Brazil there is no view like this." He stood and gazed silently, in awe.

I walked down the mountain toward Bennington. Distance walking downhill was not as easy as one might think. I was using a different set of muscles and the down slope was incredibly stressful on the knees. A couple of miles of downhill were no big deal, however, ten miles could bring one to tears. The many surgeries on my knees over my lifetime had left me with fragile knees. The extra stress of the constant downhill walking was often difficult to tolerate. The slightest misstep could be extremely painful. I had to be much more alert, as I couldn't afford to suffer an injury.

I'd say the day was going well. I had walked twenty-five miles and it was early afternoon on another ninety-degree day. As long as the terrain remained fairly flat, as it had since completing the long descent from Hogback, I should have been arriving in Bennington by 7 P.M. Generally, my forty-mile-a-day goal was demanding, but doable. But walking up and down mountains made that daily goal almost impossible. I only hoped the terrain in New York would be less challenging.

The Deerfield River, with its crystal-clear water, ran along the road to my left. I was tempted to dive in, a temptation I felt every time I passed water. Fortunately, the rich green, forested hills to my right provided me with a natural sun block, so I moved on.

For an hour, the sound of flowing water had been a delightful companion, interrupted now and then by the scream of a chain saw, and the crack of an axe splitting logs—the sounds of folks making preparations for a cold Vermont winter.

Ahead I saw a threatening sky. Another long uphill stretch found me closing in on the village of Searsburg—nothing more than a few farms and a general store. As the storm clouds headed my way, I was seven miles from Bennington, where I would spend the night. Moments later, the swift-moving storm was now overhead.

Suddenly, a strong gust of wind temporarily blinded me, blowing sand and debris into my face and eyes. Lightning was followed by deafening thunder. And then it started to rain hard—just a typical New England summer thunderstorm—but a relief for a distance walker on another 4H day.

Without warning, the storm became a mini-hurricane. The wind whipsawed me so hard I could barely stand, and the rain, moving sideways, felt like needles pricking my face and neck. Thrown by an unseen hand, a metal stop sign, like a Frisbee, flew by me—six feet off the ground. Still, I kept walking, alerted to potential dangers. It wasn't as bad as being blown off the road by a passing semi.

A bolt of lightning shattered a giant Douglas fir 100 yards to my left on the hillside, leaving a jagged ten-foot-high stump.

"Enough!" I declared.

I crawled into the van. As quickly as the storm had arrived, it passed over us and continued its track east, toward Hogback. Soon the wind abated, and the "road rivers" mellowed into trickles. After the rain stopped, the trees kept "raining" for a while. The distant thunder, rumbling off to the east, told me the storm was now tormenting someone else. In the short time I had waited out the storm, I had stiffened considerably. I was far too uncomfortable to continue.

My stopping early meant eight extra miles in the morning, but the flying stop sign and obliterated pine tree were warnings I couldn't ignore.

Danger was an integral part of walking—sometimes overt, other times subtle, but always there. Some dangers can be treated and controlled, like skin cancer and diabetes. Others, lurking unseen and unanticipated, were waiting to take me out at a moment's notice—like the Douglas fir, broken in half like a pencil. And then there were my knee, back, and heart problems, not to mention heat stroke—all exacerbated by my now diminishing 275-pound frame. As my weight continued to drop, however, I was much better off. When one is walking long distances, every pound means so much. I could sense that the strain on my body was less severe. But, I still was double extra fat.

* * *

The next morning, we were up and out by 5:00 A.M. It would be a strenuous day because I had failed to meet yesterday's mileage goal. I needed to do those remaining eight miles to Bennington before I could begin the day's planned march into New York. It was still dark. I was on Route 9, trying to get my legs loosened up. It was muggy, yet raw. Fortunately, there was almost no traffic, so I walked in the middle of the road, where it was flat. I had no sense of being tired as I moved quickly west. My exhilaration level was at A-plus. I was thrilled to soon be knocking on the door of another state.

By daybreak, I found myself in Bennington, home of Bennington College, a mecca for artists and writers. Robert Frost was buried there. Grandma Moses painted in Bennington for many years. Locals claimed this was where "Vermont really began."

For me, college towns like Amherst, Austin, Berkley, and Cambridge were unique. Bennington belongs on that list, along with places like New Haven, Ann Arbor, Princeton and Dartmouth among others. College towns are so vibrant. The presence of "things of the mind" permeates those towns. Poetry readings, book signings, concerts, street musicians and artists of all sorts abound. Energetic young people engaged in thoughtful intellectual conversations, bearded professors smoking their pipes, lounging in the myriad of sidewalk cafes. Theater, parents dragging their teenagers on college tours, bookstores, organic cafes, and pizza places are all regular sights. Sometimes it seems like those towns are utopian.

Back in colonial times, Bennington was the first town west of the Connecticut River to be settled. It was also a festering spot for the renowned Bennington Mob, known as the Green Mountain Boys, led by Ethan Allen. On this day, I felt like I was a member of the Bennington Mob, having earned my stripes walking over those Green Mountains.

I finished the final eight miles to Bennington at the lightning-fast pace of 4.8 miles per hour, but it wasn't worth it. I was soaked with sweat and needed to cool down, change clothes, and have a cold drink before moving on. I took time out for a quick interview with the local newspaper. After that, I rested for half an hour. My legs had tightened up. After a few minutes of stretching, I was ready to walk again. Reaching another state was a powerful motivator.

I strolled out of Bennington, and headed west to Hoosick, New York. It was mid-morning. I could tell I was losing weight because my clothes were noticeably looser. I felt stronger than I had felt a few days before, and I had completely stopped thinking about abandoning the walk. With the exception of the mini-hurricane on Hogback, the weather had been excellent.

My legs came back to life as I pushed along; trying to imagine what was in store for me in New York, my fifth state.

I stopped to look back at Vermont. As I stood alone in the sunshine, the silence was loud. Inhaling the fragrances of pine, I must say I loved the beauty and the state of mind of Vermont. It was where all the hippies ended up, now more seasoned and mellow. I could sense why they gravitated there.

Each day of the walk has its special moments; this was today's.

Part Two
From the Mountains

I have learned this at least by my experiment: that if one advances confidently in the direction of his dreams, and endeavors to live the life which he has imagined he will meet with success unexpected in common hours.
—Henry David Thoreau

Chapter Twenty-Nine

The Preparation

Execution is the ability to mesh strategy
with reality, align people with goals, and
achieve the promised results.

— **Larry Bossidy**

In early April of 1997, when I made the commitment to myself to begin Walking USA on July 4, 1997, I soon realized that in order for my walk to become a reality there was a virtual mountain of planning necessary. There was so much to think of, very little time to do it, and little margin for error. Luckily, the route had been mostly determined years before, otherwise, three months would never have been enough time to get myself ready.

What remained to be done was a budget that included the appropriate funding, a line item for the needed equipment and supplies that I would need to carry. A plan for publicity and media contacts was required along with the establishment of a process by which charities could benefit from the event, and the methods for folks to participate in supporting the charities had to be structured.

Budgeting was perhaps the most complicated issue for me. I had no experience in estimating the cost of things completely unknown. How much clothing? What types of clothing? How much did I need to allocate for motels, meals, laundry and photography? What about health care? Seemingly small things could add up to a big expense. The cost of laundry, for instance, would be a factor because I would be walking for months. In the heat of the summer I would have to change clothes five or six times a day, or even more. What would telephone charges be like? I would have to keep a cell phone with me. I would need to alert folks ahead of me where I would be speaking of the exact time of my arrival, Also, I always needed to have my sons be able to reach their dad. I had to guess at the amount of food and drinks to be consumed while walking—keeping it to a bare minimum—balancing what I could carry, but separate from the amount needed for eating in restaurants before and after each day's walk. But the most important budget item was to provide for my family while I was away.

My being away would be difficult enough without my wife having to worry about finances. I wanted her and the kids to continue their routine without having to sacrifice any of their normal activities. I immediately calculated a sum to cover all their expenses and deposited it in a bank account for my wife to use freely while I was walking.

Once that was done, I visited Eastern Mountain Sports to select a backpack. I had never done any walking with a pack before, so I had no idea how limited I would be carrying the things I needed. I chatted with a sales associate to determine the amount of weight I should try to carry. "Try a sixty-pound pack, that's sounds like more than enough weight," he said. We picked out and packed sixty pounds of various gear so I would have an idea of how the heavy pack would wear on my back while I walked.

The salesman helped me put on the loaded pack. It felt very cumbersome. I was used to walking long distance, but not walking with any weight on my back. The weight of the pack didn't feel tolerable, even in the comfort of the store, but I thought I should give it a road test anyway. My plan was to walk five miles and back—a total of ten miles—to analyze how well I could walk carrying this amount of weight. Surprisingly, sixty pounds was not much in the way of actual equipment and supplies, certainly less than I would need to sustain me for months.

After walking only a mile, I realized there was no way I could travel 5,000 miles with a pack on my back. I went back to the store and apologized to the guy for wasting so much of his time. "I don't know how anybody could take a walk with that weight on his back," I told him.

"When you were telling me your plan I was thinking it was going to be an awakening for you wearing a pack," he said.

My plan took a radical change that night. I realized I needed a vehicle of some kind—a "sag wagon" like you see in long-distance bicycle races—to support me in my effort. It would have to be a utilitarian vehicle that met all the varying needs of the trip. This was a considerable unplanned expense. Additionally, I would need to find a driver: someone who wouldn't mind crawling behind me at a snail's pace for thirteen hours or more each day and be my companion 24/7. If I were lucky enough to find someone to take on this job, his salary would be another huge expense. To boot, the amount of money I needed for meals, drinks and clothing would be more than doubled. The cost of gas, insurance, oil, repairs and car washes would need to be added. The budget had–overnight–become a much larger concern.

I put it all together and the cost was staggering. The driver cost was budgeted for $10,000. The motel, at only $50.00 a night, was

$7,200. Meals would cost an incredible $18,000, based on $125 a day for 144 days. The weekly cost of vehicle-related expenses was $300 a week for 20 weeks, or $6,000. The photography, film and laundry was an additional $2,000. The equipment and clothing I would need to buy added up to at least $6,000 more. I rounded off the budget at $50,000. That did not yet include the purchase of a vehicle.

The cost to fulfill my dream came out to $10.00 a mile. Many people would see this as a waste of money. For me, the issue of money was of no importance. The costs related to the trek were but a small price to pay if it meant I was to realize my dream. For so many years I had drifted in that nasty sea of uncertainty. For so many years I had let all opportunity and possibilities pass me by. Now, if spending some heard-earned money was all that was left to do, so be it.

With the budget done, I focused on the issue of raising money for charities. It was important to me that any number of charities could benefit from this. Walking events are traditionally a great way for charitable entities to raise money. I was going to walk across the country anyway, so why not make it a fundraising event? I quickly settled on six different charities that I really believed in and asked people to support what I was doing by donating to them. When I had the vehicle ready, I would stencil the names of the charities on all four sides. They were United Cerebral Palsy, The Jimmy Fund, (Children with Cancer), COPS (Children of Police Survivors), The New England Center for Homeless Veterans in Boston, The United Negro College Fund, and the Brimmer and May School in Chestnut Hill, Massachusetts (the school that my children attended, where I wanted to create a healthier scholarship fund for minorities.). Throughout the entire walk, whenever anyone would ask, "How can I donate?" I would point to the list of charities on the van and ask them to please consider one or more from my list and then call 1-800-walk1ok and give whatever felt comfortable.

It was because of the charities that the need for publicity and media involvement became crucial, as it was vital to getting people involved in giving. Secondly, the pervading thought was, given enough publicity, corporations would want to become involved as sponsors, ultimately providing the funds for the expenses of the event and additional donations for the selected charities.

Much of the publicity would happen spontaneously, especially in smaller news markets. But to get coverage by the larger markets it would be necessary to fax press releases and then follow up with phone calls to gauge interest and hopefully set up interviews.

While a cell phone company provided me free service for the entire walk, and the shoe manufacturer Rockport gave me free footwear, I wasn't able to get significant corporate sponsorship. Most corporations viewed me as too old and fat to complete the walk. I had sent sponsorship proposals to more than twenty corporations. A couple of marketing types asked me outright if I would be able to complete such an arduous event given my weight and age. Several companies promised to join in after I got to the West Coast. I expected that once I did reach the Pacific Ocean, I would find significant corporate support but starting out I had to rely on my own funds. I left Boston with $40,000 in my account, specifically earmarked for walk expenses. I had already spent $10,000 stocking up.

When I had committed to the walk, I had already been in the process of selling my interest in the medical practice management company company my wife and I had built. I wanted to get the profit from that sale to be able to afford my walk across the country.

At the closing of that sale, I pushed the investors to sponsor my walking event with a payment of $50,000 to defray the expenses I would incur. I was thrilled when they summarily agreed to contribute those additional funds by becoming the first sponsor for the event. It made it very easy for me to assure the viability of the walk. In addition, the new owners agreed to pay the health insurance premiums for me and my family until the end of the walk.

The major pieces had fallen into place. I was ready—and there was no turning back.

Chapter Thirty

I Love New York

Life is never boring but some people choose to be bored.
The concept of boredom entails an inability to use up
present moments in a personally fulfilling way.
Boredom is a choice; something you visit upon yourself,
and it is another of those self-defeating items that you
can eliminate from your life.

—Wayne W. Dyer

With a sense of buoyancy, I soared over the sun-suffused New York border, my fifth state, touching down on Route 7.

Those miles were not just lonely, exhausting, and endless, but at times very monotonous. Although I might have conquered the physical, the remaining challenge was the mental fatigue. If I could only devise tricks to manage the emotional roller coaster, I would float along the journey like a butterfly.

I found that my plan to walk forty miles a day left no time to smell the roses. If I "only" walked a marathon distance each day—about twenty-six miles—I could finish by 2:00 P.M., which would allow me to meet the locals and maybe even visit some of the attractions. Maybe someday I would be able to do that kind of a walk but I did not have that luxury on this schedule.

Still, I found ways to make my forty miles a day more enjoyable and less tedious. Sticking to a routine helped, as did recalling as many details of the previous day's walk, committing them to memory. Another was to identify the different kinds of wild animals and birds that I encountered, or to classify the many different styles of homes I passed and guess when they were constructed. Sometimes I would daydream about what I would do if I owned a home I saw. As I passed a dilapidated farm house with a barn, I imagined myself, step by step, rehabbing the place. I also kept a running survey of what percentage of passing vehicles were cars, vans, pick-ups, or SUVs. As a result, I could gauge, without any other information, what area I was approaching—rural, suburban or urban.

Late in the afternoon, I arrived in the city of Troy, New York. I was suddenly concerned about traffic. It was my first exposure to heavy traffic since I had left Boston. I was worried about Charles being able to keep to the right far enough so as not to block the flow of the other vehicles. His usual habit was to stay about 100 feet behind me, moving at the same snail's pace as me—coasting along at about four miles per hour. It must have been dreadful for him, driving part on and part off the road, with cars beeping their horns behind him.

I had developed the uncanny ability to distinguish the sounds of oncoming automobiles. I could tell, without looking, whether it was a pick-up, a semi, a sedan, a camper, bus or a van. I could tell if it was a four-, six- or eight-cylinder vehicle. Four-cylinder engines make a quiet "tinny" sound. Six- and eight-cylinder cars have louder and louder whining engines. Cars like Mercedes and BMW's have barely any noticeable engine sound. Apparently the body construction keeps the sound under the hood. Unless the Mercedes is a diesel—then it has a distinct knocking sound that is typical of that kind of engine. Busses have a muffled dull and constant roar and, as they whoosh by, the diesel fuel fumes their engines emit burn your nasal passages. Trucks have an overpowering sound that comes with great horsepower.

It was apparent that drivers in New York were taken aback when they a happened upon a walker where he shouldn't be, so I remained eternally vigilant. They would swerve unnecessarily, blast their horns, shake their fists and scream and yell. It made no sense to me why they were so upset that I was walking along on the roadway.

* * *

At 4 A.M. the next day, I was up and walking away from the town of Amsterdam, on Route 5. At one point, shortly after sunrise, I found myself walking along the Erie Canal. From my vantage point, I could see five different flavors of transportation, all right next to each other: a) Route 5, a the two-lane country road that I was walking on, full of frost heaves; b) the Amtrak railroad line; c) the New York Thruway, also called Interstate 90, which connected Boston Harbor with Seattle's Puget Sound—over 3,000 miles away—without a red light or stop sign (except at the tolls); and d) the moribund Erie Canal. With X-ray vision, I could see the Mohawk River, only a few miles to the south.

Walking west into the village of Fonda, I encountered some Native Americans, members of the Iroquois Nation, which used to rule this part of the world. There were three men, a pregnant woman who looked about ready to deliver, and a boy of about three. They were all clad in colorful and typical Native American garb. All sported long black hair in pony tails. They were walking slowly along the same route. I asked, "Is it alright if I walk with you for a while?"

The fellow who appeared to be the leader said, "Welcome! Walk with us as long as you like, but we only have a mile to go."

"What gets you out and walking so early in the morning?" I asked.

"For my wife, walking every morning will help her to not suffer when she is in labor."

When is she due? I asked.

"Yesterday," he declared.

When they reached their house a short time later, they invited me in and I accepted their hospitality. I soon discovered their home contained a wealth of Iroquois memorabilia. They ran a school in their house to help the tribe's youngsters maintain their native heritage.

Another dazzling day was coming to an end. I walked through the eastern outskirts of Utica in the ebbing light and heat of the evening. Glancing at the old freshly painted Victorians beaming in the dying sunlight, framed in shiny green leaves, I was enveloped by the powerful aromas of summer. As I advanced westward, the summer advanced too, almost keeping pace with me, the days hotter and steamier.

Chapter Thirty-One

Coopers Town

He owed a part of his inspiration to the magnificent
nature which surrounded him, to the lakes, forests,
and Indian traditions of a great State.
—Edward Everett, speaking of the departed Cooper

I had walked forty-seven miles and it was only 6 P.M. so Charles and I decided to jump into the van for a quick thirty-five-mile side trip to the Baseball Hall of Fame in Cooperstown. To get there, we followed the nine-mile-long road around Lake Otsego. The lake—like a giant mirror, nestled among thousands of majestic pines—was aptly described by James Fennimore Cooper as "Lake Glimmerglass."

This was the home of the literary giant, James Fennimore Cooper, one of my all-time favorite American writers. Cooper's books were testimony to the Noble Savage of yesteryear. He wrote about the true pioneers of the seventeenth century. His books take a reader back in time to a peaceful and quieter place. It was easy to see that the town he loved, Coopers Town, had influenced his writing greatly.

Fortunately, the Baseball Hall of Fame museum had extra-long summer visiting hours and was open till 9:00 P.M. We had gotten a late start because I lingered too long in the shower, and on the way we had stopped for a quick bite. We only had an hour left to see the display, so we had to move quickly. I was thrilled once again as I passed by the plaques of the game's greatest players, "Where the legends live forever." I first visited this museum in my teens, during my baseball-playing days, and dreamed of being honored here myself someday. Though I had put that dream to rest long ago, I was still in awe of this place. Being at a baseball fan's greatest haven, however, made me sad, too. I missed my sons. Big baseball fans themselves, they had been here a couple of times with me and really loved this place. On the trip back, I walked along the lake for a while, even though I had already put in more than my scheduled mileage for the day. I wanted to walk in Cooper's Great American Forest. In the fading twilight and heat of the evening, I stumbled upon the "Natty Bumpo Trail" and felt myself becoming a minor character in the thrilling pentalogy that includes *The Deerslayer* and *The Last of the Mohicans.*

I was out on the road by 5 A.M., heading to Syracuse from Utica. For only the third time on the walk, it was raining. Passing cars splashed me and the drumming of the rain on the pavement drowned out the usual sounds.

I drifted through several small towns and villages with lovely names, like Oneida and Canastota. I was inclined to stop and visit each, but I was soaked from the rain and perspiration. I looked awful: unshaven and unkempt. Because I was out of clean clothes, I walked most of the day without the van following behind. Charles had stopped in Westmoreland to do the laundry, get a haircut, and do personal errands.

Back in the zone, only boredom prevented me from walking far into the night. The aches and pains no longer hindered me. They were no longer symptoms of ailments, merely the fruit of great physical exertion.

Like an idiot, I had spoken too soon. As I walked into east Syracuse under an overcast evening sky, my knee was beginning to ache. One mile short of my forty-mile goal, I had to quit.

* * *

At 4 A.M. the next day, I left our motel in order to get to downtown Syracuse and beyond, hopefully before rush hour. I had to follow an interstate spur for ten miles. Despite my best effort to beat the traffic, it turned into rush hour. Thousands of cars and trucks were doing their best to blow me off the road. I sent Charles ahead ten miles to meet me at the end of the spur, where I would resume walking on an old two-lane road. It was unwise to have the van behind me on that tough stretch of highway.

The road kill was plentiful and upsetting. Dead deer, raccoons, woodchucks and skunk littered the highway. The stench of rotting flesh stained my mood and suppressed my appetite. That, I suppose, was good, considering how much weight I wanted and needed to lose.

Chapter Thirty-Two
The "Old Boy" Network

An informal system through which men are thought to use their positions of influence to help others who went to the same school or university as they did, or who share a similar social background: Many managers were chosen by the old boy network.

—Oxford English Dictionary

As the day wore on, and for no particular reason, I spent a lot of time thinking about my mother. Before she died in 1991 at the young age of seventy-two, I spoke with her—either in person or on the phone—every night of my adult life. Anything that was happening in my life or hers was fodder for discussion. In addition, I always needed to check in on her to make sure she was doing okay. She was my hero.

In my life there was nobody who cared about me the way she did. She was supportive, nurturing, understanding, kind and taught me more than the rest of the world combined. When I was troubled, she was always able to get me moving in a better direction. When I need to find jobs, she helped me get one. She taught me how to cook, do the laundry, take care of my baby sister and so many other things. She used to say to me, "You are going to make some woman a good wife someday."

One night in the spring of 1986, I had spoken to her for an hour at dinner time. Soon after I chatted with her I experienced one of the most serendipitous evenings of my life. I will never forget what I am about to tell you as long as I live.

It was a Friday night that I had spoken to her. I was nearing graduation at Amherst College. I had the entire weekend set aside to finish my American Studies thesis. I was energized. After so many months of traveling, researching, interviewing, I was about to complete what turned out to be a 253-page paper. I would personally deliver it to all three of my thesis advisors before the start of classes Monday morning.

I was busy checking footnotes around nine at night when the phone rang.

"This is the Athol Memorial Hospital calling for Donald Brown," said a somber male voice. "I am calling to let you know your mother has just been brought in by ambulance. She has had massive heart failure and is not likely to make it through the night."

"You must have the wrong Donald Brown," I said, "I just talked to my mother at dinnertime a couple of hours ago. She was fine."

"Is your mother Anita Hastings?" (I may have called her Maude, but her real name was Anita, and many years after my father's suicide, she married Henry Hastings, who was twenty years her senior.)

"Oh my God," I said. "What is being done for her? Are you her doctor? Is there something I can do?"

The caller was the emergency-room physician. In his opinion nothing could be done. He said that she was hanging on by a thread.

"How about sending her to a Boston hospital?" I asked.

"First, she would need to have a cardiologist approve that, and second she would not survive the long ride."

"Isn't there anything we can do?"

"The only possibility is a life flight, but you'd need a cardiologist in Boston willing to take her on as a patient without even knowing her. And you need one here as well. It is not possible to do all these things at this hour on a Friday night."

I was dazed. My mother sounded just fine when we chatted; now she was on death's door. I had to get there, to be with her. I was sobbing so hard I couldn't see.

As I prepared to drive to the hospital, an idea popped into my head. Dr. Frank Austen was a college trustee. He was also a director of something at Brigham and Women's Hospital. As Scriver's driver, I had often picked him up at the Brigham in Boston for campus events at Amherst. Because I had access to special directories at the college, I called Dr. Austen at home. I knew his was a Wellesley, Massachusetts, phone number from my landscaping days. Dr. Austen himself answered. I quickly explained the situation.

"Where are you?" he asked.

I told him I was in Amherst in my house across from the Admissions Office.

"I will call you back in five minutes."

I waited. Five minutes went by, then ten, and then fifteen. Finally, the phone rang. Dr. Austen told me to get in my car and get to the Athol Memorial Hospital as fast as possible.

"The CBS jet helicopter, courtesy of Tom Wyman (chairman of the board of CBS and an Amherst College trustee) is on its way to Boston to pick up a team of cardiologists and then take them to Athol. You need to be in Athol when they get there. They will be in Athol at 11:30."

It was 10:45. Only at an outrageous speed could I get there in time. I called the state police and asked if I could get an escort. The operator's said, "No, just go. Do what you have to do, but be careful."

I drove fast, at times as much as 100 miles per hour on country roads. Ten minutes after I departed on the forty-mile trip, two police cruisers were in hot pursuit, lights flashing, sirens wailing. It was like a scene from a movie. There was no way I was going to stop and explain. They kept a safe distance behind me. When I reached the highway in Orange, I drove even faster. I was driving so fast I couldn't even look down to see the speedometer. By now, there were at least six cruisers following me.

Darting off the highway into Athol, I had to slow down and the flashing blue lights began to close in. All I needed was another minute.

I turned into the hospital entrance going about eighty and screeched to a stop in front of the main entrance. As I leapt out of the car, running towards the main lobby, my car was immediately surrounded by police cruisers.

I looked back and shouted, "My mother is dying. I will face the tickets after I find out if she's still alive." I could hear the helicopter blades *thwonking* in the rear of the hospital. I ran in. I was sure I would be arrested, but I didn't care.

When I got to the hallway leading to the emergency room, my mother, who was as white as the sheets covering her and looked dead, was being wheeled on a gurney towards the back door where the helicopter was waiting. Doctors were preparing her for surgery as they were rushing down the hall with her. When they got to the helicopter, they pushed her gurney in. Then the team of cardiologists all squeezed in behind her. There must have been six of them. I signed the necessary paperwork. The operation had already begun in the helicopter. It was so cramped inside you couldn't fit in a package of gum. I was able to bend in and give my mother a kiss, all the while avoiding looking at what they were doing to her chest.

I tried to compose myself as I watched them ascend skyward. I went outside to face the army of police. Much to my surprise, they were all gone except one, a state trooper. He explained that everybody understood the situation and had agreed no tickets would be issued but I did have to sign his incident report. I turned to leave and he said, "That was a great piece of driving. I'm glad you made it without killing anybody. I hope your mother makes it."

A half hour later, the University of Massachusetts Medical Center in Worcester called to say that my mother was resting and had regained consciousness. The doctors had decided against taking her to Boston because she was in such grave condition. During the flight they had put a pacemaker in her chest. I immediately drove to Worcester.

An hour later my mother was sitting up and smiling, asking what all the fuss had been about. She had no memory of anything since dinner. She knew nothing about the ambulance, the Athol Memorial Hospital, the helicopter, or the operation that saved her life.

I explained all that had happened. I realized, as I was telling her, that because of Amherst College she was still alive. Calling Dr. Austen, who arranged for the cardiologists and the CBS jet helicopter, had certainly saved her. My respect for the Amherst network can never be diminished. In fifteen minutes, two of the college's trustees had done what the Athol doctor said couldn't be done. It was an incredible response to a student's outrageous request. I am eternally grateful for what Dr. Austen and Tom Wyman did for me and my mother that night.

I know one thing for sure. Because I had been accepted at Amherst College, I was able to save her life and spend an additional four years with her.

Chapter Thirty-Three
Tragedy Strikes

Those we love don't go away, they walk beside us every day. Unseen, unheard, but always near; still loved, still missed and very dear.

—Anonymous

One night, after I had been practicing law for about a year, I was out of town on a trip to visit my friend Peggy Stotz in Amherst. Peggy needed my help for a legal situation in her life. Estela had come with me to get away for a couple of days. No sooner had we arrived and unpacked when Peggy's phone began to ring. She answered and said, "Donald, it's for you."

My heart sank. I had left Peggy's number as one to reach me in an emergency, so I knew this could not be good. Fearful of what it might be about, I took the phone and said, "Hello?"

A voice on the other end said, "This is the South Shore Hospital calling about Anita Hastings."

She was talking about my mother and I was instantly overcome with horrible thoughts.

My mother had a myriad of health problems and was totally disabled from severe rheumatoid arthritis. She was also a "brittle" diabetic—a rare and highly unstable form of the disease—who needed constant care. In spite of all her health difficulties, she was still able to live pretty much independently. I asked, "What about my mother?"

"She had a bad fall in her apartment at 2:00 A.M. yesterday. She was on the floor until 9:00 A.M. when her home health aide showed up to cook her breakfast. She was brought here by ambulance at 9:30 A.M."

"Is she going to be okay?" I responded.

"She shattered her hip. We can't operate because she is failing rapidly. She has been put on life support, and she is in grave condition."

I began to cry. I couldn't talk. Here I was, far away, and my mother was in trouble.

Peggy realized what was going on and she took the phone. After she hung up she told me, "The hospital had trouble locating you, and you are the person named in your mother's living will. They think the

151

best thing to do is withdraw life support as her situation appears hopeless. But you have to go to the hospital to do that."

I was dumbfounded. I quickly packed my things and jumped into my car to drive the hundred miles back to the south shore of Boston to get to the hospital. What should have been a two-hour drive took me all of one hour and twenty minutes. Once I arrived, a doctor took me into a private conference room and explained, "Your mother's prognosis is very bleak; she is too weak to tolerate any intervention at this point. We think that you should consider allowing us to withdraw all her life support equipment."

"No! I can't do that to her," I said.

The doctor said, "By not doing it, you may be ultimately doing more harm than good."

"I need to talk to my sisters," I insisted.

I called my sister Beryl first. She was a nurse and had been for more than forty years. I explained the situation. She asked to speak with the doctor so I handed the phone to him. After they were done talking, I took the phone back and Beryl told me, "The doctor is right; you should let them withdraw life support."

I trusted Beryl without reservation. I signed the papers authorizing the hospital staff to end all treatment.

It was a long night, already 4:00 A.M., and I was physically and emotionally exhausted. I found a seat in the private waiting room for the visitors to the intensive care ward. I curled up in a chair and dozed off. I woke up in a daze at 7:30 A.M. I went to my mother's room, and was shocked to see her sitting up in bed, smiling when she saw me. No one could explain why, but after they had withdrawn all the life support, my mother had rallied, regained consciousness, and gotten back some of her strength.

She said, "Did they tell you I fell in the bathroom?"

I couldn't talk. I was so worried I had lost her, and here she was holding a conversation with me. I thanked God that she seemed to be okay

Unfortunately she had developed a serious sore on her hip, apparently when she was lying on the bathroom floor for so long after the fall. Being in the hospital bed, the sore had developed into a significant bed sore. "We can't operate until the bed sore heals," the doctor told me.

After a couple of weeks, the bed sore had not improved. The hospital was forced to transfer her to a nursing home across the street. The plan was as soon as her bed sore recovered, she would be transferred back to the hospital for the hip surgery. If all went well, she would then go to a rehab facility and then be able to return home.

In the nursing home she was doing reasonably well but was terribly frustrated at losing the independence she had enjoyed in her senior citizen apartment for some many years. It was frustrating to go to see her because she was always begging me to intervene and get her out of the nursing home. I wanted to help her and grant her that wish, but the doctors were adamant that she needed to be there.

I stopped going to see her regularly because it was so painful to see her in such a dependent state. When my son was born terribly afflicted with birth defects, I couldn't bring myself to tell her about Louis. I stayed away for several weeks using "I am too busy" as an excuse.

Finally, after my wife pleaded with me to go see her because she was so upset that I hadn't been there, I went for a visit. She seemed content, was smiling, and confident that she would have the necessary surgery very soon and would return to her apartment.

The conversation quickly turned to her asking, "How's my newest grandson?"

I could not respond. I was tearing up. I tried to talk but I couldn't get the words out. I began to sob. She realized that the news was not good. She knew by how upset I was that there was major problems.

Right there in front of me and my wife, she curled up into a fetal ball, and slowly slipped away from me. Watching her in that situation, I could sense that she lost her will to live. I was a basket case for the rest of the day. That evening, sleep was hard to find. I knew she was gone, it was just a matter of when.

The next day, a Monday, my wife went to see her and told her, "Don will be coming to see you on Friday morning."

She said, "I won't be here."

She died four days later, on Friday morning. I had never gotten to see her again after she had curled into the fetal ball.

When she died, I was heartbroken. I would never be whole again. The human condition is ultimately cruel. As I walked along, it hit me how much I missed her.

Even though it had been six years since her death, there were nights when I reached for the phone to call her. Often it took two or three seconds before I'd realize I needed more than a phone to reach her. "Maude the Broad," as I used to call her, would have been ecstatic to see me realizing my dream of walking across the country. I hoped she was watching.

Chapter Thirty-Four

Amherst Again

I've had some tremendous adventures,
good and bad. It's part of the novel, and
a novel isn't interesting if it doesn't have
some good and bad. And you don't know
what good is if bad hasn't been a part of your life.

—Lynn Johnston

Those memories drifted away as the early morning breeze licked my face with cool air. This was a most tranquil time, when the sweet aromas of pine and grass mixed with the pungent scents of fertilizer and cow manure. The absence of lights in the houses suggested there were no early risers. A trickling brook twinkled as the sun rose. The black sky turned blue. Thousands of birds seemed to have something urgent to say. It was these moments of tranquility that drowned out my boredom, making a 3.8-mile-per-hour pace seem effortless.

I decided to grind out some extra miles to get closer to Buffalo. By walking farther than planned, I would have extra time the next day to do a side trip to Niagara Falls, something I knew Charles would enjoy. With that in mind, I walked the extra fifteen miles to Clarence, New York, arriving at 11:30 P.M. I had walked an astonishing fifty-eight miles that day. (The farthest I walked in any one day of the entire trip). Surprisingly, I felt pretty good. I showered, shaved, and was in bed in less than five minutes—sore and sleepy as usual, but content.

* * *

I left Clarence, New York, at 6 A.M., while Charles remained behind to do the laundry. I walked through a fancy suburb of Buffalo, called Amherst, whose name, as you already know, had special significance to me.

* * *

I was truly transfigured by that school. It was at Amherst College that I began in earnest to prepare for walking across the country. At the end of my third semester there, I had undergone the last of twenty knee surgeries. With artificial joints in my legs, I was back on my feet in the early spring, several weeks earlier than expected, and I began walking. Within a few days, I pushed myself to walk twenty miles a day, ten miles up the mountain to Belchertown, and ten back down to Amherst. Those walks were some of the best of my life. I felt alive again. I walked not to go anywhere. I walked just to walk. "The special thing is to move," poet Langston Hughes wrote.

I was trying to think back through the cobwebs of memory when the idea that I could really walk across America—not just dream about it—first took root in my brain. For an American literature course, I had just finished reading *Two Years Before the Mast* by Henry Dana, Jr., and *The Oregon Trail* by Francis Parkman. Those were two New Englanders who had decided to flee Boston in order to get a taste of life outside of the parochial world of their upbringing. Since I got seasick every time I got on a boat, I decided to follow Parkman's path, not Dana's. And so, it was after reading those two wonderfully written memoirs that I finally decided that I was going to walk across America.

It was also in Amherst, New York, that I was struck for the first time by the irony that my debilitating knee injury—the worst thing that could have ever happened to me—was the best thing that could have ever happened. I was reaching goals that I had never before thought possible. If it wasn't for my injury, I couldn't imagine where I would be. Instead of suicide, which I had yearned for, I'd been reborn. Instead of treading water, I was now swimming to a distant shore just over the horizon where I could for once stand tall and be proud.

I left this well-to-do suburb behind with happy reflected memories. Soon, I found myself in the "Other Apple."

Part Three
The Rust Belt

You will recognize your own path when you come upon it, because you will suddenly have all the energy and imagination you will ever need.
—**Jerry Gillies**

Chapter Thirty-Five
The Other Apple

In all of us, there is a hunger, marrow deep, to know our heritage,
to know who we are—and where we come from. Without this
enriching knowledge, there is a hollow yearning,
there is the most disquieting—loneliness.

—Alex Haley

On the final ten miles of the morning walk, I passed through the heart of the black neighborhood of Buffalo. The difference between this and the immediate suburb of Amherst was as unjust as it was heart wrenching. Racial disadvantages are as common here as in most inner-city neighborhoods I had been in. In the area I walked, it seemed like there were no white people except me. Buffalo is a city where something like 40 percent of the population is black. You would never know it from this area—because it's all black. As I walk, block by block, the residents greet me with smiles and some high-fives.

I haven't always been so perceptive and sensitive. In my late teens and early twenties, I'd been the typical racist South Boston street kid.

Growing up in Westwood, my childhood exposure to blacks was confined to what I watched on television, a medium that depicted them as either: "Amos and Andy" types—jocular, deferential, and not well educated; the African tribal type—uncivilized and barbaric; or the superlative athletic type—unbeatable in baseball, football, basketball and track. It was hard not to get the impression—with perhaps the exception of athletics—that blacks were demeaned and ridiculed by the culture.

Later, in the playgrounds of South Boston—where at the time, no blacks dared set foot, never mind reside—I made friends with the street kids in the neighborhood. Like me, most of them had little interest in education, only the pursuit of athletics. I began hearing the word "nigger," as we competed against teams from other parts of Boston. "Niggers" were bad and disgusting. Yes, they were admired for their athletic prowess, but everything else was negative. Whenever blacks dared to venture into "Southie," the neighborhood kids would attack them with their fists and send them back to Roxbury and Dorchester, where most blacks lived. I never beat anyone up, but I certainly participated in using racial slurs. I guess I accepted everything I heard and I wanted to fit in, so I became as racist as most of my buddies.

When I joined the Marines in 1961 at age seventeen, I was sent to the recruitment depot at Parris Island in South Carolina, deep in the heart of Dixie. It was my first trip ever out of my home state of Massachusetts. Even my South Boston upbringing didn't prepare me for the hardcore "redneck" mentality that was the culturally accepted standard of behavior in that day and age. In the South, blacks were never allowed to mix with whites—nowhere, no place, no time. In Boston whites and blacks went to all the same places. Blacks and whites ate in the same restaurants, went to the same ballgames, movie theaters and rode on the same trolleys, buses and trains.

In the South I came face to face with white Southern males—the "good 'ole boy" types—who believed in the unquestioned superiority of the white race. They flew the Stars and Stripes right next to the Confederate flag without compunction.

After my first day of being demeaned and brutalized by the drill instructors, white and black alike, I was shocked to hear our black drill instructor make incredibly racist statements to the black recruits. When I took my sixty-second "shower," I made the mistake of chatting with a black recruit from Washington, D.C. Several white fellow recruits, obviously from Dixie, came in and slapped me around a bit. They informed me that white folks don't take showers with "niggers." It didn't stop there. "You Yankee nigger-lovers are disgusting. Won't you ever learn?" This was a new level of racism and I accepted it without much resistance or thought. I just wanted to get along and survive, which I did.

As the interminable boot camp continued, I saw both non- and commissioned officers, even black ones, openly taunting black recruits in my platoon, reminding them daily that they were inferior "jungle bunnies" and "spear-chuckers." "What were you thinking when you joined my Marine Corps?" they would yell. "We don't want niggers. We only want men. *Oo-rah!*"

Witnessing this kind of primitive racism from exalted authority figures during my brief stint in the Corps only left me with a more entrenched form of racism. When I got back to South Boston, I told all my friends how mistaken they were to treat "niggers" so well. "Down South," I told them, "niggers are on par with pigs and dogs, and surprisingly, they don't even stand up for themselves. You are not even supposed to talk to a black person—and you absolutely don't play sports with them."

The Other Apple

In the early 1970s, my marriage to Louise, who was my first wife, crumbled. The divorce that followed was an incredible disaster for me. I felt like such a failure. I had let my family down. I was useless. I cried like a baby for weeks. In spite of our strained relationship, I really loved my wife. Over the years I have often wished that somehow I could go back in time and correct my mistakes. I have nothing but good feelings about Louise. The penalty was severe, as my children were gone from my everyday life. I had lost my long-time driver-delivery job, as the place where I had worked for many years had been sold and they instituted a different delivery system which left their long time drivers without jobs. It was a tough pill to swallow because I had made an extraordinarily good living there over the years. I was able to buy a house at a very young age because of that job. The financial pressures that resulted and our inability to communicate had doomed the marriage. I remember Louise saying to me "You'll never change."

"You got that right." I responded. "I didn't know that I was supposed to change." Years later I would wake up to the fact that I needed to make massive changes in the way I thought and acted.

Nonetheless, I was marooned in depression, moping around, often watching television all day. One evening, the TV announcer said, "Coming up next—*Roots: The Saga of an American Family.*" I thought it sounded interesting. But soon I realized the show was about blacks, something I had no interest in. I was distracted by a phone call and the show began before I had a chance to get up and change the channel. Those were the days before "clickers" when even couch potatoes had to do at least some exercise by getting up to switch stations.

After I hung up the phone, I found myself becoming captivated by Alex Haley's story. His book *Roots* would change my life. Reading it caused me to want to read more about black history, mainly because I believed we (white Americans) never behaved the way it had been depicted in *Roots*. I came to a different realization after reading scores of books that showed white Americans had behaved far worse than I could have imagined.

I began to feel the roots of change in my own mind. I sensed that blacks were simply fellow human beings and no different from all people. I realized that skin color meant nothing. I also felt so saddened by the way I had behaved in my life. I vowed that I would change that. I also felt an enormous sense of duty to try and fix the hatred that spawns racial animosity. I had no plan, but the thoughts were rolling around in my head. Only time would tell.

Later, studying race relations at Amherst College and Harvard Law School became my passion. It was probably a reaction to the nonsensical and insensitive racism of my younger self. My biggest revelations in studying race relations was how long it took for American writers after the Civil War to write about the "real war," as Whitman put it. Writers seemed to doggedly avoid the issue that had caused the conflict in the first place and kept it burning long after. That issue was slavery. That "peculiar institution" had left behind such scarring that our nation is still reeling from its dastardly implications. Jim Crow laws, which were a response to the freeing of slaves and the 14th Amendment guarantees, are still alive and well in many places in our country.

As the writer Thomas Sowell once said: "Racism does not have a good track record. It's been tried out for a long time and you'd think by now we'd want to put an end to it instead of putting it under new management."

Chapter Thirty-Six
Liquid Thunder

Through the ear the "Mighty Thunderer" makes
First assault upon the senses. A roar,
like a thousand throbbing jungle drums, shakes
The earth, calling to see what lies in store.
                                              —**Mary A. Sheppard**

I left the black neighborhood of Buffalo and walked into the downtown area at Niagara Square, where a photographer from the *Buffalo News* met us. After the interview and photos, Charles and I set out for the Outlet Mall on Niagara Falls Boulevard, ten miles to the north. There, as planned, I picked up four new pairs of Rockport Professional Walkers. That evening, they would undergo the maize-and-water makeover, followed by some minor surgery.

I walked the final five miles to Niagara Falls. As I got closer, the endless thunder of water drowned out all other sounds. Well, not always endless. In 1848, there was a drought and the falls fell to a trickle. And in 1969, the Army Corps of Engineers temporarily dammed up the water to clear away some rocks at the bottom. I had always assumed that I would go crazy if I had to live near an airport, a fire station, or a subway line. The same for living near the continuous jet-engine roar of Niagara Falls. But apparently, after a week or two, something inside you adapts and you stop hearing the noise . . . like the loneliness of a long-distance walker. I had gotten used to the isolation. It had become normal. Of course, I had Charles constantly shadowing me.

Charles pulled off Niagara Falls Boulevard into the parking lot for Goat Island on the American side. We walked together for the last few hundred yards, moving with throngs of tourists headed for the cascade. At the falls, Charles' jaw dropped open. In seconds, the ever-present cloud of fine white mist cooled us before rising into the hot sun and vanishing.

From our vantage point, we saw a panorama of thousands of fellow tourists gawking at the endless cascade of water. On the "Maid of the Mist" boats, floating dangerously close to where the falls crashed into the lower river, the passengers were all decked out in yellow rain gear. Below us, long lines of hikers in raincoats and ponchos edged their way down to the lower gorge.

Charles enjoyed a special afternoon, as a tourist for a change; me, too, for that matter. Charles wanted to go to the Canadian side of the falls, but he lacked the proper visa to return. As we stood together in the middle of the rainbow bridge, watching a steady stream of tourists flowing into Canada to the north and the U.S. to the south, Charles was upset that he couldn't just walk into Canada and back into the States like everyone else.

Later in the afternoon, we headed back to Buffalo to walk the final ten miles of the day before finding a motel. Our lovely time in upstate New York was about to come to an end.

Chapter Thirty-Seven

Knee Alert

I learned that if you want to make it bad enough,
no matter how bad it is, you can make it.

—**Gale Sayers**

Summer had shifted. The dog days of August were upon us, even though July was not yet exhausted.

I noticed my water and juice supplies were getting low. Before I began today's walk—from the vineyards west of Fredonia, New York, to those of northeast Pennsylvania, and on to the shoreline of Lake Erie—I had to find a grocery store. The van's cooler only held about twelve gallons of fluids and then got topped off with twenty-five pounds of ice every other day. But we could store as much as fifty gallons of drinks in the van—under the bed—enough for a week. When we shopped, we didn't mess around.

We found a small market and wiped out the entire water shelf—thirty gallons—and all of its juices—sixteen gallons. The cashier seemed nonplussed, but she did ask why we were buying so much. I told her about my walk and how I used as much as seven gallons of juice or water each day. Everybody's an expert. With great authority, she declared, "Seven gallons a day is far too much for you to be drinking. You should never drink more than a gallon a day." If she spent even half a day in my Rockports, I'm sure she would revise her declaration.

Charles and I reloaded the cooler and the week's storage supply then headed back to resume the walk on Route 20 in Fredonia, where we'd left off. The heavy lifting, loading and packing left my right knee unstable and in pain. Something was wrong. I kept walking, but my apprehension grew. Knee problems were not like blisters or a perspiration rash. They often got worse.

I would soon be crossing the Pennsylvania border, the sixth state of the walk. Although a very large state, I would only be darting across its northwest corner—about twenty miles before sundown and another twenty miles in the morning—before stepping into Ohio. That was, if my aching knee didn't stop me in my tracks.

As I walked the last few miles in New York, my mind dwelt on the nearly four weeks I had completed. The first two weeks were a blur of pain, blisters, rashes, and discomforts of one sort or another. At times that was enough to make me want to quit. Of course, there were many special moments—especially visits with friends, meeting strangers and familiar places. However, once I left Vermont, I was moving farther from home, and there was less that was familiar. I realized the fight against boredom would be a never-ending challenge, but now that challenge had been superseded by my aching knee. I was obsessed by the fear that every step could be my last.

I tried to distract myself. I listened to the sounds around me. In rural places, it was mostly animals. Barking dogs, the occasional bleating sheep, not to mention birds, especially the mourning dove, which sounded like an owl with its "*who, who.*" They all distracted me somewhat from worrying about my knee.

Before I left on this journey, I had visited my orthopedic surgeon. "Do you think I can make it?" I asked Dr. Anas.

"I think you are making a big mistake doing this walk," he responded. "If I thought it would do any good to further discourage you, I would. But, knowing you, you have your mind made up and you're going to do it no matter what I say."

He was right. I don't think people, even doctors, are fully able to understand the strength of human resolve. "I am eternally grateful to you," I said. "If not for your wondrous methods of surgery, I'd still be in a wheelchair."

For a few hundred yards, I enjoyed the company of an elegant chocolate-point Siamese cat. I smiled as she allowed me to pet her, emitting that characteristic "*prrrr,*" until she suddenly darted off into the field. Ten minutes later she reappeared with a mouse in her mouth, which she generously dropped at my feet. For a couple of minutes she batted it around with her paw, and then she pranced off with her dinner, leaving me without company, except for Charles, gliding silently a couple hundred feet behind me.

I stopped to rest in the shade of a huge elm in front of a mammoth vineyard. All of the sudden, hundreds of swirling bees had taken an interest in me. I dashed to the van to escape them. Charles laughed. I'm sure he would not have found it quite as funny if they were chasing him!

Chapter Thirty-Eight
The Mistake by the Lake

We live in a fast-paced society. Walking slows us down.
—Robert Sweetgall

After crossing into Pennsylvania in the late afternoon, I was worn out. My legs and feet felt okay, but my right knee still ached.

After supper, I begin walking along the shore of Lake Erie. I was confident the worst of the walk was over. I tried not to think of failure anymore. The painful twinges in my knee, however, make me wonder who's kidding who.

As I strolled along, my goal was to reach downtown Erie before dark. I was excited to be arriving in another city. Each one was a blessing of people, unique attractions, and municipal pride.

We stumbled upon a first-class family motel called the Glass House Inn. It was a sparkling clean, colonial style, crisply painted, rambling series of Cape Cod style structures, but there was no "Glass House" anywhere in sight. The owners, Tim and Laura Merryman, managed the place with the help of their three daughters—all blonde, blue-eyed beauties like their mother. Charles seemed particularly taken by one of the girls and his eyes followed her everywhere she went. The Merrymans all lived in the large central building. The family touch throughout the inn made it feel like a home on the road. Observing and admiring their family made me realize how much I missed mine.

I had always shared everything in my life with my sons. My relationship with my wife had long ago been ruined because of serious revelations. More about that later. For the most part, if I went somewhere, be it to a store, the mall, the beach, a ballgame, a fancy restaurant or a hot dog stand, my sons were always with me. To be doing things like visiting and walking through Erie, Pennsylvania, without my sons enjoying the visit was an uncommon sensation for me. My sons were my life. My visit with the Merrymans had me longing to be with my boys.

Both Tim and Laura, natives of Erie, had left their hometown for Houston, Texas, after college, but returned in 1987 to take over the Glass House from Laura's aging parents.

Laura suggested, "You should walk to Presque Isle to get a sense of Erie." Listening to them sing the praises of Erie made me smile. For thousands of motorists passing by every day on Interstate 90, Erie is a blink of the eye, often pejoratively called "The Mistake by the Lake."

We weren't the only wayfarers checking in. The parking lot was filled with cars from ten or more states. Many of the travelers in the lobby looked weary. The men were unshaven, wearing wrinkled and food-stained clothing, and emitted body odor from too many days cooped up in a vehicle. I could only imagine how I must have looked and smelled. I hadn't shaved in days and my body odor would stop a tank.

After a delicious lasagna dinner at Spada's Family Restaurant, we felt a change in the weather. A cold wind was blowing and litter was swirling around the parking lot. Rain wasn't far off. This was called the "lake effect." If it was winter, we'd be buried in snow drifts.

We returned to the Glass House Inn just as the deluge descended. Dashing into the room, escaping the worst of it but soaked, I turned on the TV just in time to see the news. An interview Charles and I did earlier that afternoon with the ABC affiliate of Erie was a featured piece on the newscast. Charles was thrilled to see himself on television again. He had been in the States only a few months, yet he had been on TV twice in the last three weeks. He phoned his family in Brazil to tell them.

Later, Charles inspected my badly swollen knee. "You rest a few days," he advised. He hurried off to the ice machine to fill a towel to wrap around my knee. The ice reduced the pain and swelling only a little bit. I had trouble sleeping. I was tossing and turning, afraid that my trip was about to end.

We were up early to get on the road. First things first, however, as continental breakfast was included in the room rate at the inn. We joined other lodgers in the breakfast nook. Many asked questions about my adventure, because they had noticed our van in front of the motel office, or they had read the article in the morning paper about the man walking through Erie on his way to Big Sur. Many of our fellow diners, several my age, or older, were puzzled by my eccentric pursuit.

"Why in heaven's name would anyone want to do such a thing?" someone asked.

Another playfully quipped, "I have trouble walking from my RV to the motel."

"I am not a first," I said. "There have been others, so I guess it's not so eccentric.

"I never heard of anybody doing it," the man said.

"I can assure you that many have made similar treks."

It wasn't a discussion I wanted to get into, as I was antsy to get on the road.

I was ready to go as soon as Charles had the van ready. The inn was situated directly on the route so I had only to walk out of the parking lot to be on my way.

I became engrossed in thought about those walkers who came before me.

* * *

Arguably, the most prominent walker in U.S. history was Edward Payson Weston. His first reported distance walk was in 1861. At the age of twenty-one, he trekked 453 miles from Boston to Washington in only eleven days. A year later, he did the same walk, this time in eight days. In 1867 Weston walked from Maine to Chicago, 1,300 miles, in an astonishing twenty-six days, and was paid $10,000 for doing it. Weston did the Maine to Chicago walk forty years later, at the age of sixty-eight, in twenty-four days, two days less than he had done it at the age of twenty-eight. When he was seventy-one, Weston became a transcontinentalist, walking 3,611 miles from California to New York in eighty-seven days, a daily average of 41.5 miles. Challenged to do it even faster, the next year he walked from San Francisco to New York City in seventy-eight days, averaging over forty-six miles per day.

Weston completed hundreds of significant distance walks in his lifetime. It's estimated that he walked more than 100,000 miles in his career. Ironically, at the age of eighty-eight, while walking in New York City, Weston was struck by a taxi. His illustrious walking career had come to a close, and he died soon after, having walked the equivalent of more than four times around the world.

Weston weighed just 120 pounds, which was an important factor in his ability to walk with the apparent ease that he did. Walking was Weston's career, as he never did anything else.

As remarkable as Weston's accomplishments were, women soon began to walk prodigious distances. Although she didn't walk all the way across the country, in 1912 Minta Beach of New York walked from New York City to Chicago, a distance of 1,071 miles, in forty-three days, an average of twenty-five miles a day. The preface of the book she wrote, *My Walk from New York to Chicago,* alluded to the significance of her accomplishment. ". . . The story of one of the more remarkable feats of endurance ever accomplished by a woman."

Other transcontinentalists include Minnie Wood who, in 1916, walked from Washington D.C. to San Francisco. It took Minnie 140 days to become, some say, the first woman to complete a coast-to-coast walk. In 1960, Barbara Moore walked from San Francisco to New York in eighty-five days. Not only was that a speedy crossing, it may be the fastest ever by a woman. Obstacles galore threatened her walk, from weather problems like dust storms and tornados to a sprained ankle and being hit by a car. Regardless, nothing could keep her from her quest.

Peter Jenkins, widely known for his two bestselling books, *A Walk Across America* and *The Walk West*, about his five-year walk across the country, may be the most well-known of American transcontinentalists. Jenkins said of his trek, "I started out searching for myself and my country and found both." He covered 5,000 miles, stopping frequently to earn some money so that he could continue. While taking time off to work in Louisiana, he met and married his wife, Barbara, who then walked with him on the second half of his walk, from Louisiana to the Oregon Coast. While Jenkins' walk may not have been as physically demanding as walks of other transcontinentalists, it was remarkable for the way he reported it in his books, giving us all an opportunity to sense what it was like.

Gary Moore, a writer from California walked from Boston to San Diego in 1978, the same year as Peter Jenkins began his walk. During his walk, Moore learned much about the people of America. "The whole nation turned out to be amazingly, gratifyingly friendly . . ." That perspective has been experienced by walkers for generations.

Perhaps the most notable modern-day transcontinentalist to walk to fame is Rob Sweetgall. In 1985, Rob walked 11,000 miles in one year, navigating a perimeter walk of all fifty states, "For the health of it." Two years earlier, Mr. Sweetgall had completed another 11,000-mile trip. On that excursion, he ran the first 6,000 miles, and walked the remaining 5,000 miles. It was on that trip that he realized walking was just as beneficial as running, but that walking resulted in far less damage to his legs and feet. I know of no other walk, at least one completed within a year, of such significance.

Sweetgall's account of his walk, *The Walker's Journal: Experiencing America on Foot,* is like a bible for me. I have read it scores of times, especially while training for Walking USA. It's filled with advice from the road that is a must-read for any would-be transcontinentalist. *The Walker's Journal* addresses foot care, not in the textbook way, but as it applies to Sweetgall's daily experiences on the road while walking approximately thirty-two miles a day. Sweetgall discusses caloric needs, fluid requirements, weather related difficulties, and a host of other issues of interest to not just other transcontinentalists, but to all walkers. One thing for sure, after reading Sweetgall's book any walker who has a notion of doing a cross-country walk will surely be inspired to head out the door and not look back.

In the summer of 1992, when my personal struggles with depression had me in deep despair, I went to Boston one day to participate in a scheduled walking event. To my surprise, none other than Rob Sweetgall was there to lead the walk. I introduced myself, telling him about my longstanding dream of walking across the country. He invited me to walk with him so we could chat more. We walked together for most of the 6.2 mile course. When it was time to say good-bye, I knew with certainty I couldn't live out my life without taking my own transcontinental walk.

Undeniably, hundreds or perhaps even thousands of other men and women have completed similar walks, journeys that were not publicized or reported in the media, which is most often the case. It is testimony to the wanderlust that lives within our souls.

* * *

I had walked ten miles west on Route 5 thinking about my predecessors. I got refocused on the road ahead. I would reach the border of Ohio before lunch. It was only a hop, skip and a jump down the road, and on this the fourth rainy day of my odyssey, I found the rain invigorating. It beat walking in the heat and humidity.

Chapter Thirty-Nine

Cortisone

We're not crazy about the cortisone,
But it allows us to work.

—Gil Reyes

At 10:30 A.M., I called my hometown radio station in Newton, Massachusetts, to do my first live, on-the-road, talk-show interview. We chatted for almost half an hour. The radio station had noted that between newspaper articles and my website, many residents were closely following my progress. I was delighted that folks back home were so interested. I scheduled my next call-in interview for October 12, from somewhere in the state of Washington.

Walking, I passed the time thinking about what it would be like in Montana and California. I was so eager to experience the "Big Sky" and the "Big Sur." I would spend more time in those states than all the other remaining states combined. Every state had its attractions but for me, Montana and California were the icing on the cake.

After lunch, because of the earlier rain and the high humidity, my discomfort became severe. The instability and sometimes excruciating pain in my knee added to my misery. I put blinders on and kept on trucking.

It stopped raining before lunch, but I had changed my clothes six times. Brutal rashes caked under my arms and on my inner thighs from the wet clothing.

By 5 P.M., I crossed the Ohio border where Charles was waiting to take photos of me as I walked into the seventh state of the trip.

This was going to be a long day. I was many miles from our destination point. There was one relief though: no hills and no haze. It was still hot and humid, but a comfortable breeze, coming off Lake Erie, seemed to diffuse the brightness without dulling it.

In Ashtabula, I took a right and headed towards Lake Erie. If I stepped up my pace, I'd make it by sundown.

Hours later, I was sitting on a dock that jutted into placid Lake Erie, wasting time. I hated to leave, but I still had a few more miles to go. I walked along the shore toward Geneva-on-the-Lake. Although my leg muscles had tightened up, I moved at a slightly faster pace.

At almost 11 P.M., I finally stopped in downtown Geneva. It was going to be a busy night for Charles because I was going through clean clothes at a record pace. Not only was it a laundry night, but Charles said the van needed serious attention. He didn't like tooling around town in a dirty vehicle, so he headed to a car wash. While he was out, he picked up some dinner for us. I would have happily helped with the chores, but I couldn't get my body out of bed. It had been a fifteen-hour day.

I took advantage of Charles' absence to call my family in Honduras. Nick and Louis were excited to hear all the details of my peregrinations. Nine-year-old Nick said, "You are not the only one who is hot Dad. It is *really* hot down here, like more than a hundred degrees."

When LouLou got on the phone, all he wanted to talk about was the Red Sox. "I wish I was home," he said "I can't even see the Sox on TV here." As I was saying good-bye, he said, "Daddy, are you going to make it?"

I replied, "Of course—you can plan on it." Any earlier doubts I had, had been erased.

* * *

Early in the morning, the peepers—small chorus frogs, widespread throughout the eastern U.S. and Canada—helped set my pace. Their voices were like a symphony. As I walked along, a couple of red farmhouses, shaded by a cluster of apple trees, reminded me that there were people nearby, and that I was not utterly alone.

A good night's rest had helped. My legs and feet had recovered. I was not tight and was almost pain free, except for my right knee. Thanks to Charles, I had plenty of clean clothes. The van was almost unrecognizably clean—inside and out.

My route took me a few miles inland. The first destination was, appropriately, Painesville-by-the-Lake. This would be my final flirtation with Lake Erie until I reached the Toledo/Detroit area.

Sitting by the lake for a few moments, I listened to the foghorns of far-away ships unseen.

I walked through the Cleveland suburbs on the famous Euclid Avenue. In its heyday, Euclid Avenue was a neighborhood of palaces, a place where folks leaving the city proper fled to build stately and conspicuous monuments to their new-found wealth. The houses were still there, but over the years, the place they had fallen into sad and lonely disrepair and was now the home of the impoverished. Many of the homes and businesses were dilapidated and abandoned, victims of neglect. The closer I got to Cleveland, the more the scenery improved. The skyscrapers of the city were looming just up ahead.

As I arrived in the downtown area, I realized that the time had come to do something about my knee. Off to my left was the world-famous Cleveland Clinic. I walked directly into the emergency room.

After a couple of hours, an emergency-room nurse finally showed up. "Come this way, sir. We're going to start with X-rays."

My knee was X-rayed from several angles, and then I discussed the prognosis with the orthopedist. He advised, "Rest and anti-inflammatory medicine for a few days. And we'll give you a shot of cortisone That will help quell the inflammation." He went on to say, "You have a significant bone spur in your right knee, which will probably need surgery if the joint doesn't respond to rest and cortisone." I cringed at the mention of the word "surgery." I wasn't too thrilled about the need for the deeply probing needle that would deliver the cortisone.

I was so anxious. I had invested so much time, money, and effort into preparing for this walk. And now, I might wind up limping back home, a failure.

Chapter Forty

Columbus Bound

Where we love is home,
Home that our feet may leave, but not our hearts.
—Oliver Wendell Holmes, Sr.

The next morning, Cleveland looked better. The cortisone shots seemed to have had a miraculous effect. My knee had dramatically improved, although it now sounded like a squishy, wet sneaker. I got ready to walk. Charles said, "What are you doing? The doctor said rest."

"It's easy for the doctor to say do this or do that. I'm the one who has to decide what I *can* and can't do."

And so I walked through the suburbs of Cleveland toward Columbus. It was mid afternoon before I rambled into farm country on a flat, hot, straight highway, a plane of asphalt. I allowed my sensory perceptions to take charge: the red barns with their crisply painted white or black shutters and neatly trimmed hedges; the green, whispering cornfields stretching for miles with their golden tassels waving; the almost-black earth, where crops had been harvested. I was passing through a colored palette of wonder. This dazzling visual display kept me distracted from the boredom and loneliness, and from the feeling of pointlessness that sometimes stretched out before me on this often gray, interminable, and desolate trek across America.

As the late afternoon arrived, I was thrilled that my knee felt fine. The sun beat down as I headed south towards Columbus. It was hard to protect my face from the sun. I needed to find a better way to shade my head and neck.

I had picked up the pace. I was averaging fourteen minutes a mile. If I continue at that speed I would make Seville, twenty miles north of Wooster, by dark.

It was 5:30 P.M. and I had about an hour left. I stopped to take a drink break because it gave me an excuse to climb into the back of the van and out of the sun to cool off. Charles got right to work, changing my sneakers and socks. He didn't seem himself.

I spoke up. "Hey, Charles, are you all right?"

In his halting English, he said, "I homesick; it bothers me."

"Me too," I said.

I missed my boys so much that I was reluctant to even mention it because tears would well up if I did. Here we were, all by ourselves, with my children in Central America, and Charles separated from his family in Brazil, sandwiched between two cornfields south of Cleveland, Ohio.

"Charles," I said, "Hang in there; better days are coming."

He said, "I know. I wish they get here sooner."

* * *

Early the following morning we headed towards Wooster. My goal was to reach Millersburg, Ohio, by day's end, which would position us to arrive just north of Columbus the next day.

The farm country in Ohio was flatter than New York and Pennsylvania. I felt like I was walking on a slab of Formica so large it met the sky at the horizon. I was bored again, but listening to music on the Walkman helped to pass the time. The exhilaration I felt—because I would be in Columbus soon—had me walking on air. One of the most important people in my life lived there. I didn't have the remotest sensation of being tired. And, my knee felt great.

We stopped at a McDonalds when we reached Millersburg to have our dinner. As I devoured my Chicken McNuggets and fries, I watched an Amish buggy pull up. This McDonalds had a drive-through window built just for horse-drawn buggies.

I stopped in an Amish gift shop, looking for a better hat. Although a little heavy, the typical Amish man's hat—yellow straw with a prominent black band—with a brim wide enough to keep my face in the shade was what I needed. I bought one and emerged with a new identity—that of an old and fat Amish guy walking to God knows where.

* * *

I was feeling much better by late the next afternoon. My knee had reacted well to the cortisone, the prayers, the slower pace, and the lack of hills. For the first time, I was protected to the max by my new Amish hat; I was going to finish my forty miles for the day in perhaps the best condition since the walk began four weeks before. My optimism was extreme.

In the late afternoon, I stopped for a cold drink in the middle of nowhere. While standing with Charles in the shade I said, "Listen."

"I no hear." Charles whispered.

"That's just it," I whispered back. "Pure silence."

Chapter Forty-One

Lou Mitchell

No great man lives in vain. The history of the
world is but the biography of great men.
—Thomas Carlyle

We left Sunbury, Ohio, early to get to Columbus before dark. I walked south down old Route 3 into the outskirts of the city, deep in the unsullied countryside, dotted with sporadic farmhouses and rustic churches, their white spires stretching skyward. As I approached Columbus, ten or twelve miles north of the city, the plethora of fast-food eateries, gas stations, and strip malls sprouted up again like weeds.

What is it about our culture that permits us to allow the outskirts of our cities to be turned into these mindless commercial strips? The business names are always the same: McDonalds, Burger King, Pizza Hut, and of course, the ubiquitous Walmart. These cookie-cutter strips all look alike. The uniqueness of the great city of Columbus is lost. You could just as easily be on the outskirts of Chicago or Pittsburgh or Seattle. Compared to the distinctiveness of the countryside I'd walked through for days after I'd left Cleveland, this was monotonous and uninspiring.

As I headed into central Columbus on North High Street, we were met by a reporter from the local NBC affiliate, accompanied by her cameraman. The interview took place as I walked the final several miles into downtown Columbus. With his hefty equipment, Steve, the cameraman, was an imaginative professional, shooting while walking backwards, or lying in the street or on the sidewalk to get a mix of unusual angles for the segment about me. By the time he had finished, I found myself in the heart of Columbus, the capital of Ohio.

This route took me 300 miles out of my way in order to visit my dear friend, Lou Mitchell.

Mr. Mitchell has been one of Columbus' prominent citizens most of his sixty years, and has owned a major local bank for the past three decades. He was a philanthropist, eager to assist less fortunate people, especially minorities. He was a devoted husband and father of six children of his own, and three stepchildren with his current wife, Cynthia. In his younger days, he played on the Dennison University basketball team. He still held the school record for the most points scored—forty-four—in a single game. He had contributed much to Dennison and was one of its major boosters. His athletic success brought him the honor of recently being named to the Ohio Basketball Hall of Fame.

I was going to surprise Lou, who had no idea that I was walking across the country. I wanted to show up on his doorstep. Even though he was going to be the recipient, I felt like a kid waiting for Santa Claus. Many years ago Lou had been my own personal Santa Claus. He had given me a magnificent gift back in 1988 during the winter of my third year in law school.

Chapter Forty-Two
The $600,000 Cab Ride

It isn't the size of the gift that matters,
but the size of the heart that gives it.
—Eileen Elias Freeman

Back in the late summer of 1988, I had just completed my second year at law school. I needed money, so I leased a Boston Taxi during the summer months. Driving a cab long hours provided me with a weekly wage I couldn't match elsewhere.

Early one evening, I was having a bad night, working the taxi stand in Boston's financial district at 225 Franklin Street, known to cabbies and dispatchers as "two-two-five." In the late evening, it's perhaps the most desirable taxi stand in the city. Cabs line up, fifteen to twenty or more at a time, and move up, spot by spot, until becoming "top cab." Once there, obviously, you get the next fare. And that fare can be sizable, as well-heeled lawyers, accountants, executives, and brokers, enjoying the luxury of hefty expense accounts and leaving work late, often need a ride to their homes in the distant, wealthy suburbs.

There was a catch, however. As top cab, there was the risk of being called off your position by the doorman at the nearby Meridian Hotel. Many drivers would ignore the doorman's whistle, or persuade another taxi to respond. No driver was ever happy about being whistled away from top cab, because a two-two-five job often meant a $30 to $50 fare. Four or five such fares made an excellent night's pay. An evening guest from the Meridian, by contrast, is usually going around the block.

On this particular night, I'd gotten into the back of the long two-two-five line. In less than an hour, I was top cab. Just then, the Meridian doorman whistled. Annoyed, I had no choice but to take the customer, surrendering my top spot—and big fare—to the cab behind me. My passenger turned out to be a two-dollar fare, half of which was mine. I made one dollar for my hour and my gas.

I doggedly drove back to the two-two-five stand. This time I was number eighteen in the line, which was barely moving. After more than ninety minutes I was top cab again. I was there less than a minute when I heard the *tweet* of the Meridian doorman.

Fuming, I pulled over to the hotel entrance. A lovely young woman, dressed to kill, slid into the rear seat. I gritted my teeth and politely asked, "Where can I take you?"

"One Beacon Street."

Another two-dollar fare!

When I pulled over in front of One Beacon, she asked how much she owed.

With a dismissive wave, I said, "Forget it."

Looking perplexed, she got out. She had no idea what was wrong, and of course it wasn't her fault. And I didn't mind small fares. I just minded them after waiting in line for hours.

I thought of taking my cab to another part of the city. "Oh hell," I said to myself, "I'll give it another shot. My luck has to improve." It would prove to be a most serendipitous decision.

When I arrived back at two-two-five, only eleven cabs were in line. It took exactly seventy minutes to reach top cab. There, I waited ten more minutes.

Then it happened. I heard that blasted *tweet*. I wanted to scream. I couldn't ignore it because cabbies can lose their hackney license for refusing a hotel doorman's whistle.

At the Meridian, a tall, thin, very well-dressed gentleman slid into the rear seat and said, "Ritz Carlton, please."

I exploded inside. Wow, a three-dollar fare! For four hours, I'd had three fares totaling seven dollars. Since I had refused payment on the second one, I had only five dollars, of which two dollars was my cut. With cab rental at sixty-five dollars a night, plus gas, usually another thirty to forty dollars a shift, it certainly looked grim.

As I glided away from the hotel, I gritted my teeth and politely inquired, "Where are you from?"

"Columbus, Ohio," he said.

"I have a friend in Columbus; maybe you know him," I said, making small talk.

"What's his name?"

"Danny Galbreath."

After a long pause, he said, "How do you know Danny?"

"We went to the same college."

"Why on earth is an Amherst grad driving a cab?" he asked.

"Working my way through Harvard Law School," I answered.

By now, we had reached our destination. The Ritz-Carlton doorman opened the door and the man stepped out.

"I have to break a hundred," he said. "Would you mind waiting a minute?"

Oh well, I muttered to myself.

I had waited almost an hour and a half for the job, it only took three or four minutes to get there, and now he was making it worse by taking more of my time to "break a hundred."

After a five-minute wait, a long time for a cabbie, my passenger reappeared. He got back into the cab and said, "Pull up a little. I'd like to talk to you for a minute."

Thinking I had to placate him to get a good tip, I did as requested.

"Tell me, how it is that you went to Amherst and Harvard Law School at this time in your life."

I said, "The whole story, or the twenty-five-words-or-less version?"

He laughed. "I'm in no particular rush."

So, of course, I gave him the longer version.

When I'd finished an hour later, he handed me his business card.

Louis A. Mitchell
President and Chairman
County Savings Bank
Columbus, Ohio

"Send me your resume," he said. "I would really be interested in seeing it."

He slapped down a fifty-dollar bill on the top of my seat. "Take your wife out to dinner, and don't forget to send me the resume."

It was now after nine. I figured nothing much would come of my sending off my paltry resume to some stranger in Ohio.

I got home at 6 A.M., just as my wife, eight months pregnant, was getting up to go to work. She was a computer analyst at MIT the Sloan Business School. I told her about Louis Mitchell, showed her his business card, and handed her the fifty-dollar bill. A big mistake—I never saw that fifty again.

Estela said, "I feel very good about this." She offered to send out the resume when she got to work.

"Don't bother. He's just a blowhard," I said dismissively. Driving a cab I'd learned that customers often tell you they are going to do something for you but you never hear from them again.

"Okay," said Estela, "but I think it's wrong not to send it, especially since he asked you to."

I guess I'm not always such an optimist. I said, "We'll never hear from him again."

A couple of weeks later, unbeknownst to me, she sent the resume anyway.

I answered the phone a few weeks after that, now early October, and was surprised to hear Mr. Mitchell's voice. "Can you meet me for breakfast in the morning?" he asked.

Still stunned, I responded enthusiastically, "Absolutely!"

At breakfast, Mr. Mitchell related, "I'm here regularly looking after various holdings in the Boston area and I wish I had someone to do it for me." Then he asked, "Do you have any interest in banking?"

"I know nothing about it," I said. I'm glad I didn't say that banking sounded as boring as watching paint dry.

He said, "Your educational background—Amherst College and a law degree—makes you an ideal candidate for any business." He then questioned me in depth on a variety of issues. Our social visit had become a job interview.

After two hours, we went our separate ways.

Several weeks later, as Thanksgiving break was approaching, Mr. Mitchell called from Columbus. "I'll be in town tomorrow night with my son. Can you meet me at 5 P.M. at the Meridian Hotel? We can have dinner and take in a Celtics game."

"Celtics tickets are impossible to get," I said. "How did you ever manage?"

"Easy," he laughed. "I own ten percent of the team."

The next evening, Mr. Mitchell, his son, and I had a superb dinner at the Meridian and headed for the Boston Garden to watch the basketball game. Inside, we made our way to our seats in the owners' box. The legendary Red Auerbach was there, along with the equally legendary K.C. Jones. They both knew Mr. Mitchell. I was becoming a believer.

After the game, Mr. Mitchell asked, "Can you drive my son and me to the airport early in the morning?"

"Of course," I said, though I was a bit puzzled. During the visit, nothing more had been said about my working at his bank.

Next morning at the airport, Mr. Mitchell said, "Come in for a few minutes so we can talk." I left my car in the limo zone, hoping my handicapped placard would keep me from getting a ticket, and followed him into the airport.

In the first-class lounge, Mr. Mitchell explained how I could work for him as an attorney and manager of his New England operations.

186

The compensation package was generous, especially for someone who would be getting out of law school in a few months. What sealed the deal was his offer to provide my wife and me a deferred mortgage so we could buy a home.

"What price range should I look at?" I asked, slightly dazed.

"The house of your dreams," he said. "One you'd be happy with for the rest of your life."

In the meantime, I had given up driving a cab because I was deeply embedded in my third and final year of law school. I had taken a security guard job at a builder's subdivision in Hanover, Massachusetts, which gave me the freedom to pre-read all the books in my courses while getting paid $500 a week, with overtime. When I needed to take a break, I'd walk through the unsold houses. During one of those walks, I had discovered the "dream" house.

It was only a couple of months since Estela gave birth to our son, Nicholas. The possibility of having a home, rather than an apartment, was now much more important. The presence of this special little boy in our lives made it very important to have the security of the job Lou Mitchell had offered, and the opportunity of having our own place completed a feeling of "We've done it," for me and Estela.

In early December, three or four months after we had first met, Mr. Mitchell called from Columbus. He would be arriving in Boston the next day, December 15, 1988, my forty-fourth birthday. He was coming on business and asked if he could meet with us. "Have you and Estela picked out a house yet?"

I said, "We have, but there was a problem. It is way too expensive—369,000."

"It sounds about right to me, as long as you and Estela are happy with it," said Mr. Mitchell. "I have an appointment in Boston on Thursday morning. After that, I'll call and set a time for you to come pick me up so we can take a look at the house."

On Wednesday night, Mr. Mitchell called to say, "I'm not coming to Boston after all because my meeting has been cancelled." My skepticism was instantly reignited. It's hardly an exaggeration to say this all sounded too good to be true. After many weeks of believing in the things he told me, I was ready to cry.

"If you can fit it in," he said, "I'll fly to Boston Saturday morning. Pick me up at the airport and return me there right after we see your house, if that would work for you."

"You don't have to fly to Boston just for us," I said.

"I want to move this along," he said.

Saturday morning Estela and I were at the USAir terminal, waiting for the Columbus-to-Boston flight. Lou Mitchell appeared and said, "Let's go buy that house!"

We drove to the subdivision in Hanover and met the developer. He and Mr. Mitchell went off together for a tour of the brand-new, not-quite-framed, ten-room colonial. When they returned, Mr. Mitchell asked us, "Are you sure this is the right house?"

Simultaneously, Estela and I said, "Yes!"

Mr. Mitchell asked the developer, "What's the bottom line? No haggling over price."

"It's $369,000," said the developer, giving the same price he had quoted us earlier. "I already gave Don the best deal I could,"

Mr. Mitchell told him, "My bank will provide the mortgage and a ten-percent down payment will be forwarded as soon as the paper-work is completed."

Mr. Mitchell and the developer shook hands as they sealed the deal.

When we were leaving, Mr. Mitchell pulled us aside. "You're going to need $75,000 to furnish this house. The bank will put those funds into the deal as well."

I was floored. Estela looked at me with an "is-this-for-real?" look.

I said, "I don't know how to thank you for all your kindness."

"You can thank me by not working during your last year in law school, and by spending more time with your family."

"Easier said than done," I said. "I have to work. Estela and I both have used all of our credit cards up to the limit to get ourselves through school. We're deep in debt."

"How much does it add up to?"

Estela, who keeps track of our bills, said: "About $50,000."

"We'll throw in that money as well. Then you won't have to work." He told us to prepare a list of our debts and to whom they were owed, and that amount would be folded into the mortgage.

I was overwhelmed. As we drove towards the airport, I finally had the guts to say, "Lou, why are you doing so much for us?"

"It's not a lot considering how much you'll be doing for me at the bank." He added, "Besides, banks make money by lending money to people who will pay them back, and I know you'll pay me back."

I said, "I don't know what the payment is going to be or how I will afford to pay it back."

"We'll defer the mortgage payments for two years after you get out of law school. Don't worry about your monthly mortgage payment, because your stock options ought to be more than enough to help cover it."

What could I say? Now, we only had to wait to see if it all came true.

A few days later Mr. Mitchell called to invite us to come to Ohio for the holiday week between Christmas and New Year's. It was a nice thought, but we couldn't accept because we had a three-month-old baby. Besides, we couldn't afford it.

I said, "We'd love to, but we're not in the position to come."

"Why not?" Asked Lou.

"I can't afford to take a taxi to the airport, never mind fly to Columbus and back."

He said, "I didn't expect you to pay for your flight. This is a business expense. I want you to be here for some year-end meetings. Besides, I already mailed the tickets to you. I didn't get one for Nicholas because I assumed he would sit in your laps." Mr. Mitchell went on to say, "You don't have to worry about a hotel. You can stay with me. I have plenty of room."

Our first Christmas with our baby was very special. The next day we jetted off to Columbus. Mr. Mitchell met us at the baggage-claim area and swept us away to the Columbus suburb of Bexley. His home was a beautiful, brick Victorian mansion, set back from the road. Each room was as large as our entire apartment. No sooner were we in the house than Mr. Mitchell said, "Don, let's go to the bank."

On the way downtown, we stopped at a high-rise office building. Mr. Mitchell took me inside to visit Danny Galbreath, the person whose name had triggered our initial conversation. The truth was that Mr. Galbreath and I weren't really "friends." We had met several times for lunches that Amherst College had arranged for me in an attempt to get Danny active again in alumni affairs. Mr. Galbreath and I chatted about Amherst for a while, got reacquainted, and then talked with Mr. Mitchell about Columbus and his bank.

Next, it was on to the County Savings Bank. We parked the car and made our way to another skyscraper that served as the headquarters of Lou's bank. In the lobby, a framed sign on the wall read, "Owned and Managed by the Galbreath Companies." So I now understood why Lou had become inquisitive when he was a passenger in my cab and I had stated "Danny Galbreath" was the person I knew in Columbus.

I spent the next several days as an observer of the daily events in the County Savings Bank boardrooms. I didn't spend much time with

Mr. Mitchell, except after hours at his home. But he did find the time to introduce me to two of his closest colleagues.

First, there was Jess Davidson, who worked in human resources at Lou's bank. Orphaned at a young age, Jess had clawed his way to college. In the late seventies, while playing football for Capital University in Columbus, he was returning a kickoff and was hit so hard his neck was broken, leaving him paralyzed and in a wheelchair for life. Despite this, Mr. Davidson was able to graduate with his class. And over the years, he has played a major role in assisting less-fortunate minorities in Columbus. All of his efforts were aided by Lou Mitchell.

The second was Cliff Tyree. Mr. Tyree—referred to by many as the "Martin Luther King" of Columbus—had implemented a number of successful programs to assist at-risk teen and young-adult minorities. The walls of Cliff's den were filled with pictures of him with Bobby Kennedy, Martin Luther King and many other celebrities and politicians—all dedicated to the betterment of race relations in our country. Obviously, Mr. Tyree had been a major player in the Civil Rights movement of the sixties. He was continuing those efforts in Columbus.

Both Mr. Davidson and Mr. Tyree had worked closely with Lou Mitchell in a special program known as "I Know I Can." This was a foundation that guaranteed the funds to attend college for every high-school graduate in Columbus with a B average (most kids in the school system are either black or Hispanic).

On my last day, I attended a whirlwind of meetings.

My plane back to Boston was scheduled to depart in a couple of hours, but nothing had been said about the house and mortgage. I walked over to Mr. Mitchell's penthouse office. It was magnificent; with its floor-to-ceiling windows that overlooked the city. It was so large you could probably place ten or more employees in it and it still wouldn't be crowded. With some trepidation, I said to Mr. Mitchell, "It's almost time for me to leave for the airport. Should I be filling out some paperwork for the house?"

"Sure, that will only take a few minutes."

He escorted me to an office and introduced me to one of his young executives. I sat down with this gentleman and we quickly went over the details.

"I understand you need $75,000 for furniture, $50,000 for paying off debt and $36,000 for the down payment on the house, right?"

I nodded blankly.

The $600,000 Cab Ride

"Please change the $75,000 for furniture to $50,000, as that is all we are going to spend." I said. "Also, the amount of the debt is $55,000, not $50,000."

He said, "Okay, that's $141,000. When do you need the rest of the funds?"

I told him that the bank would be hiring a law firm in the Boston area to handle the closing, and that one of its lawyers would be in touch.

He said, "Okay, I will send you a check early next week for the things we've discussed."

Sure enough, a week later, there in my mailbox back in Boston was a check for $141,000.

I had never seen a five- or six-figure check before, never mind one made out to me. I picked up the phone and called Lou Mitchell to let him know how grateful we were.

The real-estate closing took place several weeks later. The bank's attorney knew little about the transaction. As we were signing all the documents, he had a puzzled look on his face.

Attorney Peter Smola—a dear friend, who represented me at the closing—asked, "Is something wrong?"

The bank's lawyer said, "I can't figure out what's going on here. The $600,000 mortgage is for much more than the $369,000 price of the house. The buyers are getting the difference of $231,000. Am I missing something?"

"You just have to pick up the right cab fare," said Smola, smiling.

After that, the lawyer didn't say another word, but the puzzled look never left his face.

All our bills were paid. The furniture was delivered the next day and we moved into our dream home.

To this day, some people think I'm embellishing or that I've made this story up. I still have a copy of the check, framed and displayed on my wall.

Two years later when our second son was born, we proudly named him Louis Mitchell Brown.

Chapter Forty-Three

Princessa Vanessa

Age is a question of mind over matter.
If you don't mind, it doesn't matter.
— **Anthony Robbins**

When I ended my walk for the day, Lou Mitchell called. He was very apologetic. "I have to fly to Boston and help my daughter."

"Well, I'll get to see Jess Davidson and Cliff Tyree—but I am so disappointed I won't get to see you."

"I'll see you the next time I'm in Boston or on your way home from the West Coast in a few months."

It was a scorcher on Saturday in downtown Columbus. I met up with my old friend, Cliff Tyree. At the same time NBC was following up on yesterday's interview, and I was doing a photo session with the *Columbus Dispatch*. Cliff, whose health won't permit him to walk any great distance, especially in the heat, walked with me for the first couple of miles toward Marion, Ohio. When we got to the campus of Ohio State University (OSU), where Cliff had gotten his degree, we stopped to rest. Cliff had begun to feel the effects of the heat. He said "Don, I wish I could do what you are doing, but I need to let you go on." We hugged as he said, "Be safe, be careful, and I'll see you when you return."

I hugged Cliff again and said, "I *will* return."

I then walked through the enormous campus and its environs. More than 60,000 students attend OSU. It is a well-known school partly because of the dozens of famous athletes that have distinguished themselves on its playing fields and parquet floors.

Former OSU teammates Jerry Lucas, John Havlicek and Larry Seigfried all went on to star in the NBA. At OSU, Lucas was the "star" and got all the ink, but it was Havlicek and Seigfried who got the rings with the Boston Celtics. What basketball fan can forget the famous "Havlicek stole the ball" while leading the Boston Celtics to one of its many championships? Running back Archie Griffin not only won the Heisman Trophy, he was the only college player in history to win it twice. Howard "Hopalong" Cassidy of the old NFL and Ed George of the Tennessee Titans also matured as players at OSU. The legendary Woody Hayes, considered by many to be the best college football coach in history, coached OSU football for what seems a lifetime. The fiery basketball coach Bobby Knight began his controversial career as an assistant coach on the OSU parquet. Jack Nicklaus attended OSU on his way to becoming one of the greatest golfers on the PGA Tour.

It was Wendy's for lunch on that hot steam bath of a day. At the counter, two customers were arguing over who would buy our meal. I loved it. Finally, the Wendy's counter employee put an end to the argument. She simply didn't charge us a thing. Life can be sweet.

Getting back on the road again, the sun made it emphatically clear that it was back in charge. The temperature had been over ninety every day of the walk so far. I was cookin' and it felt like I was headed toward medium rare.

As dusk approached, a late-model sedan stopped in front of me and the driver slowly emerged from the vehicle. He was tall, had curly hair, and looked like he played football for Ohio State. With a big smile, he said, "Hi, I'm Mikel Rivers." He was another of the many caring and friendly people I met on the walk. Mikel and his wife were from Columbus on their way to Toledo to visit her folks, about a two-hour drive north.

"Where are you heading?" he asked me.

"Hoping to make Toledo by Monday," I said.

"Driving to Toledo is tough enough. I can't imagine walking all the way there."

Mikel was fascinated with my trek and asked if he could walk with me for a while.

"I'd be delighted," I said sincerely.

Mikel's wife sat behind the wheel and pulled in behind Charles for two or three miles. As we walked together, Mikel suggested that Charles mount a magnetic flashing light on the rear of the van to increase our visibility to approaching cars—especially at dusk. He told me that we could find one at Wal-Mart or any auto-parts store. "What a great idea," I said. "Charles has had a few close calls and had been nervous about somebody rear-ending the van."

Mikel said "I'd like to do something like this myself, but I'm too busy with my business."

He and his wife were quite the entrepreneurs. They operated a "mobile" garage. They drove to a customer's home or business and repaired the client's vehicle on the spot from their roving service station.

After walking together for nearly an hour, Mikel and his wife said good-bye and drove off.

About an hour later, just as darkness was setting in, they reappeared. They had stopped at a Wal-Mart and bought us the magnetic flashing light. "How sweet it is!" I said to myself.

Continuing in the dark—with the newly installed flashing light on the back of the van—I did feel safer. I was thinking about how amazed Mikel was by my walk.

From birth, one of our first major accomplishments is to walk. Our parents make a big fuss when we do. Everyone around us is so encouraging and delighted as we take those first steps. Obviously, we seem to quickly forget that walking plays such a big role in our lives.

When I spent so much time confined to a wheelchair and crutches, the inability to walk only made my yearning to make this journey even greater.

For me, distance walking is a healthy addiction; mine began more than twenty-five years earlier when I had recovered from the surgeries that made it possible for me to walk again. The walking made me feel better and also stronger mentally, physically, and spiritually after each excursion.

Before I began this trek, my doctor said to me, "If you can *really* walk across America, you will add ten years to your life."

I challenge anybody—walk an hour a day, every day for a month—and you, too, may become an addict.

I liked to think of a sports analogy to describe walking. Imagine the thrill of a walk-off home run, a game-winning touchdown pass, a three-pointer "swish" with no time left on the clock to win the game, or a rink-length rush down the ice to score the game-winning, sudden-death goal in overtime in the Stanley Cup final. Each of those moments creates an adrenaline rush for the athletes who accomplish these feats. Even we, as mere fans, get the sense of exhilaration from those shared moments. For me, walking several hours a day rewarded me with a similar feeling because to walk—after I had been told I wouldn't walk across the room, let alone the country— is to win the World Series.

When it was time to end my typical thirteen-hour walk of the day, I hopped into the rear of the van. The interior smelled like a Dumpster. Charles went off in search of a car wash.

When he returned, the van looked squeaky clean, but the stink persisted despite deploying an entire can of "Lilac Spring" air freshener. The stench was so bad we were sure something had died in there. Charles and I ransacked the van and finally located the culprit: an open package of cheese that had somehow inveigled its way into a tiny storage hole. From the looks of the mold, it must have been there since Maine.

Once back in the room, I lay down on the comfy bed to rest. I began to read the tourist propaganda, scooped from the motel lobby back in Columbus. The long and short of Marion, Ohio, is that it held the distinction of being the hometown of our twenty-ninth U.S. president, Warren Gamaliel Harding. As a candidate, like his fellow Ohioan President Garfield, Harding conducted his presidential campaign mostly from the porch of his homestead here in Marion, which is now his final resting place.

* * *

At daybreak, we took longer than usual to move on as we had to repack the van. Our destination was Fosteria, Ohio, some forty-two miles away. It was another 3H day with temperatures in the high nineties by mid-morning. I was awed by the sight of manicured farms as far as the eye could see on both sides of the road. I could also infer that folks in Ohio take their Sabbath very seriously. There were only a few cars that passed by. On that day, however, the heat was not enervating. Mindless enthusiasm kept me moving. My weight loss and conditioning continued to improve. I was down to 265—31 pounds less than day one. My feet felt fine and my legs were moving like well-oiled pistons.

By mid-afternoon, things had changed. I craved food. I was also reeling from the diabetic implications of low blood sugar. Dizzy, I wobbled into a KFC just off the highway. I allowed myself to be suckered into the $4.99 "All you can eat" buffet. Both Charles and I pigged out. By the time I was ready to move on, I knew I had erred badly. I felt like an elephant reluctantly forced onto a treadmill.

The sun punished me. There was no breeze and only an occasional silo for shade. The freshly mown hayfields were a continuous reminder of the throes of summer. Late in the afternoon I spotted a giant elm a few hundred feet ahead and told Charles I wanted to take a cat nap. It was 5:00 P.M. and I still had several miles to go. I asked him to wake me up in exactly a half hour.

When I woke up, the night sky was saturated with stars. I caught my breath. I had overslept. I looked at my watch—it was 9:30. I had really passed out.

Charles was lying next to me. We had both slept. "Charles!" I said, "I thought you were going to wake me up in a half hour." He simply shrugged. I assumed he misunderstood me due to our language barrier. We still had about ten miles to go, all in the dark, which was not only boring but also more dangerous. It would be another late finish.

* * *

We departed Fosteria, headed toward Toledo, just after first light. Finally, the temperature had dropped and the weather was soothingly cool, mixed with a misty drizzle. It was the first day like this in a thousand miles.

As we headed into Toledo, it was surprising to be so close to a major city surrounded by nothing but cornfields—no strip malls, fast-food pit stops or motels. Instead, gargantuan farm tractors passed by regularly. At every mile, there was a sign: "Farm tractors use this road." Why the signs? There were more tractors than cars. Some of the tractors were bigger than a house.

Near downtown Toledo, Vanessa Gezari, a reporter from the local daily, met us, along with her photographer, Don Strayer. It turned out that Don had covered Rob Sweetgall's USA perimeter walk in 1985. I figured I would meet more people who had interviewed Sweetgall during his fifty-state/fifty-week walk because I had plotted my own route, at times, to coincide with his.

A breath of fresh air, Vanessa was bright, bubbly, and well-educated. Her lively personality made me want to invite her out for dinner. So I did. She accepted. The Spaghetti Factory was her choice.

Our dinner began with small talk about Toledo, dubbed "Frog Town," because of the swampland on its south side. I knew very little about the city and I was surprised to learn it was a major port, the western port of Lake Erie. Toledo was also considered the "Glass Capital of the World." Most of the glass we see or touch comes from there. Since WWII, Jeeps have been produced in Toledo. In fact, the auto industry's influence on Detroit has created a similar auto industry-based economy in Toledo.

I learned that Vanessa, whose mother was a college professor and whose father was an engineer, had recently graduated from Yale University. She came to Toledo with a remarkable maturity for a youngster just out of college and landed herself a gig as a reporter for the *Toledo Blade*, the city's major newspaper. She told me she planned to become a foreign correspondent, traveling the world and writing about issues that were important to her. She reminded me so much of the young and sophisticated women I went to college and law school with. Because I attended those schools so late in life, I found that I related to younger people better than folks my own age.

By the time dinner was over, I was enchanted. Vanessa, with her confident and articulate ways, touched me deeply. I told her—and I made sure I noted it in my journal—that if I ever wrote a book about this adventure, I would call the Toledo chapter "Princessa Vanessa."

Chapter Forty-Four

Baseball

I think about baseball when I wake up in the morning.
I think about it all day and I dream about it at night.
The only time I don't think about it is when I'm playing it.
—**Carl Yastrzemski**

I wish I could have lingered for a day or two to attend a Toledo Mud Hens baseball game. It's one of the oldest minor league teams in existence. In 1884, it was the only professional baseball team with black players, Moses Fleetwood Walker and his brother Welday. However, the Chicago White Stockings refused to play the Toledo team in an exhibition game because of them. It is disconcerting to realize that the color line would not be crossed for another sixty-three years until 1947, when the Brooklyn Dodgers signed up the legendary Jackie Robinson.

I became a rabid baseball fan when I was very young. I read everything I could find about the game. I had learned the skills for throwing and catching when my older brother Dickie, recruited me to be his catcher so that he could practice pitching. He was five years older than me and he threw the ball so hard my mother worried he would hurt me. I didn't realize he was throwing hard, I only knew he was helping me become a good player. I just did my best to catch everything he threw. It was the first and only time in my life that I had any attention from either of my brothers as a mentor. They were in different worlds than me. They were much more connected to my father than I and I rarely saw them. Likewise, I rarely spoke to them, because other than baseball, we had nothing in common.

When I got to the age where I could play Little League, I chose to be a catcher. My hero in those days was Roy Campanella, then perhaps the best catcher in all of baseball. Because of Campanella I had read a great deal about the Negro Leagues and the players who, in spite of their greatness, were never allowed to play in Major League Baseball. I remember thinking how strange it was to not let those guys play.

In Little League I found my passion. I loved catching, I loved hitting, and I loved throwing out runners, especially picking them off base. I was always very big for my age, which was a huge advantage.

The Morphine Dream

By my last year in Little League, while I was only twelve years old, I was six feet tall and weighed 200 pounds.

I was considered a very good baseball player. My baseball skills were dominant and seemed so natural. My coaches told me that I had a future and that I likely would become a major-leaguer.

The next level up was Babe Ruth League where I continued to dominate on the diamond both as a hitter and as a catcher with what was described as a "major-league arm." One of my coaches at that level had been a great baseball player. He had played in the minor leagues for several years. He said I was a "sure thing" if I continued to work hard at being as good defensively as I was with a bat in my hands.

By the time I was fifteen I was singularly focused on becoming a baseball player, with no other plans for the future. When I was seventeen I joined Marine Corps simply to get my service obligation out of the way so I could return to my only considered career. Once I came home from the Marine Corps I returned to playing baseball and played successfully for four more years until my eyesight did me in and I could no longer see a fastball. I was devastated; I would never realize my dream of playing in the major leagues.

At that time, I never realized the significance of the damage to my eyesight from diabetes. I knew nothing about the disease or my eye afflictions. All I knew was I couldn't see a pitched ball well anymore. I had no idea why. When I was cut, at the very young age of twenty-two, I never played another game of baseball.

I turned to baseball's substitute—softball. I had always thought that softball was a joke. I learned the first time I played, that it was a very significant sport. I was suddenly facing pitchers who threw the ball even faster, and from a much closer distance, than in baseball. The ball, being so much bigger, allowed me to be able to see it, and hit it. I enjoyed the sport and played in professional like fast-pitch leagues for many years. Many of my teammates, like me, had played baseball at high levels. Also like me, they didn't make it to the "bigs." The talent in those leagues amazed me. With the smaller field and the much shorter base paths, the speed of the game, much faster than baseball, took some serious effort to adjust to.

As I got older, I switched to playing in slow-pitch leagues. It was amazing how slow pitch could often be more difficult than the fast-pitch leagues. Some of the pitchers in slow-pitch softball put such a spin on the ball, it could make it nearly impossible to hit it. The fun of being on the diamond and still playing competitively was enough for me.

Baseball

I continued to be part of baseball, though not as a player. I did some high school and college umpiring. I was a batting coach for a time. I did a lot of private tutoring at a local batting cage. I was a catching coach in instructional camps. Baseball would always be such a passion for me and these non-playing roles allowed me to help many young players to hone their skills and build their love of the game, too.

Chapter Forty-Five

Motown

Keep your face to the sun and you will never see the shadows.
- Helen Keller

We left Toledo, headed to Detroit, via Monroe and Trenton, Michigan. As I walked into Monroe, I discovered that the town's claim to fame is that it was the boyhood home of General George Armstrong Custer. I had heard the very same claim somewhere in Ohio. Perhaps Custer's father moved the family around a lot.

Even though it's not wise to stop for any length of time, I agreed to a one-hour interview with Don Ayres, a reporter from the *Monroe Evening News*. As I was leaving, Don told me that their photographer would catch up with me on the road to Detroit for some "candids."

A short time later, I was startled to see a young man crouching in the weeds at the side of the road, snapping pictures of me striding toward him. Charles grabbed the camera and began taking pictures of him. I was beginning to appreciate how hard journalists and photographers work.

Soon, the traffic and congestion increased markedly. I felt as if I was in New York or Boston. At some point I turned a corner and I could see downtown Detroit off in the distance. The final ten miles to Cadillac Square were like walking through the neighborhoods of Boston, a cacophony of sounds, aromas, and sights that let you know you were in an urban neighborhood.

Detroit, to be sure, is a great city. In spite of what the media may say, it is neither dead nor dying. Nor is it what some call "Murder City." Others quip that Detroit is "America's First Third-World City." Don't be fooled by these epithets. Detroit will always be "Motown."

Some people don't realize Detroit's importance in American life. It's alleged "founders," a Frenchman named Cadillac, and Pontiac, an Indian Chief who tried to take it back from Cadillac, are names we know well. Henry Ford, the Dodge Brothers, Louis Chevrolet and Walter Chrysler created the auto industry. The Fords, Cadillacs, Pontiacs, Chevrolets, and Chryslers we drive all originated in Motown. And all of those names are on street signs, buildings, squares, and parks throughout the city. What Motown manufactures has so insinuated itself into our psyche that it's like the air we breathe. We don't even notice it.

If you're a sports fan, you know that there are four major leagues—baseball, football, basketball, and hockey. Therefore, you probably know that Detroit is one of only a handful of cities with bragging rights to teams in all four leagues. Some of the great sports names are intertwined with this city. Arguably one of the greatest hockey players of all time, Gordie Howe, proudly wore the uniform of the Detroit Red Wings for decades. Other greats include Ty Cobb, Al Kaline, Isiah Thomas, and Barry Sanders, to name a few. All brought much deserved respect to their Detroit teams.

Another significant legacy of "Motown" is the music of legends such as Smokey and the Miracles, Marvin Gaye, The Supremes, The Temptations, The Four Tops and little Stevie Wonder. The list of music makers from Detroit could fill a phone book: Wicked, Wicked Wilson Pickett, Martha and the Vandellas, Sam Cooke, Luther, Barry White, the Shirelles, and the Jackson Five. All were part of the Detroit scene. "Motown" is America. No other city—with the possible exception of Nashville and New Orleans—has had the musical impact of Detroit on our culture.

That is the Detroit I was thrilled to be walking into.

Sitting on a wall in Cadillac Square, I waited for an interview with the local NBC affiliate. The van created a lot of curiosity. A black minister came over to chat. He had noticed that among the charities I was walking for was the United Negro College Fund. He said: "You are my hero." He launched into a sermon about heroes. He declared, "Heroes are not Bill Clinton or Newt Gingrich or Roger Clemons, Barry Sanders, Michael Jordan, Larry King, Tiger Woods and Jay Leno." He went on to say, "The real heroes are people like you, and the kids who work in convenience stores and gas stations from midnight to dawn; the police, firemen, EMTs, and our men and women in the Army, Navy, Marine Corps, Air Force, and Coast Guard."

"And the truckers," I chimed in.

As the sun slipped below the horizon and the temperature dropped about twenty degrees, we were met at the monument in Cadillac Square by Joel Boykin, a reporter from NBC Detroit. We chatted while we were getting ready for the interview. "Welcome to Motown," she said.

"I couldn't be happier than to have my walk take me through Detroit," I said.

"I'm surprised that you would come here, most people seem to want to avoid Detroit."

I told her, "Many people over the last couple of months have questioned, 'Why would you go to Detroit?'

"I tell them there is no way I would miss Motown."

After the interview, Charles and I struggled to find a place to stay. It seemed as though every motel was owned or operated by people who hid themselves behind six-inch thick Plexiglas, who apparently don't trust anybody. When you entered a lobby, that Plexiglas separated you from the desk clerks. All transactions were handled through tiny windows, smaller than my hand. No credit cards accepted. After an hour, we finally found a place that agreed to take my plastic.

I quickly showered and climbed into bed. On the night table was a dog-eared copy of *Ebony* magazine. I picked it up and randomly opened it to a sweet, but corny, short story, which I'll summarize:

There was a map of the United States in a magazine. The father of a toddler carefully ripped it out and said to his son, "Let's turn this into a puzzle." He tore the page into pieces and mixed them up on the floor. He told his son that if he could put it together, he'd give him a dollar bill. Three minutes later the little boy had it all put back together. He called out to his father. The father walked over, somewhat amazed. "How did you do it so quickly?"

The little boy replied, "It was easy. On the other side of the map there's a picture of this large black family. When you get the black family right, our country's right."

I'm such a sap.

Smiling, I fell into a deep sleep.

Chapter Forty-Six
Soccer School

*Every kid around the world who plays soccer wants
to be Pele. I have a great responsibility to show them not
just how to be like a soccer player, but how to be like a man.*

—Pele

We departed from downtown Detroit, heading west on Michigan
Avenue to Ypsilanti, a well-to-do suburb. On the way, however, I deliberately walked through an aging, deteriorating section of the city.
While some neighborhoods do have beat-up looking buildings, most
still retain some of their beauty. The fact that most of the folks are
black and are often viewed as criminals, junkies, or gang members
is absurd. Just like in any neighborhood, most of the people who live
here were away at work. And I saw nothing that would make me think
the minorities in Detroit are any different from those of Boston, with
whom I became well acquainted in my capacity as a litigator on their
behalf.

I passed three black teenage girls, beautifully outfitted with corn-
rows, sitting on the curb, smiling and singing with so much animation
in front of a ravaged tenement house. Smiling, I told them how great
they sounded—"just like the Supremes"—and that they were good
enough to be on the radio. They giggled at the compliment.

Farther down the block, foul odors—strong enough to gag me—
emanated from a burned-out shell of a building. In the next block,
there were so many abandoned buildings that it was hard to call this a
neighborhood. Several blocks later, I saw some druggies out in force
hawking their wares, as openly as one might sell ice cream from a
Mister Softee truck. On the front steps of another building, a group of
middle-aged men passed a bottle, cloaked in a brown paper bag, back
and forth, swigging its contents. I wondered why they would bother
disguising it with the bag when packets of heroin were being openly
sold a block away. As dangerous as these situations might be, nonetheless, I waved to everyone and more often than not everyone waved
back. One guy asked me, "What are you doing in the hood?"

I told him: "I'm walking across the United States and I consider
the whole country my hood."

Though many of the young kids I passed looked at me and shook their heads, as if I'd escaped from a mental hospital, I nonetheless identified with them. When I was their age I had my own difficulties as a juvenile delinquent. I can understand that, for many young people, it's merely a stage of life—a part of learning lessons and growing up—becoming an adult. I had been involved in things like breaking and entering into neighbor's houses, and shoplifting with my buddies. I'm sure many people viewed me in the same way as they see the young people in disadvantaged neighborhoods everywhere in our country. The kids on the streets in Detroit were no different from youth anyplace else. Kids everywhere need to have leaders and role models who encourage them and who have positive attitudes. Education and motivation would go a long way towards helping our youth do more with their lives. The negativity that surrounds many of our inner-city kids often defeats them, causing them to follow unrewarding paths. Like it or not, these youth are our future, and we need to connect with them. I was, for a time, a victim of the same negativity. I also was a recipient of great assistance, from many folks, to eventually get on the road to a better tomorrow.

By mid-morning, we came upon a Ford factory on Bronco Lane in Wayne, Michigan, where Broncos, Expeditions and Navigators were built. Nearby, I saw a sea of thousands of Broncos, with hundreds of them being loaded onto trucks for distribution around the country.

As I arrived in Ypsilanti, I noticed a photographer taking pictures of me. John Galloway introduced himself and said, "Thank you for what you are doing." He had seen the various charities listed on the van and was pleased that my event was raising money for minority scholarships. John worked for the Ypsilanti and Ann Arbor newspapers. He went on to say, "A reporter will be catching up with you soon."

"Thank you for being interested in us," I said, as I continued westward.

As I neared a major interstate junction, Melanie Feliciano, the reporter for the *Ann Arbor News*, caught up with me for an interview. As we walked together traffic whizzed by and made turns perilously close in front of us. It was a dangerous place to be walking and conducting an interview when our focus needed to be on the traffic, but somehow we survived.

The city of Ann Arbor was next. Walking through one of Michigan's many college towns was a treat. Some refer to the university there as the "Harvard of the West." That label must have been bestowed a couple of centuries ago, when you were in the West if you were in Michigan. The schools that make this apparent claim to fame are crass. Every college ultimately stands on its own reputation, not that of Harvard. I'm sure the University of Michigan is every bit as good as Harvard and doesn't really need to use the loose association to the "Harvard of the West" to get folks to realize what a good school it is. Ann Arbor was a fairly large city, and yet one would never think it was such because it exuded a cozy, quiet and friendly feeling. It reminded me of Amherst, and the downtown area is reminiscent of Harvard Square in Cambridge.

I had started teaching college part time right after law school. Teaching brought me into regular contact with college communities. For me, these communities carried a special attraction. I had become a person who was most at home when among students and in the academic environment. Teaching became such a passion for me and in many ways, it had taken the place of baseball.

As I strutted through the west side of Ann Arbor, I spotted a Ford dealer just ahead on the right. I tried to explain to Charles that we should get the van serviced as we had put on more than 3,000 miles since leaving Boston. I couldn't break the language barrier, so I asked him to slide over so I could drive the van into Varsity Ford. Todd Lands came out to meet us. He was quite pleased that we had chosen his dealership for service. I realized that the dealer might be interested in using the van for some publicity benefit, so I asked Todd if that was a possibility. We quickly struck a deal. We traded a photo op with them for free servicing. They would use a photo of the Walking USA van in their ads later that week. Charles stayed behind while the service was being completed, so I could keep walking.

As I trekked through a long stretch of noisy road construction, I spotted a quaint, tiny gift shop called "Me and the Missus—Americana Decor and Gifts." I needed a break from the jack-hammering, so I wandered in to check it out.

Big mistake. I found so many delightful things in that little shop. From beautiful hand woven blankets and linens, to glassware and flatware, to collectible dolls; I saw many things I would've loved to buy, but my budget wouldn't allow it. Because I have such a weakness for inane aphorisms and poems, I bought a lovely, hand-woven blanket for my boys, monogrammed with a famous Irish blessing I know by heart from childhood. It begins: "May the road rise to meet you . . . "

After Ann Arbor came Chelsea. Here we came upon a soccer school being held in a large field on the side of the road. Now back on the road with me, Charles was fascinated, watching the youngsters soak up instruction in "football," as he and the rest of the world called it. "Let's take a break," I called out to Charles as I could see he wanted to check it out.

We parked and approached the adult in charge. His name was Rick and, incredibly, he and Charles knew each other immediately. They hugged and slapped each other's back and then high-fived one another. Rick was also a former Brazilian soccer player, like Charles. Apparently they had met in the past in matches in their home country.

Charles quickly got involved, helping out with soccer instruction, while I chatted with Rick's wife, Maria. Also Brazilian, she told me, "We came to this area because we had relatives here. Once settled, Rick launched a soccer school, and I started medical school."

"Are you done?" I asked.

"I am in my final year of residency," Maria responded.

"So the American dream is still alive and well?"

"America has been good to us," Maria said.

Soon, Charles hurried over and excitedly said, "Rick asked if it's okay I come back a couple of days later, on Saturday, for a game; parents against Brazilians!"

"We'll be eighty miles and two days from here by then," I told him.

He looked crestfallen. "I want come back," he insisted, pouting.

"If things go well, we can drive back," I promised, hoping it eased his homesickness.

We said our good-byes. After a couple of miles, I saw a ramp for Interstate 94 West. I impulsively decided to walk on an interstate for the first time, so I could make it to Jackson, Michigan before nightfall. By taking that route, I wouldn't be weaving through the rural towns between Chelsea and Jackson. Apparently it would save me three miles.

I sent Charles back to Varsity Ford to fix some lingering problems with the van. Fifteen minutes later, as I walked on the grass shoulder some ten feet from the pavement, I heard brakes screeching, and it sounded like a car was barreling my way. Without taking the time to look behind me, I leapt away from the oncoming sound, dove to the ground, and rolled down a slight incline, distancing myself from whatever was happening. When I finally looked back I saw several cars crashing into each other; one of them careened into the grass only a few feet from where I was walking. When all settled, fortunately, no one appeared to be hurt and vehicular damage was minimal.

As I struggled to my feet, my knees squeaked and cracked, reminding me that I was still an old, overweight man whose physical condition was precarious. Knowing how lucky I was to have escaped serious injury—if not death—I got off at the next exit and headed toward Jackson on back roads.

I called Charles' cell phone and with difficulty explained that I was now hoofing it on a byway in Leoni, a couple of miles south of, but parallel to, the interstate. After a couple of hours of back-and-forth calls, Charles finally located me. I realized how parlous the language barrier was making things. I was aware that the difficulty of communicating was becoming more and more difficult to deal with. I wondered if the tapes I had gotten for Charles were of any value. He was always listening to them, but after six weeks I certainly didn't find it any easier to chat with him. It had become the only real problem for me, but when my feet were covered with blisters and my knee was aching, I didn't really focus on the inability to communicate with Charles. More immediately, in spite of the difficulties presented by the language barrier, I was starving and about to drop dead from thirst.

* * *

On the morning of August 8, 1997, I prepared to leave Jackson to walk to Battle Creek. I began walking and had gone about a mile when I was approached by Alicia Sands, a young woman from the Jackson *Citizen Patriot*. "Can I buy you breakfast?"

"Absolutely," I immediately answered. The opportunity to have breakfast with somebody other than Charles wasn't something I would have passed up. Breakfast with Alicia meant I would be speaking with someone who spoke "normal English" instead of struggling to chat with Charles.

Together we walked into a pleasant restaurant that looked like the kind of place you might see featured in *Yankee Magazine*. Everything was red-and-white checkered: the napkins, the placemats and even the waitress' uniforms. The smell of bacon abounded. I certainly was in the mood for breakfast. Alicia conducted her lively interview as Charles and I enjoyed a huge breakfast. First I had a Belgian waffle, hidden beneath mounds of strawberries and whipped cream—to which I had added a more than generous blanket of strawberry syrup. Then I had an omelet I had never before tried: cream cheese and herbs. I ordered a side of bacon and when it came it looked like it must have been a pound. All that—and I wasn't even full.

Back on the road, an hour later, Max da Lento, a reporter for the local NBC-TV affiliate, Channel 10, in Jackson, also stopped to interview us. Since Max was a native Brazilian, he was fascinated with Charles' story about seeing America at three-and-a-half miles per hour. Charles was thrilled that the press was only interested in his story. I enjoyed watching him smile from ear to ear. He was a natural "ham." A few minutes later, Alicia's photographer showed up. Apparently people in Michigan were truly interested in what I was doing, and I also enjoyed the attention.

The walk from Jackson, Michigan to Marshal was uneventful. I realized my tenth wedding anniversary was six days away. Wouldn't it be a nice gesture to go home for a day or two, not only to celebrate my anniversary, but to see my children who had just returned from Honduras? The more I thought about it, I realized that on the entire walk so far, I hardly ever even thought of my wife. The thought of "celebrating" an anniversary had caused me to realize how completely estranged we actually were. I was becoming convinced that I was walking away from her. I didn't see another failed marriage as another failure of mine. It was just not meant to be. I was saddened though, by the thought. There was really no celebration possible.

Chapter Forty-Seven

It Ain't Over Till It's Over

So many tears I've cried
So much pain inside
But baby it ain't over 'til it's over
So many years we've tried
To keep our love alive
But baby it ain't over 'til it's over.

—Lenny Kravitz

On the solitude of this long trek, I had begun to face the fact that the marriage was essentially over. Almost never thinking about Estela seemed to prove it.. The ugly truth of the matter was that my marriage had been nothing more than a sham from shortly after we were married. It had been predicated on my wife's need to get "papers" to stay in the United States. At the time of the wedding, everybody seemed to realize that reality, except me.

I had been smitten, thrilled that such a young and beautiful lady had picked me for a husband; she was twenty-seven and I was forty-one when we met. I was fresh off a divorce and reluctant to be involved in any relationship when I met Estela.

The day before I was to start law school, my sister Nancy threw a barbecue party for me in her backyard to celebrate my going to Harvard. Estela, an enchanting and beautiful Spanish lady, was a guest of my older sister, Fran. I happened to sit down next to her not long after the party began. I was captivated by her brown eyes, and her warm smile made me melt. As we talked and shared our experiences in school, it was obvious to me that she had great courage. She had come to the states from Honduras to learn to speak English. Her job at the Port of Honduras required her to speak better English, so the Honduran government sent her to Boston to take a cram course at the English Language School. Once here, she quickly realized the wonderful educational opportunities that existed in America. She enrolled in UMass Boston and, at the time of our meeting, she was entering her final semester and about to graduate with a degree in computer science.

Given my own journey, I was highly impressed by the struggle that she had gone through to get herself a college education. It spoke volumes of the strength of character and of the courage it took to accomplish such lofty goals, especially given the language barrier.

A couple of nights later I called her and asked her to meet me in Harvard Square for an ice cream. After our Bailey's hot fudge sundae, we took a walk along the Charles River. Strolling along, I turned to her and impulsively said, "You know I am going to marry you don't you?" Although I really meant it, I was shocked that I had the nerve to say it out loud.

I was even more surprised at her answer. She said, "Yes."

We began to see each other regularly, though just on weekends. Between my law school demands and her college course work, we had no time whatsoever to see each other during the week. On Fridays, as soon as classes ended for the week, I jumped into my tiny, candy-apple red Ford Feista and drove to her apartment in East Boston, and we would spend the entire weekend together—except I had to return to my room to sleep each night as she refused to let me stay over.

In December, she finished her final semester. She soon applied for and accepted a job at MIT in Cambridge. Meanwhile I was completely buried in my first year of law school. When spring break arrived that year, we spent the week together in a mountain condo outside of San Diego.

It was a week filled with joy. We went horseback riding on mountain trails. We spent hours in the indoor pool. Instead of eating out, we got our own groceries and cooked for each other. It really was a "break." It was the first time in years that I really relaxed. We had a lot of time to think about our relationship and we decided that we would get married in August. I warned Estela that there would come a day at some point in our marriage when I would have to leave for a significant period of time to fulfill my dream of walking across the country. She understood that this was very important to me and she knew that I was totally committed to walking to the West Coast. She told me that she would never stand in the way of my plans.

That summer, while I worked for a law firm in Boston, we finalized the plans for our wedding. On August 14, 1987, we tied the knot. Our wedding was an amazing event and remains one of the greatest memories in my life. I felt like I was finally "getting married." This was real. My two earlier marriages had lacked the emotions I was feeling as I said "I do." It was as though I had been given a fresh start in life, and the errors of my past were just that.

Totally fascinated with my bride and equally fascinated by the thought of starting a family after law school, I had absolutely no reservations about my situation. I felt as though I had finally been blessed and that I was in a marriage that was perfect, with the right mate for me.

We planned to wait two years to start our family. For practical reasons, we wanted to wait until after I was done with law school before having children so that we could save some money. I even bought my bride a book four months after our wedding entitled, *How Not to Get Pregnant*. I should have asked for a refund; only a few days after my purchase Estela was pregnant with our first child.

Shortly after the beginning of my third year of law school, on what would have been my father's seventy-fifth birthday, September 21, 1988, my son Nicholas Alexander Brown was born. It was certainly the happiest day of my life. When the doctor pulled Nicholas from my wife's womb, he handed him to me after letting me cut the umbilical cord. I was overwhelmed with the wonder of my son.

When my daughters had been born some twenty years earlier, fathers were not allowed anywhere near the delivery room. It was an incredible experience to be a part of my child's birth.

In the early months of his life we had significant difficulties in locating someone to take care of Nicholas so I usually carried him on my chest to my classes in law school. It was an extraordinary experience to have that kind of time to bond with my son.

I remembered what it was like for me as a kid. The words "I love you" were never expressed in my home. There was, but not that I knew at the time, nurturing about the important things in life, i.e. music, art, books, education, family. I vowed that my son would hear "I love you" every day of his life. I promised myself I would make available all the things that I was deprived of when I was a lad. I would be a real father to my son. I certainly knew what not to do. I'm sure my father struggled with his own demons and just didn't have the capacity to fight them and be a good parent at the same time. Sadly, we were victims of his disease, too.

From the day Nicholas was born, he seemed destined to do significant things in his life. His eyes were filled with curiosity and zest and he always had a huge smile on his face. During my class breaks, with Nicholas in tow, I would take long walks, looking right in his face, talking to him about what I perceived to be the most important things in life: reading, books, education, and love of family. Nicholas would look back at me with those deep brown, absorbent eyes, drinking in everything I was saying.

Nick experience that third year of law school along with me. On graduation day, the dean of Harvard Law School handed Nicholas my Juris Doctor degree.

My son continually amazed me. He walked at seven months, and was able to carry on full conversations in two languages (Spanish and English) before he was one year old. He was able to translate English to Spanish and Spanish to English for adults, at a year old, without even being asked. He knew when translation was necessary.

By the age of two, Nicholas was a swimmer and a budding pianist and we enrolled him in piano lessons. He loved his art classes, and spent hours painting. At two and a half, we enrolled Nick in a Montessori School where he would begin his continuous trek of education. After three years in Montessori, he began kindergarten at Shore Country Day School in Beverly, Massachusetts, where he did extraordinarily well. The next years, first through third grade, he was dazzling his teachers at Brimmer & May School in Chestnut Hill where he quickly was recognized as an extremely talented artist, musician and student.

Nicholas' success didn't help the marriage. I thought that he might have made things a little better between Estela and I, but that never happened. Not too long after he was born, one of Estela's sisters from Honduras was visiting with us. One morning she called me saying that Estela had called the police on her to send her back to Honduras. They apparently had been arguing and it had gotten ugly. I immediately drove home from law school only to find them screaming at one another. To break the tension before the situation could get any worse, I asked my wife to take a break. I handed her the car keys and said, "Take a ride to the mall and relax." After she left, I eventually calmed her sister down.

I asked, "What is going on?"

Gladys responded, "I don't want to be a part of what Estela is doing to you."

"What is she doing to me? I queried.

"She don't love you. She marry you for the "papers.""

To say I was shocked and hurt was an understatement. We were basically still newlyweds and new parents. I was completely devastated. I didn't want to believe it—but why would Estela's sister lie about something like this?

I confronted Estela, hoping she would deny her sister's claims. I asked her point blank, "What is this about you marrying me for papers?"

She said, "So what?"

That response might as well have been a bullet to my heart. I thought I'd finally found the perfect mate, one who truly loved me, and then she hit me with a dismissive zinger like that. It threw me into an emotional tailspin. Even years later, the confrontation and revelation still confounds me. I never got over it—and never will.

Maybe Estela didn't realize I would be so wounded. In her culture what she did is apparently an absolutely normal occurrence—almost like an arranged marriage would be. But I am not from her culture and I didn't marry it; I thought I had married the most special woman that I had ever met. She hadn't led me to believe otherwise. I was clueless about her charade for the entire two years we had been together. Along with being a huge slap in the face, it was the beginning of the end of our marriage.

Still, I refused to give in and worked to keep the flame alive for the sake of my son. I did all I could to tolerate the marriage. I tried to act like there was nothing wrong. But, "So what" would always creep back into my mind.

Then, a couple of years later, Estela was pregnant again. I couldn't completely shake what I knew to be the truth but I wanted more than anything to make the marriage work, especially with our family growing.

Our second son, Louis Mitchell Brown, was born on May 3, 1991. He was born with very severe birth defects which plunged me into an emotional free-fall. Louis had had a stroke in *utero* and had been left with only a quarter of a brain. His head had been badly deformed by a blood clot in his skull that caused the brain matter to be forced out and his head was enlarged to far beyond normal measurements. He was in a semi-vegetative state and the prognosis was that he would likely not live twenty four hours. If he did live, doctors said that he would be in a permanent vegetative state. He was diagnosed with hydrocephalus and cerebral palsy. Basically, his brain was damaged beyond imagination.

As a family, our lives were affected in unimaginable ways that one could never be prepared for. The pain that we all experienced, of a child with such birth defects, was more severe than any pain I had ever known. The fact that I was unable to do anything to fix his problems made me feel helpless. We were consumed by a difficult and endless job—trying our hardest to persevere through the frightening experience of caring for a dramatically handicapped baby.

The Morphine Dream

The warm and tender feelings that had been a part of the short time before Nicholas was born had long ago evaporated. Estela and I not only drifted apart, we drifted *far* apart. There was a complete loss of communication. The distance was also terribly hampered by the fact that I was working a minimum of sixteen hours a day, seven days a week. I was not present for much of the struggle of dealing with Louis. Long afterwards, I came to the realization that in those first couple of years after Louis was born, I worked so hard and such long hours just to avoid the grief I felt when I was home. It was not just the grief over Louis' problems, but the grief of the lost promise of my marriage.

Estela and I stayed together but as a family, we fell into a routine that was merely aimed at getting through each and every extraordinarily difficult day. Providing care for Louis was more than a full-time job for us, including Nick, who was more devoted to his brother's needs than anybody.

As the months and years passed I reminded Estela occasionally that there would still be a day when I would leave for a long time to do my walk across America. I think she realized that it was an inevitable situation, because of my proclivity to pursue my dreams. She had her own dream—to come to America and get an education—and she had achieved it. She knew I was focused. I was doing charity walks regularly and usually walked more than fifty miles a week, ever since we had met.

In the fall of 1996, I became really sick. I had a very successful business going, in Medical Practice Management. Other than a marriage that had grown into nothing more than a matter of tolerating each other, things were going reasonably well. But, I was so ill, I finally drove myself to the hospital. I was diagnosed with prostate cancer, and warned that it was advanced. I kept the diagnosis to myself, as I was certain I was in significant trouble.

When confronted with a diagnosis like that, you know for certain that each minute of every day counts. For certain, I could not put off the final part of the Morphine Dream. Once my chemo was done, I knew it was now or never. I *had* to do my planned walk across the country.

When I arrived home after being hospitalized for a spell, I sat down with Estela and told her, "I *must* do my walk. I am past the dreaming and talking stage and need to finally just do it."

I was surprised by her reaction: there was none. She apparently didn't care what I did. I put everything out there on the table and said, "I am terribly disappointed how our marriage has turned out." She sat

218

stone-faced as I continued, "I am incredibly thrilled with my sons and being a father. But our relationship is not what I consider a marriage."

I would have expected *something* from her but I got not a word, or a facial expression, or a reaction of any kind. It was like she had heard nothing.

I explained to her that within the coming months, I wanted to sell the company that we had built together, including her shares of ownership. She had, under my guidance, created the software that ran the company. I knew what I wanted the software to do, and she knew how to get the computers to do it. In that way, we were a very efficient team. I certainly respected her knowledge and her ability to program my thoughts. What we created was cutting-edge medical billing and collection software. I had gotten several friends together to fund the start-up for the purpose of creating a solution for doctors who were experiencing a myriad of problems in getting paid by insurance companies.

The proceeds from the sale of the company would provide Estela with a significant amount of money for her to be able to maintain the household and the children's needs while I was away—and far beyond.

Selling the company was also the key to embarking on my planned walk across America. If it happened, there would be no reason not to go on the trek.

Although the handwriting appeared to be on the wall, I told Estela that once I returned, "We will need to find a way to create a much more significant and meaningful relationship together or I will not stay in the marriage." Up until then, I had stayed because I was loathe to leaving my children behind. I was equally loathe to staying in the marriage—as it was. I didn't want the misery of the last several years to become the rest of my life

When I left Boston to begin walking across the country, I knew deep inside that I was not only walking across America, but I was most likely walking away from my marriage. I could sense that it was over.

A tenth wedding anniversary should be a milestone of sorts—well past the "seven-year-itch" stage, and an implication that the marriage had some sense of validity and permanence. My marriage, however, had been built on deception, a false promise. The number ten, in my case, was simply a number with no real significance, other than the passing of time.

The Morphine Dream

As that famed philosopher Yogi Berra once said: "It ain't over till it's over." It was over.

Chapter Forty-Eight
Battle Creek

Middle age is when you choose your cereal
for the fiber, not the toy.

—Unknown

After lunch, I walked along a two-lane road off the beaten path, passing farms and small villages. It was such an improvement over the interstate. Yet I felt depressed and lonely. Charles was not the only one who was homesick; I was, too.

Finally, we reached Battle Creek, home of Kellogg's and C.W. Post. Here I was in the city made famous by Wheaties: the Breakfast of Champions, Cheerios and Tony the Tiger. It is another fabled place in our culture. If you grow up in America it's almost impossible not to know Kellogg's and Post cereals.

I took a break on the soft mattress of manicured grass under the soothing shade of a giant oak. Two men, probably my age, both in great shape and powerfully built, hurried out of the house shaded by the big tree. They appeared concerned. One asked, "Can we get you a cold drink? The other, seeing my copious sweat, said, "Do you need a doctor?"

I responded, "I'm fine, I don't need a doctor but I would love the cold drink."

After I explained my trek and said that I was just resting, we chatted about the area. They were brothers and had both been employed by the Kellogg Company all their working lives.

"Kellogg's," one of the brothers said, "has multi-billion dollars a year in sales and was founded by Dr. Jon Kellogg."

Kellogg apparently became interested in the health benefits of eating grains. His motto was "You are what you eat." Along with family members, he and a neighbor, C.W. Post, created these two giant cereal companies here in Battle Creek. The names are as synonymous with cereal as is Battle Creek.

One of the brothers suggested I come back the next June for the annual "Cereal City Festival." He said, "The town of Battle Creek hosts the largest breakfast feast in the world. We serve more than 50,000 people, who come from hundreds and some from thousands of miles away, just for a free breakfast!"

We left Battle Creek at 5 A.M., headed toward Kalamazoo. Again, there was nothing notable on the walk between the two western Michigan industrial cities. I picked up the pace so we could drive back to Chelsea at the end of the day to allow Charles to play in the scheduled "Brazilians versus parents" soccer game later in the day—with Rick and his soccer school's parents. Charles was the happiest I had seen him in a long while.

After quickly checking into a motel, we were off to the soccer battle. The game began an hour later, with great fanfare. You'd have thought it was the World Cup finals. The result? Not unexpectedly, the Brazilians crushed the parents like bugs!

* * *

The next morning, Charles woke up in agony. He could barely move. His muscles were stiff and sore. He informed me that he was in too much pain to drive.

"Charles," I said firmly, "It is hard for me to walk *every* day. You've seen me with my feet so badly blistered that I could barely stand, and yet I still walk. You have to drive. I can't walk and drive."

I also reminded him that we agreed he would not play soccer during this event. I made an exception so he could play in the game just to please him.

Charles reluctantly drove. We headed west to Kalamazoo where we would then head south to Elkhart, Indiana. Small farms dotted the countryside. Twice, I was slowed by TV interviews, one from a local station in Battle Creek and one from Kalamazoo.

I won't deny it. I loved the attention. The publicity would make it more likely that I could add a sponsor as I moved west. The problem was each interview added at least a half hour to the completion of my daily walk.

The walk that day was an unusually long one: forty-seven miles. It was 11 P.M. and I still had ten miles to go. I was not pleased with myself, being on the road so late.

The good news was that I was leaving Michigan—another state in the rearview mirror.

Part Four
Crossroads of America

It's little I care what path I take,
And where it leads it's little I care
I wish I could walk for a day and a night,
And find me at dawn in a desolate place
With never the rut of a road in sight,
Nor the roof of a house, nor the eyes of a face.
—Edna St. Vincent Millay

Chapter Forty-Nine
The House That Rockne Built

We're gonna go inside, we're gonna go outside, inside and outside.
We're gonna get 'em on the run boys and once we get 'em on the run
we're gonna keep 'em on the run. And then we're gonna go go go go
go go
and we're not gonna stop till we get across that goal line. This is a
team they say is . . . is good, well I think we're better than them. They
can't lick us, so what do you say men?

—Knute Rockne

It was 2 A.M. when we finally crossed into Indiana. While we gained an hour with the time change, interestingly, it was instantly only 1 A.M. I was disheartened to finish so late. We quickly settled into our motel in Elkhart, the "Land of the Indians," and fell asleep without bothering to eat dinner, undress or shower.

In spite of our extremely late finish, we were up at 7:00 A.M. We had a busy day ahead of us. I was scheduled to do an interview with the *Elkhart Truth*, the local newspaper. We had to meet the reporter at the Elkhart County Visitors Center.

I learned a lot of interesting, but useless stuff at the center. Elkhart claims to be both the "Band Instrument Capital of the World" and the "RV Capital of the World." Approximately 50 percent of all recreational vehicles are made there. Elkhart is also where Alka-Seltzer was invented. Many years ago, before I began to eat more judiciously, Alka-Seltzer was part of my daily meal plan!

As it turned out I could have slept a little more after all. Lisa Blair, the reporter, left word that she'd have to postpone our interview and meet us later on the Boston Post Road, when I was walking towards South Bend.

Finally, I was back to walking, headed west on Route 20—the same Route 20 that starts as the Boston Post Road in Kenmore Square in Boston. It stretches for 3,365 miles to the West Coast and is allegedly the longest road in the country. It will lead me to South Bend and, eventually, I would be on it again as I got near the Place of the Smelly Onion—Chicago.

It was raining a little, making walking easier. In the rain there was less perspiration, less exertion and it was easier on my fatigue level.

Soon, we did the scheduled interview with Lisa Blair. She asked: "Why are you walking through Elkhart?"

I had a ready answer: "No walk across the country would be complete without a trip to South Bend, and the road to South Bend goes through Elkhart."

This was also, again, Amish Country. It was like going back in time. Life for these folks—at least on the surface—was simple and peaceful. The work ethic and morality of the Amish people is uncommon. In spite of how different they seem—eschewing electricity and prancing around in horse and buggies—the Amish are extraordinarily kind, respectful, and merciful.

I remember spending a couple of weeks visiting the Amish settlement in Lancaster, Pennsylvania, several years ago. Their lifestyle is reminiscent to that of Mormons. (I am a Mormon). They are very attentive to their spiritual life, family and are extremely close-knit.

In stark contrast to the Amish horse and buggies was the Hummer factory, off to my left. There were hundreds of the huge, macho vehicles sitting in the parking lot. They were originally designed solely for military use and somehow became a sexy toy for the young and rich. You had to be well off to buy one, as they originally cost almost $100,000. With the gas mileage at allegedly eight miles to the gallon, you'd spend a small fortune filling the tank, too.

Overhead, ominous clouds threatened. The rain was returning.

In the mid-afternoon, we arrived in the outskirts of South Bend, home of Notre Dame. The mention of that school conjures up thoughts of academic excellence and the thrill of "big" college football games. The blue and gold have been national champions more than any other college football team in the modern, post-1900 era. At the time of my walk they also held the record, by far, for the number of Heisman Trophy winners, and the signs announcing that were everywhere. On the way into town, a reporter from the local NBC affiliate, owned and operated by the University of Notre Dame, met us in the drizzle for a quickie interview.

Once in South Bend, we immediately headed to and toured the Notre Dame campus—so large it felt like a city within a city. Its traditions and mystique filled me with awe. I felt transformed into one of the "Fighting Irish."

I strolled into the stadium through the famous tunnel that "Rudy" Ruettiger walked through when he first arrived at the Notre Dame campus, into the "House That Rockne Built." Coach Knute Rockne had designed this stadium, which was built in 1930. He had only one year to enjoy it as he was killed in a plane crash shortly after that season. Over the last few months, Notre Dame had been modernizing the stadium for the 1997 season. They changed the capacity from about 60,000 to something like 80,000.

The structure was unremarkable. It looked like most college football stadiums, but when I walked onto the field and smelled the scent of the gridiron grass, I couldn't help but feel the presence of Knute Rockne, George Gipp ("Win one for the Gipper"), Joe Montana, Paul Horning, Joe Theisman, Tim Brown, and Ross Browne and especially, Rudy. Except for Rudy, they were some of the greatest college players that ever lived, although because of his unique and incredible story, Rudy is perhaps better known than the others, at least by non-football fans.

This stadium was the leitmotif of *Rudy*, the 1993 inspirational film, directed by David Anspaugh. I had watched Rudy more times than I cared to admit. Based on a true story, Daniel "Rudy" Ruettiger was told he was too dumb (actually, he was just dyslexic) and too small—five foot six inches and 165 pounds—to attend college or play on any college football team. Through sheer grit, he got into and graduated from Notre Dame and played on its football team. Whenever I felt down and discouraged in my own struggles to overcome adversity during the past few years, or while trudging from sea to shining sea, I watched *Rudy*. It fired me up and got me back on track.

I remember one year, after I had began teaching college (long after I had returned from my walk across the country) I included the movie *Rudy* in a class entitled "Critical Thinking." When the movie ended, I asked the students: "What would you say that movie was about?"

A freshman football player in the back of the room raised his hand. I nodded to him, anxious to hear what he would say.

"It wasn't about football," he said, "It was more about life."

He got it.

Chapter Fifty

Football

It's not whether you get knocked down,
It's whether you get up.

—Vince Lombardi

Perhaps more than most people, I could appreciate what Rudy had done. He was only five foot six and apparently weighed only one hundred and sixty-five pounds when he became a part of the Notre Dame team practice sessions. He was on the field daily throughout the week before each game—lining up against people who weighed anywhere between 100 pounds and 200 pounds more than he did. Many of those Notre Dame linemen were as much as a foot taller than Rudy. How he was able to function in that environment was beyond my ability to comprehend.

For me, when I found myself no longer able to hit a fastball and struggled with the realization that my baseball playing days were over, I turned my attention and focus to the gridiron. I had very little experience with the game so playing football was alien to me. While I was big, six-foot tall and 265 pounds, I quickly found out that on a football field, designated as a "nose" tackle, I was very small, especially when I lined up against behemoths who often tipped the scales at 325 or more. Those linemen were bigger than NFL lineman. Because they were slowed down some by their pounds, they were usually cut by the NFL where speed rules. Rudy must have felt like a toddler.

During training camp I regularly found myself knocked senseless from the hits put on me by the offensive lineman. Like Rudy, I jumped right up, afraid to let anyone know how badly my bell had been rung. I was never going to let anyone know that I was hurt or dazed. I guess it was that "macho" thing that athletes succumb to. I made the cut and was named the starting nose tackle. I didn't know whether to celebrate or cry. This was not baseball. The physical punishment can be brutal. I needed to excel. I had always set a high standard for my athletic endeavors. I guess it was the only accomplishment I could point to. Just being on the team wasn't good enough, as it had been for Rudy.

In my first game the opposing tackle threw me all around the field, as if he were a cat toying with a mouse. I began to learn lessons, one of them being that adding more weight could increase my chance of success.

I purposely (and stupidly) began to pack on the pounds. I ate—if you can believe it—a gallon of ice cream every day, followed by weightlifting sessions lasting hours. By the end of the season I was pushing 300 pounds and my difficulties with the opposing tackles were much less. Often, I played with them like they were the mouse and I was the cat. It had been a reversal of roles that I enjoyed.

Over the winter following my first season, I played basketball for conditioning while waiting for football season to begin. I was doing well, I thought, as I put on another twenty-five pounds again using the ice cream eating and weight-training regimen. By the opening of camp I was in the best condition of my life, and I was a quick and mobile 325 pounds.

As my football career progressed I began to understand it wasn't so much about my weight and height as it was about my speed and my ability to strategize about how to get around the super-sized tackles rather than try to move them. As I learned, game by game, I found myself stunting with a linebacker lined up behind me. The result was I had many opportunities to get into the backfield unhindered leaving the offensive tackle wondering what happened.

I found it to be more of a brain game than a contact sport. Obviously, out-thinking your opponent was the key to success. So for the next few years, sacking the quarterback and blocking for the safeties and cornerbacks as they ran back interceptions became the thrill of victory for me.

It was easy to understand why football meant so much to Rudy. I developed the same passion for the game that I once had for baseball

Over those years, I became a big-time NFL fan. I religiously watched pro games whenever I wasn't playing. I realized that I would never go to that level. The speed and power of NFL players could be classified as inhuman. The ferocious hits that took place at that level caused me to think how strange it was that players weren't regularly killed. I knew that they wound up in hospitals during—and especially—after their careers because they were often my roommates in the surgical ward at the New England Baptist Hospital.

But as a young guy, restless and eager for the glamour of the athletic highs of the gridiron, I participated willingly, until my body declared "No more!"

While I still love to watch the NFL games, you could never ever get me to espouse young guys pursuing football as a means of being able to get college scholarships. You can get a college scholarship for having a good time doing good work academically. Kids don't need to have their physical quality of life destroyed in order to have a happy and successful life otherwise.

My message is, I guess, "football sucks." even though when playing it was so special to do it and do it well. If I had it to do over again, I would have never put on the pads. And especially, I would never have purposefully put on that incredible amount of extra weight. I have been struggling with weight problems ever since. My knees were always bothering me. My diabetes, with all its damaging effects, worsened. The excess weight was such a huge health hazard and except for football, it was nothing but torment.

Chapter Fifty-One

A Mild-Mannered Reporter

A mild-mannered reporter for a great metropolitan newspaper, fights for truth, justice, and the American way.

—**Superman**

I hated leaving South Bend, especially during an early morning torrential downpour. It was raining so hard it seemed crazy to be walking but nothing was going to stop me. When I contemplated the walk, I knew there'd be days like this. I thought of what the Marines said: "Pain is weakness leaving the body" or "When the going gets tough, the tough get going."

By mid-day, the rain had turned to drizzle. I had changed so many times there was a mountain of soaked clothing and shoes in the back of the van. It smelled like a football locker room after a rainy, muddy, September game.

When I finally walked into Kokomo, I was astonished at the size of the place. I had expected a small town. Instead, it was a rapidly growing metropolis. Because of all the construction going on, there were "no vacancy" signs hanging outside all the local motels. Carpenters and laborers from "faraway places with strange-sounding names" had grabbed all the rooms.

At last, we found a vacancy. The chatty desk clerk informed us that Kokomo is the "City of Firsts." (Here we go again.) It was in Kokomo that the first automobile was built in 1894 by Elwood Haynes. It was also where the first carburetor was produced, along with the first car radio and the first auto tires were manufactured. It was Kokomo where aluminum and stainless steel were first fabricated. These "firsts," if true, speak of the ingenuity of the early settlers of Kokomo.

* * *

Leaving Kokomo, I walked south toward Indianapolis. It was again a steamy 3H day. We were up and out early, before 6:00 A.M. Shortly after noon, I was met by John Flora, a self-described "mild-mannered reporter" from the *Indianapolis Star*. John was my age and close to my size—large. He was delighted that someone our age was doing something as quixotic as a cross-country walk. John said, "I do my own adventure, regularly traveling around the country, but on a motorcycle."

After chatting too long, I was back on the road, trucking toward Indianapolis. It was soon rush hour, as we crossed under the outer-belt interstate that surrounds the city. Darkness approached as we finally reached downtown Indianapolis. We stopped at the local ABC affiliate, Channel 6, for a scheduled interview. I was a day ahead of schedule, yet the folks at Channel 6 quickly got everything arranged so I could film it.

* * *

Because we had arrived in Indianapolis a day early, I impulsively decided to do what I should have done in every major city. I took a thirty-five-mile walk around the city, visiting most of its neighborhoods. "Indy" was a slice of America: glamorous and gritty, rich and poor, but almost ubiquitously friendly. For no particular reason, I suddenly felt blessed to be on this journey. No more did I ask myself, "Can I *really* do this?" Now, at the risk of sounding trite, I *was* doing it—with a smile on my face and joy in my heart.

"Savor the moment," I kept telling myself. "It won't last forever."

Chapter Fifty-Two

The Brickyard

Indy makes the race driver. You become
famous when you come here.

—**Rodger Ward**

My next day began at the Indy 500 racetrack. This is where they say: "Gentlemen, start your engines." I had written many weeks earlier for permission to walk the track itself, and it was granted just a few days before my arrival. Officials allotted me one hour, which would allow me to do one lap around, or two and a half miles. All my life I had watched the famous Indy 500 race so I felt thrilled and privileged to stroll around the track. At the first curve, I thought about the hot rods taking this turn at 200 miles per hour, as I crept along at 3.7.

This place was built almost a hundred years ago and the racing surface was created from the laying of 3.2 million bricks, thus the moniker "The Brickyard." I was told that many of the original bricks are still in place under the asphalt that now makes up the racing surface.

It was a real treat to visit the museum inside the facility. There must have been fifty vintage race cars spread around the space. Looking at them one is certainly able to see the incredible power of those vehicles. The engines of each car were about twice the size of a typical auto engine. The sleek body and the wide tires evoked visions of speed. Someday, I hope to drive one–just for the thrill.

* * *

Rick and his wife, Maria, of the Chelsea, Michigan, soccer school had driven down to join us as I walked on towards Chicago—a three-day journey headed north. When we had been at their place, Rick and Maria had asked us if they could come and walk with us when they could get free from their regular obligations. They wanted to be a part of the event. Rick, especially, wanted to have some time to visit with Charles. Maria, a rabid walker, wanted to find out if she could walk forty miles in a day. Rick settled in as co-pilot in the van with Charles, while Maria joined me for a hot and steamy perambulation out of Indy into the verdant and peaceful farmlands that surrounded the city.

Charles was delighted to have his countryman along for the ride. They must've had a great time trading war stories in Portuguese about soccer, women and Brazil. I hadn't seen Charles this upbeat since we left Boston. Even though he was well compensated and was getting a chance to see the United States, it must have been frustrating and lonely talking in broken English to an old man, with whom he had little in common, for months on end. He had told me countless times that he was lonesome for his family.

At our lunch break, Rick—who speaks English rather well—explained to me that Charles was worried about his mother. "She is apparently very ill," said Rick. He warned me that Charles may have to fly to Brazil on short notice. I was glad to know this. Charles had seemed increasingly distracted and despondent, but I had no idea why. It would be challenging to find someone who could take as good care of me as Charles had. Except for the language barrier, he had been a real asset. I would have to make some calls back to Boston later in the day to see if I could line up a potential replacement. I needed to get the word out quickly, as I realized how difficult it had been to find Charles.

After lunch, Maria wanted to talk about my sons. She and Rick had no children yet. She said, "So the oldest is Nick?"

"Yes," I said. "He is a very special child." I went on to boast about my son, and Maria didn't seem to mind at all.

"From the day Nick was born, we knew he was destined to do significant things in his life. His first few months were spent in an over-shoulder carrier on my chest while I was completing my third year at Harvard Law School. In fact on graduation day, the dean of Harvard Law School handed Nicholas my Juris Doctorate degree." I realized I had been talking a lot so I asked Maria, "Are you sure you're not bored?"

"No, no, no—continue. I love hearing you talk about him."

So I went on, "He did everything so early. He walked at seven months, was able to carry on full conversations in two languages (Spanish and English) before he was one year old. At one year of age he was able to translate, without being asked, from English to Spanish and Spanish to English for his Spanish-speaking nannies.

"By the age of two, he was a swimmer and a budding pianist. He regularly took art classes. At thirty months we enrolled him in a Montessori school where he began his formal education. After three years in Montessori, he attended Shore Country Day School in Beverly, Massachusetts, where he did extraordinarily well. The next years, first through third grade, he has attended Brimmer and May School in Chestnut Hill where he quickly was recognized as an extremely talented artist, musician and student. All the while he continued his pursuit of music, developing an affinity for the French horn along the way."

"Now tell me about your younger son," she said.

"That's enough for now. We'll continue the discussion at dinner," I responded.

We moved steadily towards the end of the day's sauntering. I was amazed how easy it was for Maria to keep pace with me and complete a forty-mile day without even looking like she had done anything. She had great endurance. She was very thin. Obviously, being thin makes everything so much easier. I didn't know if I'd ever get there.

* * *

Maria was by my side again the next day. Having her to walk and talk with had been a delightful change of pace. It was the first time I had a walking companion for more than a few miles for such an extended period of time. Despite the heat, chatting with her had made the forty-mile days feel like forty minutes. As dusk fell Maria and Rick had to say good-bye and return to Michigan. After ten minutes of hugging and kisses and tears, Charles and I were alone again. It was sad to have Rick and Maria leave; we were spoiled for two days.

Chapter Fifty-Three
Ian Vanderwall

I will cherish my walk with you
for the rest of my life.

—Ian Vanderwall

Within a half hour I was surrounded by western Indiana farmland with corn "as high as an elephant's eye." It wouldn't be long before the sun would set. I was drenched with sweat and needed some fresh clothes. As soon as I changed, I felt refreshed and invigorated.

On the outskirts of Rensselear, a minivan driven by a middle-aged man slowed to a stop. The driver asked, "Can my son walk with you for a while?

"Of course!" I said, enthusiastically.

Out of the van popped Ian Vanderwall. Tall and skinny for a ten-year-old, he reminded me of my son, Nicholas, who was about the same height and build. His complexion was very fair, with freckles, and he had sandy-colored hair; almost like a young me, only I was never skinny. Nick was also tall and skinny—but with much darker skin and brown hair.

Walking with me for a few miles, Ian posed a continuous stream of intelligent questions. Of course, he asked the typical ones: "Why are you walking across America?" "Where have you walked?" "Where will you be going from here?" Surprisingly—coming from a boy his age—he queried, "What do you hope to accomplish?" Then he followed that question with another heavy one, "What will this trip mean to you when you're finished," followed by, "How will walking across America change your life?" The more questions I answered, the more Ian's wheels turned and the more new questions he thought of, which he fired at me like a seasoned investigative reporter.

Finally I said, "If I keep answering all these questions, I won't have anything left for my book."

Ian asked, "Are you writing a book?"

"Not yet," I answered. "When I finish, I think I'll want to write a book about all the people and places of this walk—including you."

Ian smiled and said, "That would be cool."

Ian mentioned that his parents were homeschooling him.

"They are doing a great job!" I said.

It was such a pleasant experience to walk with Ian. He was so bright, inquisitive and worldly. If only all our youth could be as special as this kid. It had me thinking, *What has gone wrong? Why aren't there vast numbers of Ians?*

Two hours later it was time to part. We had walked together for more than six miles and had reached Ian's house, which was on my planned route. I had enjoyed this little guy's company so much and I was deeply touched by his goodness. Ian hugged me and told me, "I'm thrilled to have been a part of your walk." He continued, "I will cherish my walk with you for the rest of my life!"

I was so moved that I was caught off guard. Ian's sentiment left me tongue-tied and I was already emotionally fragile. The combination of the two brought tears to my eyes that I could not stifle, and soon they rolled down my cheeks. I didn't want Ian to see me crying so I just kept moving, trying to get away quickly before the waterworks really opened up. I didn't have the presence of mind to say it then, so I'll say it now: "Ian, thanks so much for walking with me. I will cherish those moments for the rest of my life."

Chapter Fifty-Four
Place of the Smelly Onion

It's wonderful to be here in the
great state of Chicago.

—**Dan Quayle**

After bidding Indiana adieu, I crossed into Lansing, Illinois, and checked into another "sybaritic" Super 8 Motel. Ahead of schedule today, I parked myself in the lobby hoping to find someone to chat with about Chicago. It happened that Renee, the night desk clerk, was an expert on the subject. She was petite, I'm guessing she was not even five feet tall and not more than ninety pounds, with cropped blonde hair, like a pixie. I could've twirled her around on one finger.

"Except for changing planes in the airport, I have never been to Chicago." I told Renee.

"Walking is the best way to see the city," said Renee, "because driving is such a nightmare." She urged me to walk the "Magnificent Mile" in downtown Chicago and make sure to go through Grant Park. Then she offered a warning: "Don't go to the South Side because it's dangerous."

Native Americans called Chicago the "Place of the Smelly Onion." Legend says that in the past the area was a place of wild onion fields that had a putrid aroma and the Indians living here had used the word "Chicagua"—the Smelly Onion Patch. We know it as the "Windy City." Renee claimed it had nothing to do with the powerful winds blowing across Lake Michigan, but rather from "The wind blowing from the lips of its politicians."

We chatted mindlessly and aimlessly until midnight.

I soon discovered that my Super 8 bed sagged to the floor. The "hot" water was lukewarm at best. And because of the noise generated by the all-night restaurant next door, I didn't get much sleep.

The free continental breakfast offered the next morning was not much of a consolation for the substandard amenities: the food was inedible, and the coffee was bitter and undrinkable. No wonder it was free; no one in their right mind would have considered paying for it.

My route this morning took me north on Halstead Street and through the "dangerous" South Side, a mostly black neighborhood. I was not surprised to find the people here friendly and pleasant. Some were actually delighted that I was fearless enough to walk this way. Of course, if I got murdered, I would be viewed as a fearless idiot.

Yes, there was rampant poverty and rows of dilapidated buildings. This was a ghetto. And yes, I saw gang members, pre-pubescent prostitutes, and too many pregnant teens. I saw young boys buying drugs from older boys, and unshaven men on door stoops drinking themselves into a stupor. I saw squatters who were apparently living in the abandoned buildings, despite the fact that they often burned down when a junkie carelessly put down his or her crack pipe.

Bad as things were though, many people here offered me a big smile or at least a non-hostile stare. *What's this old, fat white guy walking through our neighborhood for?* many must have been thinking to themselves. When directly asked that question, I said, "I decided that if I was going to walk across America, I would have to experience Chicago—all of Chicago." That seemed to satisfy the curious ones.

Suddenly, as I glanced up, I stopped in my tracks. I couldn't believe it! Attached to the side of an abandoned building was a tattered, ragged campaign poster: "Barack Obama for State Senate."

Hey! I actually knew that skinny dude, I thought. He was one of the reasons I drew my route through Chicago. When I was in my third year in law school, Barack was in his first year. Professor Derrick Bell, our mutual mentor, had introduced us.

I really liked Barack. Everybody seemed to like him. He possessed a quiet, confident intelligence. Nothing ever seemed to ruffle or rattle him. Because we were both "older" students, we had a special respect for each other. There was something about his infectious smile, framed by his short Afro and his leather jacket, which made him particularly striking, almost luminous.

During my last year of law school, when I'd often show up to class with Nicholas in tow, I'd sometimes have to leave the lecture hall whenever he started to cry. One thing that touched me about Barack was the special attention he paid to Nicholas. Barack teased me about my being the only one at school who took an infant to classes. He would put his finger in Nicholas' hand and gently shake it until he got my boy to smile. Barack clearly liked people, especially children, and they undoubtedly liked him. He stood out as one of the nicest people I had met at law school.

I remember the day Barack stopped by my "Walk for Hunger" fundraising table in the student center, known as the "Hark." The Walk for Hunger is a tradition in Boston, held every year on the first Sunday in May, since 1969. It is a twenty-mile circular walk, beginning in Boston, continuing into the western suburbs and then back into Boston. The walk raises millions of dollars each year to help feed people in food pantries. It was the first organized charity walk that I ever participated in back in 1985.

I was talking with a fellow student, Mitch Lasser, who had become my closest friend from the very first day of law school when he popped in my room to introduce himself. Obama could have easily slipped by and avoided me like so many others did. But Barack seemed genuinely interested that this older law student in his forties was doing a twenty-mile charity walk.

"Are you really going to walk twenty miles?" he asked me.

Mitch piped in, "If he says he's going to do it, he's going to do it,"

"Sounds like a long walk," said Barack.

"Well, not for me," I replied.

"Okay," said Barack, smiling, "put me down for fifty cents a mile."

As he signed my pledge sheet, he reached into his pocket and handed me a ten-dollar bill. Back in 1989, ten dollars was a lot of money for a law student, especially for Barack, who, like me, was on a scholarship and usually didn't have two nickels to rub together.

"Well," Mitch piped in, "if he's doing fifty cents, I'll have to do a dollar a mile."

I also remembered Barack's elbows. In law school, we had our own basketball court in the Hemenway Gym. Since I was no longer driving a cab, thanks to Lou Mitchell's financial assistance, I had time to blow off steam on the parquet floor after a long day of classes. The games were every bit as competitive as the NBA playoffs. Since I was older and slower than the other players I usually parked my ass under the basket so I could grab the rebounds. Barack was often there, too, jostling me for position.

He was a crafty rebounder, although he didn't look like one. He wasn't tall and rugged like the typical player under the boards. His arms were much longer than you would expect for a guy his height. He used his elbows like weapons. Even though they were skinny, they inflicted much pain on my arms, shoulders, elbows, and on several occasion my face. More than once I wanted to smack him. I finally had to stop playing because I was just too old for that kind of physical exertion.

In my third year, I had to write what's referred to as a "third-year paper." I called it "The Struggle That Must Be," a title I borrowed from a book of that name. In my paper, I examined how the law had failed to resolve the problem of racism, and I offered several legal solutions.

Professor Bell, my advisor, critiqued it. He asked if I'd consider writing another two chapters. He wanted me to describe "two scenarios, one in which race relations deteriorate severely, and the second in which America made great strides toward racial equality."

Back to work I went. My final chapter was a several-page fictional letter to the grandson of Martin Luther King, allegedly written in 2020. In it I reported to the young King, that my classmate, Barack Obama, became President of the United States. First, he got elected governor of Massachusetts. After that, he defeated the legendary Ted Kennedy and took over his seat in the U.S. Senate. Finally, I wrote, in a race against Newt Gingrich, he'd captured the White House in 2004. Of course, I knew this was utterly ridiculous, but I did it to please Professor Bell, who was also very fond of Barack, (that final thesis is housed in the permanent collection of the Harvard Law Library).

The following year, I was delighted to learn that Barack had been elected the first black president of the Harvard Law Review. The fame landed him a contract with Times Books, a publishing imprint of *The New York Times*, to write a book on race relations. It evolved into a memoir, published a couple of years later, and called *Dreams from My Father: A Story of Race and Inheritance*. Of course, I ran out and bought it, read it, and absolutely loved it, but I don't think it did all that well. It was a pity, because the guy could really write. I heard it didn't even pay back the publisher's advance.

Walking in Chicago in 1997 I found out that Barack was a first-term Illinois State Senator, probably spending most of his time down in Springfield, the state capital, which is about a three-and-a-half-hour drive south of Chicago.

I asked a few people in the neighborhood about him. One woman told me that Barack was very popular. He had run in the Democratic primary without opposition and had been elected to the Illinois Senate with around 90 percent of the vote. She also told me that his wife, Michelle, was even more popular than he was.

"Michelle? Could it be Michelle Robinson?" I opined. I had met Michelle in my first year of law school. My mentor and dear friend, Professor David Wilkins, had introduced us. Michelle was as stunning as she was bright. She was always dressed to the nines, not a hair out of place, and was the epitome elegance. At the time, we were both heavily involved in recruiting minorities for our undergrad schools. I knew she was from Chicago and I had heard that Barack had married a girl who had gone to Harvard Law School.

Moments later, someone in the neighborhood confirmed it. Until that moment, I had no idea Barack had met and married another one of my admired classmates! Michelle had graduated in 1988—the year before Barack had arrived at law school—and I knew she had promptly left the Cambridge area. Barack didn't enter until the following fall. I wondered how their paths crossed.

As I walked along, I asked a few more people and eventually found out how they met. Apparently, in the months between his first and second years in law school, Barack was a summer intern at Sidley Austin, a Chicago law firm. Michelle, who was a first-year associate at the firm, was apparently his boss. They fell in love and later got married in 1992.

Our mutual connections in law school were Professors Charles Ogletree and David Wilkins. In fact, it was in Wilkins' office where I first met Michelle. It was David's first year teaching, and he was already a very popular professor, especially as far as Michelle and I were concerned, because we were both heavily committed to racial activism, as was Professor Wilkins.

Now, I was more determined to try to reach out and catch up with Barack and Michelle while I was in Chicago.

I continued north on Halstead into downtown Chicago and took a right on Jackson Street. I immediately spotted a restaurant named "Lou Mitchell's." Since this is the name of my benefactor from Columbus, Ohio, and my younger boy's first and middle names, of course I had to stop and eat there. Interestingly, it was located between Jefferson and Clinton Streets, which are the middle and last names of our president, Bill Clinton.

After a great meal, I strolled up Michigan Avenue, along the Magnificent Mile, weaving my way to the waterfront. There, I walked to the imposing sea wall. A stiff breeze came, off Lake Michigan. It made me cold and uncomfortable, even though the temperature was in the nineties. I lay down, wrapped myself in towels to keep warm, and promptly fell asleep.

When I woke up, there was a TV camera in my face. In fact, the reporter had just completed her interview of Charles. He was beaming, obviously happy to have gotten the attention of the reporter and thrilled to be on TV.

I watched the segment later on in my motel room. The reporter's voiceover began: "If you had walked from Boston to Chicago in the heat of the summer, you'd probably be tired. He *is* tired. He is Don Brown, known as 'The Walking Man,' and he has just arrived at Chicago's lakefront." As she spoke, I was filmed sleeping on the seawall, draped in towels. Ever since then, I have been usually called "The Walking Man" whenever I have dealt with the press.

After my soporific interview, I strolled along the lakefront. It literally took my breath away. I felt like I was high on morphine again. The visual blend of man's and nature's handiwork was awe-inspiring. I could have easily lived there.

We drove to our motel, adjacent to O'Hare International Airport. At 7 P.M. I phoned Barack's office. One of his aides told me he would try to arrange for us to get together in the morning.

I picked up a book but it was hard to concentrate because of the incessant airplane noise at O'Hare

One of my sisters had lived most of her life in East Boston, a mere 500 yards from the runways of Logan Airport. Whenever I called her, at one point in the conversation she'd stop me in mid-sentence and say, "Hold on. Can't hear you. There's a plane taking off." But other than that, she claimed it didn't bother her at all. She said that a couple of weeks after she moved in, she simply stopped hearing the planes. I would later live near Boston's Logan Airport and find out for myself that you quickly learn to tune out the sound of the planes.

Around midnight I was just falling asleep when my cell phone rang. *It must be Barack or Michelle,* I thought. I was disappointed to hear, "Sorry, wrong number," when I answered the call. Hopefully I'd hear from them in the morning.

At dawn, we drove back to Grant Park where I had ended the walk the previous day. I worked my way through the park, then along the shoreline of Lake Michigan toward Evanston and Kenilworth. If I didn't hear from the Obamas soon, it would be too late to drive back to Chicago and visit them. Maybe Barack hadn't gotten the message, because he was the type of guy who would always return a call.

As I continued walking along Lake Shore Drive, I saw softball and soccer games, along with volleyball matches. I passed (or was passed by) thousands of runners, walkers and skateboarders. There were lovely sandy beaches, beautifully manicured lawns, and fancy, tall apartment buildings overlooking the park and the lake. I especially enjoyed the discrete bike paths.

The North Side of Chicago was quite cosmopolitan. Along the way, I traversed the globe—a slice of India, Russia and Asia and all of the Middle East. I heard their music and smelled their cuisines. I was suddenly very hungry.

I strutted up the western shore of Lake Michigan and crossed into Wisconsin, headed for Milwaukee.

Unfortunately, I didn't hear back from Barack. I'm not sure I ever told him of my silly prediction about his becoming president of the United States. Maybe Professor Bell told him. I had no idea.

Looking back now, knowing that my prediction had come to pass, I was so proud that I had the good fortune to attend law school with our president and first lady.

Coming full circle, in 2011 my son Nick completed an internship at the White House as part of the First Lady's staff. Maybe he knew something when he was a baby and grabbed our future president's fingers with his little hand.

Chapter Fifty-Five

Brew Town

Beer is proof that God loves
us and wants us to be happy.

—Benjamin Franklin

I began the day just outside Milwaukee and through some of its south side neighborhoods. It appeared to be a relatively small and quiet city, with many lovely Victorian homes.

In Detroit, everything is named after cars. In Milwaukee, it's beer. There's the Pabst Brewery, Miller Brewing, Schlitz, and much more. You can go to the Pabst Mansion and the Pabst Theater. Even the Major League Baseball team is called the "Brewers" and they play in Miller Park.

I knew Milwaukee mostly from being a football fan. Until the mid-nineties, the Green Bay Packers had played half of their home games in Milwaukee. When I was a lad, I used to wonder why they called the team the "Green Bay Packers." I had thought of them as a Milwaukee team because it seemed like they played there all the time.

This was back in the time of Vince Lombardi, Paul Horning, Jim Taylor, Bart Starr and Jerry Kramer. That was "smash mouth" football at its best. Those were tough teams so I related tough with Milwaukee.

The city brought back incredible memories from long ago.

When I was in junior high, late at night when the airwaves were less cluttered, I would listen to baseball games in distant cities. You could barely hear the announcers but back then, in the days long before we were so connected through the Internet and cable television, it was a thrill to listen to a broadcast from so far away. Hearing announcers in those faraway places always had me thinking about being a wanderer. One night I tuned into a Milwaukee station. The Milwaukee Braves were playing the Pittsburgh Pirates. The Braves, having moved from Boston a few years earlier, were one of my favorite teams. Little did I know I was about to hear one of the most famous games in baseball history. It was about the sixth inning when I began to realize that the Pittsburgh pitcher, Harvey Haddix, was pitching a perfect game. No batter had reached base for the Braves, which was unlikely. The Braves team was loaded with great hitters, the likes of

Hank Aaron, Eddie Mathews, and Joe Adcock to name a few. To be pitching a perfect game by itself was an incredible feat. To be pitching a perfect game against *those* players was even more incredible.

As the innings went by, Haddix continued to retire every single Braves batter he faced. There was a problem though as the Pirates hadn't scored either. The game reached the end of nine innings, still scoreless. Haddix had retired all twenty-seven batters. He had pitched a perfect game. Amazingly though, the game wasn't over.

The tenth inning was three up and three down for the Braves. The eleventh and twelfth were the same. Haddix had pitched an unbelievable twelve-inning perfect game and the Pirates still had not scored either. In the top half of the thirteenth inning the Pirates still were unable to score to enable Haddix to record the win in this incredible game. The bottom half of the thirteenth was a comedy, featuring an error. The Braves shortstop, Felix Mantilla, ended the perfect game when he reached first base on an error. It had to have been a huge disappointment for Haddix, having retired every batter he faced up until that point. If only his team had been able to score a mere one run, he would have recorded the only extra-inning perfect game in Major League history.

The comedy would soon unfold as the next batter, Hank Aaron, one of the game's all-time greatest hitters, was intentionally walked. With runners on first and second, Joe Adcock came to the plate. The lumbering first baseman was a feared power hitter and he quickly ended the game as he hit what should've been a three-run homer. The base runners lost their focus, laughing and celebrating, and Joe Adcock passed Hank Aaron on the base path, causing Aaron to be called out. Adcock was awarded only a single as he had only reached first base before he passed Aaron. Mantilla however scored, and that was the only run of the game. It was a most bizarre ending to a most incredible game. While for twelve innings it had been perfect game, in the record books it doesn't even show as a perfect game, because ultimately it wasn't. But it was perhaps the single greatest pitching exhibition in the history of Major League Baseball. Given the way baseball is today with pitchers generally only lasting five or six innings, allegedly to preserve their arms, it was a feat that will certainly never be duplicated.

* * *

Early in the afternoon, we stopped at a gas station for a cold drink. The Patriots logo shirt I was wearing was a big mistake. Several guys tending the station were drinking Old Milwaukee beers and were all slightly inebriated. Not surprisingly, they were all rowdy Packers fans. They told me, "The Patriots aren't nothin'."

They did seem intrigued about and even impressed with my walk across America. One of the drunkest among them called the local CBS affiliate to inform them about some "real" news in Beer City that day. He told the person on the phone: "Yea, and he's wearing a New England Patriots jacket, but we can't hold that against him. He just doesn't know any better."

An hour later I was back on the highway, moving west, when a crew from CBS showed up in their fancy satellite-on-the-roof van to do an interview. The reporter quickly cranked up my emotions by asking about my family. "I miss them so much," I told her as I welled up. We chatted for a few minutes about my boys. After I had finished the interview, and they were packing up the van, the reporter came back to ask me one more question. She really zinged me with her query: "Why are you doing this walk if you miss your family so much?"

My voice cracked, and tears began to roll down my face as I responded, "My life wouldn't be complete if I didn't find out if I could do it—and my family completely understands and supports me."

Half an hour later, still reeling from pondering that question, a car suddenly pulled over about 100 feet ahead of me. Out jumped a smiling young woman in her thirties. She was pretty, curvy, and a snappy dresser. She walked right up to me and announced that she wished she could join me. Despite my copious perspiration, she put her arms around me and kissed me smack on the lips, long and hard. Before I could say a word, she had jogged back to her car and drove away. She had succeeded in taking my breath away. She had taken me by surprise as I was lost in thought about my sons. I never got to say "thanks for being interested."

With dusk approaching, an older gentleman walked up to me and asked if he could join me for a few miles. His name was Rodney Schultz. He was from Waukesha, just west of Milwaukee. We walked together and talked about our love of walking, our families, and our careers. I told him about my longstanding dream of walking to the Big Sur. He said "I wish I could go with you, I know how beautiful it is."

Like me, Rodney was a prostate cancer survivor. His cancer was several years back and he had to have surgery, My scare had been the previous fall, and I was really lucky as I only had a regimen of chemo.

Rodney was very concerned about living healthy as he was so thrilled about being a grandfather. He was sixty-five and had just retired. Also an avid bicyclist, like me he also raised money for charities. Just before his bout with cancer, Rodney was a contestant in the "Trek 100," a 100-mile biking event through southeast Wisconsin. He said the heat and humidity were unbearable. After ninety miles, most riders had dropped out. Not Rodney, he wouldn't quit.

"I couldn't stand the thought of going home and telling everyone I'd quit," he said. "I did come in a distant last, but at least I finished." I completely understood.

A few miles later, after a long silence, Rodney announced that he wanted to sing a couple of songs for me. He sang "How Great Thou Art" in a rich baritone that surprisingly brought me to tears. Together, we then sang "God Bless America." It might sound corny, but walking across our country shed a whole new light on that song for me. I don't know if I harmonized vocally with Rodney, but this was one of those experiences that truly touched me.

When we reached his home, Rodney invited Charles and me to have dinner with his family and to spend the night. It was so special to be in a home instead of a hotel. It was like being a part of a family—if only for a day. Rodney's wife, Jessica, and his son Glenn's wife, Samantha, with their kids, made us feel right at home. After dinner, I called Honduras to talk to my sons. Rodney grabbed the phone and talked to them too. He told them, "Don't worry about your dad, he's doing great."

When it was time to retire, Rodney took us to the master bedroom. I had assumed they had an extra guest room so was a bit uncomfortable. "Where will you sleep?" I asked.

"The sofas," he replied. "You are my guests."

How special, I thought, *that they would give up their room for a total stranger.* Actually, strangers, plural—I had to share the king-sized bed with Charles. This was a first for me, sleeping in a bed with a man. But I was grateful to Rodney and his wife nonetheless.

In the morning, Rodney took Charles and me to his favorite breakfast place for steel-cut oatmeal. After our meal, I resumed my journey. Rodney walked six more miles with me before we said good-bye. I hugged him and thanked him. I told him, "It was a wonderful surprise for us to have a home-cooked meal and to sleep in a real home."

Time and again, the unsolicited kindness of strangers warmed my heart. These acts of generosity were spontaneous, and certainly unexpected, and they kept me moving ahead both in body and in spirit. I felt so privileged to experience the random acts of kindness. These times made me realize the goodness of most folks everywhere I walked.

Chapter Fifty-Six

Bob Ferrari

Death is nothing else but going home to God, the
bond of love will be unbroken for all eternity.
—**Mother Teresa**

On my walk toward Madison, motorcycles passed me in far greater numbers than cars. These were not the outlaw biker types but families going for a Sunday ride. In this part of the country many used bikes for recreation and others to commute.

When I was about eleven years old I got a lecture about the dangers of motorcycles from my neighbor Bob Ferrari, a retired Massachusetts State Police captain who was on the motorcycle squad. His warning stuck with me: "Donny, there are only two kinds of people who ride motorcycles—those of us who have to and the crazies. Motorcycles are dangerous. Stay away from them."

I thought back to when I first met Bob. He was probably in his fifties at the time and was forced to retire because suddenly, with no known problems or illnesses, he had lost the use of his legs. He moved around using two canes. He should not have been up and around but he was determined to stay active. My school bus stop was directly in front of Bob's house and he was out on his front lawn one afternoon when the bus dropped me off.

He spotted me and said, "Hey, kid, come over here." His voice was hostile sounding so I wasn't too keen on approaching him. At the time, I had no idea who he was. Despite my apprehension, I slowly made my way over to him as he struggled to stay upright on his useless legs.

Apparently, my reputation as a troubled kid preceded me, and Bob knew all about me. I had never talked to him before. I wondered how he knew about me. He began, "So I hear you think you're a tough guy. You don't look so tough to me."

I stood there speechless.

He continued, "You've been in all kinds of trouble, breaking into houses, mouthing off, disobeying people—and you have become well-known around town as a pain in the ass."

Obviously someone had been filling him in on my difficulties as a troubled kid. "What's it to you?" I asked sarcastically. To me he seemed like another doddering old fool and I expected that would be the end of our conversation. I turned to walk away, muttering under my breath. Bob, however, had a lesson to teach me. Before I could take my first step, he wacked me with his cane on the back of my knees and I crumbled to the ground.

"Get your ass into my house and sit down at the kitchen table," he barked.

I didn't hesitate and did what he said, terrified about what would happen if I didn't follow his orders.

When Bob sat down at the table with me he said, "I need help in the afternoon. You are going to come here every day after school and stay with me until suppertime when Kay (his wife) comes home. Then you will go home, have dinner and do your chores, help your mother, and go to bed. That way you won't be able to get into any trouble. Do you understand me?"

I was trembling but an inner voice told me this would be okay. From that day on, I showed up at Bob's house every day during the week as soon as I got off the bus. I started out by mowing the grass, shoveling the driveway, running to the store to get things for Bob. Before long, he taught me how to earn money. I wandered the entire neighborhood, picking up piles of newspapers and storing them in his garage. When the space was full, Bob called the "junkman" who loaded the papers into his truck and paid me $30 for the lot. I used my earnings to buy Christmas presents for Bob and Kay, my mother, and my baby sister, Nancy. After that, I had no money left but I was thrilled; this was the first time I ever had money to buy Christmas presents

I grew to love Bob and his family who took me under their protective wing. As Bob had predicted, I didn't get into any trouble during the year or so that I spent with him. Despite his gruff exterior, he was kind and good to me and I had grown to enjoy our time together. I had begun to practice the self-discipline I had learned from Bob. I learned how to make some money. Most importantly, I learned that when people cared about me, it made me feel good about everything. Bob was so kind and thoughtful and always guided me towards excellence. But our time together was soon cut short.

One day, I got off the bus as usual but Bob wasn't outside to greet me as he always was. I knocked on his door and Kay answered, which was also unusual. She worked at a local bank and was never home during the day. Her eyes were red and swollen, and dried tears stained her cheeks. She could barely speak and told me, "Go home, Bob doesn't need you today." I knew something was wrong but I didn't ask why. I went home wondering what had happened.

After supper, as I was climbing into bed, my mother sat down and told me what had happened. "Bob died today," she whispered.

I was devastated. I cried for hours and never went to sleep. I didn't want to believe this was true and the next day I wanted to go to Bob's house and see for myself. Maybe this was a mistake, maybe he was just sick and now he was okay. I kept thinking that I would get off the bus and find him still alive. But as the bus approached my stop I saw scores of cars, many of them police cruisers, parked all around Bob's house. I had hoped against hope that I would see Bob standing on his lawn, waiting for me as he always had. When he wasn't I knew for certain that my mother had told the truth; he had died.

Weeks passed and then months. My grief engulfed me and I felt like I was in a fog. Bob was perhaps the very first mentor in my life; a beacon of light who helped guide me through my difficult formative years. When he died, something inside me died as well. It was not too long after that when my own father died. Strangely, I had no feeling of loss then like I had when Bob died. Kay, Bob's wife, took over the duty of being my mentor. For the rest of my life, until she died in the late nineties, she was a constant source of support for me.

Chapter Fifty-Seven
Mary in the Morning

Nothing's quite as pretty as Mary in the morning
Chasing the rainbow in her dreams so far away
And when she turns to touch me I kiss her fingers so softly
—Michael Rashkov, Johnny Cymbal

Glancing at the map on my way to Madison, I felt right at home—if not a little homesick. It seemed the original settlers who named the towns near my route must have come from Massachusetts. The towns of East Cambridge, Deerfield, Milton, Middleton, Arlington, Roxbury, Merrimac, Stoughton, Belmont and Fitchburg were just up ahead.

The next morning, I walked south from Madison to Stoughton, where I stopped at a gas station to fuel up and for a cold drink. I reached into the van for my wallet. When I turned to put my credit card into the gas pump, I found myself standing face to face with a woman who was indescribably beautiful.

"Hello," she said dreamily, "I'm Mary. My boys and I saw you walking on the highway from Madison, on our way to the city and back. Tell me about Walking USA."

Her three shy boys, one large, one medium and one small, were standing a few feet away. One of them reminded me of my own son Nicholas; the next down in size, of course, reminded me of Louis. The little one was like a miniature bear, small and round, but with a perpetual smile.

We talked about my expedition for a while. She told me she was divorced and was raising her boys by herself. She didn't take her eyes off of me the entire time we spoke. I couldn't take my eyes off of her either.

Before I said good-bye and got back on the road, she gave me her phone number.

"Call me, if you feel like," she said, smiling warmly.

I then pulled her to me and kissed her. The kiss was long enough to be dangerous. Her boys had puzzled looks on their faces. I couldn't blame them as I was puzzled myself.

Off she drove, leaving me with unexpected feelings. I wanted to go with her.

Later, as I was crossing the Illinois border, I was lonely. I wanted to call her. But I was afraid.

Chapter Fifty-Eight
The Fall from Grace

I guess I thought as an American
Tragedy...It has all the elements—the
Success is larger than life, and the
Fall from grace is equally larger than life.
—Peter Guralnick

The next morning's walk was an ordeal. I hadn't slept well and I was starting the day exhausted—never a good thing. I tossed and turned all night thinking about Mary and I couldn't stop thinking about her even now. I knew this was ridiculous. Barely awake, I stumbled along, passing oceans of Illinois cornfields gleaming in all directions. I inadvertently stepped on a beer can on the side of the road and almost lost my balance. A bad fall could end my odyssey and it would all be because I found myself distracted by a woman I hardly knew. How ridiculous was that? Acting upon my impulses would be not only absurd but catastrophic. Even with the faults in my marriage I was married nonetheless, and had two young children. I didn't want to do anything that would call my character into question. *I should throw Mary's phone number away at once*, I told myself.

I had made catastrophic mistakes before. I didn't want to make any more. One per lifetime was more than enough.

The one I made in 1992 still weighed me down like a thousand kilos. It was always there, haunting every step I took. I knew there was no point in dwelling in the past, but I couldn't help it. I'd had it all—and I threw it away.

It began in 1990, the very first day I opened my law office in Dorchester, a rundown, minority neighborhood in Boston. On that very first day, I thought I'd gotten lucky. An elderly black man walking with a cane slowly shuffled in the door carrying a suitcase. "I'm John Storms," he said, introducing himself. He told me he wanted to declare bankruptcy.

"What's in the suitcase?" I asked.

"All the paperwork from my loans," he said.

I asked if he would leave the suitcase with me so I could look through the papers. "Come back tomorrow so we can talk."

Mr. Storms agreed and left the suitcase. Since I had no other clients yet, I sat down to review all the documents right away. What I found astonished me. Mr. Storms had been the victim of unscrupulous lending practices the likes of which I couldn't imagine. It took evil and callous people to exploit a poor, elderly gentleman and rob him of his home, which is exactly what the lenders were doing. Had they robbed someone of their wallet at gunpoint, they would be locked up in prison. Instead, they were extorting people of their life savings while they lived high on the hog, masquerading as legitimate businesspeople.

The suitcase was filled with documents that were obviously false and misleading. For example, the loan application stated that Mr. Storms was sixty years old when in fact he was eighty-four. The application also stated that he was white, when he was obviously black. Furthermore, his income had been greatly inflated, so that he could "income qualify" for the mortgage. Mr. Storms had included his actual federal tax returns, along with the doctored ones that had been filled out by the criminal who had engineered this scam.

Even though I was a wet-behind-the-ears lawyer, I knew that the terms of the loan were beyond usurious. The mortgage's annual percentage rate was officially 24 percent, which was in itself outrageous. But he had also been charged seven points (7 percent of the amount borrowed) by the lenders at the closing, and the loan ballooned (had to be repaid) in five years! So without even using a calculator, I knew that his APR (Annual Percentage Rate—the true interest rate of this loan) was approximately 150 percent!

The next day, Mr. Storms returned to my office. Together, we went over all the documents. He explained how the loan originators were actually home-repair contractors. They had knocked on his door and persuaded him that he needed new aluminum siding, new storm windows, and a handicap ramp.

Mr. Storms, whose home was mortgage-free, told them he didn't have the money for these improvements. They told him not to worry. They would take care of making sure he got a loan against his house to do the work. They even produced a blank loan application and assured him they would help him fill it out. Mr. Storms said he didn't even have to sign the loan application. They signed it for him.

A few weeks later, the loans were miraculously approved and the renovations began. The workmanship proved to be quite substandard. For example, the handicap ramp was too precariously constructed to be used at all. The aluminum siding had been installed by amateurs, because it was uneven and not level.

After several similar transactions, Mr. Storms had "borrowed" $150,000 against his home. He soon realized that he could not afford the monthly payments because they far exceeded his only source of income—his monthly Social Security check. When the foreclosure letters began to arrive, he decided to stuff all the papers into a suitcase and seek a lawyer. After being turned away by four, he arrived at my office.

I immediately went to the Suffolk County Registry of Deeds and began researching Mr. Storms' mortgage history. As I looked up his transactions in the grantor-grantee indices, I noticed other similar transactions. I dug deeper. I found hundreds of transactions involving the same lenders. All of the homeowners lived in the minority neighborhoods of Dorchester, Roxbury and Mattapan.

What I had stumbled upon was a cabal of predatory lenders, preying on elderly and minority homeowners. These loans all had extremely high interest rates, high prepayment penalties, balloon payments, exorbitant late fees, and single-premium credit insurance. The lenders had falsified loan applications, forged borrowers' signatures, changed the loan terms at closing, misrepresented loan terms, physically obscured key terms, and had borrowers sign documents with key terms omitted.

Within a couple of weeks, I had filed a lawsuit on Mr. Storms' behalf against eight banks and several home-improvement contractors for their fraudulent behavior.

My lawsuit got the attention of many people, including the press.

In the fall of 1990, reporter Gary S. Chafetz wrote an article that appeared in the *Boston Herald* titled, "Hammering Away: Attorney Goes to Bat for Buyers in Trouble." (Early the following year, Chafetz moved to *The Boston Globe*.)

On May 6, 1991, *Boston Globe* reporters Chafetz and Peter S. Canellos had a front-page story, whose headline read: "Elderly Poor Losing Homes in Loan Scam: Unregulated Lenders Offer High Rates, Risks." The story featured my clients Charles and Irma Sorrel, two elderly black homeowners, who were now squatting—the legal term is "tenants at sufferance"—in their former home, which had just been foreclosed by a predatory lender named Growth Mortgage Company of Brookline. The Sorrels had borrowed $88,000 for aluminum siding, which had also been improperly installed. Their monthly mortgage payment was $2,062. Their only source of income was a monthly Social Security check of $800.

The response to this story was overwhelming. I was interviewed repeatedly by the media. Later that year, those reporters were nominated for a Pulitzer Prize, based on a series of stories they published that soon became known as the Second Mortgage Lender Scandal. These stories also gained national attention because predatory lending practices were not just unique to the Boston area.

The scam quickly became the focus of my practice. Soon, I had hundreds of clients, on whose behalf I was filing multiple lawsuits.

Because of the media attention and assistance from Congressman Joe Kennedy, the publicity generated a storm of indignation. Courts quickly handed down decisions in favor of my clients. Congress held hearings on the issue and proposed and passed legislation that would forever ban the practice of so-called "home renovators"—also known as "tinmen"—from preparing loan documents for borrowers, that were then presented to banks, which funded the loans, though based on fraudulent documentation. What made this story so intriguing was that the predatory second-mortgage lenders (who quickly folded their tents and skipped town) had sold their despicable loans to conventional banks, which were more than happy to reap the high interest rates and look the other way.

To make a long and satisfying story short, these banks rued the bad publicity. Recognizing their exposure, they quickly set up a billion-dollar fund to make restitution and to provide mortgage assistance to struggling homeowners and would-be homeowners in minority communities. Most of my clients, who had lost their homes to foreclosure, got them back. Others who were about to lose their homes to foreclosure had their loans forgiven or drastically reduced.

Eventually, Massachusetts and other states across the country passed legislation to stop the predatory lending practices I had uncovered. Many states passed a "Three-Day Right of Rescission," which meant that borrowers had three days after signing a second mortgage to rescind their decision. Furthermore, legislation was passed to regulate and license contractors and to set up a fund to pay for shoddy work done by unlicensed contractors.

My law practice—Brown & Associates—was bursting at the seams. I had more business than I knew what to do with, and I didn't have the heart to turn away any of these vulnerable minority homeowners, who were about to lose their homes. I was working day and night, weekends and holidays.

It was incumbent on me to hire a lot more staff and open offices in other minority neighborhoods. But how would I finance this expansion? The banks hated my guts, of course, because I had cut into their profits and besmirched their reputations. They wouldn't lend me a cent and attorneys are barred from seeking financial investors.

Along with defrauded minority homeowners, I had also accepted some other clients. These were doctors, mostly chiropractors, who treated patients in minority communities. In many cases, insurance companies were refusing to pay the doctors, claiming that their patients' injuries were fraudulent. In a handful of cases, this was true. Nonetheless, I had been remarkably successful in threatening and bullying insurance companies into fulfilling their obligations to pay my doctor clients for services rendered. Hence, I had hundreds of thousands of dollars in clients' accounts that I was holding for those doctors.

Desperate for cash to expand my practice, I asked three doctors if I could borrow from their accounts. They all happily agreed. They told me to take what I needed. I borrowed almost $200,000 in this manner. The problem was that borrowing from clients' accounts, even with their permission, is a violation of the ethical code of conduct in the legal profession. And I knew it. I figured I'd quickly pay them back and no one would ever know or care.

I was wrong.

I quickly hired several lawyers. I opened two new offices. Before I knew it, I had spent the $200,000. As a result, we were able to accept hundreds of new victims of predatory lending.

It was also an extraordinarily stressful time in my life. My son Louis was born with a serious brain defect, and my beloved mother passed away.

A year later, one of the lawyers I had hired stumbled upon what I'd done. He was legally bound to report my transgression to the Board of Bar Overseers. All the lawyers in my firm, except three, promptly resigned. As a result, Brown & Associates was quickly shuttered.

I've often used my son's birth defects and my mother's death to make excuses for what I did. The fact is, what I did was inexcusable. I have only myself to blame. And I am deeply ashamed of what I did.

Against all odds, I had academically climbed Mt. Everest and had promptly jumped to my professional death.

The distant shore to which I had unknowingly been swimming for so many years was the magical land of the law. As an advocate for the poor, I was good at lawyering. I loved fighting for the underdog and I became a shrewd negotiator and a tough litigator.

I voluntarily gave up my license to practice law. I had already applied to the Board of Bar Overseers to have it reinstated. The hearing was scheduled in Boston for soon after my completion of this walk. As an eternal optimist, I had every reason to believe it would be reinstated, but I knew it would be an uphill battle. "The commingling of clients' funds" is considered a serious offense in the legal profession, perhaps worse than murder and drug-smuggling. After more than twenty restless years, I finally discovered what I was meant to do with my life. I became an attorney. I went on to accomplish some notable things. In my brief legal career, I revolutionized certain laws and regulations across the country that benefited many people, especially minority homeowners. I was very proud of that. But due to lack of funding, lack of the experience needed to run a thriving law practice, and a serious lapse of judgment, I blew it all up. I had achieved the impossible—and then inexplicably lit the fuse that destroyed it.

After having lost my license to practice law, I didn't waste any time getting back on my feet. I launched a medical billing company that also proved successful. Several years later, I sold the company and used the proceeds to repay the $200,000 I'd borrowed from my clients' accounts, along with any lingering debts of my former law firm. The $50,000 left over was what I used to fund my walk across America.

* * *

Reflecting on all this and what I had been through brought me back to reality and the serious consequences of acting on impulse instead of thoughtful consideration. I took the scrap of paper with Mary's phone number out of my pocket, ripped it up, and threw it away. The wind scattered the pieces into the cornfields nearby.

Walking along the verdant farmlands of central Illinois, I envied the farmer's life. It must be a simpler one. It was hard work for sure, but it can't possibly be as stressful as practicing law and then being suspended.

Somehow, I stumbled through another forty-mile day.

We arrived at our motel. I didn't have the energy to shower. I was asleep within minutes.

I wanted to be well rested for tomorrow's long walk. I was determined to reach the outskirts of Peoria, because the day after I would be meeting some people at the airport. My wife and my boys were flying in for a visit!

Chapter Fifty-Nine

Family Reunion

*Carry out a random act of kindness, with
no expectation of reward, safe in the knowledge
that one day someone might do the same for you.*
—Princess Diana

I sat at the Peoria airport, waiting anxiously for them to come out into view. I'd pictured them in my mind's eye constantly on my sojourn, replaying things they had said or places we had gone together, but it was no replacement for being with them. Seeing my boys in person again was beyond words!

Many hugs and kisses and squeals of joy later, we drove to where my walk left off the previous evening. The cross-country jaunt must continue uninterrupted. It was raining hard. Estela and I walked together for about ten miles. I'd be dissembling if I denied that my prolonged absence had not caused even more stress between us. Here I was gallivanting across the country and she was at home, holding down a full-time job while being a single mom.

The boys were having a ball in the van watching movies and visiting with Charles. When the rain stopped, they joined me, and we walked together for a couple of miles down the rural roads of western Illinois.

A few hours later I started feeling ill. I stopped to prick my thumb so I could test my blood sugar. It was extremely high, over 400. It made no sense. My diabetes was out of control, which perhaps explained why I had been feeling off my game for the past several days.

Finally, we crossed the mighty Mississippi River into Iowa. It's called the "The Father of Waters," and some say it created the Gulf of Mexico. By crossing the Mississippi, I guessed we were now officially in the West.

After a good night's sleep in a large motel room, we all walked into Mount Pleasant to plumb the depths of a giant flea market on the town common.

Two hours later, we were back on the road. Now, not only was I concerned about my diabetes, but my legs were bothering me, too. I forced myself to focus on each individual step, just putting one foot in front of the other. I was feeling depressed because I already rued the fact that my family would be leaving in a couple of days. I reminded myself not to rob myself of the moment.

The day's schedule had us walking from Burlington to Ottumwa. My wife walked with me for ten miles. Most of the way, millions of noisy grasshoppers—seen and unseen—surrounded us. They were flying and hopping in the nearby grass and on the road. Many had been squashed by cars and were now being further crunched by our shoes as we trudged along.

A few miles later there was a biological shift. There were thousands of butterflies fluttering around us. I'm sure there was a scientific reason for this but, not being a biologist, I did not know why. The butterflies fascinated my kids, who jumped out of the van and began collecting all sizes and colors of the beautiful insects. I couldn't imagine what they were going to do with them.

It was August 31, 1997, as we approached Des Moines. I was preparing for some significant media attention because I had scheduled a half-hour local-interest television news show, a radio interview, and an interview for a Sunday newspaper magazine. Suddenly, everything was cancelled. Diana, Princess of Wales, had just been killed in a car accident in Paris, France. Her death dominated the news. Like the grasshoppers on the side of the road, I was a forgotten nonentity.

I had planned to spend two full days in Des Moines but, given the circumstances, I reduced it to one.

* * *

My wife had been building up her endurance. She walked with me again the next morning, from Ottumwa toward Knoxville. We didn't have much to say to each other. It was obvious, I think, that we were on thin ice. She was beginning to appreciate the meditative soulfulness of walking, however, enjoying the peace and solitude as much as I was.

After a few miles, we stopped to rest on the side of the road by a farmhouse. I lay down on the sloped grassy shoulder and closed my eyes, listening to the breeze and the insects. A man from the farmhouse wandered down to see if we were okay. He was quickly joined by his wife and five blond children. Two of them were the same age as my kids. I explained what I was doing and the fellow talked about the travails of farm life. "Everyone has a cross to bear, and the grass is always greener," he said. He was tired of the slippery slope of farming, and worried they might lose their farm. He blamed President Clinton. I kept my mouth shut.

To help make ends meet, the father also worked part time for the Pella Corporation, the window and door manufacturer and a major employer in the area. He said, "I work so hard I barely have time to sleep or see my family."

I said, "I understand that story all too well."

We resumed the walk. After lunch, I walked alone into Indianola. From there, we drove the final few miles into Des Moines so my kids could have a night in a special room at the Embassy Suites Hotel before flying home. While the kids preferred room service and to remain behind to watch movies in the room, my wife and I dined out at The Iowa Steak House, which billed itself as the best steak house in the state.

They did offer the biggest restaurant steak I'd ever seen—a seventy-two-ounce sirloin. It was free if you could eat it all. I didn't know how anyone could ever do that, but the guy at the table next to us was making a heroic attempt.

Des Moines had the most beautiful capital building I had ever seen. It was built on a hill, overlooking the downtown area. The imposing structure had five gold domes, and, I'm told, they all glisten with twenty-three-carat gold.

Unfortunately, the time had come to take my family to the Des Moines airport. I hated to see my sons go. My long hours of solitude during the walk had made me more aware of how special they were in my life. By the same token, I also realized how little my wife now meant to me. Absence is supposed to make the heart grow fonder but my time away from Estela, and then seeing her again, made me realize that my feelings for her had dissipated over time until there was now nothing left at all.

It had been a magical visit with the kids but school started in two days and they had to get home. I kissed and hugged them for what seemed like forever. All three of us were crying. They boarded the plane with their mother and suddenly they were gone. I was not sure when I would see them again.

Distressed, I returned to the northwestern suburbs of Des Moines to resume my walk. It was back to the loneliness of a long-distance walker. Thoughts of my boys made it even more intense.

I didn't finish till after 11 P.M., exhausted, depressed, and alone—except for Charles, with whom I could barely communicate.

Chapter Sixty
The Day the Music Died

While (Buddy) Holly was touring England in 1958, he received an ominous message from Joe Meek, a British recording engineer and producer. On a night in January of that year, Meek had attended a tarot reading. The message delivered that night was "February third, Buddy Holly dies". Holly thanked Meek for the warning, but did not seem concerned since February the third (1958) had already passed. Buddy Holly would die on 3 February 1959.

—Angelfire

After a two-day walk through northern Iowa, I came to a little town called Clear Lake. I noticed an old poster on a fencepost, promoting a festival held the previous February. It was called "The Day the Music Died." My curiosity aroused, I set out to learn what it referred to. I had heard that phrase somewhere. Yes, I remembered. It was a line from the song "American Pie," which went: "Bye, bye Miss American Pie . . . the day the music died."

We stopped in a restaurant for dinner. I asked our waitress about the festival. She told me, "When I was a little girl, there was a big concert in Clear Lake one night and some famous singers were killed in a plane crash after the concert." She recalled, "One of them was Richie Valens."

Of course! In my early teens I used to listen to Richie Valens, along with the Big Bopper and especially Buddy Holly. I remembered waking up one morning to the news that a plane carrying the three of them had crashed in a blizzard. So here in Iowa was where the accident happened and thus the festival of "The Place the Music Died." The event is held every year on the anniversary of the crash to honor the memory of the trio.

As a teen, I had especially liked Buddy Holly's "Peggy Sue," "Oh Boy," "That'll be the Day," and "Maybe Baby." Richie Valens was somewhat of a newcomer. His big hits were "Donna" and "La Bamba." The Big Bopper was an even more recent arrival with only a novelty hit, "Chantilly Lace."

The waitress offered to call a friend who knew more details about the night of the crash. A few minutes later, Bill Bossy walked in. He was a jovial old guy, as round as he was tall, and sported a huge black handlebar mustache, which didn't really go with his silvery white Beatles haircut. He was a couple of years older than I was.

First, he wanted to hear about Walking USA, because he had seen the van and became curious about it when we had driven into town. After I gave him the twenty-five-words-or-less version, he promptly declared, "I'd like to quit my job and join you, but I have enough trouble walking from my car to my house."

Bill remembered the concert like it was yesterday. In fact, he attended the evening of rock-and-roll music with his high-school sweetheart, to whom he had been married thirty-six years. He remembered that the musicians were "really on" and that the crowd had loved the show.

Billy didn't find out about the crash until the next morning, the same day I had learned of it. The Clear Lake area, which was not used to national attention, was stunned. Bill remembered that there was also a commercial airliner crash that same morning in New York City. I didn't remember that.

As days went by, Bill learned what happened on the evening of February 2, 1959. "Buddy Holly, the Big Bopper (J.P. Richards), Richie Valens (Richie Valenzeula), Dion and the Belmonts, and another singer (whose name escaped Bill) arrived in town on a leased school bus as a part of their 'Winter Dance Party Show' national tour. They played here at the Surf Ballroom."

After the concert, apparently Buddy Holly was tired of traveling on an aging school bus with a marginal heating system. He also needed some extra time to wash a mountain of clothes. His wish to arrive quickly in the next town so he could visit a Laundromat cost him his life.

Holly chartered a small private plane that only seated three. His backup musicians, Tommy Allsup and Waylon Jennings, were supposed to travel with him. But the Big Bopper had the flu so he begged Jennings to give him his seat on the plane. Jennings agreed. Next, Richie Valens asked Tommy Allsup if he'd be willing to flip a coin for the remaining seat. Allsup agreed. Valens called "heads" and won the toss. Winning that toss cost him his life. Dion and the Belmonts, Allsup, Jennings, and all the other musicians departed by frigid school bus late that night for the next day's gig.

As Holly, the Big Bopper, and Valens were leaving for the airport, Holly was said to have remarked to Jennings, "I hope you freeze your ass off on the bus."

Jennings wisecracked back, "Yeah, and I hope your plane crashes."

It did. And the music died.

Bill recalled that there was no blizzard as had been often reported. It was just snowing lightly when the plane took off. People on the ground watched the plane disappear into the sky. Everything appeared normal. The twenty-one-year-old pilot apparently wasn't qualified to fly the plane at night or in the snow. When he didn't radio back within a few minutes after takeoff, the plane's owner became anxious.

It wasn't until morning that the plane was found in a nearby soybean field. It had apparently flown right into the ground. No one really knew why. Everyone on board was killed.

That evening, the surviving musicians decided to continue on tour as a tribute to their friends. They found a fifteen-year-old singer to fill in. His name was Bobby Vee. This was his big break and he went on to great fame.

Dion and the Belmonts also went on to great success, especially Dion who became a solo artist and still performs regularly. Waylon Jennings became a mega country star. In interviews, he often spoke of those last words he quipped to Buddy Holly. Those words haunted him all of his life.

In 1979, Tommy Allsup opened a club in Fort Worth, Texas. He called it "Tommy's Heads-Up Saloon," after the coin toss he lost to Richie Valens on February 2, 1959, the loss that saved Allsup's life.

Chapter Sixty-One
Mall Walking

Mall walking, or ambling around a shopping center for exercise, has become a major fitness option in the United States, and not just for senior citizens.

—Reuters

I was eating up the miles. Albert Lea was the town just across the Minnesota border we were trying to reach before quitting for the day. It had been hot, but when the sun slipped below the horizon, it became downright cold. Soon, the air was thick with fireflies. One of my favorite childhood memories was of chasing the flashing insects on hot summer nights and putting them in a jar with holes punched into the lid. I wished I could do that now, and send them to my kids.

For a distraction, I walked over to a pond. As I approached it, I disturbed a four-foot water snake. Deathly afraid of them, I jumped as it slithered away inches from my foot. My fright quickly passed as I was serenaded by a pair of loud dueling bullfrogs. Several perfectly still turtles, which had been sunning themselves on lily pads, were still in the sunning position, stacked three high. They seemed oblivious to my presence.

Not too far away, I saw a seventyish-year-old man fishing. I walked over and asked, "How's the fishing?"

He replied, "It's the best time of year to fish." He glanced at my vehicle and added, "Your van tells a story. It's a good thing you're walking through before the cold sets in, because soon it becomes real difficult to be outside."

We arrived in Northfield, Minnesota, to find the town all dressed up for the Defeat of the Jesse James Gang Celebration. I learned that on September 7, 1876, the outlaws rode into town to rob the bank. The town folk knew in advance and had prepared an ambush. Two of the gang members were killed instantly. A few days later, a posse hunted down and killed or captured four more. Only Jesse James and his brother, Frank, managed to get away.

The town of Northfield stages several reenactments of that rout each year. I guess it's their claim to fame. The itinerant carnival rides and games sprout up, drawing hordes of tourists.

From Northfield, I continued north towards Minneapolis and the Mall of America. The occupants of most passing cars went out of their way to wave hello. Minnesotans know how to welcome an outsider. Some drivers stopped to chat and congratulated me for what I was doing. It made me feel good to be appreciated, but more importantly, just to have people to talk to.

I watched planes approaching the Twin Cities (Minneapolis-St. Paul) Airport from the east. I had never seen two planes side by side gliding in for a landing. It looked dangerous. Walking suited me just fine.

Soon we reached the mall. Billed as the largest fully enclosed retail and family entertainment complex in the country, it opened in 1992. It has about 40 million visitors a year, which is about eight times the population of Minnesota. There are over 520 stores and restaurants. The food court itself could qualify as a town. In the middle of this behemoth is a seven-acre theme park—the largest indoor amusement park in the United States, including two roller coasters and many other rides. As if this place wasn't big enough already, I heard that a huge expansion was in the works: American excess at its best.

As I passed through the parking lot, I saw license plates from every state (except Hawaii) and most of the Canadian provinces. I was actually here by invitation from the local Mall Walkers Club. I guess I had arrived too late, as I couldn't seem to locate any of the members.

Although it would have been nice to have had some companions, I set off on my trek solo, as I was used to doing—but now I was in climate-controlled comfort and on perfectly level and polished flooring. I walked the seven miles and five levels of the mall in two hours. I was a bit overwhelmed by the extravagant consumerism. I must have seen twenty-five shoes stores alone. Charles was totally awed. He said, "Look like whole city in Brazil."

Chapter Sixty-Two

Twin Cities

Camping is nature's way of promoting the motel business.
—**Dave Barry**

Anxious to get on my way, I hurried outside. I had another fifteen miles to go before reaching downtown Minneapolis. Once there, I did a planned interview for the Minneapolis Sunday newspaper. The photographer walked with us for several more miles as we went away from the downtown area. We were on Interstate 394, headed west. He walked backwards, snapping photos of the van with the beautiful Minneapolis skyline in the background.

Soon after his departure, we were still on the interstate when we experienced our first flat tire of the trip. Fortunately, a friendly state trooper quickly arrived to assist us off the highway. We eventually figured out how to get the spare tire out from underneath the van. It was no small feat.

The flat tire proved to be a costly delay in time and money. After mounting the spare, we then had to drive around town to buy a replacement. The size of the tires on the van were not very common. We finally located an auto parts store that sold the size. Then we found a garage to put the new tire on the rim. We watched them struggle to reattach the spare under the van. I was glad they were doing it and not me. The chilly night had already set in by the time this problem was resolved so we called it quits for the day.

* * *

In the morning, just west of Minneapolis, I began trudging towards South Dakota. At the end of the day, I decided we would sleep in the van for the first time. I was worried that at sixty to seventy bucks a night, we would run out of money before we finished. We parked at a truck stop. I slept in the van's double bed, or at least I tried to. Charles put the back of the driver-side captain's seat down to form a lounge. When I got the van with the bed in it, I figured it would be "cool" to sleep in it. While that was great in theory, in practice it was not "cool" but cold—and uncomfortable. It had been a terrible idea to save a little motel money. Neither of us slept very well.

Still dark in the pre-dawn hours, I decided to get up and start walking. I woke up Charles and asked him to help me get out of the back door, which he did. I was shivering but the cold air didn't seem to bother him even though he was wearing only a T-shirt and shorts.

"Charles, you need to put on some clothes. You'll get sick."

"No tell me my clothes!" he barked.

I didn't know how to respond so I said nothing. I had noticed that he had become more irritable over the past several days, but he had never spoken to me like that before.

I was worried as it was becoming obvious that Charles was likely at the end of his time as my companion. I wondered how I would continue as I had no one to take his place.

I dressed and started walking in the dark. At first light, the surrounding meadows were gleaming in the early morning dew, like in a fairytale. The cool air was invigorating. I strode down the road at more than four miles per hour, but I was really hungry.

When Charles caught up with me, we stopped for breakfast at an old-fashioned art-deco diner. The jukebox was filled with golden oldies. I played some of my Motown favorites. Although the four-egg omelet breakfast hit the spot, the pleasure was greatly diminished because all the truckers in the diner were heavy smokers.

Once back outside in the fresh air, I stupidly talked to Charles again about dressing warmly. In so many words, he told me to "mind my own business." He mumbled something in Portuguese, probably "Go fuck yourself."

I lost my cool. "You're endangering the success of my walk!" I shouted.

He said nothing. This made me more upset.

Grateful to be back walking alone, I kept thinking about my options should Charles jump ship.

* * *

After a good night's sleep, I felt less anxious. Somewhat upbeat, I hoped to make it to Litchfield, forty-two miles away. It was the coldest start so far. The morning temperature was twenty degrees. I broke out some winter clothing to wear for the first couple of hours. The cool air was actually a welcome change from the hot and sultry 3H and 4H days of the first two months. There were advantages to the cold. Even though I was still sweating profusely, I didn't have to change my shirt every hour. My daily liquid consumption was down to two or three gallons, rather than five to seven.

When I reached Howard Lake a few hours later, we were met by a reporter from the local newspaper. At the next town, Cokato, we did another interview. Frankly, I was a little tired of being asked the same questions and giving the same answers. My irritability really stemmed from my worry about Charles and the possibility I might have to interrupt the walk. I was terribly out of sorts, finding fault with everything.

Every step along the way, I could see two or more lakes from the road. "What should I have expected?" I said out loud. "This is Minnesota—the land of 10,000 lakes." I learned that it really is the land of about 11,500 lakes of more than ten acres.

Next, I walked into Dassel, Minnesota, where we encountered five middle- school football players on their way home from practice. They were all very interested in Walking USA. They spent nearly an hour walking along with me, peppering me with questions about my adventure. They were all pretty large for middle school kids. *I guess they grow them big in Minnesota*, I thought. Given their age and their size, they must have eaten their parents out of house and home.

I, too, thought often about food, especially while walking during the day. I delighted in projecting ahead to the evening meal. I often changed the menu several times. In the morning, I tended to dream about sandwiches and soup. In the late afternoon, I fantasized about a thick steak with a baked potato overflowing with sour cream or melted butter or, even better, both!

* * *

The following morning appeared to be just another routine day. I started walking before 6 A.M. It was quite chilly—again—and the weather woke me up quickly. I wanted to finish on the early side so I could do some "smelling of the roses" in western Minnesota. I also had a live radio interview scheduled in Atwater.

Just outside of Atwater, Charles received a phone call from Brazil. His mother had been taken to a hospital. "My mother be dying," stammered Charles. He told me, "I must fly back Brazil."

"Of course," I responded. I understood and fully supported his need. I would have done the same if it was my mother. Though I knew this might be coming sooner rather than later, I was stunned nevertheless. *What am I going to do without a driver?* I thought. *Should I just sell the van and walk the rest of the way with a knapsack on my back?*

My test run with a pack before I started my journey proved this was not possible but I had no back-up plan in place. I never considered losing my driver mid-journey like this.

I immediately drove Charles back to the Twin Cities airport. I bought him a ticket to Boston so that he could collect some belongings there. I paid him what I owed him, along with a generous tip. Without much warmth, we shook hands and bid each other adieu. I watched him board. Just like that, he was gone. I stood frozen in place until his plane took off. I was now driverless. I certainly couldn't walk and tow the van behind me so for now I was grounded.

With bad weather and challenging terrain ahead of me I had no time to spare. I called a friend back home, Bob Fedele, and explained my desperate situation. "Don't worry," he said reassuring me. "I know just where to go to get you a driver."

"Where's that?" I asked.

"The veteran's homeless shelter in Boston," he replied, cheerily.

"That's a great idea," I volunteered. "There will probably be some guys there who are free of commitments."

Bob said, "I'll make some calls and see what I can do".

Sure enough, Bob came through. Several hours later, he called back. He had drafted Frank Aherne, a retired Capitol Police Officer from Boston. He had served in the Air Force and was, due to illness, in a tough situation—he was homeless. He gave me Frank's number so I could interview him. I felt like a million pounds of bricks had been lifted from my shoulders. "You are a magician!" I told Bob, amazed that he found me a replacement so quickly.

Frank and I spoke for a half hour. His illness, asthma, was under control. I liked what he had to say and the way he chose his words. Simply speaking English was a big plus after my language difficulties with Charles. I felt badly for Frank. How did it happen that a retired policeman could be so down on his luck that he had been reduced to living in a homeless veteran's shelter?

Frank explained that because of some unanticipated expenses, his pension wasn't enough to live on. In order to qualify for veterans housing assistance, he had to live in a homeless shelter for a specific period of time in order to get a housing voucher. Homelessness was a pre-condition for getting the voucher.

By a stroke of luck, he just happened to be doing his stint at the shelter when my friend Bob showed up asking for someone who might want the job as my driver. Frank had jumped at the chance.

I told Frank how much I would pay him *per diem*, and added that I would also pay his expenses and reimburse him for his plane ticket to the Twin Cities—which I would need to have him book immediately.

Without any haggling, Frank accepted my offer. He said, "I'll be on the first flight out in the morning."

Chapter Sixty-Three
Changing of the Guard

I don't need your organization, I've shined your shoes,
I've moved your mountains and marked your cards
But Eden is burning, either brace yourself for elimination
Or else your hearts must have the courage for the changing of the
guards.

—**Bob Dylan**

I picked up Frank at the airport the next day around noon.

I couldn't believe how quickly my predicament had been solved. We went to an airport restaurant and chatted amiably over an early lunch.

Frank was 6' 4" tall and weighed 200 pounds. Slightly younger than I, he was clearly someone you wouldn't want to mess with in a dark alley. He still retained a military air and kept his gray hair very short. Even though he'd never attended college, he was extremely articulate, bright, and knowledgeable about current events. A big plus was he had been a marathon runner, which had been ended because of his asthma. His knowledge of taking care of legs and feet would be a big help. I was worried though, about his asthma since it had been bad enough to force him into early retirement.

Later, as the trip progressed, Frank's asthma indeed became a problem. I would sometimes awaken to the sound of him struggling to breathe. He would usually ask me to pound him on his back to help jump-start his respiration. I couldn't deny that I would often fear waking up one morning to find him dead on the motel bathroom floor.

After our lunch, Frank and I drove directly back to Atwater for my re-scheduled radio interview. I was flying high. I had enjoyed some rest while waiting for Frank to arrive. The day off had brought some spring to my legs. I was excited about the difference Frank would make as I walked on. I gave my best and most spirited radio interview of the trip in Atwater.

After Frank and I spent some time reorganizing and cleaning up the van, the walk resumed.

Because of the late afternoon start, I only walked fifteen miles to Willmar, Minnesota. While I was resting on the side of the road, Frank met the first of several "cattle queens" as he called them. "I've been searching for a cattle queen all my life," he declared, laughing with glee. Her name was Sharon and she was a full-figured Native American woman. She may not have been a "looker," but as Frank noted, "At my age, who cares."

Frank and Sharon flirted for a few minutes. When Sharon realized that we weren't planning to settle down and take root, her interest waned.

I could see that I was going to have some fun. I had laughed more that day than I had for many weeks combined.

Part Five
To the Prairies

These are the gardens of the Desert, these
The unshorn fields, boundless and beautiful,
For which the speech of England has no
name—
The Prairies. I behold them for the first,
And my heart swells, while the dilated sight
Takes in the encircling vastness. Lo! They
stretch,
In airy undulations, far away,
As if the ocean, in his gentlest swell,
                                  —William Cullen Bryant

Chapter Sixty-Four

Mosquito Rain

A man thinks he amounts to a great
Deal but to a mosquito a human
Being is merely something good to eat.

—Don Marquis

We arrived in South Dakota, the fourteenth state of the odyssey. We stopped for breakfast at a little country café in Big Stone City. The owner and only employee, Millie, was a seventy-nine-year-old toothless woman. She was a one-woman band: the waitress, cook, and dishwasher. Her identical twin sister ran the bar next door. Neither had ever married. Frank played the room. He had Millie just about signed up to come with us and also engaged everyone in the diner in conversation. I don't think any of them ever experienced someone as open and witty as Frank. It was a show watching the way he got "tight-asses" to smile and talk.

We moved on. After an uneventful fifteen-mile walk, we stopped for lunch in Milbank in the mid afternoon. We were able to complete an interview over lunch without losing travel time.

Soon thereafter, I came to a detour on the highway and we were diverted onto a dirt road. This was a first. The highway was a narrow two-lane rural road, and I was forced off of it to walk many miles on a very narrow dirt road that ran west, adjacent to the highway.

I was soon able to introduce Frank to the joys of communicating with cows, a trick I had picked up along the way. As we were moving along the dirt road toward a herd of Guernsey's, I told Frank: "The cows will all soon be staring at you." As we got closer to the herd, I shouted out to the animals, getting their attention. Suddenly about 100 cows were staring right at us. After about perhaps thirty seconds, they all turned around and loped away.

For some reason, the dirt road had been especially hard on my legs. After only twenty-one miles on its surface, with only about thirty-six miles done for the day, I was in such discomfort that I stopped early.

* * *

We stumbled out of our motel room at 6 A.M. Standing outside, loading his car, Nick Overmeir introduced himself. With his Stetson and string tie looped around his neck over his Western-style shirt, Nick looked every bit the part of a cowboy. He said, "I'm from Billings, Montana. Are you headed there?"

"We'll be there in about two weeks," I said.

Affable and talkative, Nick told us he was headed home and would be there by nightfall. "I guess walking will take you a bit longer." He promised to arrange a special Montana meal for us once we got to his hometown.

Nick warned, "You're about to enter the land of giant mosquitoes as you move closer to Aberdeen."

We breakfasted at a little cafe in Bristol, South Dakota. At nearby tables, we got acquainted with a couple of female "harvesters." Amazingly, they were both in their late seventies. They looked just like the women my mother used to play gin rummy with at her senior center, but these septuagenarian ladies owned and operated huge farm combines. These contraptions cost around $160,000 and were as big as a house. Like migrant workers, they traveled all over the Midwest and the Plains states, harvesting crops for farmers. After breakfast we followed them to where their gargantuan combines were parked for a great photo op.

While trekking toward Aberdeen in the late afternoon, we wandered into a rural country club for a cold drink. The locals were so interested in my escapade that they called in reporters from the two local papers. Frank said, "I can't believe it, here we are in bum fuck Egypt, and they have *two* papers."

The reporters quickly appeared and both interviewed me. One of them asked, "How do you like South Dakota?"

I told her, "It far exceeded my expectations and I am so glad I decided to walk through your home state."

She said, "You should come back after your walk and live here."

"No way in hell!" I responded.

"Why? I thought you really liked it here."

"I do," I told her, "but there is a problem—it is called winter."

Roast beef was on the dinner menu at the country club, and the members invited us to stay for the meal, on the house. We happily obliged.

The food was tasty, filling, and much appreciated. But now we were running *very* late. By the time we got back on the road, it was 6:30 P.M. Soon, the sun was setting across a beautiful sky, streaked with pink, blue and white. The colors were so special; the scene looked artificial, like a painting.

I'd almost forgotten what Nick Overmeir had warned us about then, on the outskirts of Bath, South Dakota, the mosquitoes suddenly attacked. Swarms of them, intent on eating me alive, forced me into the van. Frank drove in search of a motel. It seemed as if heavy raindrops were striking the windshield, but actually it was thousands of mosquitoes splattering against the glass. The windshield was covered with the blood of whomever they last drank from. Finally, we stumbled upon a motel in Aberdeen, appropriately named the "Settle Inn."

* * *

In the morning, we drove back to Bath to walk the final ten miles to Aberdeen. No mosquitoes bothered us—maybe we killed them all last night. Once back in Aberdeen, we dropped off Frank's first few rolls of film for developing before we went to have a quick lunch. We again got an interview out of the way during our stop. As soon as we left, we had to visit a car wash to get rid of the dead mosquitoes obscuring the view out of the windshield. After picking up the developed photos, we departed Aberdeen, and headed north hoping to reach the North Dakota border by sundown.

After a mile or two, I noticed a shoe store across the highway. Frank had told me about a type of sock that would better protect my feet. "Thorlos," he called them. We walked into the store to see if they had any. They did and I bought a pair to try on. At $12.00 a pair, I thought they were much too expensive, but Frank assured me they were well worth it. I had come to realize the importance of socks in the battle to keep my feet healthy. Besides, when Frank said they were special I had to listen.

The Thorlo sock is part cotton and part synthetic materials. The manufacturer claimed it would keep my feet much cooler than 100 percent cotton socks and they were designed to absorb much more moisture than regular socks. I really liked the padding in the heel and toe areas, which would help prevent blisters.

I put on my sneakers to see how they felt over the Thorlos. They made my feet much more comfortable. It was a feeling like putting on fur-lined gloves. After I laced up my walking shoes, I was sold. The socks were definitely worth the extra money and I bought twelve pairs. I never imagined there would come a day when I would spend $144.00 on a dozen pairs of socks.

On the way out of town, I spotted a library that had the distinction of having both my sons' middle names: the Alexander Mitchell Library. I bought a picture postcard of the place and mailed it home to Nick and Lou.

On the road north, many giant farm combines passed us. They literally took up the entire road. At 6 P.M. we stopped to rest and took a peek at the recently developed photos. It appeared that Frank, who had never operated a camera in his life, had a natural eye for photography. His photos were an amazing keepsake.

Chapter Sixty-Five
Sunflowers

"Do not go where the path may lead,
go instead where there is no path and leave a trail."
—Ralph Waldo Emerson

We had now reached Ellendale, North Dakota, where we spent the night in the Prairie Winds Motel. It was the beginning of the twelfth week of the walk.

In the morning, we checked out and headed for a gas station. While Frank was filling the tank, I noticed that the Aberdeen newspaper was sold in North Dakota. I purchased a copy and discovered that my picture and a story about Walking USA appeared above the fold on the front page. Amazing! Back in Boston, it took saving thousands of minority homeowners from getting defrauded out of their homes by predatory lenders to land me on the front page. Here, I get front-page billing just for walking.

We dropped by the local café for breakfast. Our waitress' name was Irene. Originally from Chicago, she couldn't give us any clear reason why she ended up in Ellendale. We suspected it was a man. A "hot ticket," Irene joked with Frank about where he might find his "cattle queen." She had discouraging news.

"North Dakota definitely is not the right place to be looking," she advised. "The average age around here is senior citizen plus."

After breakfast, we moved west on Route 11 through the chilly winds of a partly sunny morning. I was walking through a relatively flat and fertile valley which, after a few miles, began to climb towards distant hills. The road was empty—no cars, trucks or people. It was a desolate world out there. Frank pulled up and said, "I've always wondered what the dark side of the moon looked like and now I know."

After five miles I was frozen to the core. The temperature was not that cold, necessarily, but the wind was getting to me. For the first time in the three months since I left Boston, I needed to get out some winter gear from the storage compartment on the roof.

Bad news. We discovered that the "waterproof" roof compartment was not waterproof at all. Most of my winter clothes were soaked and mildewed. We interrupted the walk and headed back to Ellendale to find a Laundromat to wash what little could be salvaged of my winter gear.

Once that chore was done, I was back on the bleak North Dakota road. There wasn't much to report. Occasionally, I'd see some livestock, but mostly it was just endless rolling fields, acre upon acre of sunflowers, and the scent of soil and fertilizer.

After walking ten miles in three hours, I needed a break. Both sides of the road were flanked by fields of sunflowers. Their seeds are the major crop in this part of North Dakota. Bordering the rows of flowers were bales of hay in huge rolls. Those rolls, perhaps eight or ten feet in diameter, were clumped together every several hundred feet. Tired, I decided to climb up on top of a bale of hay and catch forty winks.

As I dozed off, I marveled at the rolling pastures of the Great Plains and the resplendent mix of pink and gray clouds swirling overhead. I was mesmerized as I stared off into the sky.

When I woke up, I realized how lucky I was to be so removed from the hustle and bustle of city life. Thoreau once said, "The best thinking is done in solitude." And this is the kind of solitude he must have meant.

After walking five more miles along sunflower fields, I was climbing those no-longer distant hills. Finally, I turned and looked back over the valley. I saw the most spectacular scenery of the journey. As far as the eye could see, the northern reach of the Great Plains spread out below me. This was where the uncountable buffalo once roamed, hunted by Native Americans, who killed only what they could eat.

Regrettably, I had to move on. The damp wind was chilling me to the bone. It seemed as if the wind was always whispering to me on the prairie, along with the undulating grass. As I began to walk down the hills, off in the distance I could see an enormous body of water. The map said it was called Pheasant Lake. The road ahead seemed to vanish right into it.

Hours later, as I got closer, I realized the road wasn't swallowed by the water. It simply ran along its southern shore. As darkness fell I pushed toward Ashley, where I and my internal combustion covered wagon would bivouac for the night.

Someone once told me that the Dakotas were considered the safest place to live or visit in the country. The low crime rate is due to the fact that there's no one here to commit any crimes. Some years ago, a visitor to North Dakota supposedly remarked, "It's a beautiful land, but I doubt human beings will ever live here." Few do. Only 600,000 people live in the entire state, which is larger in area than all the New England states combined.

It also seemed to be a common misperception that North Dakota is full of Native Americans. In fact, less than five percent of the population is of that descent.

We finished rather late, checking into the Ashley Motel about an hour after dark. I had ignored severe muscular pain in my calves all day long. Now, I was really suffering. I climbed into the tub and soaked in hot water for an hour to get some relief. Soon thereafter, Frank returned with sandwiches and drinks. We were sound asleep by 9 P.M.

* * *

We got an early start. There was not a cloud in the sky, and the wind had become a gentle breeze.

We walked into a local café for breakfast and I immediately noticed how the customers were grouped. The men were all in one corner and the women in another.

The men seemed clearly distressed by our presence, hiding behind each other, hoping they couldn't be seen. They concealed their faces with their palms and spoke to each other quietly, while never taking their eyes off of us. The women, on the other hand, were quite friendly and delighted to make our acquaintance. We chatted about the trek. We learned the husbands and wives breakfasted there daily, dividing into the two groups by sex the moment they arrived. It was weird. The men appeared to go off with the other men to engage in "man talk." The women seemed to accept being neglected by their husbands.

Frank went out to fetch his new toy. When he walked back in with the camera, you would have thought he was carrying a loaded gun. The men scattered and refused to have their photos taken.

Frank was not the least bit shy and said, "Come on guys, we just want some photos of all the lovely folks we met along the way."

The women smiled and obliged us with a "Cheese!" But the men refused.

When I stopped at the cashier to pay for our breakfast, she informed me that our tab had already been spoken for. It had to have been the women—how kind— but I was careful to thank everybody.

Heading west on foot, I now felt a cold coming on. I had a sore throat and an itchy and runny nose. Feeling that way, walking had become a drag. To make matters worse I was walking into a fifteen-mile-per-hour headwind. I felt like a salmon swimming upstream.

We finally reached Route 83, where we would again head south back to South Dakota. It was once the only paved road between Canada and Mexico. I mentioned to Frank, "We should take a short side trip north to see the Lawrence Welk homestead."

He said, "It's probably the *only* famous place in North Dakota, but it's getting late." I still had ten miles to go, so we decided to pass on the Welk homestead attraction.

I was walking south for the first time since Illinois, about to cross back into South Dakota.

A sign announced that this portion of the road was part of the Lewis and Clark Trail. I was thrilled to be walking on such hallowed ground.

Chapter Sixty-Six

The Pied Piper

Out came the children running.
All the little boys and girls,
With rosy cheeks and flaxen curls,
And sparkling eyes and teeth like pearls.
Tripping
and skipping,
ran merrily after.

—Robert Browning

Herreid was the first hamlet in South Dakota we came to. Several teenage boys on bicycles gathered to chat with me and Frank as we stopped to catch our breath and grab a cold drink. Frank gave each of them Walking USA hats and T-shirts. The kids got a kick out of becoming honorary members of the jaunt, and I'm sure they didn't get many people from Boston visiting—let alone walking—through their obscure town.

Adults always seem much older to kids than their chronological age, so to these boys I probably looked ancient. It didn't completely surprise me when one youngster asked, "Aren't you too old to be walking all the way to California?"

I responded, "Why don't you follow me and we'll see who gets there first."

They all began to tag along after me on their bikes. They were laughing and having themselves a grand old time. I was moving at a fast clip and they rode right behind me, remaining as my rear guard for quite a while. I told them, "I'm not serious about you guys following me to California."

"We're going to ride protection for you until you get to Selby, a few miles up the road."

What a bunch of nice kids, I thought.

As we reached Mound City, I expected the kids would quit. To my surprise they continued to follow me. I asked, "Where are you guys going?"

One of the kids said, "If you're going to Selby, we're going to ride with you."

It was so much fun to have them. We began to chat about NFL football. They were all Broncos fans and were averse to *any* talk about the Patriots. To those kids it was the Broncos, and only the Broncos—the rest of the league didn't count.

They were all relatively small— probably less than 150 pounds—but they all played on the high school football team. They all reminded me of "Rudy" of Notre Dame fame. I asked them if they had seen the movie. The response from all was a resounding, "Yeah!"

I asked one, "What did you think of that flick?"

His response was, "It was about us."

The biggest kid, Andy, was the quarterback. He said, "Nobody else wanted to play quarterback, so I decided to volunteer."

Onward I strolled at a much faster pace than I usually would be doing at the end of a day. The kids provided me with motivation. I wanted them to see me at my best.

Though it had been warm enough throughout the day, the chilly dusk was a reminder that fall was planning to settle in. Another sign was I found I was walking in the dark a little more each day. The sun seemed to set so much earlier than it did just a couple of weeks ago. After an hour of struggling to walk in the dark, I finally gave up after thirty-nine miles and wearily climbed into the van.

The bikers seemed disappointed that I had stopped for the day. They had followed me and, when traffic allowed, ridden right next to me for almost three hours. "We'll be back in the morning to ride some more," one of them said. "What time will you be leaving?"

I answered, "Nine o'clock," knowing full well I would leave much earlier. I didn't want them to think that following me was necessary.

They told me, "We have to be in school at 8:30, we could only ride with you till 8:00."

I said, "It has been a privilege to have you guys for company. The only drawback is you're being Broncos fans."

"Hey Walking Man, don't come to Bronco country if you don't bleed Bronco orange."

They all laughed. It had been great fun. Off they rode. One kid stopped and yelled to me, "Good luck Pied Piper!"

We found a motel in Selby, South Dakota—population 707. After we checked in, we headed out in search of dinner. To our delight and relief, we found a family restaurant. A sign in the window proclaimed: "Prime Rib Dinner, All You Can Eat." We ordered the prime rib, but we were too exhausted to take advantage of the "All You Can Eat" challenge. People at nearby tables stared at us as if we'd just landed from another planet. It might be that anyplace other than Selby was another planet. We ate quickly and quietly and returned to the motel.

I was asleep within minutes, praying that I would wake up in the morning without pain in my legs.

Chapter Sixty-Seven
"The Big Muddy"

The Missouri's temperament was uncertain as the
actions of a jury or the state of a woman's mind.
—Sioux City Register, March 28, 1868

After an uneventful walk to Gettysburg, South Dakota, we spent the night in a motel that charged only $12 a night. Even at that low rate, it was overpriced.

The room smelled like it was being used as the local meeting place for lovers in hiding. After my shower, I pulled back the spread and blanket to reveal a sheet covered with recent stains—they were multicolored and made my stomach churn. There was no way I was going to sleep on that! Frank went to the front office and demanded another room. "No more rooms," was the concerned response. I really did not want to sleep in the van but we might be forced into it. As we contemplated our options an Indian woman—a breathtaking, dark-skinned beauty—showed up with fresh sheets. In fact they were brand new, along with an entire change of bedding for both beds. Still, I hardly slept a wink. The bedding might have been fresh, but the lingering images of the stained sheets and what lurked beneath them made deep sleep impossible.

I began the two-day trek to Eagle Butte, which was part of the Cheyenne River Sioux Reservation. Steve Emery, my Harvard Law School classmate, was the tribe's attorney general, and chief justice of the Oglala Sioux Nation's Supreme Court. He was also a noted singer of Native American music, had cut several CDs, and was one of the top stars in that genre. Steve had invited me to speak to the Eagle Butte High School student body.

The beautiful day was diminished by a sore throat, fever, and flu-like symptoms. After about three hours, we reached the Missouri River. It's one of the most dazzling vistas I've encountered, in which the endless flow of water carves out an enormous lazy serpent. To folks in South Dakota, it is simply "The River." It divided the state into sections referred to as "East River" and "West River." It is allegedly the longest river in the entire country, over 2,500 miles from end to end. It begins its southern flow in Three Forks, Montana, and flows to just north of St. Louis, where it meets the mighty Mississippi.

The Morphine Dream

While we were crossing the bridge over the Missouri, some Native Americans going towards Eagle Butte stopped to give us a donation. It was such a special event when people did that. Although it seldom happened, it seemed like it was always the people who could least afford it. Frank's unofficial tally of donations now stood at $220. I asked the guy who handed Frank the money, "Do you know Steve Emery?"

"Sure, he's my lawyer!" he answered enthusiastically.

"Tell him I'm only fifty miles away and closing fast," I said, glad that we had this chance meeting.

Vast seas of sunflower farms undulated around me, and I saw my first buffalo herd off to the south. I guess most buffalo in existence are now on private reserves or in national parks. Here in South Dakota, for some of the Native Americans, raising Buffalo had apparently become part of their culture.

In the late afternoon, when we were about forty miles from Eagle Butte, a car skidded to a stop in front of me. A giant and somewhat inebriated Native American unsteadily stepped out to officially welcome us to the Cheyenne River Sioux Reservation. He looked to be about six and a half feet tall, had a muscular build and leathery skin, and looked like the old chieftain on the Pontiac hood ornament. His long, straight, jet-black hair was tied in a traditional ponytail. He was a magnificent specimen of the archetypical Hollywood Native American, who could also be the starting tackle for any pro football team.

"Happy Cloud" was what Frank dubbed him. He walked a few hundred yards with me and volunteered that he was the shepherd for the nearby buffalo herd.

On the outskirts of a small village, we came across a used-car lot that stopped us in our tracks. All the vehicles were vintage cars from the forties and fifties. There was even a 1939 Chevy Master 85 with a winged-angel hood ornament and blue swirled-glass gear knob for its "three on a tree" console shifter. Unfortunately, most of the automobiles were worn out and rusting away. It was more like a junkyard. The sticker shock price on each of the cars ranged between $100 and $300.

I stopped walking about ten miles shy of my goal. We drove ahead into Eagle Butte and checked into a motel. I was unable to reach Steve Emery by phone. Because of my flu-like symptoms, I took a steamy shower and was fast asleep by 8 P.M.

Chapter Sixty-Eight

Mato Tanka

(Big Bear)

TUNES FROM THE REZ
—Title of CD by Steve Emery

I was up early and out into the rain, then we breakfasted in the Outrider Cafe in downtown Eagle Butte. The custom at this restaurant was for patrons to serve and refill each other's coffee mugs. It engendered camaraderie among friends and strangers. I liked it. I wished it would become contagious.

I left Eagle Butte to drive back to where I ended the walk the previous evening. But first, we visited briefly with Steve Emery at his office at the Cheyenne River Sioux Tribal Center. It was great to see him again! He invited us for dinner at a local restaurant as soon as I finished my walk into Eagle Butte.

After a thirty-four-mile walk, I was back at the motel to shower and change for dinner. I had walked through the most amazing signs of poverty that one could imagine. I visited with some Native Americans during that stroll. I learned that the unemployment rate on the reservation was some astonishing number—like 80 percent. The county is regarded as the poorest of all counties in the United States. Alcoholism and rampant diabetes haunt the tribal members. Unwed mothers, almost a complete lack of adequate medical care, terribly underfunded schools, lack of public transportation, lack of adequate water, electricity and other necessities of life are typical of life on the "Rez." I felt like I had walked out of America into a third-world country.

We met Steve and his wife at the Diamond A restaurant at 7:30. He had invited a reporter from the *Eagle Butte News* to join us.

Steve, who is always smiling, has a round face with a moustache, long dark Indian hair, and wears big, round glasses. I wonder how he managed to stay happy given the poverty and suffering in his environment. He stood tall and proud, at least six feet tall and somewhat bulky, which I imagine is what inspired his Lakota name, *Mato Tanka*, or Big Bear. Steve and his younger brother, Mark, who lives in Washington, D.C., are both graduates of Harvard Law. Steve told me that two years earlier his brother became an attorney for the Department of Tribal Justice, a new division at the time, of the U.S. Department of Justice.

Steve has an amazing story. His ancestors were among the most significant Native Americans in the nineteenth century. His great-grandfather, according to many sources, was the Sioux warrior who was responsible for slaying General George Custer during Custer's Last Stand. His great-great-grandfather, Martin Charger, was the founder of the "Fool Soldiers Society" in 1860. It was also known as the "Crazy Band." They acquired these names because they were ridiculed for their altruism. The goal of this group of Native Americans was to be nonviolent, and to help all people. Steve told me that Chief Charger and the Fool Soldier Band vowed not to make war on old people, women and children. Thereafter, using their horses and other personal belongings the Fool Soldier Band ransomed and rescued the white captives taken from Lake Shetek during the 1862 Sioux Uprising in Minnesota. They neither sought nor received compensation of any kind.

Steve was a high-school dropout, and had been a police officer on the Santee Sioux "Rez" in Nebraska, and on the Yankton Sioux "Rez" in South Dakota. At some point, he decided he had better get an education so that he could follow his calling to help his people. He credited his grandfather for instilling that mission in him. His grandfather once said to him: "*Takoja* (grandson), there are many people on the reservation who need help. Before you return home, learn a skill that will let you provide assistance to your relatives." That wise advice from his elder had guided Steve to a life of service to his tribe.

Steve's educational trail led him to the Marty Indian School at the Yankton Sioux Adult Education program where he got his GED in 1977. He went on to the Santee, Nebraska, branch of Nebraska Indian Community College where, in 1981, he got his associate's degree. He pursued his B.A. at the University of South Dakota shortly after his induction into USD's Alpha Chapter of Phi Beta Kappa graduating in May, 1986. I met Steve the following September and we became friends on our first day as students at Harvard Law School. At HLS, Steve was among the most respected students on the campus.

In August of 2007, Steve was named Chief of the Prairie Dwelling Lakota. That honor caused him to change his Indian name to *Wicasl-tancan Mato Tanka* which means "Chief Big Bear."

If you had told me during my life that I would someday be friends with a Sioux Indian chief, I would have thought you were tripping on LSD.

Mato Tanka (Big Bear)

* * *

The company and the buffalo steak were magnificent. After dinner, Steve invited Frank and me back home for coffee. Steve, a supremely talented musician, was soon serenading us with Native American music. He's as good as any rock star I've ever heard live, except this was a private and intimate concert. Steve played along with his singing on a beautifully engraved Dobro guitar, the likes of which I never knew existed. It is an acoustic guitar with a built-in metal resonator. Not only was the sound amazing but it was a magnificent piece of art. I couldn't even estimate its value. Steve also chanted some Lakota funeral music, which he regularly performed at funeral services. His latest CD, *Tunes from the Rez*, had recently been released. I would have to order it, so the music would be with me as a keepsake of my journey.

Chapter Sixty-Nine
Grades Are Random

In 1890 Harvard University's average GPA was 2.27. In 1950,
its average GPA was 2.55. By 2004, it's GPA, as a result
of dramatic rises in the 1960s and gradual rises since,
had risen to 3.48.

—Wikipedia

Steve and I reminisced about our days at Harvard Law School. One of the things we shook our heads about was the grading system at the elite law school we attended. Most first-year Harvard Law students are quite anxious about all the work and the pressure to do well. When our first exam period approached, we were quite surprised to see professionally printed posters hanging all over campus that read: "Fuck Studying. Grades Are Random." It was amazing to me to see that kind of profanity so routinely accepted on the campus. We had no idea what the posters meant. We soon found out.

During the second semester of my first year, I was forced to drive a cab full time, while trying to attend classes, because I had a family to support. I did most of my studying in the cab while waiting for a fare, but my research time in the library was limited. I realized I didn't have time to fully prepare for all four courses that semester. I decided to work hard in two courses and thus did little in the other two.

At the end of the term, I took the exams in the two courses I had not prepared much for. I had read the assignments, but only cursorily. I attended no study-group sessions because I simply didn't have time. When I sat down for the first exam, all I could do was write a lot of the most intelligent bullshit I could muster.

The second final exam for which I was mostly unprepared was another story. Steve was sitting next to me during that one. The professor, whose classes I only sporadically attended, was reputed to be one of the toughest graders at Harvard Law. When the proctor said we could pick up our pens, I launched into a feverish disquisition on the subject with which I was only somewhat acquainted.

After five minutes, the proctor interrupted us. He announced apologetically that the exam question had been misstated. He read the corrected version and we were told to start over. Irritated, I crossed out what I'd written and began scribbling a response to the new question.

Five minutes later, the proctor interrupted us again. This time he apologized profusely. He had been given the wrong information. The original question was the correct one. He told us to start over.

Of course, it was typical for the exam room to be filled with tension and anxiety, but now it was a pressure cooker about to blow its lid. Somehow, all of us managed to keep our cool. I glanced at Steve. He shook his head and shrugged. We collectively groaned, turned the page in the bluebook, and started again.

I know you'll think I'm making this up. About five minutes later, the impossible happened. The proctor interrupted again. "I cannot tell you how sorry I am, but the confusion about the wording on the exam question has finally been cleared up." He then proceeded to read the new version and told us to begin again.

I looked over at Steve, but I couldn't catch his eye. I wondered if this was being done deliberately to test us for the kinds of frustrations we might encounter in the practice of law. You work day and night on a brief only to learn that some new precedent has been discovered that requires you to throw all of your work away and start over. Nevertheless, I was now so upset that I simply turned the page and wrote in the book, "This is bullshit." I got up, slammed my blue book on the proctor's desk, and stormed out of the room. Once I got outside, I was shocked and ashamed at the way I had behaved. I wanted desperately to return, but once you leave the exam room, you weren't allowed back in.

For the next few days, I was worried. Of course, I must have received an F on the exam. Maybe I'd be put on academic probation, especially since I had behaved so disrespectfully and unprofessionally.

The real shocker soon arrived. The grade I received on that exam was a B. In fact, I got B's in all four courses—those that I'd prepared for and those that I had not.

It was at that point in our time at Harvard Law that Steve and I understood what "Grades Are Random" meant. They weren't random. There was an unspoken rule at Harvard Law. If you were smart enough to get in and you could breathe, you automatically earned a gentleman's B. If you really studied hard, you might actually get an A. For some of our classmates, grades were very important. For non-traditional students like Steve and I, grades were almost meaningless. Survival was our only goal.

It was after that second semester as 1Ls (first-year law student) that Steve and I decided that Harvard Law School didn't have to be taken quite so seriously. We still studied hard, but no longer around the clock. And it wasn't until my third year—thanks to financial assistance from Lou Mitchell—that I really knuckled down and got my share of A's.

Before we realized how much time had passed, it was 2 A.M. We reluctantly said goodnight. I had such a great reunion with *Mato Tanka*; I wished we could visit all night long. I gave Chief Big Bear a big bear hug. Such a special person—devoting his career to do his best to help those living on the "Rez." My evening had been filled with *wopila*—the Sioux Lakota word for "gratitude from the heart."

Frank and I trudged back to our motel.

Chapter Seventy

Red Cloud

I am poor and naked, but I am the
chief of the nation. We do not want
Riches but we do want to train our
children right. Riches would not do us
No good. We could not take them with us
to the other world. We do not want riches.
We want peace and love
—Sioux Chief Red Cloud to President Grant

In the morning, after again pouring coffee for one another at the Outrider Café, we returned to the tribal headquarters for photos with Steve and the tribal council. He then escorted me into the high-school auditorium. The entire student body was assembled and waiting.

Steve introduced me by telling the audience something I didn't know. That he and I were the only two people from our class that graduated from Harvard Law School who had not completed high school. We both had gotten a GED. That factoid was received with sustained applause. He told the kids a little about my long walks—the one across America—and the one that got me to Harvard Law School.

I spoke to the kids about a long walk by of one of their own. "In 1870, the famous Sioux Chief Red Cloud and several other notable Native Americans walked all the way to Washington, D.C., to meet with the 'Great White Father', " I told them. Red Cloud was seeking to rectify an injustice over several treaties. For some reason, however, he detoured through Boston to visit then Massachusetts Governor Claflin at his Walnut Street home in Newton. "Amazingly," I told them, "I live on the same Walnut Street in Newton, only a couple of blocks from where Red Cloud visited so long ago."

As a small boy, Chief Charles Red Cloud used to assist the original Chief Red Cloud after the old Chief went blind. Steve's grandfather, Jim Emery, was adopted into the Red Cloud family by Chief Red Cloud's grandson Chief Charles Red Cloud during a Lakota Sioux *Hunka* or "Making of Relatives Ceremony" held in 1953 at Chief Red Cloud's original allotment about two miles from what is now known as Pine Ridge, South Dakota. Steve's Grandpa was his favorite interpreter as he spoke the true, old-time Lakota.

I also spoke about how to get into the college of your choice. Basically, I gave the kids an abbreviated version of this book. When I was finished, the high-school class president presented me with a gift—a handmade Sioux quilt. It is something I will always cherish.

We were soon back at tribal headquarters, where I finished an interview with the *Eagle Butte News* reporter that I had begun the day before. Steve and I got into a long conversation about practicing law. "Boy, what they don't teach you in law school," Steve remarked.

I agreed. "I certainly didn't learn about being a lawyer at Harvard. I learned in the courtrooms, and mostly from the clerks."

I related to Steve that I had to have surgery right after our final class and was unable to take the bar exam in July like my fellow students. "When I did show up for the bar exam the following February, I was shocked to see about six of our very bright Harvard Law School classmates who were appearing for the second time to take the exam, as they had failed at in their first try."

Steve wasn't surprised. He said, "We certainly were taught the philosophy of law, but not the nuts and bolts."

The morning had passed in what seemed to be only a few minutes. A part of me didn't want to leave. I could have stayed in Eagle Butte forever. It was a place that touched my soul. But, it was time to move on. I had tears in my eyes when Steve and I hugged good-bye and promised to stay in touch.

I walked away from the hardscrabble, poverty ravished Cheyenne River Sioux Reservation just before noon. Eight of the ten poorest counties in the United States are on Indian reservations—five of them belong to the Sioux in South Dakota. Steve had verified that Ziebach County, which is wholly within the reservation was, indeed, the poorest county in the U.S.

I reached the town of Faith, late in the afternoon. We drove south to see Mount Rushmore and then landed a motel in Spearfish. We all have heard of Rushmore and most folks have seen pictures of it. I can tell you that being there, staring up at the four "heads," George Washington, Thomas Jefferson, Abraham Lincoln and Teddy Roosevelt, causes a sensation that one feels to his very core. The sculptor, Gutzon Borglum, put it aptly when he stated his mission: "A monument's dimensions should be determined by the importance to civilization of the events commemorated."

Chapter Seventy-One

Rambo

Oh, give me a home where the buffalo roam,
Where the deer and the antelope play,
Where seldom is heard a discouraging word
And the skies are not cloudy all day.

—John Lomax

We drove from our motel to Belle Fourche, South Dakota. I began walking by 7:00 A.M., toward the Wyoming border. This was to be our last day in the spectacular Dakotas. The area had surprised me. I expected to find the Dakotas a drab and barren place. This misconception couldn't have been any further from reality.

Frank went off to develop some film and to wash and gas up the van. When he caught up with me ten miles later, he told me that he didn't like the way the van was handling. We immediately drove back to Belle Fourche to get it checked out at the local Ford dealership.

Scott Peterson Ford was owned by Scott and Susan Peterson. Susan was kind enough to service our vehicle free in return for a publicity photo for the local newspaper. This was the kind of deal we liked!

As we waited for the service to be completed, Susan told us about a Chamber of Commerce luncheon at noon. She asked, "Would you and Frank like to go?"

Frank and I looked at each other and smiled. I answered, "Of course, we'd love to have a hot meal."

"Would you mind giving a talk about your trek?" Susan asked.

"Delighted," I said.

After my off-the-cuff Chamber of Commerce speech and a delicious lunch, I waved good-bye to the kind people of Belle Fourche. Frank drove me back to where I had left off and he then returned to town to do some errands.

I had only gone about five miles down Highway 212 when I spotted a large herd of small, deer-like animals in the field to my right. I'd never seen such an animal before. They were about the size of a greyhound dog and they had a white puffy ball where a tail should be. Moving quite fast, they pranced around skittishly, almost hopping.

I spotted a man hiding in the brush to my left. He was dressed in camouflage fatigues. He was carrying a six-foot, high-tech compound bow. His face was painted green and black. This guy couldn't be serious.

I shouted, "Hey, Rambo, what kind of animals are those?"

Rambo was not pleased that I had come along and spoiled his fun.

"Wyoming jackalope, asshole!" he shouted back. "Now get out of the way."

He was even less happy when I snapped his photo.

"Talking of assholes," I said, "You're the one out here trying to kill baby deer with that nuclear bow of yours."

Rambo gave me the finger and slinked away.

* * *

I had flashbacks as I walked toward the Wyoming border. When I was a kid, I was fascinated with the Old West. My childhood visions were shaped by Hollywood movies: Redskins with their faces painted like rainbows, bright colored feathers mounted in the wind blown strands of black hair; heavily loaded Conestoga wagons inching across the prairies; bronco-busting cowboys circling thundering herds of cattle; gunfighters with lightning-quick hands; and the sounding of bugles as the boys in blue and gold, led by Rin Tin Tin, came to the rescue. That was the West that captivated me as a kid.

Today's West, at least most of the "West" that I have been walking through reminds me so much of the scenes that I used to see in Western movies and on TV. The dry, rolling plains, the surrounding mountains in the distance, the dust rising behind riders and stagecoaches, all under the ever-present sun, and the long distances between civilization

It also appears that the spirit of the old West is alive and well in this part of the country, but rather than the round-ups and cattle drives, tractor-trailer trucks, with their chrome stacks belching clouds of diesel pollution, and their powerful engines stealing the silence of the prairie, haul the cattle and the porkers off to the stockyards.

There are still some bronco busters, but now they ride sport utility vehicles. The Conestoga wagons live on in the form of U-Haul trucks, still battling their way across the prairies. When you think about it, they're pretty much the same as in the old West, four wheels, all the possessions in the rear, and mom and pop and the kids huddled together on a single seat, the horses replaced by horsepower. Indians are still here, but in such small numbers or segregated on reservations, that nobody pays much attention to them.

Rambo

As I headed for my third state in one day, I was aware that it was only the second—and the last time—that I would walk in three states on the same day.

People are even scarcer here than in South Dakota. Wyoming's population when I trekked through it was about 490,000, perhaps the lowest state population in the country. The state has more livestock than people. This was also where "The deer and the antelope play," not to mention the lovely jackalope.

With the exception of a few eighteen-wheel behemoths, carrying herds of pigs or cattle, Route 212 was traffic-less. Like everybody else, the trucks disregarded the seventy-five-mile-per-hour speed limit by at least twenty miles per hour, and if I was not careful they could easily blow me right off the road and be in the next county before realizing they had passed something. But there was always plenty of warning. You could hear them five miles away and smell them a mile away.

Since leaving Belle Fourche, I had walked ten miles in South Dakota and ten miles in Wyoming. I had reached the town of Colony. According to the map, I was halfway between Belle Fourche, South Dakota, and Alzada, Montana. That's like saying I was halfway between nothing and nowhere.

I marveled at what they called a town in Wyoming. Colony appeared deserted. There was no business district and no stores, not even a gas station—only several widely scattered, seedy-looking homes and a few dilapidated outbuildings. The countryside was bleak, barren and windswept. All I saw were fenced-in pastures for pigs and cattle.

Finally, Frank showed up. I happily retreated into the van for some air conditioning and refreshments. The sun had been burning me up. I rested and rehydrated. I dozed for a few minutes. When I woke up, I was thinking about the weather I had encountered.

I had been walking now eighty-eight days and every day, except five, there had been sun. At least out here in the West, the humidity was not much of a factor. Walking in the heat without the humidity is a completely different experience. Without the humidity, my endurance was not depleted as quickly each day.

While I was nursing a third cold drink, a cattle truck approached from a distant ranch. The truck came to a stop nearby. The driver jumped down from his rig. He was dressed in jeans, a plaid shirt, cowboy hat, and cowboy boots. The turquoise belt buckle he wore was the size of a dinner plate. It was a piece of artwork, though, and it must have cost him a small fortune.

"Hi!" he shouted, "You guys need any help?"

"Thank you," I said. "Would you like a cold Diet Coke?" He gladly accepted. "I'll trade you the cold drink for that belt buckle," I quipped.

Frank, who could talk the ears off a raccoon, began telling the trucker about our journey, complaining how tough it was to follow me at 3.7 miles per hour, looking at my fat ass all day.

I sat there silently listening to their babble. After another half an hour, I was well rested and sufficiently cooled off, I jumped into the conversation.

"What's your name, friend?"

"Jim," he said, "but Jimbo to friends."

He told us that he'd never encountered a cross-country walker before, and he expressed skepticism that I was really doing it.

"Do you think I came out here just to pull your leg?"

Jimbo, who wasn't the quickest draw, didn't know what to say.

Frank came to the rescue by changing the subject. "So what do people around here do for work?"

"The big business here is cattle- and pig-ranching," said Jimbo. "But, not far from where we are sitting is the Black Thunder Mine, the largest coal mine in the USA."

He claimed that the mine's pride and joy is a behemoth coal-chewing machine, which can extract more than a ton of coal every second. "That's 28,800 tons per eight-hour shift," he said, "and it fills twenty-five trains a day, each a mile long."

Frank said, "At that rate, the entire planet should be gone in about ten years."

Jimbo used to work on that gargantuan coal-chewing machine but said, "I got bored and wanted my independence."

He had saved his pennies and bought the eighteen-wheeler parked nearby.

"Some independence," said Jimbo, "the damn thing owns me."

Just then, another trucker pulled up and hollered at Jimbo. "Hey, they's waitin' on ya at the yard."

Before he left, I inducted Jimbo into the honorary society of Walking USA, presenting him with an official Walking USA hat and T-shirt.

"You're in a very select group," I said. "You and the other guy."

Miles later, I saw another herd of jackalope, prancing and cavorting in the pasture to my right. Those poor critters had somehow gotten themselves trapped in a barbed-wire pasture. They couldn't seem to find their way out. I walked over near them and tried to coax them toward an open gate, but they were skittish and moved as far away as possible. A car pulled up and stopped. The driver shouted, "Better stay away from them. Some trigger-happy hunters may shoot at them and hit you instead."

"Thanks partner," I shouted. "Someone told me that these critters are jackalope. Is that true?"

The driver laughed so hard I thought he was going to pass out. "Where are you morons from?" He drove off without waiting for a response. Frank and I looked at each other and shrugged.

I resumed walking. Every few minutes, I looked back, hoping the jackalope had escaped. A few minutes later, they found the opening and regained their freedom.

Later, I learned why the driver had found my comment about the jackalope so hilarious. It was customary for residents of Wyoming to jerk the chain of gullible visitors like me about this animal. The jackalope was a "fearsome critter" that does not exist. It's a chimera, a mythical animal, usually described as a large jackrabbit with antlers. However, the jackalope I saw were real animals—actually pronghorns, not true antelopes.

Shortly after dusk, I trudged into the dreary, sleepy border town of Alzada, Montana, not much more prosperous than Colony, Wyoming. Frank was exhilarated. "Little Big Horn, here I come!" he announced to no one in particular.

Chapter Seventy-Two

He Died with His Boots On

... most Americans think of the Last Stand as belonging solely to George Armstrong Custer... But the myth applies equally to his legendary opponent Sitting Bull. For while the Sioux and Cheyenne were the victors that day, the battle marked the beginning of their own Last Stand...

—Nathaniel Philbrick

Although the village of Alzada seemed more like a ghost town, it did have a restaurant. We saw a sign painted on the top of a dilapidated weather-beaten barn: "Stoneville Saloon. Cheap Drinks—Lousy Food." I don't drink, so the first part of the sign didn't faze me. Since I was ravenous, neither did the second part.

We parked the van and walked inside. The place was empty. Soon, the bartender was cooking and serving us our giant burgers, which proved to be done to perfection.

As soon as we swallowed the last bite, Frank, whose mood had inexplicably darkened, said, "Let's go, old man. No lollygagging. We still have miles to go."

"Maybe we ought to hang around here tonight. They may have a hootenanny and you can dance with a Montana cattle queen."

"No, I want to get going," he insisted.

For no particular reason, I decided to be stubborn. I told Frank that I was still overheated and thirsty, "I'd like to stay a little while longer and drink another Coke or two." Turning to the bartender, I asked, "Where's the name 'Stoneville Saloon' come from?"

"Well," he began, "back when this was the Montana Territory, Stoneville used to be the name of this town. After the Civil War, it was a stagecoach stop on a section running between Deadwood [South Dakota] and Miles City [Montana]. And cattle-rustling gangs used to also operate from here in the late 1800s."

He claimed that Annie Oakley, Wild Bill Hickok, Buffalo Bill Cody, Jesse James, and Calamity Jane used to be regulars at this saloon. But there were no photos or autographs.

Clearly, the lonely bartender was thrilled to have company. He was just getting started. But I sensed that Frank's fuse was getting shorter. I interrupted, paid the bill, and we departed abruptly. I felt badly but Frank came first.

* * *

I'd been walking for hours when Frank pulled up next to me. He asked "Where are we staying tonight?"

I consulted the map. The town of Broadus seemed larger than Alzada, so that's where we'd bed down.

Broadus was located a little west of the Powder River, which had been described as "A mile wide and an inch deep—too wet to plow and too thick to drink."

When we arrived in Broadus, we discovered it was just another sleepy hamlet. Unfortunately, we had just missed the annual cattle drive. Tourists pay big bucks to follow along in covered wagons to get a taste of cowboy life.

There were no strip malls, fast-food joints, or motel chains. Our motel looked dreary. The woman at the front desk suggested we dine at "The Judge's Chambers," which was just down the street.

The steak was surprisingly delicious. The vegetables had been harvested from the fenced-in garden adjacent to the restaurant. We chatted with a couple at the table next to us about the fact that there was no speed limit on Route 212. The woman told us that three days before two Broadus teenagers were killed in an accident, driving over 120 miles per hour. She said ruefully, "Most Montanans don't like the idea of a speed limit."

Her husband piped in, "I hope you're not continuing your walk after dinner."

"Why not?" I asked.

"After the sun goes down, the rattlesnakes like to move onto the pavement for warmth," he said. "I wouldn't want you to step on one, as sure as hell they'd get ya."

I glanced at Frank, whose bad mood I hadn't been able to fathom. "I guess there'll be no more walking for you, Mr. Snake Charmer," he said, smiling for the first time that day. Frank was so good at keeping things light. From the outset, I knew how fortunate I was to have him.

During the first weeks of the walk Charles had been an able and mostly effective driver, companion, assistant and protector of my safety. Of course a huge problem from the beginning, however, was the fact it was very difficult for us to communicate. Charles spoke only Portuguese. While he did understand some words and was able to sometimes get a point across in English, for the most part we had little to say to each other. My days and evenings were virtually silent. Plus Charles was much younger than me. We were products of not only different cultures but also different generations.

Frank, on the other hand, was a kindred soul. We grew up in the same culture and in roughly the same generation, even in the same area. Frank was not only able to communicate, he could converse with anybody, anywhere, at any time. While I am somewhat reserved coming in contact with strangers, Frank's zeal to chat with people knew no bounds. I believe he could talk with rocks.

Having many years of experience as a marathon runner gave Frank a great advantage in terms of understanding the physical and mental stress of my extreme physical quest. He understood every problem, pain, ass-ache and equipment failure that I routinely encountered during my thirteen-hour days. In addition, Frank knew the right moments to give me a hand, push me when I needed to be pushed, console me when my spirits were low, and support my mission and my goals. He brought to the walk a leadership approach that Charles lacked. Basically, from the day he came aboard, he took charge. That leadership allowed me the freedom of simply walking, leaving all the rest to his discretion.

* * *

Early the next morning, I took my first step on a forty-four-mile trek to Ashland, Montana. Thankfully Frank's mood had improved. He sounded excited, and talked incessantly about George Armstrong Custer. Much of his knowledge came from three or four movies and he filled me in on Custer's military prowess. I knew little about the man. I made a mental note to purchase some guidebooks at the battle-field-site gift shop to confirm what Frank had told me.

With a little luck, we would arrive at Little Big Horn late in the day.

I was more excited about seeing Montana. I'd heard so much about "Big Sky Country" and now I was finally immersed in it.

Tramping down this "ribbon of highway," I couldn't even make out the make and models of the cars, because they were whizzing by so fast. I finally passed the sign I had been waiting to see—the world-famous Montana speed-limit sign. It would thrill the heart of any testosterone-charged teenager. It read: "Speed Limit—Reasonable & Prudent." In other words, the sky's the limit. Apparently, it was the only state at that time that had no posted speed limit on its major highways. On some of those roads, to have no speed limit is risky, as the twists and turns are sometimes sharp and dangerous, yet the "reasonable and prudent" prevailed. And therefore, since this harkened to the issue of states' rights, it's probably safe to say that Montana is close to being the reddest state of all. Indeed, it had not voted for a Democrat for president since 1964, and that was one of only five times since statehood.

Speaking of red, I was walking due west with the sun baking the left side of my face. By the end of the day, my left cheek would surely look like a ripened tomato.

Despite the fact that there are now about five billion people crowded onto this mostly blue pearl of a planet, hardly any of them seem to live in this corner of Montana. Except for a handful of speeding cars, the only sounds I heard were a few wolves and coyotes.

At about the twenty-mile mark, I walked into Custer National Forest, headed toward Custer's Last Stand. Apparently, Lewis and Clark also passed through here. And I soon learned that beneath my feet sat the earth's largest coal reserves, not to mention innumerable dinosaur fossils.

As the road ahead gained elevation, I soon passed a sign that declared this to be a "chain-up" area, which meant that during winter storms drivers are required by law to drive with chains on their tires.

With each passing mile, trees began to encroach on the road. Soon, I was surrounded by a forest of evergreens. Occasionally, a log home appeared nearby, its yard cluttered with snowmobiles, pickup trucks, spare airplane tires or pontoons, and other paraphernalia of bush survival.

After a relatively monotonous thirty miles, I waved to the blur of a van rushing by. It pulled over and stopped a few hundred yards ahead of me. It was not a van but an aged Volkswagen bus—older than the two teenagers walking back toward me. They introduced themselves—Dallas Rolnick, eighteen, and Clay Rockefeller, nineteen, from the state of Maine. They told me they had been accepted to college, but decided to defer for a year to take a "Driving USA" trip. We swapped a few stories, but it soon became apparent that they were anxious to get back to their quest. Clay claimed to be a direct descendent of John D. Rockefeller and Dallas was an heir of an equally famed and wealthy family. Before we parted, I outfitted them with Walking USA shirts and hats and away they went.

With only eleven miles left, I was walking in the iridescent glow of Big Sky twilight, feeling like I had died and gone to heaven. It was as if I was back on morphine. I clamped on my Walkman and danced down the road to the rhythm of the Four Tops, the Temptations, and then the musical from Sylvester Stallone's *Rocky* soundtrack. I was always such a sap for inspirational stories.

Finishing late, we checked into a motel right next to the Custer Battlefield National Monument and settled in.

Frank was more excited than I'd ever seen him. All he did was babble about Custer, his hero. His favorite movie is *They Died with Their Boots On*. It's the 1941 fictionalized biopic, starring Errol Flynn and Olivia de Havilland. The script was loosely based on *Boots and Saddles*, an 1885 first-person account of life with Custer, written by his devoted wife, Elizabeth. After his death, she launched a successful single-handed campaign to cleanse her husband's image and glorify his memory. (He'd been publicly censured by President Ulysses S. Grant for blundering into the massacre, which is exactly what he did.)

In 1876, Custer thought that his campaign against the Sioux would bring him greater glory. Crazy Horse and Sitting Bull had made it clear they were not keen on the imposition of the reservation system and that Custer needed to be put in his place.

Frank showered me with fascinating tidbits about Custer. "Did you know that he finished last and had the most demerits in his class at West Point and yet went on to become a Civil War hero?"

"No, I didn't know that."

"Did you know Custer was temporarily promoted to general at age twenty-three—the youngest general in the Union Army—three days prior to the battle of Gettysburg?"

"No, I didn't know that either."

"Did you know that Custer was there with General Grant when Lee surrendered at Appomattox?"

The only thing I could recall about Custer was a tasteless joke I heard in junior high school: "How much would you like to contribute to the Indian Relief Fund, Mrs. Custer?"

With each of Frank's assertions, I was becoming more impressed with his hero.

"Did you know that Hollywood has produced more films about Custer's Last Stand than any other story?"

I loved his enthusiasm and I appeared riveted to everything Frank had to say, but I couldn't help but sneakily do some quick calculations in my journal as he held forth about Custer.

I had now walked 3,365 miles in twelve weeks.

* * *

We were standing in the middle of the Custer Battlefield National Monument. This was where Native Americans killed and mutilated 263 U.S. soldiers. However, it wasn't just Custer's last stand; it was also the last stand for the briefly victorious Lakota Sioux, Arapaho, and Cheyenne Native Americans. It is a little known fact that the day of Custer's Last Stand spawned enormous change in our country, and that day should be viewed as one of the most significant days in our history.

Because of the humiliating rout, President Grant sent thousands of troops into the area, ordering them to systematically wipe out the Indians with a ferocity commensurate with what they'd done to Custer and his men. The lives of Native Americans were irrevocably altered and tribal life was tragically destroyed.

As was usually the case, Custer was not the unadulterated hero that Frank imagined. The reputation of Custer, a complex and controversial man, had suffered notable revisions, especially in the face of our growing collective guilt over the treatment of the original settlers of the New World.

Yes, Custer was a somewhat flamboyant cavalry commander during the Civil War, but he did ride his horse in front of his men into battle, while many of his peers "led" their men safely from the rear.

And Custer did play a somewhat significant role in the battle of Gettysburg. After hours of charges, counter charges, and hand-to-hand combat, he led his cavalry in what seemed a foolhardy assault, which finally crushed a Confederate attempt to flank the Union position. Custer lost 257 men, the highest loss of any Union Cavalry brigade. Never humble, Custer later wrote in his report, "I challenge the annals of warfare to produce a more brilliant or successful charge of cavalry."

Although reputed to be reckless, he always thoroughly scouted out and carefully planned his military assaults during the Civil War.

Most of his earlier accomplishments, however, were overshadowed by what happened here. At Little Big Horn, on June 25, 1876, Lieutenant Colonel George Armstrong Custer goofed, believing he was invincible. (We all make mistakes.) And basically, that's all he's remembered for.

Today, a twelve-foot-high, white obelisk overlooks the battlefield with the names of the soldiers who died here. The gravestones of Custer's cavalrymen, buried where they fell, are scattered over the hillside. Custer's remains were later exhumed and re-buried at the U.S. Military Academy at West Point.

There is an effort afoot to build another monument here, recognizing the Native American version of events.

Before Interstate 90 was built in the sixties, which passes right by the battlefield, very few tourists visited the battlefield. Now, they flock in vast numbers.

While I stood next to the obelisk, I heard an elderly gentleman remark to his wife, "Usually you have to be a hero and win a great victory to have a monument named after you. Here, we honor a complete loser."

Like in Northfield, Minnesota, where residents reenact the defeat of the Jesse James Gang, in nearby Hardin, Montana, there is an annual re-enactment of Custer's Last Stand.

I guess it's a good excuse to have fun and haul in a few tourist dollars.

Part Six
Purple Mountains Majesty

I grew up in Idaho, on the flat, sagebrush-dotted Snake River Plain.
My horizons were bounded by mountains eighty miles to the north
and thirty miles to the south. In a certain light the jagged lines of the
distant ranges took on a purple hue.
Besides, I knew the words to "America the Beautiful":
Oh, beautiful for spacious skies,
For amber waves of grain,
For purple mountains majesty . . .
—Cathryn Wellner

Chapter Seventy-Three
The Last Best Place

I'm in love with Montana. For other states I have admiration, respect, recognition, even some affection. But with Montana it is love. And it's difficult to analyze love when you're in it.
—John Steinbeck

We had breakfast the following morning in a gambling casino in the town of Hardin, just a couple of miles from the Custer Battlefield. Casinos were apparently sprouting up all over Montana. These were nothing like the Las Vegas variety—usually just a few of slot machines. Unlike casinos in other states, in Montana they were apparently operated by corporations and not solely by Native American tribes.

Starving, I told the waitress, "Burn the bacon and double up on the eggs, pancakes, and English muffins."

Frank chimed in, "If you're going to eat all that I guess we won't be getting to Billings today."

I knocked off a large carafe of orange juice before the food arrived.

When the bill came, I realized I was down to my last hundred-dollar bill. I had spent $10,000 in cash since leaving Boston. That was just the cash. I had charged a lot more than that. I was upset. I was spending far more than I had anticipated.

I asked Frank "Can you lend me a couple of thousand until we get to California?"

"Here you go old man," he said as he reached into his money belt and handed me twenty, one-hundred-dollar bills.

After breakfast, I decided to walk along an old deserted highway nearby that ran along Interstate 90 that also went to Billings. It would be safer than the interstate.

Down the road a few miles, we lost one of our flags to the heavy wind. We always flew four flags, one on each corner of the van. We had an American flag, A black POW/MIA flag, a state flag (from whatever state we happened to be in) and of course, a New England Patriots flag. We lost the Patriots flag. It was a bad omen.

After forty-four miles of getting shoved around by heavy fifty-mile-per-hour winds, we arrived in Billings and found a motel. It seemed like every few steps I took, I was blown back one step. I had to wear goggles to keep flying debris out of my eyes. My face hurt from the sting of flying sand. We were fortunate though, as Indian summer was still hanging around. In early October, the wind often brought colder weather and early snows to Montana.

I called Nick Overmier. He's the guy we had met in South Dakota a couple of weeks before who told us to call him when we got to Billings. Nick had left on another trip, but he made good on his promise of a dinner. He had told his son Ray to make sure we got the best of Billings for dinner when we arrived. Within an hour, Ray delivered our "special Montana meal" right to our motel. It was a tasty broiled chicken dinner with salad, mashed potatoes and broccoli. It would have been easy for Nick to simply say, "Sorry, I'm out of town." His consideration for us was noteworthy. A shout-out to Ray and Nick! Thank you guys so much!

After dinner, we visited a sporting-goods store to pick up some winter gear, including boots, in case vicious old man winter descended on us unexpectedly even though it was only October. I had lost most of my winter gear when the storage bin on the top of the van had proven to be leaky. As I was checking out, the store owner called the local TV station to tell them about my walk and within minutes I was doing an impromptu interview. The reporter had trouble accepting the fact that I planned to walk all the way across Montana, nearly 600 miles.

I told him, "But I've already walked over 3,000 miles."

"But this is Montana," he said. "It's far too big to walk across."

Guess that's Montana, I thought.

After that interview, during our meals people constantly came up to our table to welcome us and they often stopped us on the road to say that they had seen us on TV. In a place devoid of the typical media fare found in more populous areas—murder, mayhem and corruption—we were minor celebrities. Many were fascinated by the fact that I was walking all the way across Montana—something they all believed to be impossible.

The next day, I passed through the hamlet of Laurel. For some reason, my olfactory sense had come alive. The roadside scent of flowers and grasses were intoxicating, but they were occasionally drowned out by the foul odor of diesel fumes whenever an eighteen-wheeler zoomed by. I especially loved the smell of the pine trees—it was like the aroma of Christmas.

The reminder of Christmas caused me to take a break and have a cold drink. I thought back to the many special Christmas days I had spent with my boys. Nicholas was only three months old when I took him in my arms and held his hands so that together we could decorate the Christmas tree. He giggled with delight in spite of how young he was, fascinated by the bright, shiny ornaments and lights.

By the next year when he was only one year and three months old, I put the lights and decorations on the top foot or two of the ten-foot tree. Then Nicholas took over. I held the ladder for him and he did the rest of the decorating. As the years passed, Nicholas always took care of decorating for Christmas in our home. On the day after Thanksgiving he would ask, "Dad, can you take me to pick out the Christmas tree?" Together, we would bring the tree home and set it up in the living room. Nicholas wouldn't allow anyone else to touch it. The next day, after it had dried and the branches had spread out, without any help, he'd decorate the tree and the entire house. His "takeover" of Christmas became the tradition in our family. To this day, Nicholas still rules Christmas.

* * *

One of the really incongruous things I had noticed in Montana was all the litter strewn on the side of and in the middle of the highway. I'm sorry to say I had to rate Montana tops on the "Worst Litter" scorecard of the trip, and someone told me it is ranked one of the deadliest states for debris-caused motor vehicle accidents. It was reminiscent of walking through Honduras or other Central or South American countries, where folks use the side of the road as their own personal trash barrel.

To the north, I saw dark storm clouds and flecks of lightning, but over my head there was nothing but sunshine. However, the winds were howling. Some of the gusts were hurricane force. I was probably exaggerating, but the winds made it seem colder, so I wore gloves, a facemask, and my red-white-and-blue New England Patriots parka.

All of a sudden, off in the distance, reaching high into the sky, I saw the Rockies. They were capped with snow that looked like whipped cream. I was like a little boy who had just gotten a puppy for Christmas!

Not too long after, a Montana State Trooper pulled up behind us. He was the first police officer I had seen in Montana. He was very courteous and just wanted to make sure we were okay. "What are you doing on the interstate?" he asked.

"We are going all the way across the state, so we have to use the interstate—there is no other route from town to town."

"You had best be real careful. Traffic moves real fast here," he told us.

"I am always vigilant," I responded.

Locals had warned me against walking very early in the morning, because that's when one is most likely to make the acquaintance of bears, wolves, mountain lions and snakes. While I was more attentive than usual, the only dangerous fauna that had threatened me so far were gophers, pronghorns, deer, pheasants and wild turkeys. However, I'd rather bump into a grizzly or a mountain lion than a snake. (Indiana Jones and I have something in common—a preternatural fear of snakes.)

On my right I spotted another small herd of pronghorns. They were running in pairs, moving in circles like hockey players warming up for a game, prancing in rhythm to some music only they could hear.

I signaled Frank to stop the van. I opened the side doors and sat down to watch the agile, elegant creatures. There were at least twenty of them, playing in the meadow below. At one point they all stopped their playful antics and looked directly at the van. After fifteen seconds, two of them turned away and raced off like bullets. A second later, the others followed. Moments after that, they had vanished into the tall grasses.

A few miles down the road, I saw smoke billowing from a farmhouse chimney. The home was surrounded by enormous fenced, but empty, pastures. Nearby stood giant rolls of hay next to long rows of firewood. Everything was covered with white tarps. This rancher was preparing for winter, in which the deadly chinook winds howl, and even though the chinook brings warm air, it would feel cold. Soon the temperatures would drop to sub-zero for weeks on end. Montana boasts the lowest temperature ever recorded in the continental United States—seventy degrees Fahrenheit below zero. Ouch!

I heard so much about Montana cattle and ranching, yet as I passed countless acres of grazing land, I'd seen hardly any cattle or sheep or horses.

At the end of the day, we checked into a typical aesthetically depressing Super 8. Their rooms are so plain and uninviting but they had one attractive feature: the right price.

After two days of walking directly into the stiff headwinds, my face was so raw and chapped we had to visit another sporting-goods store, where I bought a better mask—a hunter's mask. I was using Vaseline on my entire face, not just my lips. The guy behind the counter said his fiancée was the editor-in-training at the local paper.

"Would you let her interview you?" he asked. It seems everywhere we stopped, someone knew someone who would want to get a scoop on the old, fat man walking all the way across Montana.

I was really not in the mood, but I agreed to do it anyway.

I had walked an extra seven miles, so I was really beat. Oddly enough, I was not hungry. I just wanted to lie down and die. A down-in-the-dumps feeling was starting to settle in. I think it started in Eagle Butte, South Dakota, on the Sioux reservation. I had done my best to ignore the sense of sadness. I am noted for always seeing the glass half full, or even completely full. In Eagle Butte, the reality had confronted me head on. I didn't want Steve Emery to know how badly I felt about all the squalor, alcoholism and poverty I saw on his reservation. I had repressed my feelings of despair and that was probably not a healthy thing to do. Maybe I shouldn't have quit my anti-depressant medicine.

I quickly fell asleep. After two hours, Frank shook me awake. "Time to get some chow," he said.

After a quiet and peaceful dinner, I was still very tired, but I couldn't sleep. My legs were jerking involuntarily, keeping me awake. After about three hours, I woke Frank. "I'm really worried," I told him. "My legs are twitching and I can't make them stop."

Frank watched for a few minutes and said, "You need to go to the hospital, old man."

At the emergency room, the nurses and doctors seemed more interested in my walk than my health. After a pretty thorough examination, the doctor said, "You have restless leg syndrome." Also known as RLS, the nurse told me. The Doc said, "You need to have bed rest for a week." He also prescribed a muscle relaxant and iron and magnesium pills. "Your problem might well be a type of RLS caused by nutritional deficiencies, given the extreme exercise you are doing."

I asked him, "Please tell me more about this RLS."

"Most times RLS can be a very significant problem if it's related to unknown genetic causes. People who develop RLS typically have rheumatoid arthritis, lupus and other such problems in their family history. Their symptoms are the same as yours. The urge to keep moving your legs usually becomes a problem when you lie down to rest and your legs are relaxed. As you've described your symptoms that's what happened to you. By lying down to rest with your legs relaxed, you can't stop moving your legs," he responded.

How long will it take to get rid of the symptoms?" I asked.

"Well, the sudden onset makes me think that this is all related to either iron or magnesium deficiency. That is easier to deal with than other forms of RLS and it should clear up quickly, I think, with the supplements I've prescribed. You should be okay in a few days."

I smiled, I nodded, I thanked him, but I was not going to stop. I swallowed the pills.

We didn't get back to our motel room until 5 A.M. I told Frank, "I've decided to take one day off." I stayed in bed the entire day, updating my website and my journals.

Frank was very concerned. He advised "You really ought to follow the doctor's orders and stay in bed for a week."

"If I did, I'd probably just give up and go home."

After the day's rest, my legs felt much better and the twitching had subsided. Apparently the medicine had done what it was expected to do. I was ready to go.

Next morning, In spite of the doctor's orders, I was up and out, walking by Crazy Mountain. "What an odd name." I thought to myself. "Look at this!" Frank shouted, "The crazy man walking by Crazy Mountain!"

Later, I learned that more than 100 years ago, Indians allegedly attacked a wagon train right in front of the mountain. All the white settlers were apparently killed, except one woman. She went berserk and in her crazed state somehow managed to kill several of the attackers. The others barely escaped with their lives. Legend has it she then wandered off up into the mountain, where she lived by herself for many years; hence, the moniker "Crazy Mountain."

The following morning I was on the road again, heading west to Livingston. For no apparent reason, I soon began to encounter an unusual number of motor homes passing me, headed west. They were usually driven by either an elderly man or woman with the other spouse as co-pilot. The license plates were from Texas, New York, California, and a score of other states. There was a disproportionate number from Florida. For some reason, none of them stopped to say hi.

Hours later, as I began to ascend the foothills of the Rocky Mountains, Frank noticed a bicyclist approaching rapidly behind us. Moments later, a seventy-six-year-old man named Gordy introduced himself. He lived in Big Timber. He told us that two or three times a week he rode to Livingston and back, which is about seventy miles round trip "to get a little exercise." Gordy also told us, "I routinely cycle to Phoenix, Arizona, and back—a roundtrip of about 2,600 miles—to visit family." Wow!

As Gordy rode off he declared, "You are crazy to be doing this."

"You're the pot calling the kettle black."

"I know!" he laughed

About twenty-five miles later, as I reached the outskirts of Livingston, we bumped into Gordy again. He was pedaling back to Big Timber. I stopped him and give him a Walking USA shirt and a hat to remember us by. From the look of his overalls, the brand-new shirt would be a big change for Gordy. He surprised me by putting the shirt over his outfit and replaced his worn and filthy Denver Broncos cap with the bright white Walking USA cap.

Gordy put the Broncos hat in his pack. I told him "Gordy, the best advice I can give you is to toss that ugly orange hat into the trash—it doesn't do you justice."

In Livingston, I sauntered past a Hummer. Someone told us it belonged to the actor Steven Segal. It seems lots of famous people were buying up land in the Livingston area for permanent or vacation homes, including Segal, Ted Turner, and Tom Brokaw. Only Brokaw seemed to be accepted—apparently because he is from neighboring South Dakota. Native Montanans are not thrilled about the invasion of the wealthy, especially those from California. They don't like big-money outsiders driving up land prices.

Staring up at the Rockies, I could see why this particular part of Montana has long captured the hearts of photographers, artists and moviemakers. It was so spectacular I hated to see the sun go down.

* * *

Early the next morning, I was beginning a twelve-mile hike up to Bozeman Pass, which is just below 6,000 feet. Because of my slow ascent, the increasingly higher altitude didn't cause me to have breathing problems. I guessed my body was able to slowly adjust to the change.

Locals say in 1860, John Bozeman came down with a bad case of gold fever. He abandoned his wife and three daughters in Georgia and headed west. Three years later, he allegedly blazed a trail from Fort Laramie, Wyoming, all the way to Virginia City, Montana, "discovering" the pass that would later bear his name. Not surprisingly, Native Americans had used this pass since prehistoric times. And Sacagawea, the Shoshone teenager who guided Lewis and Clark, led their expedition through this pass in 1806.

Bozeman later died at the hands of Native Americans. I guess you could say that karma caught up with him for leaving his wife and children. It was a message of "What goes round, comes round."

The Morphine Dream

Once I reached the scenic vista up at the top of the pass, the view was beyond description. Above were the snow-covered mountains. Below were the serpentine rivers, the sweeping grasslands, the ranches, the highways, and the train tracks. Unfortunately, the scenic lookout area was littered with trash.

As we began the twelve-mile descent into the city of Bozeman, we were interviewed by Dennis Carlson, the anchor of the local Fox News affiliate. I guess I spoiled the interview by complaining to Carlson about the mountains of litter. He said, "It's such a disgrace, and the fines are huge, but people still do it."

Fortunately, that part of the interview was not on the segment on television that evening. The broadcast was notable for the portion devoted to Frank. The reporter asked him, "What's it like for you on the thirteen-hour days?"

Frank responded, "If you think what he's doing is hard, think again. Following him at three and a half miles an hour—looking at his ass all day—is *much* more difficult."

* * *

The next day I left Bozeman in the pre-dawn hours. It was the fourth-largest city in Montana but it's really just a small town. There would be no mountain walking on this day, thank God.

Around lunchtime, I strolled into the tiny town of Manhattan. Transplanted New Yorkers must have named it. We dined at "The Cafe on Broadway."

Several hours later, I walked into Three Forks. Three rivers converged there, the Jefferson, the Madison and the Gallitan—and they together formed the famed Missouri River. The rivers were named by Meriwether Lewis while crossing Montana as part of the Lewis and Clark Expedition. In the town's center, a statue stands to honor the Native American woman, Sacagawea, who had been the interpreter, guide and liaison to Native Americans for Lewis and Clark as they explored the Native American lands. Without the presence of Sacagawea, Lewis and Clark probably would never have been allowed the access by Native Americans to complete their trek.

It was cold, raw and windy at the confluence of the rivers. "Enough is enough. Let's hang it up for the day," I said to Frank. We checked into The Broken Spur Motel. We quickly found a place to eat and gulped giant burgers and slurped down icy and frosty root beers at Custer's Last Root Beer Stand.

336

The Last Best Place

* * *

I was back mountain-climbing as I traveled from Three Forks towards Butte. While the altitude was not affecting my breathing, it had not been a normal day. I wasn't feeling good emotionally. I had no explanation—just had the blues.

At noon, I reached Homestake Pass, where the famous Continental Divide was located. This natural boundary line, which runs from Alaska to Mexico, is the point from which all water either flows into either the Atlantic Ocean (or Gulf of Mexico) or the Pacific Ocean. It would be easy to miss the divide, because there were only a couple of small signs off to the side of the road noting that we were at it.

Two hours later, I decided to quit for the day. I was disappointed in myself. I was having problems with my diabetes, and I was not reacting well to the medication the doctor had prescribed for my restless legs. To top it off, I was feeling really down. Maybe it was related to diabetes. Perhaps the strain of being away from home and my boys was overwhelming me. Whatever it was, it didn't feel good. I felt like I was drowning.

We drove to a motel in Butte where I spent the afternoon trying to get my blood sugar under control. I also watched three *Rocky* movies and some video of my sons in an attempt to quash my dark mood.

* * *

Feeling a little better, I was up and on the road by 7:00 A.M. A mile ahead, I saw six-and-twenty blackbirds attacking a road-kill prairie dog. They were so focused on their task that they didn't even bother to look up as I quietly drifted by.

I noticed somebody walking on the highway up ahead of me. It turned out to be a guy about my age, with a pack and a sleeping bag. He was as tall as me, but frighteningly skinny. He had not had a shave, haircut or—if aroma was any indication—a bath for a long time. "Where are you headed?" I asked as I slowed down to walk with him.

"Anywhere and nowhere," he said. "I'm homeless, penniless and just keeping moving."

"You are a long way from the next town. Are you okay? Can you make it?"

"That's why I got the sleeping bag. When I get tired, I just roll it open, lie down and rest."

"Would you like to ride in the van for a while?" I asked him.

"No. you guys move too fast for my blood."

I grabbed a couple of Walking USA shirts and a cap for him from the van. The new duds brought a big toothless smile to his face. "There still is a Santa Claus," he said. "Thank you, thank you, thank you!"

The afternoon dragged and I felt unusually fatigued. Uncharacteristically, I wanted to quit for the day but Frank was snapping the whip, telling me that, "Quitting is out of the question." I dug deeper and pushed on for the remaining ten miles. For some reason, the magical beat of the Four Tops and the Temptations didn't do the trick. I felt miserable. Maybe, it was my diabetes, the loneliness, fears about the future, and perhaps, the pointlessness of it all. I was thinking about the homeless guy and how, in some ways, I wasn't much different than him. For the time, I was without a home, even though I had one. On the road, I was so far removed from my life it almost seemed like it was gone. Besides, I was certainly acutely aware that my marriage was falling apart. I would not know what was going to happen in that regard until I returned home after the walk.

* * *

My morning was difficult. I was struggling just to complete my twenty miles before lunch. Frank was on my case: "Keep moving' old man." Finally, I ignored him and took a rest in the van. Unfortunately I was thus forced to listen to Frank's favorite radio talk show—Rush Limbaugh. He was spewing about moral decay in America, after a sixteen-year-old student had shot two classmates and his mother in Pearl, Mississippi.

To me, these random acts of violence did not suggest moral decay. They were the extreme exceptions. I had experienced something quite different on this epic odyssey. Call me a delusional optimist, but I had found the opposite of moral decay on this walk of thousands of miles. It was the many selfless random acts of kindness from people living normal lives that were so uplifting: the Shultzes in Waukesha, Wisconsin; the Mitchells in Columbus, Ohio; the Ringhands in Oregon, Wisconsin; and the Boyles in Iowa. They were just a small sampling of anonymous people who, in their own quiet way, made our country better every single day. Their stories didn't make the newspapers or the TV screens, but it was they who tell the true story of America, not the mentally deranged guy with a gun who "goes postal."

And finally, even though I agreed with Walt Whitman that America is "the greatest poem," I also knew that nothing was quite so simple, including my platitudes about all the wonderful people I'd met on this trip. America is a complex place, often praised or vilified for mistaken reasons, and in need of continual reinterpretation and excavation.

* * *

I had been walking in Montana for several days. It had all become a visual blur—the hamlets we passed through, the motels we stayed at, the taverns we dined in.

I was finding out why Montanans called it "The Last, Best Place." As I walked along, it was a no-brainer. Nearly two centuries ago, Meriwether Lewis and William Clark were equally mesmerized, wandering across this magical landscape, in search of an all-water route from the Missouri River to the Pacific Ocean. What they ended up doing, among so many other things, was germinating Manifest Destiny—the arrogant notion that the United States was fated to extend itself all the way to the Pacific, without regard for the Native Americans.

Lewis faced some daunting challenges upon his return home. He had been plagued with depression for most of his life. Some speculate that after the thrills of his "discovery" quest, he became despondent because of the lack excitement in the times after he completed his remarkable expedition across the vast plains and mountains of the northern territory of the country.

When Lewis returned to Missouri, he had been named Governor of the Louisiana Territory. As governor, he was apparently deeply troubled by President Madison's refusal to reimburse him significant sums for checks he had used to pay for valid expenses of the territory. He wrote notes to William Clark, which Clark thought to be "suicide notes." He had written more of these apparent suicide notes to several other people as he was preparing to embark on a trip to Washington, D.C., to convince the government to pay him back for the money he had spent on official business. On that trip, it has been alleged that he committed suicide by shooting himself twice. There are many who claim he was murdered. Whatever happened, one of America's genuine heroes was dead at the young age of thirty-five.

Although I couldn't wait to end my own journey at Big Sur, I also dreaded reaching it, because I, too, would have to deal with the let-down that seems to prevail after arduous quests. I would have to return home and face the music. As I had already said, I had applied to have my license to practice law reinstated. The hearing was slated for February 1998. The outcome was at best uncertain. *What if I get turned down? What will I do?* I thought. I would be confronting again the daunting challenge of how support my family. That was the constant in life since my early teens when my father died.

Early in the morning, I had stepped out of another nondescript motel room. It was still dark outside. I heard howling in the distance. I smiled at the pleasant memory—reading Jack London's *The Call of the Wild*. (His gift for the bold use of language was amazing.) Of course, that book didn't take place in Montana. In preparation for visiting this wondrous state, I had read Norman Maclean's *A River Runs Through It* and Larry McMurtry's *Lonesome Dove*.

As I approached the front desk to check out I said "What is the howling outside?"

"It's from one of those million-dollar wolves," he answered.

"Huh?" I said.

He explained. "It's the federal government's program to re-populate the area with wolves. They were virtually wiped out around here. The cost of the government program translates into about a million dollars per wolf." He said he could think of more sensible ways to spend the money. "Most Montana farmers are not thrilled about the government's program, because wolves like to prey on their livestock."

"Do they have a habit of bothering people?" I asked as I was a little leery about how close they might be to the interstate.

He responded "With the van traveling behind you it's probably not likely they will come anywhere near you, as the sound of the vehicle will keep them away."

We left—and I was less troubled by the sound and the danger. Walking along, I continued to listen to the distant howling, It seemed to be too close for comfort. I was still somewhat worried about one of those wolves discovering me walking along in the dawn.

After twelve days in Montana, the most beautiful state of them all, ironically, I was more depressed than ever on this trip. I couldn't explain it. Thank God I had Frank to talk to.

I began to think my depression was due to missing my sons. Every day, I thought about them for much of time. I had been blessed as they had never done anything to cause my concern. They had been extraordinarily close and completely devoted to one another.

I remember when Nick was in first grade and LouLou was in nursery school. Nick often came home with projects to complete for school. LouLou always would have to complete the same project. Nick was so patient with his little brother, and would help him, always being a "teacher" to Louis. Nick's attention helped Louis to advance from the significant deficits related to his birth.

Nick was a musician from two years old, playing the piano. Louis had great difficulty moving his fingers because of his cerebral palsy. Doctors and therapists said he would never be able to use his hands effectively. That meant, I assumed, no piano for Louis. Yet he wouldn't accept that. Nicholas was playing, so Louis had to play. And play he did, overcoming many of his disabilities so that he, too, could make music.

* * *

I decided to shorten my daily walks for a while to give my diabetes and my RLS some recovery time. I had built a couple of extra days into the schedule for crossing the huge state of Montana. I was able to cut back and still stay on schedule.

I set out for Deer Lodge, forty miles from Butte. After about twenty miles, it got very cold. I was struggling against a fifty-mile-per-hour headwind. After thirty-five miles, I was beaten. We drove ahead to Deer Lodge to find a place to rest and to do some laundry.

The extra rest helped, as always. I had come to realize that no matter how beat I was, a rest period would bring me back quickly. Each night I would go to bed with legs so sore, I thought I would never walk again. After a night's rest, I would wake up pain free. I would be stiff—for sure—but a mile or so into my daily walk, I would loosen up and feel normal.

* * *

In the morning, I headed out to Drummond, only thirty-five miles away.

The weather started out sunny and cold. After a few miles, it changed to cold, rainy and windy. It was a miserable day for walking.

We met G. E. Keith, a Montana State Trooper. He stopped to see if we needed help and then circled back a couple hours later. The three of us spent an hour or so chatting about nothing much at all.

I asked Trooper Keith, "How come I never see any cattle?"

"They are here," he responded. The ranchers have them grazing in remote grasslands till late October when they are rounded up and brought back to the farms, which are visible from the highways." He told me.

Mystery solved, I thought.

I said, "Someone has told me that the ranchers in this day and age still have to worry about cattle-rustling. Is that true?"

Trooper Keith said, "You need to understand, at a dollar a pound, a single cow could be worth $2,000—and the temptation is a problem."

He also advised us, "Clear out of Montana fast! The weather is about to make a big change. It's something you don't want to experience."

A UPS truck stopped to make sure all was okay. I asked him about his daily route, realizing houses were few and far between.

He told me, "I drive about 400 miles a day to make only thirty to forty deliveries. People here depend on getting most of their needs shipped to them, because most everyday consumer goods are not locally available."

"Can't they just drive to the cities around here?" I asked.

"The nearest real city for Montanans is Seattle, and it is eight hours away."

Our roadside gathering broke up as Trooper Keith got a call to respond to an accident. The UPS driver had to move on to his 400-mile daily trip.

The journey continued. I thought often about the parents and children who walked before me or rode in covered wagons 150 years ago. They all did it without sneakers or Rockports. There were no roads, maps, motels, cell phones, or restaurants. No friendly state troopers to offer assistance. No UPS trucks to bring supplies. They often walked twenty to thirty miles a day. They forded rivers and climbed mountains, and fought Native Americans and wild animals. And they had no idea of what was up ahead. How in God's name did they do it? And people told me what I am doing is tough?

I don't want to sound repetitive, but I continued to see breathtaking mountains, tumbling streams, misty waterfalls, and millions of trees along the way. It never got old or tiresome. The aroma of the forest was always with me. The icy clean water in the streams made me think I could drink it. The sound of those streams never leaves your ears.

As I finally approached Drummond, Frank and I saw a fabulous billboard next to the road. "Welcome to the Annual Testicle Festival. Come Have a Ball." Around here, breaded and fried bull's testicles are considered a delicacy, referred to as "Rocky Mountain oysters."

We headed for the festival. I certainly was not interested in tasting the "oysters." Frank, on the other hand, was considering trying them out. I said, "Please don't do it while I'm around." The thought of eating one made me sick.

* * *

The following early cold, brisk morning, I left Drummond to walk to Missoula, the last of the Montana cities on my route. At our ten-mile rest stop, we met a family of three from West Virginia. They were traveling with all their worldly possessions stuffed into their little eleven-year-old Toyota, headed to Spokane to seek a new life. They certainly didn't have a penny to spare, but nevertheless they give me a $1 donation for Walking USA. Some people were truly amazing.

We made it into Missoula in time for the Patriots-Broncos Monday Night Football game. In Missoula, of course, everybody was a Denver Broncos fan. My Patriots jacket drew a lot of attention as we ate dinner. Everybody playfully disparaged the Patriots. Frank and I smiled at each other. *We'll show them tonight*, we thought.

We should have kept walking. The "big" game was a disaster. The Patriots got their butts kicked. It was embarrassing. John Elway did what he always did, rising to the occasion, throwing impossible passes and eluding defenders, turning a certain loss of yards into a first down. Having led the Broncos to at least five AFC Champions and four Super Bowls during his storied career, he was no stranger to clutch performances. That year the Patriots were really playing well and most football fans expected them to dominate the Broncos. Elway didn't hear that news I guessed.

In a bad mood over the loss, Frank and I lay awake comparing Montana and Boston. In Boston, it was Mercedes, BMWs, and Audis. Here, it was pick-up trucks with mounted rifles and a couple of hunting dogs in the back. Back East, we watched teenagers going out on dates; here, the youngsters are often married with kids before graduating from high school. In Boston we used planes and trains and buses to travel wherever we wanted to go. In Montana, according to the locals, most folks on the ranches didn't do much driving other than around the ranch. Usually they traveled on horseback, on an ATV or snowmobile, or in a their "pick-em-ups." As Easterners, we had Social Security numbers and paid taxes. Here, many people were hiding from the government. Bostonians lived in fancy homes and condos. Here, folks lived in log cabins. Most Bostonians bought their food in supermarkets. Here, according to Trooper Keith, most people went out into their yards for vegetables and shot or trapped game for dinner. Many have fishing spots on their land or very close by.

In contrast, in Massachusetts, we had thousands of state police. Here, in a state that covers 147,000 square miles—compared to 10,000 square miles of Massachusetts—they had only 250 state troopers. My hometown of Newton, larger than any city in Montana, is a smallish suburb of Boston with a population of nearly 100,000. Only 25,000 souls lived in Helena, the capital of Montana. Incredibly, Massachusetts, my home state, would fit into Montana an amazing fourteen times. Only California, Texas and Alaska are bigger. We got tired of talking about all the differences and fell asleep.

* * *

At breakfast I was reading about Missoula. It was the cultural center of Montana. Although it is officially a city, it seems like a small town—a college town. There is a symphony here, well-regarded libraries and bookstores, like one finds in Harvard Square in Cambridge. It was apparently the home of many artists, musicians and writers. After having walked all the way through Montana, this place was a neat surprise.

I was on the interstate by 7 A.M. I was only two days from the Idaho border. Later that morning, Jeff Powers of the *Missoula Independent* pulled up and snapped a few photos for an article.

Later, trudging along, not paying much attention, I was startled by a ring-necked pheasant that emerged from the high grasses on the shoulder next to me. Actually, we were both startled. The bird darted off right over me, dropping—probably intentionally—a massive poop that barely missed my head.

We stopped for lunch in Alberton at the Side Track Cafe. I quickly got another point of view on Montana. We chatted with Ron Banner, a self-proclaimed "Militia Man." Ron happened to be a white supremacist. He bragged, "I never paid taxes in my life."

"How do you do that?" I asked.

"I don't have no Social Security number and everything I earn is under the table. Ain't never gonna let the government know where I am."

"If everybody did as you do, the country would fall apart," I told him.

"That's okay with me," he said. "I don't need no government."

Fully expecting an equally bizarre response, I purposely asked him, "Can you tell me why I haven't seen any blacks in Montana?" I wanted to see if he also would admit to blatant racism.

He told us, "There are two kinds of people in Montana—assets and deficits. The blacks are deficits—and they don't last long in Montana." He continued, "We know how to handle our deficits in Montana."

He continued, telling us about the militia and the fact that many folks in Montana keep their existence unknown to any government, state or federal. He said "I'm a real Montanan."

I wanted to tell him sarcastically, "It's been such a treat meeting a white supremacist," but I just smiled and wished him well.

The day wound down. I was walking into a spectacular sunset, and I could attest to the fact that I was feeling better, despite my encounter with a racist, anti-government, white supremacist.

Later, at our motel, a reporter from the *Atlanta Journal-Constitution* phoned me. The journalist, Paula Schwed, was doing a Sunday magazine story titled "On the Road for a Reason" about my cross-country walk. The story would appear in the next Sunday issue, October 19, 1997. The interview went well.

Paula asked the hard questions. "Isn't this very selfish of you—leaving your family responsibilities and doing this walk?"

My answer to that hardball question: "All my life I've taken care of other people, my ex-wife, my present family, my mother, my business partners, my employees and my friends. Now I'm taking a year off to do something I've always wanted to do, taking care of me. And I'm going prove that one step at a time, you can do anything want to do."

* * *

In the morning, I was off to Haugan, the last town before the border. The morning was frigid, but it warmed up in the early afternoon under the Big Sky sun.

On our last night in Montana, we stayed at Lincoln's 10,000 Silver Dollar Inn. We were told that at one time, there actually were only 10,000 silver dollars embedded in the bar and glued to walls. The original owners, Gerry and Marie Lincoln, started the collection in 1952. Because people have kept adding to the collection over the years, the assortment allegedly boasted 32,000 silver dollars.

To me, it seemed like a robbery waiting to happen. But Frank pointed out, "It would take the perps too long to pry all the money off the wall before the police showed up."

* * *

Finally, the last day in Montana was underway. As I strolled along, I reflected on the great eighteen-day experience of walking through the most beautiful state I had seen thus far. Replete with spectacular snow-covered peaks, including the Northern Rockies and many other mountain ranges; a kaleidoscope of rivers and streams—thanks to the "Triple Divide"—that empty into the Pacific, the Atlantic, and the Arctic Oceans; stunning buttes; idyllic cattle ranches; and amazing views of grazing range. The jaw-dropping Glacier National Park was here, and three of the five entrances to Yellowstone National Park were also in this state. It was a nature lover's paradise, and Montanans would prefer that it remain a secret. Photographers must have a genuine love affair when visiting Montana. One would never be at loss for a stunning vista to record. I was being told daily: "Don't tell anybody about Montana. It's The Last Best Place."

Chapter Seventy-Four

Coeur d'Alene

French for "Heart of the awl,"
Abundant life, fish or foul.
Northern Rocky's hidden gem,
A slice of heaven, Canadian friend.
William Sherman's claim to fame,
Lakes and shores of Coeur d'Alene.

—Kevin Mooney

A quick change of shoes and I was ready to launch myself into the anonymous state of Idaho—I had no clue what to expect. Walking out of Haugan, the view was breathtaking.

As I moved up onto Lookout Pass, it was snowing lightly and the trees in the higher elevations were snow-covered, a beautiful sight. Below, clouds glided across the forested mountains like an armada of eighteenth-century warships.

Walking up the steep grade, I found I was able to move along faster than the mighty eighteen-wheelers with their 600-horsepower engines, sucking up a gallon of fuel every couple of miles. As I reached the pass and saw a beckoning sign that stated "Celebrate Idaho," I began my descent. The grade was much steeper headed down than it was coming up from Montana. The walk down from Lookout Pass was about seven miles long, and it included a sequence of spectacular hairpin turns. I was glad I wasn't going in the other direction.

Because I would be crossing the narrow Idaho panhandle, it suddenly dawned on me that I would be in this state for only fifty miles before I set foot in Washington. It was an exciting thought. I'd soon be in a state contiguous to the Pacific Ocean. But my excitement quickly faded upon further reflection. The second part of my Morphine Dream—walking from Boston to Big Sur—would soon no longer be a dream, but a thing of the past. This journey had been a great escape. Soon, I would have to confront a tougher reality back home.

The first part of the dream, going to law school, had proven to be extraordinarily difficult given the fact that I was so unprepared academically to deal with the challenges of attending college, getting a bachelors degree and doing well enough to meet the entrance requirements of the fabled Harvard Law School. The selection process for getting into Harvard was a seemingly insurmountable obstacle by itself.

It would take eight long years of incredibly difficult attention to academic excellence for me—a late thirties, formerly uneducated blue-collar worker—to achieve my first dream. It was also an extremely difficult experience to attend college for the first years in a wheelchair or on crutches.

The second part of the dream, walking across the United States, may seem to many to be an overwhelming physical challenge. In fact many friends and family told me it was impossible. For me, walking forty miles a day for a few weeks was far easier than the struggle to complete college and law school. That didn't make it easy, just easier. Realizing that I was very close to completing the second part of my dream was a constant motivator to keep moving and to get it done.

What I had come to realize, though, was the real motivating factor for finally doing my walk across America was my desire to escape home because of the state of my marriage and my complete failure to establish any relationship with my wife. Finally realizing the dream was causing strange feelings as it was almost time for me to go back home.

The thought of going home was, at times, uncomfortable. My reinstatement hearing, which would hopefully result in getting my law license back, was a scary proposition. The Board of Bar Overseers had given me a laundry list of items I was required to do before I could reapply. Before I left on the walk cross country I had completed all the items on that long list. Left to do was only the preparation of the actual hearing petition and various supporting documents. The uncertainty of the outcome of that hearing was always on my mind. Also weighing me down was figuring out how I was going to generate an income and resume my duty of supporting my family. I had no idea what I was going to do. I only knew that I certainly had best figure it out quickly. I wasn't going home to a rose garden, but while out here in the middle of the beauty of the astonishing Northwest, I simply couldn't force myself to concentrate on those decisions. I realized that I could not resolve these situations unless I was home.

Just before the final switchback on my way down the mountain, I could see Mullan, the first town I would visit in Idaho. That was where I would have lunch. The sky had turned ugly. Within a few minutes, it began to rain. At least it wasn't snow, but walking was miserable.

In addition to the sound of my footsteps, I occasionally heard the roar of those always present 600-horsepower engines, straining to carry their behemoth loads up the pass, or the whine of a low-gear, slowing the huge logging trucks on their way down the mountain.

Once in the valley, I struggled into Mullan, where Frank was waiting. We had agreed it was too dangerous for him to follow me at such a slow speed down the hairpin turns, so he went ahead. I couldn't wait to have a good meal, but first I changed my clothes, because I was soaked.

After lunch, I was back on the road. The temperature was the same as before, but after resting at lunch for almost an hour—though now wearing dry and comfy duds—it felt thirty degrees colder. The rain had stopped, but the wind was blowing pellets of water off the forest trees that lined both sides of the road, so it was essentially still raining. Worse, the shoulders were narrow and somewhat steep.

After three hours and ten difficult miles, slogging through the horrible weather and the winding and hilly terrain, I reached the town of Wallace. Its homes were scattered along the sides of the hills overlooking the highway. I took the first exit and immediately came across a coffee shop. I stepped inside and sat down; I needed some tea and warmth. Unfortunately, the place was freezing. It seemed that the folks in Wallace didn't like to turn on the heat until it was well below zero.

A friendly old-timer in blue jeans and a flannel shirt approached my table. He asked, "What's this Walking USA business all about?"

I spent a few minutes, explaining. He hadn't shaved in days and looked unkempt, but he was curious and surprisingly articulate. He pulled out his wallet and handed me a twenty-dollar bill.

"I admire what you are doing," he said. "I always wanted to walk across the country, but I was too busy working and raising a family. Now, I'm too old."

He didn't appear to have a lot of money, which made his donation even more meaningful. I felt guilty taking it. I considered giving it back, but I didn't want to insult him. As I got up to leave, we shook hands, but he didn't let go.

"Damn," he said, "What I would give to go along with you."

* * *

Idaho, like the Dakotas, was so different from my preconceptions. Sure, there are plenty of potatoes, but not in this part of the state. There was timber, mining, ski areas, tourism and beautiful mountain passes, pristine streams and lakes, and tiny waterfalls cascading from cliff tops as I wandered along Interstate 90. As the sign instructed when I crossed the state line, "Celebrate Idaho." That's what I was doing.

Late in the day, I ran into a severe storm—high winds and heavy horizontal rain. As I hunched my shoulders against the wind, the downpour was so thick I couldn't see my feet. But I could tell that my shoes were slogging through ankle-deep puddles. The wind-chill factor had to be around zero. There was sweat and rain frozen on my glasses. I could barely see. Without glasses, I'm essentially blind. A voice from a passing pick-up truck shouted, "Hey, idiot, get off the road!" Although the interstate is not the best place to be, I had no other choice.

At every rest stop, Frank counseled me not to tough out the extra ten miles I'd vowed to walk. When the storm took a turn for the worse, and visibility ceased, I climbed into the van and we made tracks for Coeur d'Alene.

As an eternal and unapologetic romantic, I'd always loved the name of this small city, whose population is around 30,000. I'd always imagined that some French fur trapper must have named it for his sweetheart, Alene. Actually, I only got the first part right. In the late eighteenth century, French Canadian fur traders named this region after the Awl, a tribe of Native Americans who lived along its lakes and rivers. In English, it meant "Heart of the Awl." Nevertheless, the name still made me smile.

Hours later after our take-out dinner, eaten in bed under the covers with our clothes on, I glanced at the thermometer outside my motel-room window. It was sixteen degrees. When we had turned in the room was hot, now it seemed like there was no heat. By the time we woke up, it would probably be zero.

In the middle of the night, I heard thrashing outside our door. It was too cold to get up, but I was curious. When I opened the door a crack, I was suddenly eye-to-eye with a beautiful black-and-white skunk, its hidden aerosol bomb ready to make my life far more miserable. Frank had put our trash just outside the door, a mistake we wouldn't repeat. And our night visitor, who had been happily feasting on our leftovers, didn't look too pleased about the interruption. I gently closed the door and slithered back under the covers.

"Dress for winter, old man," yelled Frank as he prepared the van for the day's journey. "You'll freeze your balls off if you don't."

We drifted away from the poetic Coeur d'Alene at 4 A.M., heading for Spokane. We stopped for a quick breakfast at a small diner. Giant muffins, the size of a softball, filled with tons of blueberries were the fare. The aroma was enough to satisfy me. But I shoveled down two, washed down with a giant cup of coffee.

An hour later, there was heavy traffic on Interstate 90. Apparently, Idahoans who work in Spokane get up real early and get on the road to work. It seems that many of the folks of Coeur d'Alene drive the forty miles to Spokane because that's where the jobs are.

In the first two hours, at least twenty drivers had pulled over, ready to lend a hand. In Boston, twenty cars wouldn't pull over in twenty days. There seemed to be a more considerate breed of *homo sapiens* in the great Northwest.

Within seven miles, the Idaho State Police had twice warned Frank and me that walking on Interstate 90 was unsafe. They were right. Soon, the traffic got even worse. It was definitely too dangerous for me and the van to continue safely on I-90. We pored over the map, searching for a different route. I took the next exit and walked into Post Falls, the last town in Idaho. I found an alternative route that would take me directly into Spokane.

By now, the gloomy fog was being devoured by the rising sun. In the blink of an eye the landscape lit up as the chilly air eased. I removed my winter coat, scarf, hat and gloves and took a deep breath.

The state of Washington was a mere few steps away, the Pacific Ocean a few more steps after that.

Part Seven
Amber Waves of Grain

Water has an endless horizon; there is no limitation when you look out into the water. There's nothing to interfere with the mind's eye projecting itself as far as it can possibly imagine. I suppose it's the same way people in the Midwest feel about watching amber waves of grain or endless rows of cornfields. There is something exhilarating about it.

—Billy Joel

Chapter Seventy-Five
Drysiders

There's more to life than increasing its speed.

—Ghandi

I was finally standing in the state of Washington. When I reached Seattle, I would be heading south for the remainder of the journey.

The Cascade Mountain Range divides the state into separate climatic zones. Those living to the east of the Cascades are known as "Drysiders" because the mountains block the Pacific's humid air from reaching central and eastern Washington. Hence, it doesn't get much rain on that side of the mountains.

I was headed to Spokane, which many call the "Heart of the Drysiders." Two hours after crossing the border I began to see the modest skyscrapers of Spokane. A billboard touted the Spokane Pump Company: "We Fix Things That Suck!" It's the cleverest sign I had seen in 4,000 miles.

Except for my ongoing foot, knee and leg muscle problems, which are from over-exercise, I felt terrific. I had successfully fought off the depression that was consuming me several days previous. Most of the time I didn't need to take my diabetes pills, as my sugar level had remained low and stable. I had lost a lot of weight. And walking must have done wonders for my immune system, because I'd hardly gotten sick. It's no secret that I'm a little crazy, and walking provides a natural Prozac. I escaped into a less stressful world; life at three-and-a-half miles per hour. It was serene and contemplative.

I didn't think I had mentioned how Frank continually made fun of my snack choices. I know they must sound awful. Being on the road, with such extreme physical demands, required a different kind of diet. Since I had to compensate for significant sodium loss, I often feasted on sandwiches of Spam and cheese. It was a great pick-me-up snack. The van also carried cases of light pears and peaches, so I could easily have fruit without worrying about perishability.

I reached Spokane by mid-afternoon. The city claimed to be the nation's friendliest. I was forewarned in Coeur d'Alene that the most welcoming and affable people were those in western and central Washington. Is it the food they eat? The climate? Or do they all take Prozac?

And sure enough, many friendly and generous folks did stop to visit with Frank and me. They bragged that Spokane is the home of Gonzaga University, whose most famous alumnus is Bing Crosby. I'm fascinated by the way people boast about and sing the praises of their particular city or town.

We stopped in downtown Spokane's Riverside Park. Its centerpiece was a huge replica of the "Radio Flyer" red wagon that was a popular children's toy when I was young. Apparently, those red wagons are built in Spokane. I once had my own red wagon just like it. Back when I was a newspaper delivery boy I used to pull it all over town, filled with tied stacks of daily and Sunday tabloids and broadsheets.

I resumed walking west on Route 2, toward the Fairchild Air Force Base in the suburb of Airway Heights. A few blocks down the road, a car stopped, and a woman thrust her arm out the window, holding a handful of crumpled greenbacks. She said, "I think it's great what you're doing, and I'm giving you all my tips from lunch hour. I wish I had more to give you, but now I'm broke." It turned out her tips amounted to $49. God bless her!

Soon, it was sundown. One more forty-mile jaunt was drawing to a close. Today, my legs had been moving like clock pendulums. I felt strong and healthy. I was down to about 225 pounds. I had shed nearly 100 pounds since I began training, and seventy-five of them walking across America.

I climbed into the van's oversized bucket seat and we headed back toward Spokane because we had spotted a place for dinner.

At the Buckhorn Restaurant, I inhaled a big bowl of pea soup and a huge steak dinner. I topped it off with an oversized piece of homemade apple pie à la mode. When we asked for the check, the owner informed us that dinner was "on the house." This was probably the fiftieth time this had happened since I left Boston. I continued to be flabbergasted by those acts of generosity and kindness. Rush Limbaugh, you are an overpaid, misinformed blowhard.

We checked into the All Seasons Motel, a few hundred yards from the restaurant. Wow! The owner gave us two rooms for the price of one. Spokane had been very good to us, indeed. I decided I could live here, too.

Into a cold wind I walked at five the next morning. The suburb of Airway Heights now seemed like such a dreary place. I loved walking before dawn. The quiet time gave my mind a chance to free associate.

It was a cleansing process. It's also a time before vehicular traffic, which impinged on my space and crowded me further off the road.

After I passed the Air Force base, I found myself surrounded by the wheat fields of eastern Washington. A cold wind blew across the open fields. As far as the eye could see, there was wave after wave of golden stalks, ebbing and flowing, reminding me what a tiny and insignificant dot I was. The wind and hilly terrain, however, made this dot's morning walk unexpectedly exhausting.

In the middle of the day, a van passed by heading east and honked. A few hundred feet later, the van pulled over and stopped. Two women emerged. They were not dressed for the cold wind. They started jogging toward us, so Frank pulled over to the side of the road. The women had seen a story about me on television and wanted to say hello. They decided to walk with me a while. But after a few minutes, they realized they were not dressed for the occasion. The four of us huddled together while they prayed for our safety and good health. They were Mormon missionaries. They kindly left behind a small donation.

The area around the towns of Reardon, Harrington, and Davenport are the second-largest wheat producing region in the world. I was thrilled to see, everywhere I looked, amber waves of grain. As a child, I loved the *National Geographic* photos of America, and I often dreamed of seeing those places in person. The melodies of patriotic songs were now playing in my head: " . . . from the mountains, to the prairies, to the oceans, white with foam . . ." and " . . . purple mountain majesties above the fruited plain . . . " My walk had transformed those lyrics into a goose-bumped reality, and I realized how those songs must have gotten written. All the authors had to do was walk where I was walking.

For much of the day, I'd seen the road ahead for ten or twenty miles, oceans of golden wheat, a rouge autumn sun. Now, that fiery beach ball—over a million times the size of the earth—was staring me right in the eye as it inched toward the horizon.

Suddenly, I saw fast-moving, foreboding clouds streaking toward me from the west. In a blink of an eye, I was in a blinding snow squall. Moments later, the snow became a torrential, drenching rain. If that didn't make me miserable enough, I was suddenly pelted by marble-size hail, which then changed back to heavy snow. And then, suddenly, it all vanished. The last sliver of sun was peeking over the horizon like a yellow diamond. I heard the shriek of a train whistle. I looked to my left. I saw an incredible double rainbow blessing a slow-moving freight train. It was as if I'd just gone on the most exciting carnival ride of my life.

At the end of the day, we couldn't find a motel. We drove more than sixty miles searching for one. Discouraged, we ended up all the way back at both the All Seasons Motel and the Buckhorn Restaurant.

I was exhausted more from the long ride than the day's walk. The next day was the Sabbath, the day God rested. I decided to follow his lead. My legs needed a break. Besides, it was NFL Sunday!

* * *

Interspersed among the football games, I did six loads of laundry. I also took a slow six-mile walk to stretch out my legs. I had learned long ago that the legs need to move every day. If you take days off and don't do at least some miles, your legs will seemingly forget their job.

Afterwards, Frank said, "You look beat. You look like you've lost your spark."

No, I'm fine. I'll have my spark back tomorrow," I said, confidently.

Frank was a godsend. He helped me in so many ways. He was a wise advisor and my closest confidant. He kept me smiling and tended to my needs. He recognized when I was having trouble with my diabetes. He knew when I needed to sleep late, and he motivated me when I shouldn't. He fetched supper when I was too sore to venture out. He was a superb official photographer. He did everything, except walk with me. He was willing to do that, too, but someone had to drive the van.

It may be that the only thing harder than walking forty miles a day is driving behind me—half on the road, half on the shoulder—at less than four miles an hour, watching my butt for twelve or thirteen hours a day, seven days a week.

While watching the football games, I used my laptop to send and respond to e-mails and to update my website.

What a remarkable time we live in. Historians may view the Information Revolution as the most extraordinary one in human history—more important than fire, the wheel, and sliced bread. If I'd undertaken this walk twenty-five years earlier, I would have been essentially incommunicado, except for pay phones and stamped mail. But in this day and age, my sons take what the mailman drops off at my home in Newton, scan it, and e-mail it within seconds to my motel room nearly 3,000 miles away. When my boys wanted to talk, they just called my cell phone.

I did surf the Internet a little, but it's such an unwieldy farrago. It takes too long to find whatever I'm looking for. I wished the heck someone would invent a search engine that would make finding things easier. I had heard of this new company that sold books online. I think it was called Amazon; what a weird name for a business. Why would anyone ever buy a book, pay for shipping, and then wait several days for it to arrive, when all you have to do is walk down to your local bookstore? *There's no way that company is going to survive*, I thought.

Chapter Seventy-Six

Hotel Waterville

*Truly great thoughts are
conceived while walking.*
—Friedrich Nietzsche

In the chilly pre-dawn wind, I pushed myself into Coulee City, which also claimed to be "The Friendliest City in the West." I wouldn't have the chance to find out, because I was through it before the rooster crows.

By the time the sun appeared, I was walking across the Dry Falls Dam. It blocked the Columbia River, creating Banks Lake. It took me a half hour to walk along the road on top of the dam. Oddly enough, even though the sun had just come up, it was already over eighty degrees and climbing.

Speaking of climbing, all I could see on the far side of the dam was the highlands of central Washington. Soon, I was walking up switchbacks carved into the hillside of Route 2. The steep grade and switchbacks continued for eight miles. The terrain seemed scorched, arid, and unfriendly to agriculture. When I finally reached the top, I'd already trudged twelve miles and it wasn't even 8 A.M.

By prearrangement, I called WNTN, a radio station back home in Newton, for a live on-the-road interview. They'd been following my progress since I left Boston. The half-hour interview gave me a chance to rest.

I was fighting inertia. I didn't want to move. It sickened me to think I still had twenty-six miles to go before I arrived in Douglas.

As I headed down into a canyon, I was once again surrounded by acres of windswept golden wheat. There were hardly any cars, and no houses, barns, farm equipment, or telephone poles.

Four hours and fifteen miles later, the scenery and the weather hadn't changed a bit. It was sunny, clear, and still in the eighties.

Hours drifted by. Not a single car passed in either direction. Finally, I recognized the sound of an RV coming up from behind me. I stepped off the road to let it pass. The behemoth motor home pulled over and stopped. An older man and woman jumped down from their seats. Bill and Barbara introduced themselves and we chatted for a while. I asked, "Do you know the name of the canyon we're in?"

Bill said, "It's not a canyon, it's a coulee," which is a small valley created millions of years ago in the Ice Age. This one is "Moses Coulee," named after a legendary Native American leader.

I turned my attention to their RV. "You must get four gallons to the mile."

Bill laughed, "You're close; four miles to the gallon."

"So you stop at every gas station?" I asked.

"Nope, we've got a 350-gallon gas tank, so we go a long way between fill-ups."

After working four decades for the state of Georgia, Bill retired, sold his home outside of Atlanta, and bought this motor home. He and his wife had been on the road ever since. They had no real destination. They just kept moving around, avoiding the winter. We said good-bye and they were gone—on to the Oregon Coast.

At the end of the long day's walk, I was in the town of Douglas—exactly where I planned to be. Surprise! There was no town of Douglas, just a few rundown buildings and a couple of boarded-up shacks.

Feeling grumpy, I jumped into the van and we headed for the next "town" on the map, called Waterville. It was only five miles away.

My feet were hurting so I took off my sneakers. I noticed there was only a few millimeters of tread left on that pair of shoes, so I'd have to throw them away. As lousy as my feet felt, it was nothing compared to the blisters of the early days in Maine and New Hampshire.

When we reached Waterville, I was delighted to discover the turn-of-the-nineteenth-century downtown district. It was in pristine condition. Unfortunately, I saw no motels on the way into town. I stopped and asked a teenage boy, "Hi there, do you know where there is a motel?"

"Sorry," he said, "no motels around here."

He saw my disappointment.

"But," he brightened, "we've got a hotel!"

I asked for directions. He pointed directly across the street.

I didn't really see what he was pointing at. I did see a large evergreen mostly blocking a Jacobethan revival brick building. It looked like a private home.

Frank and I wandered across the street. Once we passed by the evergreen, we spotted the sign, which had been hidden from our view: "Hotel Waterville."

The structure was an ornate architectural masterpiece. It had flattened, cusped Tudor arches, stone trim around the windows and doors, carved brick detailing, steep roof gables, and high chimneys. I was pleasantly surprised.

"I hope we can afford a room," I mumbled.

Frank went back to stay with the van, as I walked in. The lobby was filled with late nineteenth- and early twentieth-century antiques. At the front desk, I was greeted by a tall, slender, middle-aged man with wispy blonde hair.

"Welcome to the Hotel Waterville," he said. "My name is Dave Lundgren. I'm the desk clerk, the janitor, the chamber maid, and the owner."

I told him "I'm Don Brown, a fat old man walking across the country, and my driver and I want a non-smoking room with two beds."

He smiled and said "If you don't mind walking down the hallway for your shower, we can certainly accommodate you."

The cost of the room, however, was prohibitive—a whopping $69 a night.

"Ouch," I said. "That's the most I've been quoted for a double room in almost 100 nights of motels."

He politely corrected me. "But this is a hotel." He explained that he had meticulously refurbished the place and proudly informed me that it's on the National Register of Historic Places. I was duly impressed.

He led me to a second-floor room, filled with exquisite antiques. The four-post beds were a bit wider than a twin and about a foot longer. Come to think of it, this was just like my paternal grandmother's home, which I used to visit more than fifty years ago. All of her furniture had been given to her when she got married in the early 1900s.

I took the room, even though it had no television or radio.

Back at the van, I told Frank the bad news. The room I had rented lacked modern conveniences. He crankily grunted. We unloaded our stuff from the van and transferred it to the room.

I found Dave and asked him to recommend a good restaurant in town. He rattled off three names.

"Which is the closest?"

"They're all close, but I suppose the closest is Knemeyer's Saloon." He pointed, saying, "It's right over there."

We walked back across the street and entered the saloon. The bar/restaurant was somewhat busy and people were curious about who we are. But we were too hungry and tired to socialize. I studied the menu and choose the chicken soup and a big T-bone steak.

I kiddingly asked the waitress if there was any MSG in the soup.

"What's MSG?" she asked.

"It's monosodium glutamate."

"Honey," she says, "If I never heard of it, there can't be any in the soup."

Back at the room after dinner, Frank immediately fell asleep. It meant he was probably sick. Usually, he spent hours writing postcards to friends back home. Not wanting to disturb him, I went back downstairs to the lobby to watch the Dallas Cowboys on Monday Night Football.

After the game, I crawled into bed. I noticed some magazines on the night stand. They looked odd, so I investigated. They were all from the 1920s. It was fascinating reading magazines from yesteryear. It took me more than an hour to finally put them down, shut off the light and bury my head in the pillow.

In the morning, we awoke to the aroma of coffee and pastries wafting up from the lobby. When we got downstairs, our places were set at the table. On my plate was an envelope with my name on it. I opened it. Inside was a note from Dave. He apologized for abandoning us this morning, but he had to run some errands out of town. He also told me that he was not charging us for the room at the Hotel Waterville! Hey, Dave, what can I say? Thank you so much!

The antique town of Waterville slowly faded into the mist as I walked down the road. Two miles later, I came to a scenic overlook. Down below, I saw Pine Canyon. I spiraled down for seven miles, from an elevation of more than a half mile high, through a desert-like terrain with sparse vegetation. I was concerned about some precarious-looking boulders that seemed ready to roll down and crush me if given a gentle nudge.

After I passed through the village of Orondo, we were stumbling along the Columbia River on Route 2, heading toward Wenatchee, "Apple Capital of the World."

For many miles along the river in this magnificent valley, there was an abundance of apple and pear orchards. Everyone seemed too busy picking and packing fruit to notice me as I drifted by. I liked being noticed. I missed the attention.

I learned that an estimated 30,000 boxcars of fruit are shipped from this area during the harvest season. Along the highway, all I saw and heard were tractor trailers loaded with apples and pears, passing by in both directions.

Just before we arrived in downtown Wenatchee, I stopped to sample some apples. They were delicious. I loaded up.

Hotel Waterville

At the end of the day, we ended up in the mock Bavarian town of Leavenworth where we spent the night. This tiny town—with only about 1,500 residents—was visited by over 2 million gullible tourists every year. If ever a place could be identified as a tourist trap, this was it. The design and layout of the town was expressly done so as to attract tourists and give them ample reasons to spend their money.

* * *

The next day was long and uneventful. I limped along Route 2, worn out from the narrow, sloping shoulder on the side of the road. My feet, ankles, shins, and knees were quite sore.

I stopped early, as ahead of me loomed a steep climb up to Stevens Pass, elevation 4,061 feet. I thought it was better to wait till morning. I'd get up before the sun did and conquer the pass no later than 7 A.M.

Chapter Seventy-Seven

Wetsiders

As God is almighty and moves mountains at will
He has love of His people and their big hearts to fill

Let angels and snow flakes Climb Mountains on high
For I love all mountains that reach to the sky
　　　　　　　　　　　　　　　　　—Alice Mae

As I began the climb up the steep, winding road in the early morning darkness, it was really cold, but I felt fine. I had no real problems. The uphill trek only took a couple of hours. Yet I was exhausted when I reached the top of Stevens Pass.

I discovered there was a major ski resort up at the top that had co-opted the name of the pass. I was almost a mile high and everything above me was snow-covered. The ski trails flowed down like octopus tentacles all around me. I stopped and chatted with a mechanic who was tuning up one of the high-speed, quad chairlifts. He told me, "Heavy snowfall usually closes the pass for more than 100 days every winter."

"How do the skiers get here?" I asked.

"They don't. When the snow flies you *can't* get here."

As I made my way down the western side of the pass, I noticed that the railroad tracks were covered by a slanted roof. I asked some folks at a scenic overlook about the strange looking roof. A guy explained: "This is the site of worst avalanche in U.S. history. On March 1, 1910, two Great Northern Railway trains—the "Seattle Express" and the "Fast Mail" train—which had been marooned for five days on the tracks due to heavy snow, were crushed in an avalanche." Workers apparently had labored feverishly to feed the passengers and free the trains. But on the sixth day, the half-mile-wide avalanche bulldozed both trains 150 feet down into the valley below, allegedly killing ninety-six people. Some report that many immigrant workers were never accounted for and the death toll was much higher. Because of the tragedy, the railroad built either tunnels or roofs over the tracks to prevent it from happening again.

In the next hour, I slalomed my way down to the bottom of the pass. I was so relieved to be back on level ground. Route 2 was nestled among thousands of pine trees. Occasionally, I passed a lovely green pasture. In the next two days, we slept in the town of Skykomish and then in the village of Index. Day and night, it seemed I was constantly serenaded by the sound of rushing or trickling water of nearby streams.

A few miles west of Index, I was still surrounded by high reaching mountains, but I was walking on relatively flat roads. Three hours and thirteen miles later, I was slicing my way through the eastern suburbs of Seattle. To avoid traffic, we turned south only to find the traffic was ubiquitous. It's like I was back in Chicago. I later learned that Seattle—famous for its geeks and environmentalists—is one of the most car-congested urban areas in the country. I could tell—I was being pushed off the roads. I had to avoid Seattle because the traffic was too much to bear.

The weather was dark, dreary, and drizzling—typical of the Seattle area. On average, it is cloudy or partly cloudy nearly 300 days a year, and 150 of those days have measurable rainfall. Since the drizzle doesn't actually add up to much, Seattle actually gets fewer inches of rain per year than New York, Atlanta or Boston.

For hours, I walked south. Late in the day, the fog burned off a little and I caught a faint glimpse of Mount Rainier, the highest peak in the Cascades. They say that on a clear day—a rare event around here—the snow-covered 14,441-foot mountain can be seen from as far away as Portland, Oregon, and Victoria, British Columbia. A still active volcano, Mount Rainier is considered one of the most dangerous in the world. If it blew its top, tens of thousands of people living in its shadow would die and it would do many billions of dollars in damage.

After spending the night in the quaint town of Eatonville, I grunt my way for two days toward Mount Saint Helens. I never saw Mount Rainer again. I had looked forward to the beauty of Rainer. Even though I walked right by its base, I saw only clouds.

I was beat. My right hamstring was bothering me. I decided to spend the day in bed, putting Mineral Ice on my sore muscles. But the real reason, again, for the day of rest is that the NFL is offering up a couple of football games.

Early Monday morning, I was back on the road. Yesterday's respite was just what my body and soul needed. The football was a welcome diversion from my steady dose of walking.

Late in the day, I finally arrived at Mount Saint Helens—one of the 160 active volcanoes that constitute the Pacific Ring of Fire. I stood before it in awe.

As many may recall, on the morning of May 18, 1980, it exploded with a force equivalent to 50 Megaton Hydrogen bombs, resulting in the deadliest and most costly volcanic event in U.S. history. Fifty-seven people lost their lives. The death toll would have been much higher had it not been a Sunday, because the area would have been teeming with loggers. Two hundred fifty homes, forty-seven bridges, fifteen miles of railways, and one hundred eighty-five miles of highway were destroyed. Millions of acres of pristine forest were turned into a brown wasteland. In an instant, the 9,677-foot summit lost 1,312 feet of elevation, causing the largest landslide in recorded history. It left behind a one-mile wide scar of a horseshoe-shaped crater, and the prevailing winds blew so much ash into the sky that Spokane, 250 miles to the east, was enveloped in total darkness in the middle of the afternoon.

* * *

My day was spent chatting with people who were there on the day Mount Saint Helens erupted. It was an amazing experience to visit with people who had experienced—close-up—the devastation of that fateful day. One lady, June, told me that, "Everybody seemed oblivious to the warnings. Some of my friends died although they had plenty of notice of the danger."

"Did you get out of here before it actually blew?" I asked.

"I left about two hours before, and I thank God I did, otherwise I would have been one of the victims."

* * *

Two days later, I sauntered across the Oregon border—my twentieth state—and walked into Portland. It was a quiet, clean, peaceful, and very environmentally friendly city, but for me it held no appeal. I figured staying overnight wouldn't hurt, so we checked into the downtown Hilton. I wanted a night of luxury and comfort, unlike most of the nights spent in somewhat dreary motels as I made my way across America.

I had originally planned to walk from Portland through central Oregon and then through central California to Sacramento where I would turn west, headed to the bay in San Francisco. Because of the horrendous flow of traffic on Interstate 5 and the roads feeding off it—the ones I had to walk on—I decided to make a major change in the route. Instead, I would walk southwest toward the coast.

Interstate 5 brings millions of tourists from California and places beyond. Oregonians would rather have no exit ramps on I-5 in Oregon. The sentiment was: "Drive right through; let Californication happen to Washington."

I moved on from Portland the next morning and spent a harrowing day in heavy traffic, making my way southwest, through the congested Portland suburbs, to the sleepy town of McMinnville. I was thrilled that I was going to be walking on the coast, where the traffic had to be less of a problem. The roads were flat all day and my legs noticed the difference. I was becoming keenly aware that it was better to avoid cities. The traffic that came with walking in or near a large city had become terrifying for me after thousands of miles in rural America.

I was very excited about finally reaching the ocean tomorrow. I picked up some tourist propaganda in the lobby and busied myself reading about the Oregon Coast.

Pacific Coast U.S. Highway 101 connects the resort towns and fishing towns of Oregon. Many of the towns are at the mouths of rivers that flow from the coastal mountains and further east into the Pacific. A multitude of state and national parks provide tourists with access to the beaches. Route 101 grips the fringe of the Pacific coastline and it is a world-class scenic wonder, but it is incredibly dangerous for a walker, especially one being followed by a very slow-moving van. While climbing the mountains, the views were spectacular. The downhill portions usually led to extraordinary bridges and into idyllic beaches, sleepy coastal towns, mostly filled with "Ma and Pa" restaurants, motels and gift shops.

Tomorrow was a momentous day, indeed. I would arrive at the big pond.

Part Eight
To the Oceans,
White with Foam

*When you are inspired by some great purpose,
some extraordinary project, all your thoughts
break their bonds; your mind transcends
limitations, your consciousness expands in
every direction, and you find yourself in a new,
great and wonderful world. Dormant forces,
faculties and talents become alive, and you
discover yourself to be a greater person by far
than you ever dreamed yourself to be.*
—Pantanjali

Chapter Seventy-Eight
War of the Woods

*The battle we have fought, and are still fighting for the forests
is a part of the eternal conflict between right and wrong,
and we cannot
expect to see the end of it. ... So we must count on watching and
striving for
these trees, and should always be glad to find anything so surely
good and noble to strive for.*

—**John Muir**

The walk from McMinnville to the Oregon coast was mostly through flat, rural countryside until I was close enough to sense the smell of the Pacific. As we got closer to the water, I was suddenly and unexpectedly climbing mountains again. Going from sea level, grunting up a steep grade, I found myself back up to 3,500 feet—mountain climbing again. Then, just as quickly, coasting downward for five or six miles, we finally arrived in Lincoln City. The air blowing in from the ocean was filled with mist and laden with salt. I could hear the waves rumbling on the beach; the unmistakable sound of the ebb and flow of the ocean. A few minutes later, I was facing the vast Pacific Ocean. It took my breath away—not so much that the view was overwhelming, and it was, but that I had walked all the way from sea to shining sea. It was a welcome relief to be cooled off some by the steady breeze coming from the west. I was crying softly when Frank walked up to me and said, "Are you gonna be all right, old man?"

It was such an emotional moment—to know I had made it all the way from the Atlantic to the Pacific, and I couldn't really answer Frank. I knew if I tried to talk I would burst into tears. I just stood there watching, almost not believing I was at the Pacific Ocean. I could only imagine how Lewis and Clark must have felt when they reached the Pacific after their journey, which was a thousand times more difficult than mine had been.

Before long I was on the beach and I headed for the water. I took off my shoes and socks and dipped my toes into the briny foam. It had been 109 days since I walked away from the Atlantic.

Frank strolled along, kicking up sand, examining an occasional piece of driftwood or shell. It was his first-ever look at the Pacific

Ocean. The beach was so serene in the early morning hours. Nobody was there. I stopped and listened to the surf and watched it lap at my feet. Despite being fully dressed, I waded out further. When the waves were lapping at my waist, I dove forward into the seemingly warm ocean water. I stayed under water for as long as I dared. I realized I was freezing. When I dove in, the water seemed refreshing and comfortable, now my bones were like ice. I rose to the surface, having swum in the Pacific for the first time ever, in joyful celebration at having made it.

About half an hour later, with my "baptism" complete, I realized I needed to get back on the road. This was a milestone on my journey but I still had a lot more ground to cover. I went to the van and immodestly stripped off my wet clothes. I took out a brand-new pair of shorts, a long-sleeved T-shirt, and a pair of Thorlos. With fresh clothes, dry sneakers and a euphoria that caused me to be unable to even see the hands of my watch. I was in a trance, yet I was shivering. Walking would get me out of both. I headed south to explore Oregon. Now it was on to the Big Sur, the end of the road.

I had never been to Oregon. As I walked over a bridge and out of Lincoln City, I noticed how neatly houses were nestled in the hills overlooking the ocean. A church steeple sliced through the treetops, reaching for the sky. Every kind of boat you could imagine—houseboats, pontoons, kayaks, canoes, yachts, fishing boats—were scattered in the harbor below. Recreational vehicle camping sites were the most common roadside entity. I stopped to chat with a visitor at one of the sites.

"How far away is the next town?" I asked.

"It's not walking distance. That's for sure," he said. "It's about a half mile or more."

Smiling, I said, "That's a long way to go."

Apparently, he didn't connect me with the Walking USA T-shirt I was wearing or the Walking USA van following close behind. "Walking distance" is such a relative term and, sadly, I'm sure there are more people using his definition than mine. If only Americans would get out of their cars and walk more; they would see life from a much different and healthier perspective.

"What's the big attraction for all the RV parks?" I asked.

"This part of Oregon has the best weather for fall and winter of anyplace in the country," he said.

In the next hour, I passed through two small towns without stopping. The road got narrower and also more congested.

We had found a number of scenic overlooks. However, there were no rest areas set aside for vehicles to pull over and admire the views. As a result, some RV drivers just stopped their vehicles in the middle of the road, got out, and wandered around, without consideration for traffic in either direction. I guess the drivers here are so used to this lack of consideration, some didn't even appear to be upset by the sudden and unexplained little traffic jams. The snarls of traffic often created a cacophony of sounds: horns of the cars and other motor homes tooting; screaming drivers, and the ear-shattering air horns of the semis.

Soon, I was quite alone. The color of the land was changing with the movement of the sun. Chatty birds, coming to roost for the night, were abundant.

I began walking a very steep incline. On my right, perhaps a hundred feet below, was a bay. It was almost a complete circle and surrounded by high cliffs except for a narrow opening through which the ocean waves surged. As I reached the top of the hill, I was surprised to see some folks standing on the shoulder. They had come out of a restaurant called "The Whale Cove Inn" especially to greet me. They all worked there and Amy, a waitress, offered us cold drinks.

We decided to stop and have lunch, before heading on to Newport. We sat at a window that overlooked the bay that I had been walking by for the last hour. "It's called Depoe Bay," Amy told us. "It has an interesting history."

Amy was really interested in my journey—so much so that she called a radio station and a newspaper in Newport to alert them to my story. As we savored our seafood dinner, Amy stopped by between other customers to chat some more. "Where are you guys from?"

"Boston," Frank and I said in unison.

"Wow," said Amy, "I'm from the North Shore, but when I got married I came to Oregon."

I thought I had detected a Boston accent when Amy was chatting with us.

After a fabulous and tasty lunch, I began walking along the coast, taking in the beautiful scenes offered by the ocean and beaches. Pretty quickly, we came to an overlook known as "Cape Foulweather," The road was nonstop up, up, up. I was back into serious mountain climbing. I had been overly optimistic thinking that this kind of terrain was behind us. Clearly, Oregon had its share of mountains, many extending right to the water. At Cape Foulweather, the surf sounded like a train—no subtle ebb and flow like in the east. The waves arrived every few seconds from Japan 6,000 miles away. This land/seascape has a Jekyll and Hyde personality: it can be calm or it can be brutal.

Over the next few hours, I was treated to a sampling of the natural beauty of Oregon: mountains, gentle valleys, caves, old-growth forests, wild rivers, glorious beaches and deserts. I also passed farms and orchards, along with fast-growing towns and high-tech companies. Even with man's imprint on the land, the wilderness was always close at hand. No wonder all the Oregonians I met had no desire to leave their state—and assumed everyone else would want to move there, too, if they knew what an awesome place it was.

In the late afternoon, we arrived in Newport. As prearranged, we went directly to the local radio station. Live and on the air, I was interviewed by Don Cohen. It went well, until he asked why I had dedicated the walk to my son, Louis. Unexpectedly, I choked back a sob.

In 1991, Louis was born after suffering a stroke in utero. An MRI revealed that three quarters of his brain was missing. For several days, doctors at Children's Hospital in Boston were certain he would only live a few days. A vast array of tubes and wires attached to his tiny body kept him alive. The doctors pleaded with me to remove his life support so that Louis' organs could be harvested to save the lives of other children. I came close to caving in. I went into to see Louis. I saw the seemingly hundreds of tubes and wires connected his tiny body. His arms both had IVs pumping medicines of some kind into his body. I put a finger is his tiny hand and suddenly he smiled. There was no way I would consent to pulling the plugs. Seeing him smile meant so much. It seemed like he could express what he was feeling. Miraculously, he didn't die.

Next, I battled with the hospital about whether Louis should come home or be transferred to an institution. I decided to bring him home. After a lengthy debate the doctors informed me that they would transfer Louis back to my hospital so that he could be taken to his mother. If Lewis was able to feed at the breast they said they would allow him to go home with us.

I had not really talked to my wife about any of this because she was so stressed about having Louis taken away from her when he was moved to Children's Hospital. She was still an in-patient at the Mount Auburn Hospital, healing from complications because of the emergency surgery she underwent when she arrived at the hospital many days before.

I drove several miles back to the Mount Auburn Hospital, following the ambulance which carried my son. We were all soon reunited in my wife's room. When a nurse brought Louis to my wife, we all watched nervously to see if he could feed from my wife's breast. Louis, thank God, immediately began suckling. This meant he would go home with us.

As we were preparing to leave the hospital, the nurse told us we should call Kennedy Intervention Center in Plymouth, Massachusetts as soon as we arrived home. The Kennedy Center, created by Joseph P. Kennedy, the Kennedy family patriarch, was noted for intervening with brain-damaged children, providing a wide range of medical and other assistance to the families of children in need of assistance not normally available through hospitals..

Once I arrived home I called the Kennedy Center and spoke to a kind and considerate intake specialist. After some discussion, the specialist agreed to accept Louis on an outpatient basis as soon as space was available. I asked "How long is the waiting list?"

"It's about six months to a year," she said.

My temper erupted. I screamed, "My son might not even have six days, never mind six months!" I was so frustrated but I also felt guilty taking my disappointment out on this very polite young lady who was only trying to be helpful. I knew I had to get significant help and I had to get it fast. I apologized sincerely to the young woman.

I hung up the phone and immediately dialed Congressman Joe Kennedy's office in Boston. Joe is the son the son of the late Senator Robert F. Kennedy, and grandson of the late Joseph P. Kennedy. I had worked with Congressman Kennedy on several occasions on neighborhood issues in Dorchester, where I practiced law. Congressman Kennedy had known about the difficulties that I was going through with my newborn son. I said to him, "Joe, I just got off the phone with the Joseph P. Kennedy Intervention Center for brain-damaged children. They told me they were happy to accept our son as a patient, but that we would have to wait at least six months before services could begin."

Congressman Kennedy asked, "Where are you now?"

"In my office," I told him.

He responded, "Go home, they will be there when you arrive."

By the end of the day we had completed arrangements through the Kennedy Intervention Center for a nurse to come every morning. After that, a physical therapist would arrive at noontime, followed by an occupational therapist in the midafternoon. It was an awesome response to a family confronted with such a monumental challenge. We never received a bill for those services, which continued for years.

When I hear people speak derogatorily about the Kennedy family I tell them the story of how the Kennedy's generosity and consideration created a meaningful life for my son. "Don't disrespect the Kennedy family when you talk to me about them," I say. I have felt their goodness over all the years of my life, and especially during my son's struggle to survive."

For many months, Louis was like a rag doll. He just lay there in his crib without moving. He made no progress and the situation seemed hopeless. But I was dogged. I had never been one to just concede—and I certainly wasn't going to give up on my son. After a couple years of daily physical and occupational therapy, and almost daily chiropractic treatment, Louis began to show signs of moving out of a vegetative state. His chiropractor, Steve Galena, said to me one day, "He's going to come out of it, just be patient."

We took Louis to his pediatrician for a checkup just before Thanksgiving in 1993. We were getting ready to leave for Honduras to visit with my wife's family for several months. I asked the doctor, "Is Louis ever going to be able to walk?"

The doctor responded, "He is never going to talk and walk. Just love him the way he is." He continued, "Louis seems to be pleasant and he seems to be enjoying life despite his deficits."

On one hand I felt very disappointed by the medical prognosis. On the other, I believed the care that Louis was getting from so many wonderful people was going to make a difference in his progress.

Arriving in Honduras the day before Thanksgiving, we quickly settled into a peaceful and restful routine at my mother-in-law's home in San Pedro Sula. One morning, about a week later, I carried Louis over to the door and set him down. It was his regular post, watching the cars and the people passing by the house. He would stand there sometimes for a couple hours simply watching. I had moved to the couch about twenty-five feet away so I could keep an eye on him. A few minutes later, all of a sudden Louis started walking towards me and said,"Dada."

I burst into tears of absolute joy. With one two-syllable word, my son had come to life, and suddenly the future didn't look so bleak. My spirituality had been severely tested by the events of his birth and the ensuing couple of years. Seeing Louis walk and hearing him talk had been a gift from God.

Over the next few days Louis started walking and talking all the time. Apparently the remaining quarter of his brain had begun compensating for what was missing. It was nothing short of a miracle, and many other miracles would follow.

When we returned home several months later, I immediately took Louis to his pediatrician. When he realized that Louis was walking and talking, he was shocked and surprised to say the least. After a long discussion about all the different care that Louis had received, the doctor said, "It seems likely that it was the chiropractic care that might've made the difference."

For all those hundreds of people who at various times make disparaging and disrespectful remarks about chiropractors and chiropractic care, I respond, "Don't refer to chiropractors and chiropractic care as 'quackery' because my life and my son's life have been blessed by chiropractors and the care they have provided to us."

Over the years, Louis was slowly able to overcome many of his early deficits. Except for a slight limp, he was able to live a relatively normal life. Although admittedly there were difficulties at times for him in school, he was fortunately mainstreamed throughout his school years. I was always very proud of him and all he has accomplished in spite of the difficult obstacles and challenges he was forced to deal with.

* * *

After the interview, I was still quite emotional. The memory of those bleak days after Louis' birth was always a bummer. I needed to clear my head so I decided to grunt my way to the next town, which was ten miles away. We arrived in South Beach and located a motel. I dove under the covers without dinner. I couldn't eat. I was still thinking about Louis and I buried my head in the pillows, embarrassed as I cried myself to sleep.

Two days later, as I passed through Gardiner, I couldn't help but notice how the highway was clogged with logging trucks. I learned that the International Paper Company had a factory here. The trucks came frighteningly close to me, doing speeds of seventy to eighty miles per hour. I walked as far as I could to the side of the road, but it was still a hair-raising experience. The wind created by the passing trucks almost knocked me over and the noise they made was deafening. I couldn't make them disappear; all I could do was try to ignore them and keep moving, trying not to think about what could happen to me if the drivers weren't playing close attention. Walking on the

Pacific Coast Highway in Oregon means that you have to coexist with these passing monster trucks.

Many hours later, I reached Coos Bay, an exquisite, small city nestled into the mountains on the edge of the Pacific Ocean. The bay was filled with ships loaded with lumber, apparently destined for Japan.

A great deal of Oregon timber is sold to Japan, which manufactures products like plywood and things made out of particle board. Then Japan's products are sold back to markets in the United States. Oregon has become a battleground over logging and clear-cutting. On the one side are the environmentalists. On the other are the logging companies, jobs and the local economy. This controversy—called "The War of the Woods"—came up in conversations everywhere I went. And, of course, this issue is not unique to Oregon.

Walking along the Pacific Coast Highway, I saw no evidence of any environmental damage, except for the high-speed logging trucks that repeatedly rattled my nerves and threatened my existence. Apparently, the logging companies were shrewd enough to do their dirty work deep in the forests, far out of sight.

From Coos Bay, I walked toward Port Orford. Again, I noticed many more freighters loaded with lumber, also apparently on their way to Japan.

As with many mornings along the Oregon coast, I had begun the day trekking in the darkness mixed with fog, which made walking hazardous. Later that morning, after the fog burned off, I came upon a farmer burning brush near the road. The smoke hampered highway visibility, not to mention my breathing. I covered my mouth with a wet cloth and picked up the pace.

On the way to Gold Beach, we met Robin and Andy Jerue. They hailed from Ypsilanti, Michigan. They told us they were biking around the world. Of course, that depended on how you defined it. They and their Trek 7200 hybrids were going to be airlifted across the Pacific—and later the Atlantic—by commercial jet, so I'm not sure what the *Guinness Book of World Records* would say about that. But I greatly admired them for their effort. They were basically doing what I was doing—reaching for and striving to complete their dream. As they readied to move on, I hugged them both, wished them well, and told them I would pray for their success.

About twenty-nine miles later, we reached Gold Beach. There we feasted at a Dairy Queen. I'm ashamed to say I've been a lifelong devotee of this not-so-swanky chain. The tasty treats notwithstanding, every time I see one, I am reminded of its extraordinary significance.

After all, it was a promised trip to DQ that snookered me into visiting and then enrolling at Mount Wachusett Community College, so many years earlier. That was the ruse that changed my life.

My hamstrings were really bothering me. I needed a day off. By some amazing coincidence, tomorrow would be Sunday and it just so happened that there were a couple of NFL games on the tube.

After a lovely and relaxing day of watching mindless competition on the gridiron, I catapulted myself out of the motel on Monday morning with a high level of energy and a renewed spirit.

Around noon, I marched into Brookings, the last town in Oregon. Just as I was about to break for lunch, I came across an historical marker that stopped me in my tracks. It stated something I didn't know. On the night of September 9, 1942, a Japanese plane, launched from a submarine, dropped two incendiary devices in the forest near here. Luckily, the resulting fires did little damage. This was the only time the continental United States had ever been bombed by an enemy plane during wartime. A much different story from what we were taught in school about how America had never been attacked.

After hiking for several more hours, I finally stepped across the border into sun-kissed California, the twenty-first and final state of my little excursion!

Frank was so excited about arriving at the California border, he wanted to celebrate. I got out my baseball gloves and a ball. With Frank standing in California and me standing in Oregon, we played catch. It was corny, but we had fun. We laughed as cars passed by tooting their horns. We brought smiles to more than a few faces.

Chapter Seventy-Nine

Land of the Giant Trees

This land is your land, this land is my land
From California to the New York Islands;
From the redwood forests to the Gulf Stream waters
This land was made for you and me.

—Woody Guthrie

I felt invigorated as I left the motel room at 5 A.M. The earlier the start meant less walking in the dark at the end of the day. I had to walk in the dark for more than an hour in the morning, but I was fresh, eager to walk and alert. I was usually accompanied by the sounds of nature waking up. I heard roosters, barking dogs, the yipping of coyotes and the ever-present peepers. It was chilly, yet I was sweating, which made me more miserable until the sun came up. Knowing I was in California, closing in on Big Sur, gave me a big rush of adrenaline. I felt like I was high on drugs as I took to the road.

By early afternoon I found myself in Crescent City, the northernmost town in California, which is tucked away by a lovely crescent-shaped bay. It's really more a village than a city. As I was walking along, I noticed some stenciled words on a concrete wall thirty feet above me. They said, "water line." Pointing up at it, I asked a passing woman, "What is the 'water line' all about?"

Her answer was a shock. She said, "Crescent City was destroyed by a tsunami back in the sixties." She continued her narrative, "We were hit four times in a couple of hours. The first two were bad enough but the third one was catastrophic. It wiped out the city."

She went on to tell me that on March 27, 1964, the "Good Friday Earthquake" struck near Anchorage, Alaska, triggering a tsunami that raced down the West Coast. Because of a number of factors peculiar to its geographical location, Crescent City was struck ninety minutes later by four huge waves that destroyed thirty city blocks, 289 buildings and businesses, 1,000 cars and twenty-five large fishing boats. Twelve people were confirmed dead and hundreds injured. For some reason, Crescent City received more damage than Anchorage.

I glanced down at the small, gentle waves rolling into the bay. It was hard to believe they ever reached that "water line" so high above me.

Speaking of earthquakes, there was a minor one, only 3.3 on the Richter scale, that hit the San Francisco area a couple of days earlier. Some news commentators were saying the "Big One" was coming soon. Well, I would be passing through San Francisco in a few days and now I was really getting nervous. Beside snakes, I have another phobia: I'm deathly afraid of earthquakes.

I found out that folks in Crescent City worry more about the near-by Pelican Bay State Prison. It was the lock-up for the most violent of criminal offenders in California. Apparently it got the name because it had allegedly replaced Alcatraz. The name Alcatraz means Pelican. While it provides many jobs in this otherwise economically depressed area, some residents are understandably uncomfortable having this employer so close to home.

I pressed on toward the giant redwoods, just south of Crescent City. My walk took me through a thickening fog that blanketed the road and obscured the forest up ahead. The magnificent trees grow to dizzying heights because of this damp climate. They are northern California's skyscrapers.

Soon I was in Redwood National Park, walking through the mountainous forest of the coastal redwoods (*Sequoia sempervirens*). Towering over me were the tallest trees on the planet. Only its close relative, the giant sequoia of central California, had more mass. A sign told me that I was in the place "Where the Redwoods meet the sea." I was fascinated. These special and almost surreal forms of life are something you can only believe when you see them. Nothing in nature that I had ever seen matched their glory. In fact, I believe once you have seen a redwood nothing can ever match the sensation: no video or photo will portray them as you first experience them. They are like we think of dinosaurs, from a different age and larger than imaginable. They are the dinosaurs of plant life, yet they are still around. The silence of the forest was total as the giant trees acted as a "roof" for the forest keeping all other sounds away.

Twenty minutes later, I was standing under "Hyperion," the tallest tree in this park, hence in the world. It was 379 feet high. You could build a single house using only this tree. It almost felt like nighttime, walking under the canopy of these trees that block out the sun. Occasionally, though, the sunlight peeks through the pine needles in slivers of light, almost like laser beams.

What really blew my mind was that a handful of these trees were around when Christ was born, making them some of the oldest living organisms on earth. Sadly, 96 percent of all old-growth redwoods, which had existed along the northern California coast for at least 20 million years, had been logged. What little are left are protected in a few national and state parks. It is a great credit to California and America that we cherish these natural wonders the way we do. As travelers, we get to celebrate their beauty because as a people we seem to have come to our senses and now protect this beauty.

* * *

The following afternoon, we were parked on the side of the road, mindlessly munching on sandwiches. A car pulled up behind us and a man stepped out. Without saying hello, he slinked away with his camera. I saw he was headed toward what had appeared to be a bunch of rocks about 100 yards away. We quickly realized that what we had thought to be rocks were now moving. It was a large herd of wild animals with huge antlers that had been lying in the grass. Several of them had stood up. They were bigger than any animal I ever saw, except elephants. They were certainly much bigger than horses. *How could we have missed seeing them?* I wondered. As the photographer stealthily approached them, some more of the animals warily stood up.

Frank grabbed the camera and we rushed out to the pasture. The photographer warned Frank "Don't get any closer. They might charge." Somewhat excitedly, he told us, "They are the only herd of endangered "Roosevelt Elk" left in the world."

We walked backwards all the way to the van, watching to make sure we were not in danger. As soon as we were safely in the van we watched for a while as the elk that had risen up had laid back down and seemed like they were at peace.

Apparently this is their sole grazing area at least for now. They're more of a tourist attraction although they don't seem to notice. Such magnificent animals. It seemed as though the herd was about fifty or sixty in number. Other than this herd, you can't see them anywhere else in the U.S.

Just ahead and far below was a beautiful cove. Sitting there, in a quiet nook above the tiny bay listening only to the magnificent waves of the Pacific crashing out in the distance, I became so fully absorbed in the beauty of the sounds and smells of the ocean, that, for a time, I forgot all else.

Within a couple of miles, I was again gazing down below where the waves were pounding the beach. Along the road were signs warning people of extremely dangerous currents and declaring the beach "Closed." With binoculars, I saw "Off Limits" signs posted right at the beach, due to "Dangerous Currents." Apparently the surfers down there were illiterate because, by the hundreds, they were paddling out to ride the waves.

As we watched them, we saw a group of young guys, clad in their wetsuits, bounce out of their old Volkswagen bus, grab their surf-boards and make their way to the beach. They didn't get to tackle the waves though as a California Highway Patrol officer pulled up, exited his cruiser and politely but forcefully asked them to get back in the bus and stay out of the area.

I asked the cop about all those surfers already in the water. He said: "I'm certainly not going in the water to get them. If they feel like risking their lives, and they are already in the ocean, all I can do is give the cars hefty tickets for being parked here. So they will pay big-time fines—if they survive the rip-currents."

I could appreciate these surfers probably knew what they were doing with respect to understanding rip currents and the dangers. That being said, the example they may be giving to people less educated about the dangers of the currents to cause less experienced swimmers and wannabe surfers to duplicate what they are seeing.

I know this to be true because in the late seventies I experienced this kind of situation myself. I was vacationing in Hawaii and I decided to go to the North Shore of Oahu, home to some of the world's largest waves and therefore a mecca for professional surfers. To those watching from the beach, these surfers' stunts look enjoyable and almost effortless because they are so skilled. My then wife Susan and I watched as monster twenty-five to thirty-five-foot tall waves crashed on the beach. The surfers laughed and seemed to be having a great time so Susan I decided to join in the fun.

We walked out to where the waves were breaking and watched as a giant wave approached us. It was such a rush watching this wave ready to crash on us, but it was hardly like the small waves we had experienced at home. The force of this was tremendous and it felt like a building had fallen on us instead of water. Both Susan and I tried to stand up, get out of the water and get back to the beach only a few feet away. But the receding wave pulled us back into the ocean and the next wave crashed over us and threw us down on the beach again. We tried our best to get out of the water, but the sand was pulled out from under us again and we were again washed back out further. Again, we fought our way towards the beach and safety. We almost made it, but almost didn't count. The next wave crashed us back down and dragged us back to sea. It was like we were a couple of plastic toys. After several attempts we finally made it to the dry beach. We immediately discovered that our frolic had cost us our bathing suits. We were naked and completely covered with sand, which also got in our ears, mouths, and noses.

Once we had calmed down and grabbed some clothes to wear, we turned toward the crashing ocean and watched the surfers still having a great time. We both know that we had survived something that could easily have taken our lives. The power of the ocean waves was something that I will certainly never forget—and always respect. There is no way I would ever again do what I did on that day in Hawaii.

* * *

Early the next morning, I was back on the road, headed south toward the town of Scotia. A couple of hours later, Andy and Robin Jerue, the around-the-world bikers we met in Oregon a few days before, pulled up behind us. We shared a cold drink with them. They told us their plan for the day was to ride on a special road that ran alongside the highway called "The Avenue of the Giants," so named because it was lined with thousands of giant redwoods. "It's the next exit," Robin said.

"We'll be there," I said.

* * *

Walking on I spotted a teen-age girl hitchhiking. While this was a long-lost art back East, in California it seemed to be a standard practice. This was the third hitchhiker I had seen already this morning. I had seen several others in the last couple of days.

This brought back memories of my younger days. As a teenager, I used to hitchhike everywhere. My first time was when I ran away from home, just after my father died. My older brother, who was about twenty, seven years older than me, had apparently decided that as the oldest boy it was his right to replace my father as the dictator in the house. I didn't fall into line, thumbed my nose at his power grab and was relentlessly defiant of his attempted tyranny.

I spent a few weeks trying to figure out how to live within this newly imposed system of rule without caving in to my brother's authoritarianism; but I came to the conclusion that leaving home was my best option. I packed a duffel bag, walked down to the highway a mile from our house, and began to hitchhike. About twenty-four hours later I was on the outskirts of Pittsburgh, Pennsylvania, when reality began to set in. I was without money, a plan, or any knowledge of where I was going. The more I thought about it, the more I realized I had to turn around. In the next twenty-four hours I hitchhiked all the way back to Boston. In those days it was easy to stick out your thumb and get a ride.

I finally made it home and found my mother frantic. She couldn't imagine why I would run away. I told her that my older brother had caused me so much grief, that I felt it was my only option. She immediately told my brother to cease and desist. She said, "You are not his father, stop acting like you are." He rarely bothered me after that.

Since leaving Boston, memories from way back—forty years or more, when I was so young and naïve—came flooding in constantly, triggered by something I saw or heard, smelled or touched. They were often pleasant, but I also remembered many things that were not so great. Being on the road for thirteen hours a day allowed plenty of solitude and time for reflection, both good and bad.

* * *

The Avenue of the Giants was a stunning boulevard indeed. I tried to focus on their exquisite beauty instead of the sharp pain that was developing in my right shin. My lower leg was swollen and extremely uncomfortable. This was a new and different problem. Out of the blue, no warning, and I was having trouble. What supremely bad timing!

I tried to grin and bear it and focus on the magnificence of nature. These gigantic trees are awe-inspiring, like the Grand Canyon or Niagara Falls. The smell of the pine, the sereneness of the forest, the brilliant green—not to mention the sheer size of the trees—envelops you and all your senses. As you walk into the forest, it is like entering a house of worship. You feel your insignificance and the power of Mother Nature. Try as I might, there are no words in the English language grand enough to adequately convey the feeling of being with them.

From time to time I would pass by huge redwood stumps. I learned that some of the trees were purposely cut down—before falling down on their own and posing a major threat to tourists. These remnants of the world's largest plant served as a reminder of the enormous size of these grand trees; many were so large we could easily have parked the van—maybe even two vans—on their surfaces.

The best part of the first day with the "giants" was our visits to two of the small towns along the way. It was Halloween day and the locals were dressed in costume. In Myers Flat (The town's slogan is "Myers Flat is where it's at.") we met Howard Baker, a man who was euphoric because he had recently appeared on the *Tonight Show* with Jay Leno after winning a lookalike contest. (I never got to find out who he looked like because he was in a full costume—as a witch).

Denise White was another member of the Myers Flat community. She not only provided us with lots of laughs, she also gave us a donation for our charities and walked with me for a few miles. She was a collector of old Indian arrowheads and similar objects from the ground. She presented me with four arrowheads for me to give to my sons.

At the next small town, Miranda, we went into the local cafe and found the waitress dressed up as a pumpkin. She informed us that the cafe was closed but she would love to give us any cold drink we desired. We took the "pumpkin lady," as we called her, up on her offer, ordering up a couple frosty glasses of root beer. We stayed for almost an hour, chatting with her and some other customers who wanted to hear about our trek across the States.

I wanted to know about life among the redwoods. One guy quipped, "Oh, nothing ever happens here worth talking about." He continued, "But having you guys here is a treat; everyone coming through here usually just breezes through in their cars."

That night I was early to bed, using a ten-pound bag of ice to try and reduce the swelling in my right calf. It had gotten so big it looked like I had an extra thigh above my foot. In all my years of long-distance walking, I had never experienced this kind of leg problem. The swelling made my right leg feel like I was dragging around a heavy cast.

* * *

Thankfully, my calf felt much better when I woke up the next day, but the swelling was still a problem. I decided to walk with a cane, trying to keep weight off the swollen leg as much as possible. Ambulation was extremely difficult, but the joy of walking among the beautiful redwoods kept my mind off my leg problems.

The Morphine Dream

All my life I had dreamed about walking among these giants, and here I was, actually doing it. I remember being unable to comprehend trees could ever grow so large. In my youth I had done many land-clearing jobs with my father and brothers. We would cut down hundreds of trees of all sizes in one day and do it day after day. All of those trees combined wouldn't add up to one of the giant redwoods I regularly saw in my old *National Geographic* magazines. My joy to finally be walking among them manifested as tears. "Are you okay?" Frank asked—several times.

"I'm fine," I said. "It's so special to be here, I am simply stunned."

Struggling all the way, I somehow reached Garberville at the southernmost end of the Avenue of Giants. It had been thirty-one miles of walking with the great trees. We found a motel and I was lying down within minutes, exhausted and with an aching leg that was seriously worrying me. Frank immediately wrapped my lower leg in ice and helped me to elevate it. By late evening, I was again experiencing less pain but, strangely, more swelling.

* * *

In spite of the leg difficulties, in the morning I was not only up and about, but out walking on the Pacific Coast Highway. After twenty miles, the pain and discomfort was so disturbing, I had to stop. It was constant and from deep within my shin. Each step had been a challenge. Frank said, "Time for a hospital old man." I didn't argue. We drove about fifty miles in search of one. In this part of California, nothing in the way of services is routine.

In the town of Willits, I hobbled into the emergency room of the Frank Howard Memorial Hospital. I wondered if it was named after a famous baseball player of the sixties by the same name.

After an exam, blood tests and X-rays, Dr. Jon Goldstern gave me the bad news: "You have cellulitis, an infection in your leg; that means complete bed rest with your right leg elevated for seven to fourteen days."

I told him, "That's impossible."

"Okay," he said. "Try resting and antibiotics for four days. If your symptoms have eased up, then you can begin walking again, but not forty miles right away. If your symptoms reappear, call me back." He went on: "This problem at its worst, can last for months when it reaches deep veins—you must take it seriously.

I asked, "How could I have gotten this?"

Dr. Goldstern answered, "Given that you have no appearance of a skin problem, it was most likely an insect bite. Around here there are often instances of spider bites causing celluitis, but there is no way for us to pinpoint what happened."

So, some bug I errantly swatted at by the side of the road was responsible for this much misery. It's always the things you are not expecting that can take you down.

I asked the doctor if the hospital was named after Frank Howard, the baseball player. He told me that the facility bore the name of a wealthy rancher from the area, Charles Howard. Among other things, Howard owned the world famous racehorse "Seabiscuit" and had donated the money to build the hospital. "His teenage son Frank was injured in an accident. There was no hospital to provide care for him, and he died." Thus the donation and the building of a hospital, named for his son, where there had been none.

Reluctantly, we checked into a motel. For the next four days, I followed the doctor's orders, took the prescribed medicine, and elevated and iced my right leg. These were the four most restless and boring days of the trek. There was nothing much to do but watch the daytime soaps and all my *Rocky* movies—twice. But at least my shin felt much better and no longer looked like an extra thigh.

* * *

The four-day rest experiment finally came to an end. After a hearty breakfast, I was finally ready to test my ability to walk again. At 8 A.M. a local TV reporter from Santa Rosa caught up to me just as I started out, having apparently been tipped off by the motel desk clerk. I wasn't really in the mood for an interview, as I was really worried about how my leg was going to react to the strain of walking on it. I answered all the reporter's queries and moved on.

To make matters more difficult, the only route available was on the freeway—no viable options existed. I was on and off the freeway, over and over again, as the police were emphatic about my not walking on it, especially with the slow-moving van behind me. In some places I made use of frontage roads that ran right alongside the freeways. Other places, I had to venture farther away. Several times during the day I found myself back on the freeway for lack of an adequate route to walk. I tried walking in the grass or the dirt off to the right of the pavement. Still, my mere presence there caused such a distraction to drivers that every step was taken at significant risk.

It was in this part of California that I encountered extremely heavy traffic for the first time since Seattle. It was very uncomfortable to walk with thousands of cars per hour whizzing by at speeds of seventy-five miles per hour and over. Unfortunately, I would have to deal with it for many days as we were getting closer and closer to large population centers.

After flirting with the freeway for two or three hours, a Califonia Highway Patrol (CHIP) officer drove up and ordered, "Get off and don't get back on or you will be arrested!" I was convinced.

Many hours later, walking on curving and lightly traveled byways, not having completed my normal forty miles, I bagged it for the day. I only walked thirty miles, but it was a victory of sorts, having not walked for several days. I don't think the doctor would have been pleased about the exertion, but for my mental well-being, I had to push myself. Besides, I was only twenty-two miles from the Golden Gate Bridge—another place I had dreamed of walking over for many years.

The Golden Gate was a significant goal because of its status as one of the most famous of bridges in America, if not the world. My pace had slowed though, because my shin was swelling again. Even more problematic, for the first time since leaving the Portland area, the traffic made me even more anxious. When the traffic was at its heaviest, it seemed like the drivers were more crazed. Some shouted obscenities at me, others blew their horns. It was obvious I was a real problem for those commuters rushing to work.

* * *

The weather was warm, about seventy degrees and partly sunny. I walked through some lovely towns—Novato, San Rafael, and Corte Madera. The beauty of these enclaves made me forget about the pain in my leg. I did feel better, but the problem had not run its course.

Each of these northern bedroom suburbs of San Francisco had its own Spanish charm, vast open spaces for nature lovers, places for fishing and camping, all so close to a major city. I was having such a wonderful time walking through these picturesque small towns, nestled in the coastal hills. The downtown areas, were filled with vintage shopping spots, yet without crowds. It was easy to understand why people come here to stay. Only thirty minutes from San Francisco, forty from Oakland, and sixty from San Jose—places where the population must have totaled over ten million—it must feel like a privilege to live here in the peace and small-town atmosphere. I'm sure the real estate market reflects all the advantages in extremely high priced homes.

Chapter Eighty
San Francisco

*It is a good thing the early settlers landed on the East Coast;
if they'd landed in San Francisco first, the rest of the country
would still be uninhabited.*

—Herbert Mye

I had trouble sleeping. My still-twitching and swollen leg was bothering me. I woke Frank up at 4:30 AM. "It's still dark out," Frank complained as he got up and got ready.

The real reason I couldn't sleep was excitement: I was about to enter the city where my maternal grandmother was born and raised.

My mother used to regale me with her mother's terrifying stories about the 1906 earthquake—a catastrophic event that she somehow managed to survive. Though she lived through the terror, I somehow ended up with the phobia, not only about earthquakes, but about San Francisco.

While my grandmother made it through the quake, she died at the very young age of twenty-two, just a couple of years after my mother had been born. My grandmother and her brothers were all afflicted with severe diabetes, and they all died young. This was a time when there was no such thing as insulin. Additionally, there was very little knowledge of the disease. In those days, diabetics would just die, often without significant signs of illness.

This genetic defect was passed on to my mother and to all my siblings. During my athletic career I was forever experiencing low blood sugar, which would cause me to get extremely light-headed. Sometimes those difficulties occurred at crucial moments in a game. It was a constant reminder that "some things are written in your blood." By sheer coincidence, my father's mother was also a severe diabetic so that same gene was passed down to us through his side of the family. With this gene pool, of course, our offspring are all doomed to deal with this terrible disease. While as youngsters, we may not have had issues with it, by the time we were teens, or approached middle age, we were all afflicted.

* * *

Sleepless, I was out on the road early. A couple of hours later, I walked into the eye-candy town of Sausalito: a wonderful little place situated just across the bay from San Francisco. This was the one-time home of the great Otis Redding. It was while living in Sausalito that he composed perhaps the most well-known of all his songs "The Dock of the Bay." There were breathtaking vistas in every direction. Everywhere you looked there were beautiful homes. Some were what you'd expect, the typical stucco, Spanish style with red clay roof tiles. There were also New England-style Victorians, along with contemporary sprawling Western- style ranches. All were majestically landscaped— gardens ablaze with bright multi-colored flowers, usually surrounded by shrubs all shades of green, and a variety of shapes—all stunning.

The town was surrounded on three sides: by the bay, the mountains and the ocean. It was connected on its only open side to San Francisco by the Golden Gate Bridge. This wealthy and artistic enclave used to be a major transportation hub. Sausalito was the terminus for the car ferry to San Francisco, which was abruptly put out of business when the bridge opened in May 1937.

I had miscalculated the distance to San Francisco; I was ten miles closer then I had thought. So I was not prepared for what happened when I turned a corner and found myself with a spectacular view directly across the bay. I was taking in, for the first time, the undulating city of San Francisco. And, for the first time, in person, I was staring at one of the most recognizable engineering marvels of the modern world—the reddish bronze vastness of the Golden Gate Bridge! It's on par with the pyramids of Giza, Stonehenge, the Roman Coliseum, the Great Wall of China, the Taj Mahal, and the Eiffel Tower. I could also see the prosaic Bay Bridge that connected San Francisco to Oakland. And finally, I saw what must be the infamous Alcatraz Island, the former federal prison, home to "The Birdman of Alcatraz," where Al Capone and Whitey Bulger, Boston's most infamous gangster, spent some down time.

From Sausalito, I walked several mountain miles. Since there was no room on the narrow switchbacks for both the van and me, I sent Frank on ahead. There were no shoulders, and if he remained behind me, it would have created dangerous conditions for other drivers, and thus dangerous conditions for me.

Finally, when I was high in the hills, the road suddenly emptied down onto the Golden Gate Bridge. I know it sounds trite, but the view took my breath away. I had only seen it in pictures before this. While it had always captivated me, it was far more magnificent in person—especially at the speed of walking. Had I been in a car, I would have sped along, viewing it through the glass of the windshield. On foot, all my senses were able to slowly capture its glory: the fresh, salty aroma of the bay; the sunlight striking and changing the unique color of the painted steel; the spires rising into the sky, punctuating the clouds. I had come across many bridges but this was unlike anything I had ever seen.

Coming out of my reverie, I saw Frank and the van, parked far below at a rest area approaching the bridge. A few minutes later I joined up with him again. Because I had miscalculated the distance, I had arrived here far earlier than expected, which created a scheduling problem. Two weeks earlier, I had promised to meet NBC News on the far side of the bridge at 1 P.M. Now I was going to have to kill two hours before walking across. This trip had taught me that you just have to go with the flow so we relaxed, talking to other tourists about the magnificent Bay area, which we would soon experience.

I grabbed a few towels from the van, used them as a pillow, and lay down on the grass and napped. I woke up refreshed and ready to cross the bridge. I counted Volkswagen "Bugs" parked nearby. Most were not of recent vintage, but were those from the sixties. My second car, in my late teens, was a brand new Volkswagen Beetle which cost me only $900 back then. Except for memories of the dealer's lot back in 1963, I had never seen so many Bugs in one place. There were eleven of those classic cars in the parking area just to the north of the bridge.

Finally, it was time to cross the Golden Gate. The pedestrian walkway looked like a road. It must be eight feet wide and thousands of folks cross it every hour. I made my way slowly across the bridge as the crowd of striders, trekking in both directions, made it difficult to walk my normal quick pace. The slow walk gave me the time to savor every moment. I peered over the railing. A container ship was passing below me. Up close, I examined the two towers. They didn't look special from this vantage point: just a bunch of riveted steel plates—more orange than red. What was so awe-inspiring was their height. It hurt my neck to keep looking up at them. The diameter of the cables slung from the towers was astonishing. They seemed as thick as my legs. What a difference to see this all close-up—another thing I would have missed if I were driving.

At the time of construction, it was the longest suspension bridge—4,200 feet—in the world, a distinction it held until 1964. And at 692 feet above the water, its two towers are still the world's tallest.

Oddly enough, this beautiful structure is a suicide magnet. Over 1,100 people have jumped to their deaths from here, far more than any other place in the world. In four seconds, you drop 245 feet to the water below, reaching speeds of seventy-five miles per hour. People die of impact trauma when they hit the water. Those few that survive usually die moments later of drowning or hypothermia. Only a handful had actually survived the jump and lived to tell about it. One jumper who recovered from her injuries jumped a second time to her death. Another survivor swam to shore and drove himself to the hospital.

As I reached the south side of the bridge, an NBC reporter and cameraman were waiting. The interview went well. I answered all the usual questions.

At one point, the reporter asked, "When did you realize how big this country is?"

"Well," I replied, "I have walked more than 400 miles since crossing into Northern California and I am still in Northern California! Pretty big, I guess."

Adjacent to the bridge I immediately walked into the Presidio, one of the largest urban green areas in the United States.

The Spanish built a fort here in 1776, which was the northernmost military outpost of its New World Empire. When Mexico won independence from Spain in 1821, it became a Mexican fort. It was then seized by the United States in 1848 during the Mexican-American War. And after 219 years of continuous military service, it was decommissioned and transferred to the National Park Service in 1994.

This beautiful, heavily wooded northeast corner of the city, with its manicured rolling lawns, overlooks the entrance to both San Francisco Bay and the Golden Gate Bridge. There were Civil War cannons, parade grounds, and military barracks built two hundred years ago. The park had an abundance of pine and eucalyptus trees. It was notable for its curving roads and acres of plush green grass, thick with shrubs and trees of all varieties. It was certainly a favorite of hikers and bikers, because hundreds of them were swarming around me as I paused to jot down my thoughts in my journal.

After more than two hours of purposely meandering through the Presidio, I walked out into the neighborhoods adjacent to the park, toward the downtown area. Spending a few hours as a common tourist, I descended Russian Hill along the flowered switchbacks of Lombard Street. I climbed Telegraph Hill and mounted the stairs of the Coit Tower. At the corner of Haight and Ashbury Streets, I saw a completely naked man strolling down the sidewalk as if nothing were amiss. Nudity, while officially not authorized by law in San Fran, except on various remote beaches, seems acceptable. Violations of the laws against it are apparently not uniformly enforced throughout many parts of San Francisco. At press time of this book, the San Francisco Board of Supervisors had voted to ban all public nudity, though a lawsuit seeking to overturn the ban is in the courts.

After spending very little time in the tourist trap of Fisherman's Wharf, I hopped on a cable car clacking up Nob Hill. I saw cars parked sideways on the streets, which must be among the steepest in the world. The conductor told me that there was an occasional runaway car, which would come crashing down the street, often doing considerable damage—no doubt!

When I got off the cable car, I strode into the Mark Hopkins Hotel as if I was the King of Prussia. No one challenged me as I took the elevator up to the hotel's famous restaurant, "Top of the Mark." I could never afford to eat here, but the maître d' didn't charge me for taking in the mesmerizing view overlooking the emerald bay and the now fog-enshrouded Golden Gate Bridge. I realized the validity of a truism I had heard long ago: "Most who come here wish they could stay longer."

As I drank it in, I tried to imagine the early morning hours of April 18, 1906, the day the Great San Francisco Earthquake hit. My grandmother was a teenager, but she never forgot what happened. She had been jarred awake, she thought, by the "roar of a train." Soon the family home began to crumble. She fell to the floor and couldn't get up. Suddenly her father appeared and scooped her up into his arms and ran from the house as it fell around them. Her mother and her brothers were already outside. Their home was lost, totally destroyed, as were the homes of most of her neighbors and many of her friends. Buildings collapsed all around her. Broken gas lines ignited fires that raged for days and could not be extinguished because all the main water lines were ruptured by the quake. Most of the city lay in ruins. Thousands lost their lives. Hundreds of thousands were left homeless. Her father sheltered the family under a makeshift tent where they huddled together for weeks in Golden Gate Park.

It made me shudder to think about it, and I knew the San Andreas and Hayward Faults were nearby. As I had mentioned, there was a minor earthquake in the area just a few days before my arrival here. So, as much as I was awed by the mix of beaches, landscaping, architecture, the bay, Fisherman's Wharf and the urban beauty—I wanted to get the heck out of here!

For all of my life I had thought that Boston—with its Common and the public gardens and the grassy malls of Commonwealth Avenue, Fenway Park, the universities, the Government Center, its many museums, the Esplanade and the Emerald Necklace—was the most spectacular city in existence. San Francisco changed all that in a mere few hours.

I hurried back down to the bottom of Market Street and did a U-turn and headed west along miles of commercial clutter and nightmarish traffic, all the while treading up and down the hills of San Francisco.

I had a strong sense of the gay presence, something that San Francisco had been known for in recent years. In my youth, one of the reasons I had avoided the place was because of my pronounced homophobia—having been raised in a culture where gays were seen to be "mamma's boys," "queers" and "fags." In the service, during boot camp, we recruits listened to drill instructors go on and on about the "sickos" and how there "Better not be any faggots in my Marine Corps!" I had always avoided contact with gays. It was at Amherst College where I learned that gay was not something to fear.

On my first day on the college campus, I met a young lady, Marie, who happened to be a great basketball player, a great musician and an excellent student and a noted softball player. We quickly became good friends. We were both on the campus the entire summer as work-study participants. We enjoyed many meals together, many interesting discussions, and we often played softball with other students and staff. I was quick to realize what a gifted human being she was.

Just before the semester began in September, I attended an event where there were campus groups attempting to recruit students for their clubs. I listened to the speeches of the Black Students Association, the Asian Students Association, the Christian Student Group, and the Jewish Student Group, among others. The final presentation was from the Gay and Lesbian Student Group on campus. I was surprised when my friend Marie stepped up to the podium. I was incredulous when she began to talk about her time at Amherst. She spoke about being a fine student, an athlete, and a musician. But she followed that with, "In spite of those accomplishments, I'm only known as the 'Campus Lesbian.'" She went on, "That doesn't seem like the term that should be used to describe me."

My jaw dropped. I was dumbfounded. I sat through the rest of her talk as she encouraged gay and lesbian students to reach out for the support of the Gay and Lesbian Student Group. As I sat there I had a profound realization: "If this girl is gay then there can be nothing wrong with 'gay' because she's was such a special young lady." At that moment I had another one of those life-altering learning experiences. I never had a homophobic thought from that moment on. In fact, I often felt guilt for the nasty things I had often said about gays or, even worse, said directly to gays during earlier years.

* * *

Throughout the day, I had a strong sense of being with my mother. At my age I knew it wasn't a manly thing to say, but I missed her terribly. And I especially needed her now, as the time was fast approaching when I would return to Boston and learn whether or not my law license would be restored. If not, I didn't know what I was going to do. I had no plan B. I was never one to have a plan B because I had the confidence that Plan A would always work for me. I was counting on getting back my license so I could return to the practice of law. That was my calling. I would not allow any other possibilities to enter my mind. I had somehow learned over the years since the Morphine Dream, to never plan for failure.

* * *

It had been a very grueling day for me. The hills of San Francisco had been the steepest hills I had climbed on the entire trip. It had also been the most spectacular day of the entire trip in terms of all that I saw and the emotions I felt in this very special city. Having returned to my mother's roots made me feel a special bond with this magical city. I too, "Left my heart in San Francisco," at least for this day.

Upon reaching Pacifica we couldn't locate a decent motel so we drove to the next town, Montara, where we found a great bed and breakfast place called the Farallone Inn. Our room was unlike any other I had encountered on the adventure. The room was huge, had beautiful modern Scandinavian furniture, and the people who managed the Inn were exemplary in every respect. The hospitality reminded me so much of Dave Lundgren's Waterville Hotel, but its contemporary architecture and presentment was very different than the historic, antique-filled Waterville Hotel.

* * *

I rose to the smell of the ocean and the sound of waves thundering against the beach. Montara Bay was a quiet secluded place, in spite of its proximity to San Francisco. I reached the amazingly beautiful beach—silent, secluded and pristine—from a lane that sprouted off the coastal road. After taking in the sights, I headed south along the coast. I had to walk a few miles to Half Moon Bay before I would jump into the van to go to a speaking event. We had to go east, over the mountains and across the San Mateo Bridge over San Francisco Bay to Oakland where I had agreed to speak at a private school, the Redwood Country Day School. I had spoken to students many times across the country but what was unusual about this appearance was the age of my audience. The kids went from kindergarten up to middle school. Thus it was a very difficult group in terms of figuring out what kind of presentation to do, given the breadth of the ages. It turned out to be a special experience as even the youngest of the kids seemed to enjoy my regaling them was stories about things that happened on my way across the country.

After my talk ended the kids were more interested in the van than talking with me. They all gathered around it, from the youngest to the early teenagers, as Frank opened the doors and gave them a ten-minute talk of the van's esoteric amenities. Most of the kids had never seen anything like it. They were fascinated that I had a computer, a television and a VCR. Many climbed up on the bed to see if it was comfortable or not—they were surprised to find that it was.

While Frank showed off the van, I discussed my trip with one of the teachers, who said that it was very kind of me to go out of my way to come and talk to the kids. He said, "Often, nobody wants to come to Oakland because apparently local fable holds that 'when you get *here* in Oakland, there isn't any *here*'."

I responded, "If somebody is interested enough to ask me to speak, I would go far out of my way to reach where they are." Besides, I told him, "I also came to Oakland because I wanted to visit the Mormon Temple."

We bid the faculty and students farewell, and then Frank and I drove the van a few miles to visit the Mormon Temple of Oakland. It sits high atop a hill overlooking the San Francisco Bay Area. Surrounded by palm trees that appear to reach for the stars, colorful gardens and is graced with several fountains, it is as beautiful a temple as I've seen.

Because of its elevation and since it is all lit up at night, I was told that the entire Bay area is able to gaze up after dark to see this architectural wonder. I was not going to be around long enough to see it at night myself but I imagined that it must be an incredible sight.

I remember hearing a lot about this temple and the obstacles surrounding its construction. It took twenty years for the Mormon Church to be able to begin building. The delays allegedly stemmed from prejudice about the Mormon religion. Finally, the church was permitted to build what was to become only the second Mormon Temple in California.

Because I am a Mormon, I had a particularly keen interest in this temple. I was attending the Cambridge Ward of the Mormon Church in Massachusetts when we had a guest speaker from Salt Lake City by the name of Truman Madsen, who was a high-ranking church official based in Utah. He regaled us with stories of how the great citizens of Oakland had finally relented and allowed the Temple to proceed with construction. He was leaving Cambridge the next day to attend the opening in Oakland. Near the end of his presentation someone asked Madsen a question—and has answer has stayed with me ever since. He was asked, "When are the latter days?" (The official name of the Mormon Church is The Church of Jesus Christ of Latter Day Saints.)

His answer was, "Many of you in this room (there were a couple of hundred of us) will see the latter days." While I've never really worried about it, I have always kept it in my conscious mind. For me, Madsen was telling us that the world as we knew it would end.

We descended from the church and quickly headed back to the San Mateo Bridge. We traveled back over San Francisco Bay, and over the mountains to Half Moon Bay. I stepped down from my comfortable captain's chair and began walking again.

My muscles were very stiff, after having spent several hours on the road visiting Oakland, and having not moved my legs appropriately for all that time. I pushed through the discomfort and focused on my relationship with the Mormon Church.

I have not been a practicing Mormon since my early twenties, and my struggles with the faith came from my inability to buy into the total beliefs of the church. I was trying to understand my own relationship with God, and contrast it with the knowledge the church bestowed upon me and many others. While some beliefs made perfect sense, like the tenets that prohibit the use of drugs, alcohol and the like. I was plenty confused that members of the church were allowed to sell alcohol all over the world—The Marriot Hotels, worldwide, for instance. It seemed as though that was a double standard that did not coincide with the Mormon teaching of "God's way."

I was also significantly influenced by the great family values, and dazzled by the many Mormon missionaries who were ubiquitous during my youth, always trying to lead teenagers down the right path. Given the difficulties I had struggled with as I grew up, much of the church's teachings provided me an alternative perspective of how we mortal beings should live.

I was probably about nineteen or twenty when one of the bishops of the Mormon Church in the Weston, Massachusetts, Ward of which I was a member, came to see me one night. He said, "In spite of your good deeds and good behavior within and around the church, you can no longer be a part of the church if you don't disavow your friendships with many of your Godless teenage friends."

It was true that some of my friends drank, some did drugs, some gambled, some were promiscuous, and some were all of the above, most of them were ordinary, run-of-the-mill Americans teenagers. I had grown up without a lot of friends, so at this point in my life I was especially glad to have a few. The bishop had issued an ultimatum—making me choose between my friends and the church. I was put in a terrible spot. I loved the church and the people who were part of my Mormon life; I also appreciated and was deeply loyal to my friends.

I pondered the dilemma, but turning my back on my friends just didn't seem right. They were good and decent people and, in my estimation, didn't need to adhere to the strict Mormon beliefs to fall into that category.

As I grew older I began to realize that my relationship with God was between me and God, and the church was merely a place where people came together to be grouped with others who believed in the lifestyle demanded by the Mormon tenets. After the bishop had drawn that line in the sand, I determined that I would follow my own way to my relationship with God.

To me we are all part of the "church" and we are free to celebrate our relationship with God as we see fit. All of my life I've considered myself a Mormon. I rarely attend the Mormon Church and rarely have contact with other Mormons, nonetheless I am proud of my Mormon beliefs and my own spirituality, which has always been the core of my being.

When we reached the tiny town of San Gregorio, I walked right into the San Gregorio General Store. As its name implied it sold everything under the sun—and then some. It was a drug store, a food store, the five-and-dime, a book store, a saloon, a plant store, the feed-and-seed store, the farm equipment store, a toy store, and a U.S. Post

Office. It sold raccoon traps and eighteen flavors of tequila. There was an in-tune piano if you cared to sit down and play. And on Saturday and Sunday nights, there was live music. Wow!

What the store lacked was a motel. The town didn't have one either. It took us an hour to find one—all the way back to Montara Bay and the Farallone Inn.

Chapter Eighty-One

Big Sur

It's not the waves you catch,
How hard or how strong.
It's the wind in your hair,
The ocean's song.

—Sasha Walker Mills

I walked south for several days and I was swept away by the ocean views, constantly there on my right, contrasted with the mountains on my left, which were sprinkled with magnificent homes. Seeing those houses made me think back to the poverty and squalor of many inner city neighborhoods I had walked through: Buffalo, Cleveland, Detroit and Chicago, to name some of them. The same memories plagued me when I thought back to the Indian reservation in South Dakota. I can imagine how the homes I was walking by would be even more special if they could be home to the folks from the poor places I had seen all the way across the country.

It must be tiring to hear me use the same adjectives over and over—splendid, dazzling, spectacular, mesmerizing, awe-inspiring, breathtaking. The truth is that language cannot do justice, especially along the California coastline, to describe the visual beauty I had encountered on this journey. I was so envious of all the people living up in those homes with their unencumbered views of the shimmering Pacific.

Every day the surfers were out in full force, even when storms were on shore or approaching. It seems to be a way of life here on the coast. One fortyish blonde, blue-eyed surfer told me that, "When the storms are coming in, that's when the waves are special."

The music of the Beach Boys often emanated from the cars parked along the roads or from boom boxes on beach blankets. I'd periodically take a break just to watch the fun. Life was certainly filled with more joy-seeking in this part of America. One of the Beach Boys albums is entitled *Endless Summer*. It seems apropos for the people of this region—the picnics, cookouts and surfing seemed to go from dawn till dusk, every day, and was like nothing I'd ever seen before in my trek cross country.

Amazingly, at least half the cars parked along the winding ocean front were old Volkswagen Microbuses or Beetles. Back East, they would be considered "classic" cars and would stop people in their tracks. Out here they seemed ordinary. Apparently the old campers were standard equipment for many of the surfers. I saw many other cars from a different era, the hot rods of my teens: a '57 Chevy, a few GTOs and Oldsmobile 440s, along with a Comet Caliente 390.

As I reached Santa Cruz, the water was filled with hundreds of wet-suited surfers—so many I thought there was a convention or competiton. Their surfboards, of all colors, shapes and sizes, was a cacophony of sensual delight. I stopped to take it all in and lost track of time. A couple of hours must have passed and darkness had settled in around me. I needed to finish my day and get to a motel. I had five miles left—not too far in the grand scheme of things but hardly just around the corner either. I felt like I was leaving a party to go to work, but duty called. I got up, so stiff I didn't think I could walk.

I found Frank sound asleep, laying in his captain's chair in the van with the back of the seat in the full recline position. I woke him up and he smiled groggily. When he realized it was dark he shouted, "Why didn't you wake me up old man?" Within an hour and a half, I was limber and trucking into Santa Cruz, one of California's many famous playgrounds.

* * *

The next day I started out on the freeway. It was Sunday morning and the traffic was quiet and sparse. Unfortunately, after only an hour of walking, the California Highway Patrol showed up and gave me the polite message I had heard before: "Off the freeway." The cop was really nice about it and even drew up a map for me to follow all the way to Monterey Bay. I hated to go off the main highway, because I always seemed to get lost. The directions led me to and through stunning neighborhoods of really classy homes. Then, about halfway through the day, the directions had me walking through the farm country of the California central coast. There were thousands of acres of brussels sprout. I would never have thought the world needed so many (I never eat them) but they were everywhere—as far as the eye could see, looking east. To the west, nothing but the Pacific.

We finally reached Monterey, What made this exquisitely beautiful town so famous were John Steinbeck's novels set in or near here— *East of Eden, Cannery Row,* and *Of Mice and Men,* among others.

Unsurprisingly, my favorite Steinbeck book is *Travels with Charley*. Monterey was also the capital of California from 1777 to 1846 under Spain and Mexico. The first thing the Spanish built in 1770 was a fort to defend the port against an expected invasion by Russia, which would have been launched from Alaska, its then American colony.

Since I was looking rather shaggy and disheveled, we paid a visit to the local barbershop. As the barber was cutting Frank's hair, I was forced to listen to him hold forth about the lawyers in the O. J. Simpson case and the lawyers in the Louise Woodward case back in my hometown of Newton, which was getting national attention (She was the British nanny accused of shaking to death the eight-month-old baby in her care.). The barber finally declared how much he loathed all lawyers. Frank winked at me. He could see I was stewing.

I climbed into the barber's chair. I could sense he was probably thinking he was about to cut the hair of someone a notch above a hobo, he asked, "And what do you do for a living?"

"I was a lawyer before I became a walker."

He turned beet red and didn't utter another word

When my haircut was finished, I paid and walked out without a word. I climbed into the van. Frank said, "To quote George Burns: 'It's too bad that all the people who know how to run the country are busy driving cabs or cutting hair.'"

I said, "To be fair to him, there are a lot of lawyers that cause ordinary folks to think that all lawyers are worthless." But, I continued, "Some lawyers do a lot of good, yet many people fail to recognize that fact."

I first realized I wanted to go to law school when I had my accident on the factory floor that nearly cost me the ability to walk. During one of my early recoveries I picked up a book titled, Your Rights As an Injured Worker. After reading it several times, I realized that I needed a lawyer to represent me against the factory and the insurance company.

I soon traveled to Boston to visit the office of the only attorney I had ever had any contact with. His name was Bernard Rome, and he had represented my brother-in-law in many tough situations. He had quite a reputation and was feared by many. When I got to his office Bernie realized that my case would be better handled by his associate and son-in-law Ed George.

Ed was something near my age, I presumed, and listened intently to the saga about my injuries and the company's subsequent strange behavior toward me . He told me that the case was significant and that he would be glad to represent me. I knew I was in good hands when

George encouraged me to follow through with my plans to continue my education at community college. In the meantime, Ed assured me he would battle with the factory and insurance companies and would certainly get a reasonable result for me and my family. For my part, the only reasonable result I cared about was getting the education.

I began to get a sense that there were many people like me who are injured on the job and for whatever reason weren't treated appropriately or fairly compensated for their injuries and loss of wages. It seemed that an injured worker was most often labeled a malingerer. Of course in most cases that is the farthest thing from the truth, yet almost every injured worker in this country apparently is treated inappropriately. The reason is simple; the almighty dollar. Insurance companies never want to pay claims. Their methods usually include calling into question the veracity of any injured workers claims.

I vowed to myself that when my day came, and I was able to practice law, I would be a lawyer who stood up for injured employees against insurers. People certainly don't want to get injured and sit at home unemployed, confined to a bed or wheelchair. Injured people simply want to get better and return to work.

For me, being so well represented by Ed George was a godsend to me and my family, It proved to me that a good lawyer representing a lay person against the employer/insurance establishment makes all the difference in the world. My case was eventually settled to my family's satisfaction. It was timely, also, as it was at the same time when I received word that I had been accepted at Amherst College.

When I was fortunate enough to become a lawyer, I kept my promise to dedicate my practice to people who were physically injured by accidents at work or in motor vehicles, and those injured financially by the wrongful behavior of banks and insurance companies. I was always unyielding in standing up for their rights. I enjoyed countless celebrations with my clients over victories that gave them great satisfaction. It is a most profound blessing to be able to advocate for someone's misfortunes and turn them into fortune.

* * *

The following day I walked into the neighboring town of Carmel. With my new haircut, a fresh shave for the first time in days, and my slimmed down physique—now at 220 pounds—I felt downright suave and debonair. Ever since we left Little Big Horn, all Frank had talked about was getting to Carmel so he could track down his other hero: actor Clint Eastwood. At least this one was alive.

Eastwood, Carmel's former mayor, is apparently still active in the community and owns a lot of property. Among other things, he apparently owns a resort called Mission Ranch, only a few blocks away.

Frank dragged me to the Hog's Breath Inn, because he had been told that's where "Make My Day" often relaxed and had a drink. Frank was hoping to catch a glimpse of "Dirty Harry," but apparently he was elsewhere. We wasted an hour there, nursing Diet Cokes. For some reason, I didn't think most people ordered Diet Cokes at the famed Hog's Breath, because the waitress wasn't friendly. Maybe she was worn out by people like Frank who were just there looking for Clint Eastwood. She kept asking, "Do you want anything else?" It seemed like she wanted us to leave.

"You have such a pretty smile," I lied. For the first time, she actually produced a smile. I left her a big tip, hoping to keep it there.

Carmel was another of the exquisitely beautiful, but frighteningly expensive, California coastal towns, drawing thousands of well-heeled tourists from miles away. Speaking of heels, some women don't care for the place because they are prohibited from wearing high heels without a city permit. Part of the town's aesthetic charm include its irregular cobblestone walkways—apparently a civil lawsuit waiting to happen should someone catch a stiletto between them and injure themselves. While Frank talked to some locals about Clint Eastwood, I wandered like a bull into one of the high-priced boutiques, of which there are many, careful-not-to-break-anything items. The prices made me gag. I wouldn't be shopping in those kinds of places.

Having killed as much time as possible for Frank's benefit, I found him again, crestfallen at not having had an Eastwood sighting. I dragged him back to the van so I could resume walking. On the outskirts of town, we reached Highway 101. As I turned south I immediately encountered a sign that warned: "Caution: Next 74 Miles Dangerous Curves and Steep Grades." Thank you. I've just walked 1,500 miles of dangerous curves and steep grades without ever having been given a single word of warning.

But, as usual, I soon discovered that the scenery was again worth the effort. We were now in the outlying area north of Big Sur. For more than forty years I had been carrying images in my mind of Big Sur—one of nature's finest creations. As a preteen, I used to lie in bed many nights with my dog-eared copies of *National Geographic* magazine. While part of the publication's appeal to me were the pictures of naked African women, I'd also flip through the photos of far-away places with strange sounding names, and dream of going to them. I remembered the Great Wall of China as another "must see" place for me to visit, along with the Grand Canyon, the Pyramids, Moscow, the Eiffel Tower, the Irish coutryside, and the Mayan Ruins. They all seemed so exotic and exciting.

Big Sur, however, was perennially tops on my list. For some unknown reason, I found the big trees fascinating. Maybe it is because I had done a lot of tree work as a youngster, working with my father, cutting them down to clear land for subdivisions. I had thought they were big—but they were toothpicks compared to the trees of California and the Big Sur.

I spent a few hours stumbling along, thinking about my father. Luckily it was daylight and I was moving forward. There have been times when thoughts of him pop into my head an any given night. Those usually become restless and often sleepless nights. When they happen I often think about what could have been. I'm always left with an overwhelming sense of how much I missed having my father's presence ever since that fateful day when he took his own life with back in 1958.

I often wonder what his being there would have meant in my own life as I grew from a boy of thirteen to a man in my sixties. Certainly if he was around I would have stayed in school because he would never have allowed me to drop out. Had he been around I probably would've graduated from high school with high honors. I had always been a good student before he died and certainly would've continued to be one under his strict guidance. I think he realized that he had never been given any real opportunities for a college education and he absolutely demanded it for his children. At the time of his death, my two older sisters had just graduated from college.

If I had graduated from high school, with good grades and my natural athletic ability, I surely would have gone on to college and would have done well and would have made a name for myself as an athlete Yet after he died, with the exception of baseball, I hardly ever participated in organized sports anymore. I took up football seriously, only as an adult. When I did begin my twelve-year football career, I was told several times that I had the size, speed and football "smarts" to be an NFL defensive lineman, but that I lacked the coaching of the formative years, Who knows how having my father around would have helped during my teen years when I was in a perpetual state of limbo.

Big Sur

When a boy loses his father, he also loses his role model. My father taught all of his children an uncommonly spectacular work ethic. He was well-liked and well-respected by neighbors, employees, and family members. In spite of the good qualities, he came from generations of a family that had never seemed to seek more for themselves. He didn't seem to have any sense of the opportunities that existed in this country. He seemed satisfied with being less than he could have been. When he died, at such a young age, I had inherited from him the good things, like the work ethic and a generally pleasant nature which allowed me to get along with people like he did. Unfortunately, I also inherited from him the same inability to recognize my capacity to create opportunities for myself. In that way, the cycle of "like father, like son" was my reality for many years.

I learned to unconditionally respect my mother from my father. As far as I knew, they never argued. If they did, they hid it very well. Although my mother had remarried in 1966 and was married for another twenty-five years when her heart gave out, her dying wish, was that she wanted to be buried beside my father. "Why? I asked her, "What about Henry (her second husband)?"

As sick as she was, she was able to tell me, "Your father was the only man I ever loved and I never stopped loving him. You were blessed to have him as your father. I want to be with him again."

I believe I grew up in a world where there was no such thing as sexism, no such thing as racism, and absolutely no such thing as laziness. These were my father's core beliefs. He believed in absolute equality. Back then, there were very few people who thought like that. He taught that unique tolerance to all his children. Later, in my teens I adopted ugly racial attitudes. I have often regretted that time in my life. I can only assume that "peer pressure" caused me to succumb to the ugly influence of what was happening all around me.

During the long, restless nights, that come more frequently than I would like, I mourn not only for the years lost but for the fact that my father's illness would have been manageable in today's world. Back in the fifties, nobody knew what to do for him. That illness robbed him of the joy of watching his children grow up. It prevented him from ever having the joy of playing with his grandchildren, which now number twenty-four, I often weep for his losses. My son Nicholas was born on September 21, 1988, on what would have been my father's seventy-fifth birthday, if not for that dreaded disease. As I celebrate the birth of my son every year, I also shed tears for my father and the lost opportunities—what could have been, for him and for my siblings, and for me.

In some ways I feel like I'm living his dream for him. With Nicholas and Louis, I have strived to be the best father that I can, and know what an extraordinary gift it is to have children and watch them grow into adulthood. Because of that I think back with regret about playing no significant role in the lives of my two beautiful daughters, In my own mental anguish and uncertainty, I left them adrift. It was a different method, but I left them, just as my father left me and my brothers and sisters. I pray that someday, they can forgive me as I have forgiven my father.

* * *

For forty miles and thirteen hours, I navigated the hairpin turns of the up-and-down mountainous terrain—the Pacific Ocean to my right and the beautiful forest-covered mountains to my left. My legs ached and I was emotionally drained from the constant battle to be safe on the crowded yet very narrow coast road. Drivers weren't expecting to encounter a wandering old man. When they did there were close calls and cat calls. "Get off the road asshole!" was a common "greeting" from aggravated drivers that day.

After dinner, we found a motel. I should have slept soundly, given my physical effort that day and the beauty and tranquility that was all around me. Instead I had a fitful night, tossing and turning no matter how much I tried to quiet my mind. The more I tried to will myself to sleep, the more awake I got. The night seemed eternal.

Tomorrow, another forty miles within Big Sur, would be the final day of this wondrous excursion. Sometimes realizing your dream—in this case the last goal of a two-part dream—can be more disconcerting than setting a goal and failing to reach it. I should have been elated; instead I was distraught. Maybe it was the sense of not knowing what the future had in store for me. I had planned every step of this long journey to the Pacific. But for the much longer journey that was ahead, my life after this dream's end, I had no idea.

* * *

I was usually pretty hungry in the morning, but on my last day I couldn't stomach breakfast. All I had was two cups of black coffee. I bravely launched myself onto the road fueled only by caffeine.

Big Sur

My day was not much different from yesterday or the day before, except that now I was deeper into Big Sur. It was just as stunningly beautiful as all the *National Geographic* photos I remembered. The cliffs along the ocean, the waves crashing relentlessly against them, the constant danger of the switchbacks and fast-moving cars while trying to take in all the beauty was all I had expected it to be, and more. My life would never have been as fulfilled if I never came to experience the majesty of this place.

Yet something was missing. I couldn't put a finger on it. It had nothing to do with the scenery. With a heavy heart, I kept trudging. It seemed as if weights were strapped to my ankles. I could barely lift my feet. My emotions were battered. It was not what I had expected for a reaction as I achieved what had been seen to be impossible.

I was there. I had done it. My Morphine Dream was completed. Why did I feel so hollow? Why was I sad? It should have been a moment of great euphoria, yet I was depressed, empty, clueless and despondent. Tears streamed down my cheeks, mixing with the sweat from my face, together dripping on the road.

All of the sudden Frank beeped the horn and pulled the van up beside me. "You just hit 5,000 miles old man, are you ready to pack it in?"

"No," I said. "I want to stop when I can easily walk into the ocean."

I continued on for a mile, then two. I was not only tired, but the emotional push needed to continue was gone. I hoped there would be a spot soon where I could simply walk out into the water and sit down and be absorbed by the gentle rolling waves.

Part Nine
From Sea to Shining Sea

O beautiful for patriot dream that sees beyond
the years
Thine alabaster cities gleam Undimmed
by human tears!
America! America! God shed his grace
on thee,
And crown thy good with brotherhood From
sea to shining sea!
—**Katharine Lee Bates**

Chapter Eighty-Two

San Simeon
(Las Cuestas Encantada)

You start life with a clean slate. Then you begin to make your mark. You face decisions, make choices. You keep moving forward. But sooner or later there comes a time where you look back over where you have been and wonder who you really are.

—Unknown

I had exited Big Sur and was skirting cliffs and coves, pocketed beaches and parks on the old coastal Highway 1. I couldn't imagine a route elsewhere in the country as scenic as the California coast. Spanish explorer Juan Rodriguez Cabrillo called this area on the central coast "The Land of Endless Summers."

High up on a hill overlooking the Pacific, about a half mile up the road, I could see the incredibly ostentatious Hearst Castle. I had seen many spectacular hillside mansions since I got to California, but this was in a league of its own. It was often referred to as "The Magic Kingdom," a title Walt Disney apparently borrowed for his Disney World theme park. The castle's origin is an interesting story.

The land on which it sat was originally 250,000 acres that the family of William Randolph Hearst used as a place for camping trips. In fact, in the time before WWI, it was called "Camp Hill." The Hearsts were quite wealthy from his father's holdings in the mining business, so these were not your typical family camping adventures; they had separate tents for sleeping and cooking and had the servants doing all the heavy lifting and real work.

William was an only child and inherited the land. By this time he had acquired his own wealth, having built a newspaper publishing empire. At his peak he owned over two dozen newspapers nationwide. At the time, nearly one in four Americans got their news from a Hearst paper.

In 1919, Hearst asked his architect, Julia Morgan, to design what came to be the Hearst Castle. He wanted to recreate the magnificent castles he had toured in Europe, though his instructions were not quite that lofty. His message was simple "Miss Morgan, we are tired of camping out in the open at the ranch in San Simeon and I would like to build a little something."

Together, they built more than a "little" something. Hearst and Morgan's collaboration was to become one of "the world's greatest showplaces." During the construction of his dream home, Hearst would later come up with a new name: *La Cuesta Encantada* or The Enchanted Hill. It took until 1947 to complete the castle. Some actually lament that it never was completed. What a castle. It was built to contain 165 rooms. Surrounding the magnificent home were over 100 acres of gardens, and many pools and terraces, all connected by a labyrinth of walks.

Images of the film *Citizen Kane* washed through my mind. The classic Orson Welles movie masterpiece was allegedly about William Randolph Hearst, a newspaper tycoon with a never-ending desire for power. On his deathbed Kane utters the word "Rosebud." This was reference to the character's childhood sled, and represented his past and his boyhood hopes and dreams for the future.

Suddenly, my own "Rosebuds" danced like apparitions before me: my father's suicide, walking my paper route, working in the dry-cleaners, being held back in the ninth grade, dropping out of school at seventeen to join the Marines, playing semi-professional baseball and football, driving a delivery truck for Lechmere Sales, severely injuring my knee at thirty-six, being told I would never walk again, getting the telephone call from Mount Wachusett Community College, being hoodwinked by the promise of a Dairy Queen ice-cream cone!

While I had originally planned to visit the interior of the castle my significant feelings of being down erased any desire to see it.. It was the ocean I wanted. With every undulation onto the beach, it sounded like the Pacific was calling me.

I did my best to focus and stay strong but I just couldn't fight the tears that started welling in my eyes and streaming down my face. Moments later, I was sobbing. I swept right by the castle, as though it were a dilapidated shack instead of one of the world's great architectural masterpieces. A couple of miles later, I found my opening to the beach. I stopped and walked back to the van and asked Frank, "How many miles?"

"Five thousand and four, old man," he said.

With that, I was done.

I climbed in the van for the air conditioning. I was hot. Frank passed me the morning paper and pointed out a front-page story about another "dreamer."

San Simeon (Las Cuestas Encantada)

Apparently a couple of days ago, as I walked from Santa Cruz to Monterey, a man had been swimming across the twenty-five mile bay—for charity. I think I would much rather be walking than swimming such great distances. I, for one, couldn't swim one mile, let alone twenty-five miles. What made me take note of this is that the swimmer had begun his twenty-five mile swim that day at the same time I began my forty-mile walk and, remarkably, we had finished at about the same time—6:30 P.M.

It was time to go to the sea. I reached the water's edge as a big wave crashed onto the beach. The tide was coming in. The foamy water raced toward me. I stared off at the horizon. I didn't even bother to take off my shoes. I simply walked right in. I kept walking until the water was almost waist high.

I stood there for a moment. I decided that it would be appropriate to say something. A whisper was all I could muster: "I've done it." I only said it once. I should have been more excited, right? I should have been jumping up and down, and shouting with joy. This should have been one of the happiest moments of my life. The truth was I was numb. I couldn't even feel the icy cold ocean water. I was beginning to understand the adage: "It's the journey, not the destination."

Now what?

The late-afternoon sky was filled with wispy red and blue clouds. I heard foghorns far away and the cries of seagulls nearby. Every once in a while I saw spouting whales in the distance. I wished they were closer. The briny water slapped against my pants. I felt the sand being pulled away from under my feet—the feet that had just carried me those 5,004 miles across the United States of America. I moved back toward the shoreline and when I was knee deep, I sat down in the water.

I thought back to the summer of 1981, when the Morphine Dream became the driving force in my life. As I sat in the water, I felt one enormous burden lift, but it had been replaced by an even heavier one. I had no plan for life after the Morphine Dream. I felt so drained, I almost wished that the waves would just take me, and then the struggles of life would be over. I sat for a long time. Worried, Frank kept coming out to check on me. He knew I was in a fragile state. He kept pushing me, "Come on old man, it's time to get on the road. We have to be in L.A. by 8:00 P.M. for your dinner with your friend Karl." Karl was another Harvard Law School classmate, now practicing in Los Angeles, whom I wanted to see on my way back to Boston.

The Morphine Dream

I couldn't speak. After perhaps more than two hours in the water, I was able to get up and wade back toward the van. I walked out of the water and plopped down on the sand. My sun-baked legs were suddenly shivering. I was soaked to the bone. Rather than cleanse and invigorate me, it seemed the ocean had sucked the life out of me. I certainly felt like a different person than the man at the beginning of this trip, the one who had a plan, a goal, and was full of energy and zest for the quest and the promise. That person had "left the building" as the saying goes. Who was this man at the end of the journey? I hadn't a clue. It was like everything was erased from my mind.

I dried off and put on clean clothes. Frank saw that I was in no mood for conversation so he let me be. Soon we were on the road to L.A. but we drove in silence. I felt broken. The end of this journey was more than just closing a chapter; it was like finishing an epic novel and starting a whole new book, except there was no new book. It was a new life now, and it wasn't starting on a promising note. Maybe it was post-partum blues. But I knew my undaunted optimism would come charging back in a day or two. At least I hoped so.

Chapter Eighty-Three

Finally

Free at Last, free at last,
Thank God almighty,
We are free at last
—**Martin Luther King**

What I had dreamed while on morphine so long ago had become reality. I had graduated from Harvard Law School and I had walked across the country. Despite a chorus of skepticism, even from my own family, I had done both. Not my age, my weight, or other factors were enough to disqualify me from this arduous trek. I had worked all my life. I realized that all that toil was a prerequisite to accomplish my dreams. I had been successful beyond my wildest imagination. Having been faced with the uncertainties, the risks, wild animals, speeding vehicles, the scorching sun, my diabetic problems, aching knees, blisters and bugs, it had all worked out. I had accepted the challenges of the unknown, and somehow, managed to complete the seemingly impossible.

In 137 days, I had taken some 11 million steps and had lost nearly eighty pounds. I had walked through all or part of twenty-one states, dozens of cities, and more than a thousand towns. There were only eleven days in which I did not walk—five for minor medical problems, three to rest and watch the Sunday football games, and two for business reasons. For the remaining 126 days I strode an average of 41.3 miles a day. My longest day was fifty-eight miles. I was finished. The walk, only a fantasy for many years, was finally over.

My daily fare of jockeying for position on the roads with cars, SUVs, semis, the scary logging trucks and gargantuan farm equipment was behind me. I had enjoyed most of my 300 meals eaten in restaurants of all kinds across the miles. I had consumed over 400 gallons of water and another 100 gallons of juices. Amazingly, I had used eighteen large containers of Vaseline; more than I—or I imagine anyone—had used in a lifetime. We had spent 112 nights in motels or hotels. Sleeping in the van was not pleasant so we spent only two nights trying that method. Friends had let us stay overnight with them on the few remaining nights.

We had participated in a significant amount of media interviews. We were featured on local and national TV news shows nineteen times. Walking USA made the front page of newspapers thirty-two times. Live radio interviews, my favorite media meets, occurred six times as we made our way along the route. On most days, folks knew about us due to that extensive media coverage, and they waved and tooted and often stopped to shake hands and say hello.

While the walk was over, it resonated with me that I had been privileged to have such an awesome opportunity. I got to see America in an uncommon way. Every morning had been like having another turn in the batter's box, another swing at the ball, another home run. It was exhilarating. The adrenaline rush was present for most of the miles. Each day brought great excitement and genuine joy. The thousands of vistas, once seen, became memories to last my lifetime

The best part was the people I met along the highways and byways. I was treated with kindness and respect every step of the way. I had been warned before I left that my walk would be "dangerous." Nobody ever gave me reason to be in fear of harm. Many had said, "Make sure you take a weapon for protection." I saw no need to have any weapon as I was never worried about anyone harming me, especially with Frank traveling close behind me.

I had uncovered a country long hidden from me. After walking 5,000 miles across America, I can tell you, first hand, that the majority of people that I got to meet and know a little, hundreds of folks, men and women, black, white and red, young and old, rich and poor, the overwhelming majority were just ordinary, good American citizens. The doomsayers like Limbaugh, and others in the media, be damned. We are not a country permeated by "moral decay." Instead we are a country of good citizens, many working diligently to repair the flaws in our combined social character.

There was also a somewhat somber realization on my part that there would be no more forty-mile days, no more ma and pa restaurants, no more of my new addiction—soup—no more surprises around the next bend, no more mountains to climb, no more of those dammed logging trucks, no more of the overwhelming sense of freedom that was a product of the walk. I had learned a lot about myself during the adventure and even more as I wrote about it. For certain, I was so filled with memories it would take all of the remaining years of my life to fully appreciate what I had experienced while Walking USA.

I am so fortunate that I'll live the rest of my life with the memories of the wondrous experience. The word "Montana" or "Idaho" will never sound the same again. The word "Oregon" will bring the fear of the logging trucks back to my conscious mind. The sound of the train passing by will take me back to the trek. The smell of the Pacific was embedded in my memory—forever. The feeling of the salty mist coating my face is permanently etched into my being. Anytime I hear the waves pounding on the beach, I will be brought back in time. My attachment to Amherst College and Mount Wachusett Community College and Harvard Law School were deepened by my visits to the campuses.

Many had asked, "What will you do after the walk?" Certainly I'd be going back to the familiar typical routine of work, children and sleep, but I'd be doing it as a different person. The days of total freedom and not being responsible for anything while on the expedition would now be memories, though never to be forgotten. I would hold on to the hope that I'd be able to do another walk someday, but if that never happens, I would die happy, knowing I had lived my most profound dream.

Yes, it was done. I was tired and needed to rest. And, as the quest ended, something else would begin, I'm sure. I would dream again. As Thoreau once declared, "Dreams are the touchstones of our character," and as long as I had "character" I would continue to dream.

* * *

At dawn, after a good night's sleep, we packed up and headed east toward home, more than 3,000 miles away. Our goal was to be in Massachusetts in time for Thanksgiving. I missed my boys so much. Perhaps it was a blessing in disguise that the walk had come to an end and I could be back with them.

The van hadn't run at highway speeds for any considerable distance for a long time, I hoped it was up to being pushed. We wanted to make Vegas by nightfall. Frank drove and I reclined the seat and chilled. I thought about what I had done. Following my string of days of extreme exertion, and silence and solitude, riding east on the interstate, gave me time to unwind, time to reflect, and time to be grateful for the wondrous blessing of Walking USA.

After a night on the town in Vegas, we stayed in a really nice room for a change at Caesar's Palace, an extraordinary change from the months on the road staying in no-tell motels. We slept in and got moving by 9:00 A.M. We made it to Albuquerque by 8:00 P.M. It was on to Missouri the next morning.

In St. Louis, we visited the famous archway, "The Gateway to the West." Frank had never seen it before and had been excited to finally get to visit it. We got in a little tour of the ballpark that was home to the St. Louis Cardinals. We were halfway home and it was time to move on to Columbus.

When we reached Columbus, we dropped off the van at a Ford dealer for service and a good cleaning. While we waited, I called Lou Mitchell to find out if we could visit for a while. Soon we were sitting in his living room, enjoying his hospitality.

Lou asked the hard question that had been plaguing me for the last part of my journey: "What are you going to do when you get back to Massachusetts?"

Lost for an answer, tears rolled down my cheeks. Lou seemed taken aback by my emotional fragility.

"You are going to have some tough times," Lou declared. He knew about the battle I faced over my law license as soon as I returned home. He also knew about the problems with my marriage and the potential unraveling of that part of my life.

"I know," I said, finally getting some words out. "I'll get my bearings back. I just need to somehow get focused."

"Let it come naturally," said Lou "Don't push yourself."

Obviously Lou understood the significance of the difficult emotions I was dealing with. I felt better. I was so glad to see Lou. I felt so fortunate for his friendship.

When the call came that the van was ready, I was actually anxious to leave. I gave Lou a big bear hug. I told him, "It's on to the next dreams, whatever they are."

"Go slow, let things come to you in time. Drive safely and hug the boys for me."

We made it to Buffalo, our last stop before home. The knowledge that with about ten more hours of driving, I would be in Newton had me tossing and turning all night. It seemed like I had only slept for a few minutes when Frank pushed me to get up. "Come on, old man— the last day," he said.

Five hundred miles of driving and we'd be done. It was November 18, 1997. I had left home on July 4th and had been gone for 137 days. I was hours away from a more significant unknown. Frank was anxious to get back because he would be able to move into his own place upon returning. While we were away, his VA housing stipend had been awarded to him and he was thrilled to be getting out of the shelter.

Finally

For me, being home was going to be a larger challenge than the 137 days on the road had been. I didn't know how I was going to manage settling into a "normal" lifestyle again. I had walked away from life as I had known it. Now I was driving back to what would have to be a much different existence.

If I could, I would spend the rest of my life walking. There were so many places to explore, both in this country and around the globe. My legs were up to it and my spirit was more in tune with it. As much as I longed for the freedom and the adventure, however, I knew that the road would always be there; my boys would not. They were what I most longed for when I was traversing the country and I thought of them constantly. I loved being a lawyer but being a father was the best job I could ever hope to have. My sons needed their father—but I needed them more.

Epilogue

It's been almost fifteen years since I returned from my adventure across the country. It's also been about that same amount of years that I've attempted to write this book. I wanted to tell this story as soon as I returned home but as I soon learned, it isn't that easy to write a book.

During my academic days, writing papers in an academic setting became second nature to me. During my days as an attorney, legal writing, a different kind of writing, also became rote—it was easy. Later as a writing professor, helping young people learn how to express themselves without reservation became an incredibly rewarding occupation.

This venture has been altogether different and has turned out to be one of the most difficult chores, yet satisfying accomplishments I've ever taken on during my life. I put it in the same category as the rest of my Morphine Dream. If someone had tried to tell me at any time during my life before my late thirties that I would someday write a book, or several books, I would've thought they were smoking funny little cigarettes. However, once the doors to higher education opened to me many years ago, I began to realize that not only could I write a book, but that all human beings can routinely accomplish extraordinary things. Sadly people often never realize how able they are.

During those years of receiving the benefits of a fantastic education, I was completely focused on realizing The Morphine Dream. I put all my energy and attention on fulfilling that promise I made to myself. It was my "true compass." Over those years I was blessed in so many ways and at so many times that I was able to do the seemingly unattainable. I *lived* the impossible dream. Yet when I was finished, having graduated from Harvard Law School and completed my arduous trek across the continent, I was quick to discover that I had made a large mistake—I had forgotten to dream beyond that dream. I learned many things, though, as a result of that walk. I realized that I had completed the most significant journey in my life. It wasn't the walk across the country that was the real journey; it was getting to know myself.

It was after I was safely home in Massachusetts, back in the daily routine of family and home; I knew that I had to begin dreaming again. I certainly recognized that dreaming meant more than talking. In order for dreams to happen, there has to be a carefully formulated plan. And, once you have the plan in place, then you have to execute the plan. It's the plan and the execution that often never gets the attention, resulting in missed opportunities. The African-American literary great, Langston Hughes, once wrote, "Hold fast to dreams. For if dreams die, Life is a broken-winged bird that cannot fly . . . "

It was only days after arriving home that I firmly established the first of my new dreams. That dream was to write and publish a book about The Morphine Dream. While I have been either thinking about writing, or actually writing the book for most of those fifteen years, I knew for certain, just as with The Morphine Dream, this new dream, too, would come to pass.

I was no sooner home then I found myself back at my regular and most important job; being a father to my sons. When I returned Nick was ten and Louis was seven. They had grown up so much while I was away. It was almost as if they were two different children. Nick was more into music than he had been when I left. Louis was beginning to understand more about the nuances of sports, so much so that he taught me much about the New England Patriots, the Boston Red Sox and the Boston Celtics. They were both doing well in school and they seemed to be achieving very high levels. I was so proud of them, my two little men. In fact I routinely called Louis "Little Big Man."

It was only a few weeks later when my long-awaited hearing to find out if I was going to get my law license back was held. I suffered through the embarrassment and humiliation of having my request for reinstatement turned down. I had so much pent-up desire to return to the practice of law as my calling. As I saw it, I was helping folks less fortunate than I was. It was terribly frustrating to be told I would have to reapply again. I took it quite badly for a few days but, within a week, I woke up to the fact that whatever happens badly, always turns out good. I wasn't going to let a disappointing outcome drag me down. I wasn't going to allow self-pity to take over my days. I simply turned my attention to positive events.

When spring rolled around, the boys began playing Little League baseball. It was so special going to watch these little guys, while they were playing the game that had meant so much to me when I was that age. Louis was *really* into the sport, and developed into a pretty good southpaw pitcher in spite of his various handicaps. While he certainly had significant deficits, especially when it came to his sight, his heart and soul were 150 percent dedicated to baseball, and he was dead serious about his work ethic. His effort was extraordinary.

Epilogue

Nicholas, on the other hand, wasn't really interested in playing baseball—or any other sport for that matter. I thought I detected in him an abundance of natural athletic ability. At the same time I certainly noticed that his heart wasn't in it. I grew to believe he was playing only because he thought I expected him to play. That was not at all the case, but he did try. He was good, too, but not dedicated.

The two of them were placed on different teams. That created a scenario whereby they'd eventually have to play against each other. When that day came, all the parents at the field were watching to see how it played out; brother against brother. Louis was only eight years old, but had a great arm and could pitch like kids who were much older. Nicholas was ten, and in spite of his apparent lack of interest, was developing into a very good hitter.

The day of the confrontation arrived. It was a bright and sunny Saturday morning. Nick was dressed in his green uniform and Louis in red. The crowd teased both of them relentlessly. Louis was pitching an excellent game. In fact in the third inning he still had a no-hitter going. It was still a scoreless tie. Unfortunately he lost his command of the strike zone and started walking people and walked the bases full, still having given up no hits. It was the moment everybody was waiting for. Nicholas picked up his aluminum bat, and made his way towards the plate.

Stepping into the batter's box, Nick pawed the red clay with his spikes. He was trying so hard to act nonchalant, but one look at his face and you could see that he was doing all he could to restrain himself from laughing.

Louis scuffed up the dirt on the mound, looking for a sign from the catcher, who probably didn't even know what a sign was. Louis was obviously anxious, wanting nothing more than to strike out his brother.

Louis threw two quick strikes. Nick, now in a hole, 0 and 2, glared out at Louis, anticipating the pitch. Again Louis pretended to take a sign from the catcher who never quite realized that Louis was looking for a sign. He went into his motion and threw the pitch with every ounce of strength he could muster. It was not to be. "Mighty Casey struck out" as Nicholas smashed the ball, sending it sailing between the left-fielder and the center-fielder. It went so far that he should have been able to walk around the bases for a home run. By the time the outfielder retrieved the ball to throw it back into the infield, Nicholas should have scored and been back sitting on the bench. Instead, as he was rounding the bases, he laughed so hard he fell on the ground between second and third and rolled on the ground, delirious with laughter.

Louis wasn't upset. He, too, was rolling on the pitcher's mound, laughing and enjoying the moment as much as everybody else. While Louis' no-hitter was gone, and the game was lost, the joy of that moment is something that I'll never forget. The three of us often reminisce about that great moment. Sometimes, I can be resting in my recliner or laying down for a nap and I'll think back to what it was like for me, sitting on the sidelines, watching my two beautiful sons share such a wonderful moment.

As more years passed, both boys would excel in music and academic pursuits. Nick went on to study music and history at Brandeis, while serving in the U.S. Army Band. He would travel to England to attend King's College in London, receiving his Masters in Musicology. His next stop was in the White House as an intern in the Obama Administration. He has now settled in to a great job as a Music Production Specialist at the Library of Congress in Washington, D.C.

Meanwhile Louis, who in his younger years seemed destined for nothing more than a special needs education, was mainstreamed all the way through his twelve years in school. On his own, he then applied for and got accepted at Loyola University in Chicago. He is now a senior at Loyola and is prepping to hopefully attend Harvard Law School next year. His rise in overcoming his handicaps and deficits are an extraordinary story and an incredible conquest.

So here I am, an old man who got married at the age of forty-two and fathered two youngsters somewhat late in life. I was forty-three when Nick was born and forty-seven when Louis was born. That put me at an unusual age to be dealing with toddlers and also in dealing with the joys and sorrows children often encounter in growing up. Conversely, being a parent in the autumn of my years has been the most rewarding experience of my entire life. There is nothing in this world that is any more significant than sitting back in retirement, watching my children as they chase their dreams.

Oftentimes the joy I feel is not unlike that long ago day on the Little League diamond, which had to have been one of the simplest, yet most wonderful sensations a father could experience. I am usually incredibly fascinated by how these two young men handle decisions in their lives. Sometimes, when I think of my own youth, I realize that I grew up in confusion and dysfunction. I do not know whether that dysfunction and chaos were a product of the times or was because of something being seriously amiss in my family's dynamics.

Epilogue

What I do know is that I witnessed my father, obviously a good and decent man, who suffered from hidden demons because of the cycle of uncertainty in his life. The lack of opportunity to pursue his own dreams must have crushed his spirit as it had the spirits of his forbearers'. The sea of uncertainty he found himself in and the lack of identifiable opportunity, obviously contributed to the hopelessness he felt that resulted in him taking his own life.

As the years have passed since I returned from my coast-to-coast walk, many important events have transpired in my life, some joyous and some sad. Yet there's no need to recount them in this Epilogue. Because, as I look back now and I think of the achievements that seemed to be extraordinary, I'm not at all moved by anything I've done except for the fact that I believe I have broken the cycle of the "Sea of Uncertainty" that plagued me and those that came before me.

Nothing equates with the significance of breaking that cycle. I can assure you with 100 percent certainty that when I leave this earth, I will have a smile on my face. It will be there not because of the things I did for myself in my pursuit of education, walking, business or anything else. The accomplishment that plants that smile on my face is my children, their well-being and their freedom from the cycle of limbo.

The Best and the Worst of Walking USA

The selections that follow are only my opinions. No scientific study was employed in arriving at these conclusions, only my opinion, for whatever that's worth. These opinions were formed, for the most part, along the route of Walking USA. Once I had visited twenty-one states, I went over my notes and pondered the possible choices for several weeks. There will be, I suppose, some who feel they should have been "the best" but if I named all of the places that were special to me during my four and one half months on the road, the list would fill hundreds of pages. That said, the results of my personal survey is as follows:

PLACES

Best Small Town:	Chelsea Michigan
Most Unique Town:	Leavenworth, Washington
Best City: Tie	Boston, Massachusetts, and San Francisco, California
Most Generous City:	Spokane, Washington
Biggest Urban Sunrise:	The Splendor of Detroit
City Experiencing Most Growth:	Kokomo, Indiana
Most Spectacular State	
Capital Building:	Des Moines, Iowa
Most Spectacular Bridge:	The Golden Gate San Francisco, California

Most Spectacular River View: The Missouri from Route 212
West of Gettysburg,
South Dakota

Most Spectacular Inland Lake: Lake Coeur d' Alene
Coeur d' Alene, Idaho

Most Spectacular Skyscraper: John Hancock Building
Chicago, Illinois

Best "Comeback" City: Cleveland, Ohio

The Best of New York: The "Other Apple" Buffalo

Best College Campus: Amherst College
Amherst, Massachusetts

Most Beautiful Urban Green Space: Tie
The Lakefront
Chicago, Illinois

The Presidio
San Francisco, California

Most Spectacular View: Bozeman Pass
Interstate 90
Bozeman, Montana

LODGING

Best Hotel: The Waterville Hotel
Waterville, Washington

Best Bed and Breakfast: The Farallone Inn
Montara, California

Best Motel: The Glass House Inn
Erie, Pennsylvania

Biggest Rip-off Motel   The Country Inn
Northfield, Minnesota

RESTAURANTS

Best Steak House: The Judge's Chambers
Broadus, Montana

Best Lasagna: Spada's Italian Restaurant
Erie, Pennsylvania

Best Seafood: The Whale Cove Inn
Depoe Bay, Oregon

Best Breakfast: Lou Mitchell's Restaurant
Chicago, Illinois

Best Soup: Cream of Tomato
4B's Restaurant
Missoula, Montana

Most Unusual Restaurant: Tie
Drive-through Window for Amish
Horse and Buggies
McDonald's
Millersburg, Ohio

Just for the Name
"Custer's Last Root Beer Stand"
Three Forks, Montana

MISCELANEOUS

Funniest Sign Seen While Walking: Tie
"We Make Things That Suck"
Pump Manufacturer
Spokane, Washington

"Annual Testicle Festival,
Come Have a Ball"
Rock Creek Lodge, Montana

Most states walked in one day:	Tie —Three Massachusetts, New Hampshire and Maine
	South Dakota, Wyoming and Montana
Most Unusual Place Walked:	The Mall of America Minneapolis, Minnesota
Best Interstate Walking:	Interstate 90 from Billings, Montana to Idaho
Closest Brush with Death:	Walking Interstate 94 Chelsea, Michigan
Toughest Uphill Climb:	The Streets of San Francisco
Best Walk with Company:	Ian Vanderwall Rensellear, Indiana
Walk That Produced Goosebumps:	The Avenue of the Giants Northern California
Most Emotional Walk:	Crossing the Boston Marathon finish fine as I began Walking USA, the Marathon in reverse, and later in the day crossing the Marathon starting line in Hopkington, Massachusetts.
Worst Place for Walking Safety:	California
Best Place for Walking Safety:	Washington with the exception of metropolitan Seattle
Most Memorable Agri-walk:	The wheat fields of central & eastern Washington

The Best and the Worst of Walking USA

Best Campus Walk:
Through the runway
into Notre Dame Stadium
South Bend, Indiana

Worst Walking Conditions
Saturday, September 27, 1997
60 to 70 mile-an-hour winds,
head on Billings to Columbus,
Montana

Best Live Radio Interview:
KYTE Radio
Newport, Oregon

Best Television Interview:
Tie
NBC Affiliate
Sonia, Holly and Cameraman
Columbus, Ohio

NBC Affiliate
Joel Boykin
Detroit, Michigan

Best Newspaper Interview:
Tie
The Toledo Blade
Vanessa Gezari
Toledo, Ohio

The Indianapolis Star
John Flora
Indianapolis, Indiana

Best Example of Western
Hospitality:
The Overmier Family
Billings, Montana

Friendliest People:
Myers Flat, on the Avenue of
Giants
California

Nicest Family Met on the Route:
The Shuttz Family
Wakeshua, Wisconsin

Best Home Cooked Meal: The Ringhand Family
Madison, Wisconsin

Best Audience for a Speech: The Redwood Day School
Oakland, California

Nastiest Person Encountered: Hunter with face paint and
fatigues upset because I
walked between him and the
antelopes he was hunting Route
212, Belle Fourche, South Dakota.

Worst Police Encounter: While walking at 6:00 A.M. in
Tilton, New Hampshire

Best Police Encounter: Tie
All of the Montana Highway
Patrol from Billings to the
Idaho Line

California Highway Patrol
From Oregon Border to
Monterey

Best Ford Service: Tie
Scott Peterson Ford
Belle Fourche, South Dakota

Patalano Ford
Franklin, Massachusetts

Best General Merchandise Store: Walmart

Best Place to Develop Film: Walmart

Highest Prices for Food: The Oregon Coast

Lowest Prices for Food: Upstate New York

Highest Prices for Motels:	Tie
	Route 1 in Maine
	Skykomish, Washington
Lowest Prices for Motels:	The Oregon Coast
Worst Weather Encountered:	Route 9
	Searsburg, Vermont
Best Weather:	Everywhere
Worst Place for Bugs:	Tie
	Route 202
	Shutesbury, Massachusetts
	Route 12, fifteen miles from Aberdeen, South Dakota
Best Places for a Nap:	Tie
	The Seawall at Lake Michigan Chicago, Illinois
	Amidst several bales of hay, Ellendale, North Dakota
Most Interesting Wildlife:	Herd of Roosevelt Elk Trinidad, California

Sources

This narrative is based on my own observations and on talks with locals as I walked across America for four and a half months. Some of those conversations provided vast details. Others—such as chatting with folks during lunch in restaurants—were brief but still informative. Much of what I culled from those conversations are merely the viewpoint of those folks I talked with. When feasible, I read materials from local libraries, newspapers and tourist pamphlets. I read many books by and about other "dreamers." No, make that "doers." Those accounts helped me to rouse memories of my journey. Those books are listed here, for those of you readers who love the stories of other dreamers or doers. The difference? Dreamers talk and doers dream, plan and execute their plan.

Abraham, Marilyn J. *First We Quit Our Jobs*
Dell Publishing, New York, 1997

Ambrose, Stephen *Undaunted Courage*
Touchstone, New York, 1996

Aspen, Jean *Arctic Son*
Menasha Ridge Press, Birmingham, Alabama, 1995

Barich, Bill *Big Dreams*
Pantheon Books, New York, 1994

Berger, Karen & *Where the Waters Divide*
Smith, Daniel Harmony Books, New York, 1993

Brill, David *As Far As the Eye Can See*
Rutledge Hill Publishing, Nashville, Tennessee, 1990

Bryan, Mike *Uneasy Rider*
Alfred A. Knopf, New York, 1997

The Morphine Dream

Bryson, Bill
The Lost Continent
Harper & Row, New York, 1987

Cantor, George
Where the Old Roads Go
Harper and Row, New York, 1990

Codrescu, Andre
Road Scholar
Hyperion, New York, 1994

Conover, Ted
Rolling Nowhere
Viking Penguin, New York, 1985

Conover, Ted
Coyotes
Vintage Books, New York, 1987

Doerper, John
Pacific Northwest
Compass American Guides, Oakland, California, 1997

Fergussen, Gary
Walking Down the Wind
Falcon Press Publishing Co., Helena, Montana, 1989

Fletcher, Colin
The Man Who Walked Through Time
Random House, New York, 1989

Gale, Bill
The Wonderful World of Walking
Dell Publishing, New York, 1988

Hartshorn, Nick
Catch: A Discovery of America
MacMurry & Beck, Inc., Denver, Colorado, 1996

Irving, Stephanie
Northwest Best Places
Sasquateh Books, Seattle, Washington, 1998

Jenkins, Peter
Walk Across America
William Morrow & Co., New York, 1979

Sources

Walk Across America II
William Morrow & Co., New York, 1981

Along The Edge of America
Houghton Mifflin, New York, 1997

Jenson, Jamie   *Road Trip USA*
Moon Publications, Chico,
California, 1996

Krakauer, Jon   *Into Thin Air*
Anchor Books, New York, 1997

Kuralt, Charles   *A Life on the Road*
G.P. Putnam's Sons, New York,1990

Dateline America
Harcourt Brace Jovanovich, Inc.,
New York, 1979

Lamb, David   *Over the Hills*
Random House, New York, 1996

Lilliefors, Jim   *Highway 50: Ain't That America!*
Fulcrum Publishing, Golden,
Colorado, 1993

Malcolm, Andrew   *Unknown America*
Quadrangle/New York Times Book
Co., New York, 1974

Mathews, T.S.   *O My America: Notes on a Trip*
Simon and Schuster, New York, 1962

Moon, Gypsy   *Done & Been*
Indiana University Press,
Bloomington, Indiana, 1996

The Morphine Dream

Moon, William	*Blue Highways: A Journey into America* Fawcett Crest, New York, 1982
Parfil, Michael	*Chasing the Glory: Travels Across America* Macmillan Publishing Co., New York, 1988
Pern, Stephen	*The Great Divide* Viking Penguin, New York, 1988
Steinbeck, John	*Travels with Charley* Penguin Books, New York, 1962
Yardley, Jonathan	*States of Mind* Villard Books, New York, 1993

About the Author

Don Brown was educated at Mount Wachusett Community College, Amherst College and Harvard Law School. At Amherst College, Mr. Brown's academic record earned him high distinctions, including the John Woodruff Simpson Fellow in Law and the First National Bank of Amherst Centennial Fund Fellow in Law. While at Harvard, Mr. Brown contributed to an article entitled, "Racial Reflections," published in the University of California at Los Angeles *Law Review*.

At Harvard Law School, Mr. Brown's third-year law paper, The Struggle For Racial Harmony, was recommended for the Permanent Collection of the Harvard Law School Library by his mentor and advisor, Professor Derrick Bell. In that paper, Brown predicted that his classmate, Barack Obama would be elected president in 2004.

In his legal career, Mr. Brown saved the homes of scores of elderly minority residents in Boston's neighborhoods during the Second Mortgage\Home Improvement Scam which plagued Boston in the early nineties.

Other Books by
Bettie Youngs Book Publishers

On Toby's Terms

Charmaine Hammond

On Toby's Terms is an endearing story of a beguiling creature who teaches his owners that, despite their trying to teach him how to be the dog they want, he is the one to lay out the terms of being the dog he needs to be. This insight would change their lives forever.

"Simply a beautiful book about life, love, and purpose."
—**Jack Canfield, compiler,** *Chicken Soup for the Soul* **series**

"In a perfect world, every dog would have a home and every home would have a dog like Toby!"
—**Nina Siemaszko, actress,** *The West Wing*

"This is a captivating, heartwarming story and we are very excited about bringing it to film."
—**Steve Hudis, Producer**

ISBN: 978-0-9843081-4-9 • ePub: 978-1-936332-15-1

The Maybelline Story

And the Spirited Family Dynasty Behind It

Sharrie Williams

Throughout the twentieth century, Maybelline inflated, collapsed, endured, and thrived in tandem with the nation's upheavals. Williams, to avoid unwanted scrutiny of his private life, cloistered himself behind the gates of his Rudolph Valentino Villa and ran his empire from a distance. This never before told story celebrates the life of a man whose vision rocketed him to success along with the woman held in his orbit: his brother's wife, Evelyn Boecher— who became his lifelong fascination and muse. A fascinating and inspiring story, a tale both epic and intimate, alive with the clash, the hustle, the music, and dance of American enterprise.

"A richly told story of a forty-year, white-hot love triangle that fans the flames of a major worldwide conglomerate."
—**Neil Shulman, Associate Producer,** *Doc Hollywood*

"Salacious! Engrossing! There are certain stories, so dramatic, so sordid, that they seem positively destined for film; this is one of them."
—*New York Post*

ISBN: 978-0-9843081-1-8 • ePub: 978-1-936332-17-15

449

The Count, My Mother, and Me

Jane Congdon

The terrifying legend of Count Dracula silently skulking through the Transylvania night may have terrified generations of filmgoers, but the tall, elegant vampire captivated and electrified a young Jane Congdon, igniting a dream to one day see his mysterious land of ancient castles and misty hollows. Four decades later she finally takes her long-awaited trip—never dreaming that it would unearth decades-buried memories, and trigger a life-changing inner journey.

A memoir full of surprises, Jane's story is one of hope, love—and second chances.

"Unfinished business can surface when we least expect it. *It Started with Dracula* is the inspiring story of two parallel journeys: one a carefully planned vacation and the other an astonishing and unexpected detour in healing a wounded heart."
—**Charles Whitfield, MD, bestselling author of *Healing the Child Within***

"An elegantly written and cleverly told story. An electrifying read."
—**Diane Bruno, CISION Media**

ISBN: 978-1-936332-10-6 • ePub: 978-1-936332-11-3

The Rebirth of Suzzan Blac

Suzzan Blac

A horrific upbringing and then abduction into the sex slave industry would all but kill Suzzan's spirit to live. But a happy marriage and two children brought love—and forty-two stunning paintings, art so raw that it initially frightened even the artist. "I hid the pieces for 15 years," says Suzzan, "but just as with the secrets in this book, I am slowing sneaking them out, one by one by one." Now a renowned artist, her work is exhibited world-wide.

A story of inspiration, truth and victory.

"A solid memoir about a life reconstructed. Chilling, thrilling, and thought provoking."
—**Pearry Teo, Producer, *The Gene Generation***

ISBN: 978-1-936332-22-9 • ePub: 978-1-936332-23-6

Blackbird Singing in the Dead of Night

What to Do When God Won't Answer

Updated Edition with Study Guide

Gregory L. Hunt

Pastor Greg Hunt had devoted nearly thirty years to congregational ministry, helping people experience God and find their way in life. Then came his own crisis of faith and calling. While turning to God for guidance, he finds nothing. Neither his education nor his religious involvements could prepare him for the disorienting impact of the experience.

Alarmed, he tries an experiment. The result is startling—and changes his life entirely.

"In this most beautiful memoir, Greg Hunt invites us into an unsettling time in his life, exposes the fault lines of his faith, and describes the path he walked into and out of the dark. Thanks to the trail markers he leaves along the way, he makes it easier for us to find our way, too."

—**Susan M. Heim, co-author,** *Chicken Soup for the Soul, Devotional Stories for Women*

"Compelling. If you have ever longed to hear God whispering a love song into your life, read this book."

—**Gary Chapman, NY *Times* bestselling author,** *The Love Languages of God*

ISBN: 978-0-9882848-9-0 • ePub: 978-1-936332-52-6

DON CARINA

WWII Mafia Heroine

Ron Russell

A father's death in Southern Italy in the 1930s—a place where women who can read are considered unfit for marriage—thrusts seventeen-year-old Carina into servitude as a "black widow," a legal head of the household who cares for her twelve siblings. A scandal forces her into a marriage to Russo, the "Prince of Naples."

By cunning force, Carina seizes control of Russo's organization and disguising herself as a man, controls the most powerful of Mafia groups for nearly a decade. Discovery is inevitable: Interpol has been watching. Nevertheless, Carina survives to tell her children her stunning story of strength and survival.

"A woman as the head of the Mafia, who shows her family her resourcefulness, strength and survival techniques. Unique, creative and powerful! This exciting book blends history, intrigue and power into one delicious epic adventure that you will not want to put down!"

—**Linda Gray, Actress,** *Dallas*

ISBN: 978-0-9843081-9-4 • ePub: 978-1-936332-49-6

Living with Multiple Personalities

The Christine Ducommun Story

Christine Ducommun

Christine Ducommun was a happily married wife and mother of two, when—after moving back into her childhood home—she began to experience panic attacks and a series of bizarre flashbacks. Eventually diagnosed with Dissociative Identity Disorder (DID), Christine's story details an extraordinary twelve-year ordeal unraveling the buried trauma of her past and the daunting path she must take to heal from it.

Therapy helps to identify Christine's personalities and understand how each helped her cope with her childhood, but she'll need to understand their influence on her adult life. Fully reawakened and present, the personalities compete for control of Christine's mind as she bravely struggles to maintain a stable home for her growing children. In the shadows, her life tailspins into unimaginable chaos—bouts of drinking and drug abuse, sexual escapades, theft and fraud—leaving her to believe she may very well be losing the battle for her sanity. Nearing the point of surrender, a breakthrough brings integration.

A brave story of identity, hope, healing and love.

"Reminiscent of the Academy Award-winning *A Beautiful Mind*, this true story will have you on the edge of your seat. Spellbinding!"   **—Josh Miller, Producer**

ISBN: 978-0-9843081-5-6 • ePub: 978-1-936332-06-9

Truth Never Dies

William C. Chasey

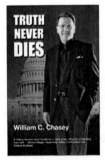

A lobbyist for some 40 years, William C. Chasey represented some of the world's most prestigious business clients and twenty-three foreign governments before the US Congress. His integrity never questioned.

All that changed when Chasey was hired to forge communications between Libya and the US Congress. A trip he took with a US Congressman for discussions with then Libyan leader Muammar Qadhafi forever changed Chasey's life. Upon his return, his bank accounts were frozen, clients and friends had been advised not to take his calls.

Things got worse: the CIA, FBI, IRS, and the Federal Judiciary attempted to coerce him into using his unique Libyan access to participate in a CIA-sponsored assassination plot of the two Libyans indicted for the bombing of Pan Am flight 103. Chasey's refusal to cooperate resulted in the destruction of his reputation, a six-year FBI investigation and sting operation, financial ruin, criminal charges, and incarceration in federal prison.

"A somber tale, a thrilling read."   **—Gary Chafetz, author *The Search for the Lost Army***

ISBN: 978-1-936332-46-5 • ePub: 978-1-936332-47-2

Out of the Transylvania Night

Aura Imbarus

A Pulitzer-Prize entry

"I'd grown up in the land of Transylvania, homeland to Dracula, Vlad the Impaler, and worse, dictator Nicolae Ceausescu," writes the author. "Under his rule, like vampires, we came to life after sundown, hiding our heirloom jewels and documents deep in the earth." Fleeing to the US to rebuild her life, she discovers a startling truth about straddling two cultures and striking a balance between one's dreams and the sacrifices that allow a sense of "home."

"Aura's courage shows the degree to which we are all willing to live lives centered on freedom, hope, and an authentic sense of self. Truly a love story!"
—**Nadia Comaneci, Olympic Champion**

"A stunning account of erasing a past, but not an identity."
—**Todd Greenfield, 20th Century Fox**

ISBN: 978-0-9843081-2-5 • ePub: 978-1-936332-20-5

Hostage of Paradox

A Qualmish Disclosure

John Rixey Moore

Few people then or now know about the clandestine war that the CIA ran in Vietnam, using the Green Berets for secret operations throughout Southeast Asia.

This was not the Vietnam War of the newsreels, the body counts, rice paddy footage, and men smoking cigarettes on the sandbag bunkers. This was a shadow directive of deep-penetration interdiction, reconnaissance, and assassination missions conducted by a selected few Special Forces teams, usually consisting of only two Americans and a handful of Chinese mercenaries, called Nungs.

These specialized units deployed quietly from forward operations bases to prowl through agendas that, for security reasons, were seldom completely understood by the men themselves.

Hostage of Paradox is the first-hand account by one of these elite team leaders.

"A compelling story told with extraordinary insight, disconcerting reality, and engaging humor."   —**David Hadley, actor, *China Beach***

ISBN: 978-1-936332-37-3 • ePub: 978-1-936332-33-5

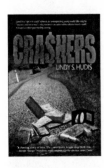

Crashers

A Tale of "Cappers" and "Hammers"

Lindy S. Hudis

The illegal business of fraudulent car accidents is a multi-million dollar racket, involving unscrupulous medical providers, personal injury attorneys, and the cooperating passengers involved in the accidents. Innocent people are often swept into it. Newly engaged Nathan and Shari, who are swimming in mounting debt, were easy prey: seduced by an offer from a stranger to move from hard times to good times in no time, Shari finds herself the "victim" in a staged auto accident. Shari gets her payday, but breaking free of this dark underworld will take nothing short of a miracle.

"A riveting story of love, life—and limits. A non-stop thrill ride."
—Dennis "Danger" Madalone, stunt coordinator, *Castle*

ISBN: 978-1-936332-27-4 • ePub: 978-1-936332-28-1

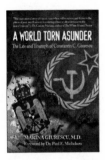

A World Torn Asunder

The Life and Triumph of Constantin C. Giurescu

Marina Giurescu, M.D.

Constantin C. Giurescu was Romania's leading historian and author of the seminal *The History of the Romanian People*. His granddaughter's fascinating story of this remarkable man and his family follows their struggles in war-torn Romania from 1900 to the fall of the Soviet Union. An "enlightened" society is dismantled with the 1946 Communist takeover of Romania, and Constantin is confined to the notorious Sighet penitentiary.

Drawing on her grandfather's prison diary (which was put in a glass jar, buried in a yard, then smuggled out of the country by Dr. Paul E. Michelson—who does the FOREWORD for this book), private letters and her own research, Dr. Giurescu writes of the legacy from the turn of the century to the fall of Communism.

We see the rise of modern Romania, the misery of World War I, the blossoming of its culture between the wars, and then the sellout of Eastern Europe to Russia after World War II. In this sweeping account, we see not only its effects socially and culturally, but the triumph in its wake: a man and his people who reclaim better lives for themselves, and in the process, teach us a lesson in endurance, patience, and will—not only to survive, but to thrive.

"The inspirational story of a quiet man and his silent defiance in the face of tyranny."
—Dr. Connie Mariano, author of *The White House Doctor*

ISBN: 978-1-936332-76-2 • ePub: 978-1-936332-77-9

Electric Living

The Science behind
the Law of Attraction

Kolie Crutcher

Although much has been written about how the Law of Attraction works, Electric Living: The Science Behind the Law of Attraction, is the first book to examine why it works—for good or bad. Skeptics and adherents alike will find Kolie Crutcher's exploration of the science behind this this potent law a fascinating read.

An electrical engineer by training, Crutcher applies his in-depth knowledge of electrical engineering principles and practical engineering experience detailing the scientific explanation of why human beings become what they think. A practical, step-by-step guide to help you harness your thoughts and emotions so that the Law of Attraction will benefit you.

"Electric Living: The Science Behind the Law of Attraction is the real deal when it comes to the Law of Attraction. Kolie's philosophy of Consciousness Creates is the key that unlocks the door to tremendous wealth. This book is a must-read for anyone who wants to be successful in his or her personal or professional life."

—**Freeway Ricky Ross**

ISBN: 978-1-936332-58-8 • ePub: 978-1-936332-59-5

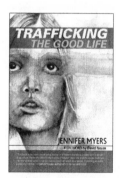

Trafficking the Good Life

Jennifer Myers

Jennifer Myers had worked long and hard toward a successful career as a dancer in Chicago, but just as her star was rising, she fell in love with the kingpin of a drug trafficking operation. Drawn to his life of luxury, she soon became a vital partner in driving marijuana across the country, making unbelievable sums of easy money that she stacked in shoeboxes and spent like an heiress.

Steeped in moral ambiguity, she sought to cleanse her soul with the guidance of spiritual gurus and New Age prophets—to no avail. Only time in a federal prison made her face up to and understand her choices. It was there, at rock bottom, that she discovered that her real prison was the one she had unwittingly made inside herself and where she could start rebuilding a life of purpose and ethical pursuit.

"A gripping memoir. When the DEA finally knocks on Myers's door, she and the reader both see the moment for what it truly is—not so much an arrest as a rescue."
—**Tony D'Souza, author of *Whiteman* and *Mule***

"A stunningly honest exploration of a woman finding her way through a very masculine world . . . and finding her voice by facing the choices she has made."
—**Dr. Linda Savage, author of *Reclaiming Goddess Sexuality***

ISBN: 978-1-936332-67-0 • ePub: 978-1-936332-68-7

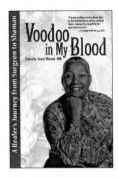

Voodoo in My Blood

A Healer's Journey from Surgeon to Shaman

Carolle Jean-Murat, M.D.

Born and raised in Haiti to a family of healers, US trained physician Carolle Jean-Murat came to be regarded as a world-class surgeon. But her success harbored a secret: in the operating room, she could quickly intuit the root cause of her patient's illness, often times knowing she could help the patient without surgery. Carolle knew that to fellow surgeons, her intuition was best left unmentioned. But when the devastating earthquake hit Haiti and Carolle returned to help, she had to acknowledge the shaman she had become.

"This fascinating memoir sheds light on the importance of asking yourself, 'Have I created for myself the life I've meant to live?'"
—**Christiane Northrup, M.D., author of the New York Times bestsellers:** *Women's Bodies, Women's Wisdom* **and** *The Wisdom of Menopause*

ISBN: 978-1-936332-05-2 • ePub: 978-1-936332-04-5

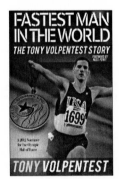

Fastest Man in the World

The Tony Volpentest Story

Tony Volpentest

Foreword by Ross Perot

Tony Volpentest, a four-time Paralympic gold medalist and five-time world champion sprinter, is a 2012 nominee for the Olympic Hall of Fame

"This inspiring story is about the thrill of victory to be sure—winning gold—but it is also a reminder about human potential: the willingness to push ourselves beyond the ledge of our own imagination. A powerfully inspirational story."
—**Charlie Huebner, United States Olympic Committee**

"This is a moving, motivating and inspiring book."
—**Dan O'Brien, world and Olympic champion decathlete**

"Tony's story shows us that no matter where we start the race, no matter what the obstacles, we all have it within us to reach powerful goals."
—**Oscar Pistorius, "Blade Runner," double amputee, world record holder in the 100, 200 and 400 meters**

ISBN: 978-1-940784-07-6 • ePub: 978-1-940784-08-3

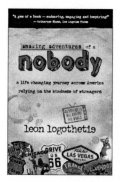

Amazing Adventures of a Nobody

Leon Logothetis

From the Hit Television Series Aired in 100 Countries!

Tired of his disconnected life and uninspiring job, Leon Logothetis leaves it all behind—job, money, home, even his cell phone—and hits the road with nothing but the clothes on his back and five dollars in his pocket, relying on the kindness of strangers and the serendipity of the open road for his daily keep. Masterful storytelling!

"A gem of a book; endearing, engaging and inspiring."
—Catharine Hamm, Los Angeles Times Travel Editor

"Warm, funny, and entertaining. If you're looking to find meaning in this disconnected world of ours, this book contains many clues." **—Psychology Today**

ISBN: 978-0-9843081-3-2 • ePub: 978-1-936332-51-9

MR. JOE

Tales from a Haunted Life

Joseph Barnett and Jane Congdon

Do you believe in ghosts? Joseph Barnett didn't, until the winter he was fired from his career job and became a school custodian to make ends meet. The fact that the eighty-five-year-old school where he now worked was built near a cemetery had barely registered with Joe when he was assigned the graveyard shift. But soon, walking the dim halls alone at night, listening to the wind howl outside, Joe was confronted with a series of bizarre and terrifying occurrences.

It wasn't just the ghosts of the graveyard shift that haunted him. Once the child of a distant father and an alcoholic mother, now a man devastated by a failed marriage, fearful of succeeding as a single dad, and challenged by an overwhelming illness, Joe is haunted by his own personal ghosts.

The story of Joseph's challenges and triumphs emerges as an eloquent metaphor of ghosts, past and present, real and emotional, and how a man puts his beliefs about self—and ghosts—to the test.

"Thrilling, thoughtful, elegantly told. So much more than a ghost story."
—Cyrus Webb, CEO, Conversation Book Club

"This is truly inspirational work, a very special book—a gift to any reader."
—Diane Bruno, CISION Media

ISBN: 978-1-936332-78-6 • ePub: 978-1-936332-79-3

457

The Search for the Lost Army
The National Geographic and Harvard University Expedition

Gary S. Chafetz

In one of history's greatest ancient disasters, a Persian army of 50,000 soldiers was suffocated by a hurricane-force sandstorm in 525 BC in Egypt's Western Desert. No trace of this conquering army, hauling huge quantities of looted gold and silver, has ever surfaced.

Nearly 25 centuries later on October 6, 1981, Egyptian Military Intelligence, the CIA, and Israel's Mossad secretly orchestrated the assassination of President Anwar Sadat, hoping to prevent Egypt's descent—as had befallen Iran two years before—into the hands of Islamic zealots. Because he had made peace with Israel and therefore had become a marked man in Egypt and the Middle East, Sadat had to be sacrificed to preserve the status quo.

These two distant events become intimately interwoven in the story of Alex Goodman, who defeats impossible obstacles as he leads a Harvard University/ National Geographic Society archaeological expedition into Egypt's Great Sand Sea in search of the Lost Army of Cambyses, the demons that haunt him, and the woman he loves. Based on a true story.

Gary Chafetz, referred to as "one of the ten best journalists of the past twenty-five years," is a former Boston Globe correspondent and was twice nominated for a Pulitzer Prize by the Globe.

ISBN: 978-1-936332-98-4 • Epub: 978-1-936332-99-1

The Tortoise Shell Code

V Frank Asaro

Off the coast of Southern California, the Sea Diva, a tuna boat, sinks. Members of the crew are missing and what happened remains a mystery. Anthony Darren, a renowned and wealthy lawyer at the top of his game, knows the boat's owner and soon becomes involved in the case. As the case goes to trial, a missing crew member is believed to be at fault, but new evidence comes to light and the finger of guilt points in a completely unanticipated direction.

Now Anthony must pull together all his resources to find the truth in what has happened and free a wrongly accused man—as well as untangle himself. Fighting despair, he finds that the recent events have called much larger issues into question. As he struggles to right this terrible wrong, Anthony makes new and enlightening discoveries in his own life-long battle for personal and global justice.

V Frank Asaro is a lawyer, musician, composer, inventor and philosopher. He is also the author of Universal Co-opetition.

ISBN: 978-1-936332-60-1 • Epub: 978-1-936332-61-8

News Girls Don't Cry

Melissa McCarty

Today the host of ORA TV's Newsbreaker, and now calling Larry King her boss, Melissa McCarty worked her way up through the trenches of live television news. But she was also running away from her past, one of growing up in the roughest of neighborhoods, watching so many she knew—including her brother—succumb to drugs, gangs, and violence. It was a past that forced her to be tough and streetwise, traits that in her career as a popular television newscaster, would end up working against her.

Every tragic story she covered was a grim reminder of where she'd been. But the practiced and restrained emotion given to the camera became her protective armor even in her private life where she was unable to let her guard down—a demeanor that damaged both her personal and professional relationships. In News Girls Don't Cry, McCarty confronts the memory-demons of her past, exploring how they hardened her—and how she turned it all around.

An inspiring story of overcoming adversity, welcoming second chances, and becoming happy and authentic.

ISBN: 978-1-936332-69-4 • ePub: 978-1-936332-70-0

GPS YOUR BEST LIFE

Charting Your Destination and Getting There in Style

Charmaine Hammond and Debra Kasowski

Foreword by Jack Canfield

Obstacles and roadblocks can detour us on the way to success, or even prevent us from getting there at all. GPS Your Best Life helps you determine where you are now, and, through practical strategies and assessments, helps you clarify what you want in your personal and career life, and shows you how to expertly navigate through hidden fears and procrastination so as to get on the road to your best life—now!

A most useful guide to charting and traversing the many options that lay before you.

Charmaine Hammond is the bestselling author of On Toby's Terms, and speaks to audiences around the world. Debra Kasowski is founder and CEO of the Millionaire Woman Club, and a professional speaker.

"A perfect book for servicing your most important vehicle: yourself. No matter where you are in your life, the concepts and direction provided in this book will help you get to a better place. It's a must read."
—**Ken Kragen, author of** *Life Is a Contact Sport*, **and organizer of** *We Are the World*, **and** *Hands Across America*, **and other historic humanitarian events**

ISBN: 978-1-936332-26-7 • ePub: 978-1-936332-41-0

Universal Co-opetition

Nature's Fusion of
Co-operation and Competition

V Frank Asaro

A key ingredient in business success is competition—and cooperation. Too much of one or the other can erode personal and organizational goals. This book identifies and explains the natural, fundamental law that unifies the apparently opposing forces of cooperation and competition.

Finding this synthesis point in a variety of situations—from the personal to the organizational—can save our finances, our family, our future, and our world.

V Frank Asaro is a lawyer, musician, composer, inventor and philosopher. He is also the author of *The Tortoise Shell Code*.

ISBN: 978-1-936332-08-3 • ePub: 978-1-936332-09-0

Last Reader Standing

Archie Willard
with Colleen Wiemerslage

The day Archie lost his thirty-one year job as a laborer at a meat packing company, he was forced to confront the secret he had held so closely for most of his life: at the age of fifty-four, he couldn't read. For all his adult life, he'd been able to skirt around the issue. But now, forced to find a new job to support his family, he could no longer hide from the truth.

Last Reader Standing is the story of Archie's amazing—and often painful—journey of becoming literate at middle age, struggling with the newfound knowledge of his dyslexia. From the little boy who was banished to the back of the classroom because the teachers labeled him "stupid," Archie emerged to becoming a national figure who continues to enlighten professionals into the world of the learning disabled. He joined Barbara Bush on stage for her Literacy Foundation's fundraisers where she proudly introduced him as "the man who took advantage of a second chance and improved his life."

This is a touching and poignant story that gives us an eye-opening view of the lack of literacy in our society, and how important it is for all of us to have opportunity to become all that we can be—to have hope and go after our dreams. It will also help parents, educators, and medical practitioners to better understand their roles in supporting and providing opportunity for the reading challenged.

ISBN: 978-1-936332-48-9 • ePub: 978-1-936332-50-2

The Girl Who Gave Her Wish Away

Sharon Babineau

Foreword by Graig Kielburger,
Co-Founder, FREE THE CHILDREN

The Children's Wish Foundation approached lovely thirteen-year-old Maddison Babineau just after she received her cancer diagnosis. "You can have anything," they told her, "a Disney cruise? The chance to meet your favorite movie star? A five thousand dollar shopping spree?"

Maddie knew exactly what she wanted. She had recently been moved to tears after watching a television program about the plight of orphaned children in an African village. Maddie's wish? To ease the suffering of these children half-way across the world. Despite the ravishing cancer, she became an indefatigable fundraiser for "her children."

In The Girl Who Gave Wish Away, her mother reveals Maddie's remarkable journey of providing hope and future to the village children who had filled her heart.

A special story, heartwarming and reassuring.

ISBN: 978-1-936332-96-0 • ePub: 978-1-936332-97-7

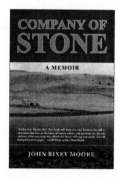

Company of Stone

John Rixey Moore

Say what you will, but the spirit of a place takes on an important role in the affairs of humans. Whether in an old house, an empty theater, a cemetery, where there was some past conflict a tangible energy haunts such places, and it can attach itself to a visitor from the present...

With yet unhealed wounds from recent combat in SE Asia, John Moore undertook an unexpected walking tour in the rugged Scottish highlands. With the approach of a season of freezing rainstorms he took shelter in a remote monastery—a chance encounter that would change his future, his beliefs about blind chance, and the unexpected courses by which the best in human nature can smuggle its way into the life of a stranger. He did not anticipate the brotherhood's easy hospitality or the surprising variety of personalities and guarded backgrounds that soon emerged through their silent community.

Afterwards, a chance conversation overheard in a village pub steered him to Canada, where he took a job as a rock drill operator in a large industrial gold mine. The dangers he encountered among the lost men in that dangerous other world, secretive men who sought permanent anonymity in the perils of work deep underground—a brutal kind of monasticism itself—challenged both his endurance and his sense of humanity.

With sensitivity and delightful good humor, Moore explores the surprising lessons learned in these strangely rich fraternities of forgotten men—a brotherhood housed in crumbling medieval masonry, and one shared in the unforgiving depths of the gold mine.

ISBN: 978-1-936332-44-1 • ePub: 978-1-936332-45-8

Bettie Youngs Books

We specialize in MEMOIRS

. . . books that celebrate

fascinating people and

remarkable journeys

VISIT OUR WEBSITE AT
www.BettieYoungsBooks.com
To contact:
info@BettieYoungsBooks.com

CPSIA information can be obtained at www.ICGtesting.com
Printed in the USA
BVOW05s1539280314

348990BV00002B/4/P